Genesis / Bereshit

Genesis / Bereshit

by Daniel A. Elias

Tzeruf Co.

Author: *Daniel A. Elias, J.D.*

Publisher: Tzeruf Co   (tzeruf.com)
               235 S Lyon Ave #39
               Hemet, CA 92543   USA
               mail@tzeruf.com

SAN Number   853-0203

© 2012 by Tzeruf Co.
Printed in USA

First Edition Published December 2012

Publisher's Cataloging-in-Publication data

Author: Elias, Daniel Aaron

Title: Genesis

English Paperback   ISBN 978-0-9792826-2-1

Table of Contents

Table of Contents v
Author's Preface viii
Intro 1
Chapter 1 3
1 BERESHIT 3
Chapter 2 8
Chapter 3 13
Chapter 4 17
Chapter 5 21
Chapter 6 27
Chapter 6 cont 29
2 NOAH 29
Chapter 7 31
Chapter 8 35
Chapter 9 39
Chapter 10 44
Chapter 11 48
Chapter 12 54
3 LECH LECHA 54
Chapter 13 57
Chapter 14 61
Chapter 15 65
Chapter 16 68
Chapter 17 72
Chapter 18 78
4 VAIERA 78

Chapter 19 84
Chapter 20 91
Chapter 21 95
Chapter 22 101
Chapter 23 106
5 CHAI SARA 106
Chapter 24 110
Chapter 25 122
Chapter 25 cont 126
6 TOLEDOT 126
Chapter 26 129
Chapter 27 135
Chapter 28 144
Chapter 28 cont 147
7 VAYEITZEI 147
Chapter 29 149
Chapter 30 156
Chapter 31 164
Chapter 32 (Torah) 174
Chapter 32 (King James)   174
Chapter 32 cont 176
8 VAYISHLACH 176
Chapter 33 181
Chapter 34 185
Chapter 35 191
Chapter 36 196
Chapter 37 203
9 VAYEISHEV 203

Chapter 38..................... 210
Chapter 39..................... 215
Chapter 40..................... 220
Chapter 41 225
10 Mikeitz 225
Chapter 42..................... 235
Chapter 43..................... 242
Chapter 44..................... 249
Chapter 44 cont.......... 254
11 Vaigash 254
Chapter 45..................... 257
Chapter 46..................... 263
Chapter 47 269
Chapter 47 cont.......... 276
12 Vaiki 276
Chapter 48..................... 277
Chapter 49..................... 281
Chapter 50..................... 287

AUTHOR'S PREFACE

The objective of this book is to;

1) make the reader more fluent in the reading of the Hebrew Language,

2) to feed the soul with the effects of reading the hebrew letters and the bible code,

3) to learn the Hebrew vocabulary,

4) to help memorize verses that are interesting to a person,

5) to foster kavanah.

One Hebrew word of a verse contains so much subtle information. There is the root, the prefix, the affix, dropped weak letters, gutturals, dagesh lene, dagesh forte, it's sentence grammatical name, etc. There is only space for a one word translation. Much of the English grammar has been left out by necessity; ie. the translation "the" was put in only when there was a specific prefix letter Heh.

Every expression in the [ongoing] present tense can variably be expressed in the future tense as well as in the past tense. This is because anything that is ongoing is in the present and has already happened and will continue to happen.

I would have preferred to translate the tenses of the verbs as they actually appear instead of looking to the sentence meaning to infer the past, present or future. However in order to make the translations simple to understand for the majority of people who do not understand this concept I have inferred verb tenses to optimize understanding.

The vast majority of the Hebrew words in the Bible are very easy to translate. Generally everyone agrees on their meanings and these words are used in everyday life in Israel. But many the hard Hebrew words with uncertain roots are such that even experts question their meanings and translations.

The Eskimos have 20 words for snow. This same principle applies to the Hebrew words found in the Torah. There may be 20 Hebrew words that have been translated with the same English word, but each of these similar Hebrew words have an extensive detailed specific and differing explanation.

When I was translating verses I listed hard to translate words and made notes on what other translators have put for a meaning and what possible roots the word could be derived from. In the end on those words it's a best estimate as to their meanings.

INTRO

The oldest existent manuscripts of Genesis are the twenty-four fragments found among the Dead Sea Scrolls, dating from between 150 BC and AD 70. The next oldest are the Greek Septuagint manuscripts of the Codex Sinaiticus and Vaticanus, produced by the early Christian church in the 4th century AD. The oldest manuscripts of the Masoretic Text, which forms the basis of Jewish worship and many Western Christian bibles, date from around AD 1000.

Date of authorship of Genesis is likely between 1440 and 1400 B.C., between the time Moses led the Israelites out of Egypt and his death.

In Hebrew the book is called Bereishit, meaning "in the beginning." This title is the first word of the Hebrew text - a method by which all five books of the Torah are named. When the Torah was translated into Greek in the 3rd century BC to produce the Septuagint, the name given was Γένεσις Genesis, meaning "birth" or "origin". This was in line with the Septuagint use of subject themes as names of the books.

The first part deals with the history of creation of the earth, the heavens, plants, animals, and man. It also deals with the fall and the Eden curse, the great flood and the descendants of Noah.

The second part of Genesis deals with the patriarchal history of Israel. It gives the history of Abraham and Lot, Ishmael and Isaac, Jacob and Esau, and Joseph and his brethren in Egypt.

1 Bereshit

Chapter 1

[פרשת בראשית]

בְּרֵאשִׁית בָּרָא אֱלֹהִים אֵת הַשָּׁמַיִם וְאֵת הָאָרֶץ:
the earth   and that   the heavens   that   Elohim   created   in beginning

1 In the beginning God created the heaven and the earth.

וְהָאָרֶץ הָיְתָה תֹהוּ וָבֹהוּ וְחֹשֶׁךְ עַל פְּנֵי תְהוֹם
deep   face   upon   and darkness   and void   without form   it was   and the earth

וְרוּחַ אֱלֹהִים מְרַחֶפֶת עַל פְּנֵי הַמָּיִם:
the waters   face   upon   hovered   Elohim   and spirit

2 And the earth was without form, and void; and darkness was upon the face of the deep. And the Spirit of God moved upon the face of the waters.

וַיֹּאמֶר אֱלֹהִים יְהִי אוֹר וַיְהִי אוֹר:
light   and let be   light   let be   Elohim   and he said

3 And God said, Let there be light: and there was light.

וַיַּרְא אֱלֹהִים אֶת הָאוֹר כִּי טוֹב
good   like   the light   that   Elohim   and he saw

וַיַּבְדֵּל אֱלֹהִים בֵּין הָאוֹר וּבֵין הַחֹשֶׁךְ:
the darkness   and between   the light   between   Elohim   and he divided

4 And God saw the light, that it was good: and God divided the light from the darkness.

וַיִּקְרָא אֱלֹהִים לָאוֹר יוֹם וְלַחֹשֶׁךְ קָרָא לָיְלָה
night   he called   and to darkness   day   to light   Elohim   and he called

וַיְהִי עֶרֶב וַיְהִי בֹקֶר יוֹם אֶחָד:
one   day   morning   and there was   evening   and there was

5 And God called the light Day, and the darkness he called Night. And the evening and the morning were the first day.

פ

וַיֹּאמֶר אֱלֹהִים יְהִי רָקִיעַ בְּתוֹךְ הַמָּיִם
the waters   in midst   firmament   let there be   Elohim   and he said

וִיהִי מַבְדִּיל בֵּין מַיִם לָמָיִם:
to water   water   between   divide   and let it

6 And God said, Let there be a firmament in the midst of the waters, and let it divide the waters from the waters.

וַיַּעַשׂ אֱלֹהִים אֶת הָרָקִיעַ
firmament   that   Elohim   and he made

וַיַּבְדֵּל בֵּין הַמַּיִם אֲשֶׁר מִתַּחַת לָרָקִיעַ
to firmament   beneath   which   the waters   between   and he divided

וּבֵין הַמַּיִם אֲשֶׁר מֵעַל לָרָקִיעַ וַיְהִי כֵן:
so   and it was   to firmament   above   which   the water   and between

7 And God made the firmament, and divided the waters which were under the firmament from the waters which were above the firmament: and it was so.

וַיִּקְרָא אֱלֹהִים לָרָקִיעַ שָׁמָיִם
heaven   to firmament   Elohim   and he called

וַיְהִי עֶרֶב וַיְהִי בֹקֶר יוֹם שֵׁנִי:
second   day   morning   and it was   evening   and it was

8 And God called the firmament Heaven. And the evening and the morning were the second day.

פ

וַיֹּאמֶר אֱלֹהִים יִקָּווּ הַמַּיִם מִתַּחַת הַשָּׁמַיִם אֶל מָקוֹם אֶחָד
one   place   unto   the heavens   beneath   the water   let gather   Elohim   and he said

וְתֵרָאֶה הַיַּבָּשָׁה וַיְהִי כֵן:
so   and it was   the dry land   and it will see

9 And God said, Let the waters under the heaven be gathered together unto one place, and let the dry land appear: and it was so.

וַיִּקְרָא אֱלֹהִים לַיַּבָּשָׁה אֶרֶץ וּלְמִקְוֵה הַמַּיִם קָרָא יַמִּים
seas   he called   the water   and to gathering   earth   to dry land   Elohim   and he called

וַיַּרְא אֱלֹהִים כִּי טוֹב:
good   like   Elohim   and he saw

10 And God called the dry land Earth; and the gathering together of the waters called he Seas: and God saw that it was good.

וַיֹּאמֶר אֱלֹהִים תַּדְשֵׁא הָאָרֶץ דֶּשֶׁא עֵשֶׂב מַזְרִיעַ זֶרַע
seed   sprouting   herb   grass   the earth   it vegetate   Elohim   and he said

עֵץ פְּרִי עֹשֶׂה פְּרִי לְמִינוֹ אֲשֶׁר זַרְעוֹ בוֹ עַל הָאָרֶץ
the earth   upon   in it   it's seed   which   to its kind   fruit   making   fruit   tree

וַיְהִי כֵן:
so   and it was

11 And God said, Let the earth bring forth grass, the herb yielding seed, and the fruit tree yielding fruit after his kind, whose seed is in itself, upon the earth: and it was so.

וַתּוֹצֵא הָאָרֶץ דֶּשֶׁא עֵשֶׂב מַזְרִיעַ זֶרַע לְמִינֵהוּ
to it's kind   seed   sprouting   herb   grass   the earth   and it brought forth

וְעֵץ עֹשֶׂה פְּרִי אֲשֶׁר זַרְעוֹ בוֹ לְמִינֵהוּ
to it's kind   in it   it's seed   which   fruit   making   and tree

וַיַּרְא   אֱלֹהִים   כִּי   טוֹב:
good   like   Elohim   and he saw

12 And the earth brought forth grass, and herb yielding seed after his kind, and the tree yielding fruit, whose seed was in itself, after his kind: and God saw that it was good.

וַיְהִי   עֶרֶב   וַיְהִי   בֹקֶר   יוֹם   שְׁלִישִׁי:
third   day   morning   and it was   evening   and it was

13 And the evening and the morning were the third day.

וַיֹּאמֶר   אֱלֹהִים   יְהִי   מְאֹרֹת   בִּרְקִיעַ   הַשָּׁמַיִם
the heavens   in firmament   reflections   let be   Elohim   and he said

לְהַבְדִּיל   בֵּין   הַיּוֹם   וּבֵין   הַלָּיְלָה
the night   and between   the day   between   to the separation

וְהָיוּ   לְאֹתֹת   וּלְמוֹעֲדִים   וּלְיָמִים   וְשָׁנִים:
and years   and to days   and to seasons   to signs   and they were

14 And God said, Let there be lights in the firmament of the heaven to divide the day from the night; and let them be for signs, and for seasons, and for days, and years:

פ

וְהָיוּ   לִמְאוֹרֹת   בִּרְקִיעַ   הַשָּׁמַיִם   לְהָאִיר   עַל   הָאָרֶץ
the earth   upon   to the shine   the heavens   in firmament   to reflections   and they were

וַיְהִי   כֵן:
so   and he was

15 And let them be for lights in the firmament of the heaven to give light upon the earth: and it was so.

וַיַּעַשׂ   אֱלֹהִים   אֶת   שְׁנֵי   הַמְּאֹרֹת   הַגְּדֹלִים
the great ones   the reflections   two   that   Elohim   and he made

אֶת   הַמָּאוֹר   הַגָּדֹל   לְמֶמְשֶׁלֶת   הַיּוֹם
the day   to rule   the great   the reflection   that

וְאֶת   הַמָּאוֹר   הַקָּטֹן   לְמֶמְשֶׁלֶת   הַלַּיְלָה   וְאֵת   הַכּוֹכָבִים:
the stars   and that   the night   to rule   the small   the reflection   and that

16 And God made two great lights; the greater light to rule the day, and the lesser light to rule the night: he made the stars also.

וַיִּתֵּן   אֹתָם   אֱלֹהִים   בִּרְקִיעַ   הַשָּׁמַיִם   לְהָאִיר   עַל   הָאָרֶץ:
the earth   upon   to the shine   the heavens   in firmament   Elohim   to them   and he gave

17 And God set them in the firmament of the heaven to give light upon the earth,

וְלִמְשֹׁל   בַּיּוֹם   וּבַלַּיְלָה   וּלְהַבְדִּיל   בֵּין   הָאוֹר   וּבֵין   הַחֹשֶׁךְ
the darkness   and between   the light   between   and to the divide   and in night   in day   and to rule

וַיַּרְא   אֱלֹהִים   כִּי   טוֹב:
good   like   Elohim   and he saw

18 And to rule over the day and over the night, and to divide the light from the darkness: and God saw that it was good.

וַיְהִי   עֶ֥רֶב וַיְהִי   בֹ֖קֶר יוֹם רְבִיעִֽי׃

fourth   day   morning and it was evening and it was

19 And the evening and the morning were the fourth day.

וַיֹּ֣אמֶר אֱלֹהִ֔ים יִשְׁרְצ֣וּ הַמַּ֔יִם שֶׁ֖רֶץ נֶ֣פֶשׁ חַיָּ֑ה

living   soul swarm the water they swarm Elohim and he said

וְעוֹף֙ יְעוֹפֵ֣ף עַל־הָאָ֔רֶץ עַל־פְּנֵ֖י רְקִ֥יעַ הַשָּׁמָֽיִם׃

the heavens firmament face upon the earth upon flyer and bird

20 And God said, Let the waters bring forth abundantly the moving creature that hath life, and fowl that may fly above the earth in the open firmament of heaven.

פ

וַיִּבְרָ֣א אֱלֹהִ֔ים אֶת־הַתַּנִּינִ֖ם הַגְּדֹלִ֑ים

the big ones the sea giants that Elohim and he created

וְאֵ֣ת כָּל־נֶ֣פֶשׁ הַֽחַיָּ֣ה הָֽרֹמֶ֡שֶׂת אֲשֶׁר֩ שָׁרְצ֨וּ הַמַּ֜יִם לְמִֽינֵהֶ֗ם

to their kind the water they swarm which the creepers the living soul all and that

וְאֵ֨ת כָּל־ע֤וֹף כָּנָף֙ לְמִינֵ֔הוּ

to their kind winged bird all and that

וַיַּ֥רְא אֱלֹהִ֖ים כִּי־טֽוֹב׃

good like Elohim and he saw

21 And God created great whales, and every living creature that moveth, which the waters brought forth abundantly, after their kind, and every winged fowl after his kind: and God saw that it was good.

וַיְבָ֧רֶךְ אֹתָ֛ם אֱלֹהִ֖ים לֵאמֹ֑ר פְּר֣וּ וּרְב֗וּ

and you multiply you be fruitful to say Elohim to them and he blessed

וּמִלְא֤וּ אֶת־הַמַּ֙יִם֙ בַּיַּמִּ֔ים וְהָע֖וֹף יִ֥רֶב בָּאָֽרֶץ׃

in earth it multiply and the bird in seas the water that and you fill

22 And God blessed them, saying, Be fruitful, and multiply, and fill the waters in the seas, and let fowl multiply in the earth.

וַֽיְהִי־עֶ֥רֶב וַֽיְהִי־בֹ֖קֶר יוֹם חֲמִישִֽׁי׃

fifth day morning and it was evening and it was

23 And the evening and the morning were the fifth day.

וַיֹּ֣אמֶר אֱלֹהִ֗ים תּוֹצֵ֤א הָאָ֙רֶץ֙ נֶ֣פֶשׁ חַיָּה֙ לְמִינָ֔הּ בְּהֵמָ֥ה

beast to it's kind living soul the earth it bring forth Elohim and he said

וָרֶ֛מֶשׂ וְחַֽיְתוֹ־אֶ֖רֶץ לְמִינָ֑הּ וַֽיְהִי־כֵֽן׃

so and it was to its kind earth and its life and creepers

24 And God said, Let the earth bring forth the living creature after his kind, cattle, and

creeping thing, and beast of the earth after his kind: and it was so.

פ

וַיַּעַשׂ אֱלֹהִים אֶת חַיַּת הָאָרֶץ לְמִינָהּ

to it's kind   the earth   living beings   that   Elohim   and made

וְאֶת הַבְּהֵמָה לְמִינָהּ וְאֵת כָּל רֶמֶשׂ הָאֲדָמָה לְמִינֵהוּ

to it's kind   the ground   creepers   all   and that   to it's kind   the beast   and that

וַיַּרְא אֱלֹהִים כִּי טוֹב:

good   like   Elohim   and he saw

25 And God made the beast of the earth after his kind, and cattle after their kind, and every thing that creepeth upon the earth after his kind: and God saw that it was good.

וַיֹּאמֶר אֱלֹהִים נַעֲשֶׂה אָדָם בְּצַלְמֵנוּ כִּדְמוּתֵנוּ

like our likeness   in our image   Adam   we make   Elohim   and he said

וְיִרְדּוּ בִדְגַת הַיָּם וּבְעוֹף הַשָּׁמַיִם

the heavens   and in bird   the sea   in fish   and they dominate

וּבַבְּהֵמָה וּבְכָל הָאָרֶץ וּבְכָל הָרֶמֶשׂ הָרֹמֵשׂ עַל הָאָרֶץ:

the earth   upon   the creeper   the creepers   and in all   the earth   and in all   and in beast

26 And God said, Let us make man in our image, after our likeness: and let them have dominion over the fish of the sea, and over the fowl of the air, and over the cattle, and over all the earth, and over every creeping thing that creepeth upon the earth.

וַיִּבְרָא אֱלֹהִים אֶת הָאָדָם בְּצַלְמוֹ

in his image   the Adam   that   Elohim   and he created

בְּצֶלֶם אֱלֹהִים בָּרָא אֹתוֹ זָכָר וּנְקֵבָה בָּרָא אֹתָם:

to them   he created   and female   male   to him   he created   Elohim   in image

27 So God created man in his own image, in the image of God created he him; male and female created he them.

וַיְבָרֶךְ אֹתָם אֱלֹהִים וַיֹּאמֶר לָהֶם אֱלֹהִים

Elohim   to them   and he said   Elohim   to them   and he blessed

פְּרוּ וּרְבוּ וּמִלְאוּ אֶת הָאָרֶץ וְכִבְשֻׁהָ

and subdue it   the earth   that   and you fill   and you multiply   you be fruitful

וּרְדוּ בִדְגַת הַיָּם וּבְעוֹף הַשָּׁמַיִם

the heavens   and in bird   the sea   in fish   and you dominate

וּבְכָל חַיָּה הָרֹמֶשֶׂת עַל הָאָרֶץ:

the earth   upon   the creepers   life   and in all

28 And God blessed them, and God said unto them, Be fruitful, and multiply, and replenish the earth, and subdue it: and have dominion over the fish of the sea, and over the fowl of the air, and over every living thing that moveth upon the earth.

וַיֹּאמֶר אֱלֹהִים הִנֵּה נָתַתִּי לָכֶם
to you   I give   here   Elohim   and he said

אֶת כָּל עֵשֶׂב זֹרֵעַ זֶרַע אֲשֶׁר עַל פְּנֵי כָל הָאָרֶץ
the earth   all   face   upon   which   seed   seeder   herb   all   that

וְאֶת כָּל הָעֵץ אֲשֶׁר בּוֹ פְרִי עֵץ זֹרֵעַ זָרַע
seed   seeder   tree   fruit   in it   which   the tree   all   and that

לָכֶם יִהְיֶה לְאָכְלָה:
to food   it be   to you

29 And God said, Behold, I have given you every herb bearing seed, which is upon the face of all the earth, and every tree, in the which is the fruit of a tree yielding seed; to you it shall be for meat.

וּלְכָל חַיַּת הָאָרֶץ וּלְכָל עוֹף הַשָּׁמַיִם
the heavens   bird   and to all   the earth   living things   and to all

וּלְכֹל רוֹמֵשׂ עַל הָאָרֶץ אֲשֶׁר בּוֹ נֶפֶשׁ חַיָּה
life   soul   in it   which   the earth   upon   creeper   and to all

אֶת כָּל יֶרֶק עֵשֶׂב לְאָכְלָה וַיְהִי כֵן:
so   and it was   to food   herb   green   all   that

30 And to every beast of the earth, and to every fowl of the air, and to every thing that creepeth upon the earth, wherein there is life, I have given every green herb for meat: and it was so.

וַיַּרְא אֱלֹהִים אֶת כָּל אֲשֶׁר עָשָׂה וְהִנֵּה טוֹב מְאֹד
very   good   and it was   he made   which   all   that   Elohim   and he saw

וַיְהִי עֶרֶב וַיְהִי בֹקֶר יוֹם הַשִּׁשִּׁי:
the sixth   day   morning   and it was   evening   and it was

31 And God saw every thing that he had made, and, behold, it was very good. And the evening and the morning were the sixth day.

פ

Chapter 2

ספר בראשית פרק ב

וַיְכֻלּוּ הַשָּׁמַיִם וְהָאָרֶץ וְכָל צְבָאָם:
their hosts   and all   and the earth   the heavens   and they finished

1 Thus the heavens and the earth were finished, and all the host of them.

וַיְכַל אֱלֹהִים בַּיּוֹם הַשְּׁבִיעִי מְלַאכְתּוֹ אֲשֶׁר עָשָׂה
he did   which   his work   the seventh   in day   Elohim   and finished

וַיִּשְׁבֹּת בַּיּוֹם הַשְּׁבִיעִי מִכָּל מְלַאכְתּוֹ אֲשֶׁר עָשָׂה:
he did   which   from his work   from all   the seventh   in day   and he rested

2 And on the seventh day God ended his work which he had made; and he rested on

the seventh day from all his work which he had made.

אֹתוֹ   וַיְקַדֵּשׁ הַשְּׁבִיעִי יוֹם אֶת אֱלֹהִים וַיְבָרֶךְ
to it   and he sanctified it   the seventh   day   that   Elohim   and he blessed

כִּי בוֹ שָׁבַת מִכָּל מְלַאכְתּוֹ אֲשֶׁר בָּרָא אֱלֹהִים לַעֲשׂוֹת׃
to make   Elohim   he created   which   his work   from all   he rested   in it   like

3 And God blessed the seventh day, and sanctified it: because that in it he had rested from all his work which God created and made.

[שני]

אֵלֶּה תוֹלְדוֹת הַשָּׁמַיִם וְהָאָרֶץ
and the earth   the heavens   begetings   these are

בְּהִבָּרְאָם בְּיוֹם עֲשׂוֹת יְהוָה אֱלֹהִים אֶרֶץ וְשָׁמָיִם׃
and heavens   earth   Elohim   ihvh   makings   in day   in causing their creation

4 These are the generations of the heavens and of the earth when they were created, in the day that the LORD God made the earth and the heavens,

וְכֹל שִׂיחַ הַשָּׂדֶה טֶרֶם יִהְיֶה בָאָרֶץ
in earth   was   before   the field   plant   and all

וְכָל עֵשֶׂב הַשָּׂדֶה טֶרֶם יִצְמָח
it sprouted   before   the field   herb   and all

כִּי לֹא הִמְטִיר יְהוָה אֱלֹהִים עַל הָאָרֶץ
the earth   upon   Elohim   ihvh   caused to rain   not   like

וְאָדָם אַיִן לַעֲבֹד אֶת הָאֲדָמָה׃
the ground   that   to work   isn't   and Adam

5 And every plant of the field before it was in the earth, and every herb of the field before it grew: for the LORD God had not caused it to rain upon the earth, and there was not a man to till the ground.

וְאֵד יַעֲלֶה מִן הָאָרֶץ וְהִשְׁקָה אֶת כָּל פְּנֵי הָאֲדָמָה׃
the ground   face   all   that   and caused to irrigate   the earth   from   it ascended   and mist

6 But there went up a mist from the earth, and watered the whole face of the ground.

וַיִּיצֶר יְהוָה אֱלֹהִים אֶת הָאָדָם עָפָר מִן הָאֲדָמָה
the ground   from   dust   the Adam   that   Elohim   ihvh   and he formed

וַיִּפַּח בְּאַפָּיו נִשְׁמַת חַיִּים וַיְהִי הָאָדָם לְנֶפֶשׁ חַיָּה׃
life   to soul   the Adam   and there was   lives   breaths   in his nostrils   and he blew

7 And the LORD God formed man of the dust of the ground, and breathed into his nostrils the breath of life; and man became a living soul.

וַיִּטַּע יְהוָה אֱלֹהִים גַּן בְּעֵדֶן מִקֶּדֶם
from east   in Eden   garden   Elohim   ihvh   and he planted

וַיָּ֣שֶׂם שָׁ֔ם אֶת־הָֽאָדָ֖ם אֲשֶׁ֥ר יָצָֽר׃

he formed	which	the Adam	that	there	and put them

8 And the LORD God planted a garden eastward in Eden; and there he put the man whom he had formed.

וַיַּצְמַ֞ח יְהוָ֤ה אֱלֹהִים֙ מִן־הָ֣אֲדָמָ֔ה

the ground	from	Elohim	ihvh	and he sprouted

כָּל־עֵ֛ץ נֶחְמָ֥ד לְמַרְאֶ֖ה וְט֣וֹב לְמַאֲכָ֑ל

to food	and good	to sight	pleasant	tree	all

וְעֵ֤ץ הַֽחַיִּים֙ בְּת֣וֹךְ הַגָּ֔ן

the garden	in midst	the lives	and tree

וְעֵ֕ץ הַדַּ֖עַת ט֥וֹב וָרָֽע׃

and evil	good	the knowledge	and tree

9 And out of the ground made the LORD God to grow every tree that is pleasant to the sight, and good for food; the tree of life also in the midst of the garden, and the tree of knowledge of good and evil.

וְנָהָר֙ יֹצֵ֣א מֵעֵ֔דֶן לְהַשְׁק֖וֹת אֶת־הַגָּ֑ן

the garden	that	to the irrigate	from Eden	went out	and river

וּמִשָּׁם֙ יִפָּרֵ֔ד וְהָיָ֖ה לְאַרְבָּעָ֥ה רָאשִֽׁים׃

heads	to four	and was	it separated	and from there

10 And a river went out of Eden to water the garden; and from thence it was parted, and became into four heads.

שֵׁ֥ם הָֽאֶחָ֖ד פִּישׁ֑וֹן

Pison	the one	name

ה֣וּא הַסֹּבֵ֗ב אֵ֚ת כָּל־אֶ֣רֶץ הַֽחֲוִילָ֔ה אֲשֶׁר־שָׁ֖ם הַזָּהָֽב׃

the gold	there	which	the Havilah	earth	all	that	the encircled	it

11 The name of the first is Pison: that is it which compasseth the whole land of Havilah, where there is gold;

וּֽזֲהַ֛ב הָאָ֥רֶץ הַהִ֖וא ט֑וֹב שָׁ֥ם הַבְּדֹ֖לַח וְאֶ֥בֶן הַשֹּֽׁהַם׃

the onyx	and stone	the pearls	there	good	the it	the land	and gold

12 And the gold of that land is good: there is bdellium and the onyx stone.

וְשֵֽׁם־הַנָּהָ֥ר הַשֵּׁנִ֖י גִּיח֑וֹן ה֣וּא הַסּוֹבֵ֔ב אֵ֖ת כָּל־אֶ֥רֶץ כּֽוּשׁ׃

Cush	land	all	that	the encircled	it	Gihon	the second	river	and name

13 And the name of the second river is Gihon: the same is it that compasseth the whole land of Ethiopia.

וְשֵׁ֨ם הַנָּהָ֤ר הַשְּׁלִישִׁי֙ חִדֶּ֔קֶל ה֥וּא הַֽהֹלֵ֖ךְ קִדְמַ֣ת אַשּׁ֑וּר

Assyria	towards east	the goes	it	Hiddekel	the third	the river	and name

וְהַנָּהָ֥ר הָֽרְבִיעִ֖י ה֥וּא פְרָֽת׃

Euphrates	it	the fourth	and the river

14 And the name of the third river is Hiddekel: that is it which goeth toward the east of Assyria. And the fourth river is Euphrates.

וַיִּקַּח יְהֹוָה אֱלֹהִים אֶת הָאָדָם
and he took   ihvh   Elohim   that   the Adam

וַיַּנִּחֵהוּ בְּגַן עֵדֶן לְעָבְדָהּ וּלְשָׁמְרָהּ:
and he guided him   in garden   Eden   to serve it   and to heed it

15 And the LORD God took the man, and put him into the garden of Eden to dress it and to keep it.

וַיְצַו יְהֹוָה אֱלֹהִים עַל הָאָדָם לֵאמֹר
and he commanded   ihvh   Elohim   upon   the Adam   to say

מִכֹּל עֵץ הַגָּן אָכֹל תֹּאכֵל:
from all   tree   the garden   eat   you eater

16 And the LORD God commanded the man, saying, Of every tree of the garden thou mayest freely eat:

וּמֵעֵץ הַדַּעַת טוֹב וָרָע לֹא תֹאכַל מִמֶּנּוּ
and from tree   the knowledge   good   and evil   not   you eat   from it

כִּי בְּיוֹם אֲכָלְךָ מִמֶּנּוּ מוֹת תָּמוּת:
like   in day   you eat   from it   death   you die

17 But of the tree of the knowledge of good and evil, thou shalt not eat of it: for in the day that thou eatest thereof thou shalt surely die.

וַיֹּאמֶר יְהֹוָה אֱלֹהִים לֹא טוֹב הֱיוֹת הָאָדָם לְבַדּוֹ
and he said   ihvh   Elohim   not   good   existing   the Adam   his alone

אֶעֱשֶׂה לּוֹ עֵזֶר כְּנֶגְדּוֹ:
I will make   to him   help   like his opposite

18 And the LORD God said, It is not good that the man should be alone; I will make him an help meet for him.

וַיִּצֶר יְהֹוָה אֱלֹהִים מִן הָאֲדָמָה כָּל חַיַּת הַשָּׂדֶה
and he formed   ihvh   Elohim   from   the soil   all   life   the field

וְאֵת כָּל עוֹף הַשָּׁמַיִם
and that   all   bird   the heavens

וַיָּבֵא אֶל הָאָדָם לִרְאוֹת מַה יִּקְרָא לוֹ
and he bought   unto   the Adam   to see   what   he called   to him

וְכֹל אֲשֶׁר יִקְרָא לוֹ הָאָדָם נֶפֶשׁ חַיָּה הוּא שְׁמוֹ:
and all   which   he called   to him   the Adam   soul   living   it   his name

19 And out of the ground the LORD God formed every beast of the field, and every fowl of the air; and brought them unto Adam to see what he would call them: and whatsoever Adam called every living creature, that was the name thereof.

וַיִּקְרָא הָאָדָם שֵׁמוֹת לְכָל הַבְּהֵמָה
and he called   the Adam   names   to all   the beast

וּלְעוֹף הַשָּׁמַיִם וּלְכֹל חַיַּת הַשָּׂדֶה
and to bird   the heavens   and to all   life   the field

וּלְאָדָם לֹא מָצָא עֵזֶר כְּנֶגְדּוֹ:
and to Adam   not   found   help   like his opposite

20 And Adam gave names to all cattle, and to the fowl of the air, and to every beast of the field; but for Adam there was not found an help meet for him.

וַיַּפֵּל יְהוָה אֱלֹהִים תַּרְדֵּמָה עַל הָאָדָם וַיִּישָׁן
and he fell   ihvh   Elohim   deep sleep   upon   the Adam   and he slept

וַיִּקַּח אַחַת מִצַּלְעֹתָיו וַיִּסְגֹּר בָּשָׂר תַּחְתֶּנָּה:
and he took   one   from his ribs   and he closed   flesh   in place of

21 And the LORD God caused a deep sleep to fall upon Adam, and he slept: and he took one of his ribs, and closed up the flesh instead thereof;

וַיִּבֶן יְהוָה אֱלֹהִים אֶת הַצֵּלָע אֲשֶׁר לָקַח מִן הָאָדָם לְאִשָּׁה
and he built   ihvh   Elohim   the rib   which   taken   from   the Adam   to woman

וַיְבִאֶהָ אֶל הָאָדָם:
and brought her   unto   the Adam

22 And the rib, which the LORD God had taken from man, made he a woman, and brought her unto the man.

וַיֹּאמֶר הָאָדָם זֹאת הַפַּעַם עֶצֶם מֵעֲצָמַי
and he said   the Adam   this   the once   bone   from my bone

וּבָשָׂר מִבְּשָׂרִי לְזֹאת יִקָּרֵא אִשָּׁה
and flesh   from my flesh   to this   he called   woman

כִּי מֵאִישׁ לֻקֳחָה־זֹּאת:
like   from man   this - to taken her

23 And Adam said, This is now bone of my bones, and flesh of my flesh: she shall be called Woman, because she was taken out of Man.

עַל כֵּן יַעֲזָב אִישׁ אֶת אָבִיו וְאֶת אִמּוֹ
upon   thus   he leaves   man   that   his father   and that   his mother

וְדָבַק בְּאִשְׁתּוֹ וְהָיוּ לְבָשָׂר אֶחָד:
and cleaves   in his wife   and they are   to flesh   one

24 Therefore shall a man leave his father and his mother, and shall cleave unto his wife: and they shall be one flesh.

וַיִּהְיוּ שְׁנֵיהֶם עֲרוּמִּים הָאָדָם וְאִשְׁתּוֹ
and they were   two of them   naked ones   the Adam   and his wife

וְלֹא יִתְבֹּשָׁשׁוּ:

and not	they ashamed

25 And they were both naked, the man and his wife, and were not ashamed.

CHAPTER 3

ספר בראשית פרק ג

וְהַנָּחָשׁ הָיָה עָרוּם מִכֹּל חַיַּת הַשָּׂדֶה

and the serpent	he was	cunning	from all	life	the field

אֲשֶׁר עָשָׂה יְהוָֹה אֱלֹהִים

which	made	ihvh	Elohim

וַיֹּאמֶר אֶל־הָאִשָּׁה אַף כִּי־אָמַר אֱלֹהִים

and he said	the woman - unto	then	like - said	Elohim

לֹא תֹאכְלוּ מִכֹּל עֵץ הַגָּן:

not	you eat it	from all	tree	the garden

1 Now the serpent was more subtle than any beast of the field which the LORD God had made. And he said unto the woman, Yea, hath God said, Ye shall not eat of every tree of the garden?

וַתֹּאמֶר הָאִשָּׁה אֶל־הַנָּחָשׁ מִפְּרִי עֵץ־הַגָּן נֹאכֵל:

and she said	the woman	the serpent – unto	from fruit	garden - tree	we eat

2 And the woman said unto the serpent, We may eat of the fruit of the trees of the garden:

וּמִפְּרִי הָעֵץ אֲשֶׁר בְּתוֹךְ־הַגָּן אָמַר אֱלֹהִים

and from fruit	the tree	which	the garden - in middle	said	Elohim

לֹא תֹאכְלוּ מִמֶּנּוּ

not	you eat it	from it

וְלֹא תִגְּעוּ בּוֹ פֶּן תְּמֻתוּן:

and not	you touch it	in it	unless	you die

3 But of the fruit of the tree which is in the midst of the garden, God hath said, Ye shall not eat of it, neither shall ye touch it, lest ye die.

וַיֹּאמֶר הַנָּחָשׁ אֶל־הָאִשָּׁה לֹא־מוֹת תְּמֻתוּן:

and he said	the serpent	the woman – unto	death – not	you die

4 And the serpent said unto the woman, Ye shall not surely die:

כִּי יֹדֵעַ אֱלֹהִים כִּי בְּיוֹם אֲכָלְכֶם מִמֶּנּוּ

like	he knows	Elohim	like	in day	you both eat	from itself

וְנִפְקְחוּ עֵינֵיכֶם וִהְיִיתֶם כֵּאלֹהִים יֹדְעֵי טוֹב וָרָע:

and it be opened	you both eyes	and you both be	like Elohim	knowing	good	and evil

5 For God doth know that in the day ye eat thereof, then your eyes shall be opened, and ye shall be as gods, knowing good and evil.

וַתֵּרֶא הָאִשָּׁה כִּי טוֹב הָעֵץ לְמַאֲכָל
and she saw   the woman   good   like   the tree   to taste

וְכִי תַאֲוָה־הוּא לָעֵינַיִם וְנֶחְמָד הָעֵץ לְהַשְׂכִּיל
and like   it - pleasant   to eyes   and desirable   the tree   to the intelligence

וַתִּקַּח מִפִּרְיוֹ וַתֹּאכַל וַתִּתֵּן גַּם־לְאִישָׁהּ עִמָּהּ וַיֹּאכַל׃
and she took   from it's fruit   and she ate   and she gave   to her man - also   with her   and he ate

6 And when the woman saw that the tree was good for food, and that it was pleasant to the eyes, and a tree to be desired to make one wise, she took of the fruit thereof, and did eat, and gave also unto her husband with her; and he did eat.

וַתִּפָּקַחְנָה עֵינֵי שְׁנֵיהֶם וַיֵּדְעוּ כִּי עֵירֻמִּם הֵם
then it opened   eyes   two of them   and they knew   like   naked ones   them

וַיִּתְפְּרוּ עֲלֵה תְאֵנָה וַיַּעֲשׂוּ לָהֶם חֲגֹרֹת׃
and they sewed   leaf   fig   and they made   to them   aprons

7 And the eyes of them both were opened, and they knew that they were naked; and they sewed fig leaves together, and made themselves aprons.

וַיִּשְׁמְעוּ אֶת־קוֹל יְהוָֹה אֱלֹהִים מִתְהַלֵּךְ בַּגָּן לְרוּחַ הַיּוֹם
and they heard   voice – that   ihvh   Elohim   strolling   in garden   to spirit   the day

וַיִּתְחַבֵּא הָאָדָם וְאִשְׁתּוֹ מִפְּנֵי יְהוָֹה אֱלֹהִים בְּתוֹךְ עֵץ הַגָּן׃
and he hid   the Adam   and his wife   from face   ihvh   Elohim   among   tree   the garden

8 And they heard the voice of the LORD God walking in the garden in the cool of the day: and Adam and his wife hid themselves from the presence of the LORD God amongst the trees of the garden.

וַיִּקְרָא יְהוָֹה אֱלֹהִים אֶל־הָאָדָם
and he called   ihvh   Elohim   the Adam – unto

וַיֹּאמֶר לוֹ אַיֶּכָּה׃
and he said   to him   where are you

9 And the LORD God called unto Adam, and said unto him, Where art thou?

וַיֹּאמֶר אֶת־קֹלְךָ שָׁמַעְתִּי בַּגָּן
and he said   your voice - that   I heard   in garden

וָאִירָא כִּי־עֵירֹם אָנֹכִי וָאֵחָבֵא׃
and I was afraid   naked – like   I am   and I hid

10 And he said, I heard thy voice in the garden, and I was afraid, because I was naked; and I hid myself.

וַיֹּאמֶר מִי הִגִּיד לְךָ כִּי עֵירֹם אָתָּה
and he said   who   caused to tell   to you   like   naked   you

הֲמִן־הָעֵץ אֲשֶׁר צִוִּיתִיךָ לְבִלְתִּי אֲכָל־מִמֶּנּוּ אָכָלְתָּ׃
the from - the tree   which   I commanded you   to nothing   eat - from it   you ate

11 And he said, Who told thee that thou wast naked? Hast thou eaten of the tree,

whereof I commanded thee that thou shouldest not eat?

וַיֹּאמֶר הָאָדָם
the Adam · and he said

הָאִשָּׁה אֲשֶׁר נָתַתָּה עִמָּדִי הִוא נָתְנָה־לִּי מִן־הָעֵץ וָאֹכֵל:
and I eat · the tree - from · to me – gave · she · with me · you gave · which · the wife

12 And the man said, The woman whom thou gavest to be with me, she gave me of the tree, and I did eat.

וַיֹּאמֶר יְהוָֹה אֱלֹהִים לָאִשָּׁה מַה־זֹּאת עָשִׂית
you did · this – what · to woman · Elohim · ihvh · and he said

וַתֹּאמֶר הָאִשָּׁה הַנָּחָשׁ הִשִּׁיאַנִי וָאֹכֵל:
and I eat · deceived me · the serpent · the woman · and she said

13 And the LORD God said unto the woman, What is this that thou hast done? And the woman said, The serpent beguiled me, and I did eat.

וַיֹּאמֶר יְהוָֹה אֱלֹהִים אֶל־הַנָּחָשׁ כִּי עָשִׂיתָ זֹּאת
this · you did · like · the serpent – unto · Elohim · ihvh · and he said

אָרוּר אַתָּה מִכָּל־הַבְּהֵמָה וּמִכֹּל חַיַּת הַשָּׂדֶה עַל־גְּחֹנְךָ תֵלֵךְ
you walk · your belly – upon · the field · life · and from all · the beast – from all · you · cursed

וְעָפָר תֹּאכַל כָּל־יְמֵי חַיֶּיךָ:
your life · days – all · you eat · and dust

14 And the LORD God said unto the serpent, Because thou hast done this, thou art cursed above all cattle, and above every beast of the field; upon thy belly shalt thou go, and dust shalt thou eat all the days of thy life:

וְאֵיבָה אָשִׁית בֵּינְךָ וּבֵין הָאִשָּׁה
the woman · and between · between you · I put · and enmity

וּבֵין זַרְעֲךָ וּבֵין זַרְעָהּ
her seed · and between · your seed · and between

הוּא יְשׁוּפְךָ רֹאשׁ וְאַתָּה תְּשׁוּפֶנּוּ עָקֵב:
heel · you bruise his · and you · head · he will bruise your · he

15 And I will put enmity between thee and the woman, and between thy seed and her seed; it shall bruise thy head, and thou shalt bruise his heel.

אֶל־הָאִשָּׁה אָמַר הַרְבָּה אַרְבֶּה עִצְּבוֹנֵךְ
your sorrow · I will increase · the increase · he said · the woman - unto

וְהֵרֹנֵךְ בְּעֶצֶב תֵּלְדִי בָנִים
sons · you bear · in sorrow · and your childbearing

וְאֶל־אִישֵׁךְ תְּשׁוּקָתֵךְ וְהוּא יִמְשָׁל־בָּךְ:
in you – he will rule · and he · your will crave · your man – and unto

16 Unto the woman he said, I will greatly multiply thy sorrow and thy conception; in

sorrow thou shalt bring forth children; and thy desire shall be to thy husband, and he shall rule over thee.

וּלְאָדָם אָמַר כִּי שָׁמַעְתָּ לְקוֹל אִשְׁתֶּךָ

your wife	to voice	you listened	like	he said	and to Adam

וַתֹּאכַל מִן־הָעֵץ אֲשֶׁר צִוִּיתִיךָ לֵאמֹר לֹא תֹאכַל מִמֶּנּוּ

from it	you eat	not	to say	I commanded you	which	the tree – from	and you ate

אֲרוּרָה הָאֲדָמָה בַּעֲבוּרֶךָ בְּעִצָּבוֹן תֹּאכֲלֶנָּה כֹּל יְמֵי חַיֶּיךָ:

your life	days	all	you will eat it	in sorrow	in your serving	the ground	cursed

17 And unto Adam he said, Because thou hast hearkened unto the voice of thy wife, and hast eaten of the tree, of which I commanded thee, saying, Thou shalt not eat of it: cursed is the ground for thy sake; in sorrow shalt thou eat of it all the days of thy life;

וְקוֹץ וְדַרְדַּר תַּצְמִיחַ לָךְ וְאָכַלְתָּ אֶת־עֵשֶׂב הַשָּׂדֶה:

the field	herb – that	and will you eat	to you	it will sprout	and thistles	and thorns

18 Thorns also and thistles shall it bring forth to thee; and thou shalt eat the herb of the field;

בְּזֵעַת אַפֶּיךָ תֹּאכַל לֶחֶם עַד שׁוּבְךָ אֶל־הָאֲדָמָה

the ground – unto	you return	till	bread	you will eat	your face	in sweat

כִּי מִמֶּנָּה לֻקָּחְתָּ כִּי־עָפָר אַתָּה וְאֶל־עָפָר תָּשׁוּב:

you will return	dust – and unto	you	dust – like	you were taken	from it	like

19 In the sweat of thy face shalt thou eat bread, till thou return unto the ground; for out of it wast thou taken: for dust thou art, and unto dust shalt thou return.

וַיִּקְרָא הָאָדָם שֵׁם אִשְׁתּוֹ חַוָּה כִּי הִוא הָיְתָה אֵם כָּל־חָי:

life – all	mother	was	she	like	Chavah	his wife	name	the Adam	and he called

20 And Adam called his wife's name Eve; because she was the mother of all living.

וַיַּעַשׂ יְהֹוָה אֱלֹהִים לְאָדָם וּלְאִשְׁתּוֹ כָּתְנוֹת עוֹר וַיַּלְבִּשֵׁם:

and he clothed them	skin	coats	and to his wife	to Adam	Elohim	ihvh	and he made

21 Unto Adam also and to his wife did the LORD God make coats of skins, and clothed them.

[רביעי]

וַיֹּאמֶר יְהֹוָה אֱלֹהִים

Elohim	ihvh	and he said

הֵן הָאָדָם הָיָה כְּאַחַד מִמֶּנּוּ לָדַעַת טוֹב וָרָע

and bad	good	to know	from us	like one	was	the Adam	thus

וְעַתָּה פֶּן־יִשְׁלַח יָדוֹ

his hand	he send out - lest	and now

וְלָקַח גַּם מֵעֵץ הַחַיִּים וְאָכַל וָחַי לְעֹלָם:

forever	and live	and eat	the life	from tree	also	and take

22 And the LORD God said, Behold, the man is become as one of us, to know good and evil: and now, lest he put forth his hand, and take also of the tree of life, and eat, and live for ever:

וַיְשַׁלְּחֵהוּ יְהוָה אֱלֹהִים מִגַּן־עֵדֶן

Eden – from garden   Elohim   ihvh   and he sent him

לַעֲבֹד אֶת־הָאֲדָמָה אֲשֶׁר לֻקַּח מִשָּׁם׃

from there   he taken   which   the ground – that   to work

23 Therefore the LORD God sent him forth from the garden of Eden, to till the ground from whence he was taken.

וַיְגָרֶשׁ אֶת־הָאָדָם

the Adam – that   and he drove out

וַיַּשְׁכֵּן מִקֶּדֶם לְגַן־עֵדֶן אֶת־הַכְּרֻבִים

the cherubim – that   Eden – to garden   from east   and he dwelled

וְאֵת לַהַט הַחֶרֶב הַמִּתְהַפֶּכֶת לִשְׁמֹר אֶת־דֶּרֶךְ עֵץ הַחַיִּים׃

the life   tree   way - that   to heed   the turning around   the sword   flame   and that

24 So he drove out the man; and he placed at the east of the garden of Eden Cherubims, and a flaming sword which turned every way, to keep the way of the tree of life.

CHAPTER 4

ספר בראשית פרק ד

וְהָאָדָם יָדַע אֶת־חַוָּה אִשְׁתּוֹ וַתַּהַר וַתֵּלֶד אֶת־קַיִן

Cain – that   and she begat   and she conceived   his wife   Chavah - that   knew   and the Adam

וַתֹּאמֶר קָנִיתִי אִישׁ אֶת־יְהוָה׃

ihvh – that   man   I acquired   and she said

1 And Adam knew Eve his wife; and she conceived, and bare Cain, and said, I have gotten a man from the LORD.

וַתֹּסֶף לָלֶדֶת אֶת־אָחִיו אֶת־הָבֶל

Abel – that   his brother – that   to beget   and she continued

וַיְהִי־הֶבֶל רֹעֵה צֹאן וְקַיִן הָיָה עֹבֵד אֲדָמָה׃

ground   worker   was   and Cain   flock   shepherd   Abel – and he was

2 And she again bare his brother Abel. And Abel was a keeper of sheep, but Cain was a tiller of the ground.

וַיְהִי מִקֵּץ יָמִים וַיָּבֵא קַיִן מִפְּרִי הָאֲדָמָה מִנְחָה לַיהוָה׃

to ihvh   offering   the soil   from fruit   Cain   and he brought   days   from end   and it was

3 And in process of time it came to pass, that Cain brought of the fruit of the ground an offering unto the LORD.

וְהֶבֶל הֵבִיא גַם־הוּא מִבְּכֹרוֹת צֹאנוֹ וּמֵחֶלְבֵהֶן

and from fat of them   his flock   from first born ones   he – also   the brought   and Abel

וַיִּשַׁע יְהֹוָה אֶל־הֶבֶל וְאֶל־מִנְחָתֽוֹ׃

his offering – and unto   Abel – unto   ihvh   and he lifted

4 And Abel, he also brought of the firstlings of his flock and of the fat thereof. And the LORD had respect unto Abel and to his offering:

וְאֶל־קַיִן וְאֶל־מִנְחָתוֹ לֹא שָׁעָה

respect   not   his offering - and unto   Cain – and unto

וַיִּחַר לְקַיִן מְאֹד וַיִּפְּלוּ פָּנָֽיו׃

his face   and he fell it   greatly   to Cain   and it angered

5 But unto Cain and to his offering he had not respect. And Cain was very wroth, and his countenance fell.

וַיֹּאמֶר יְהֹוָה אֶל־קָיִן לָמָּה חָרָה לָךְ

to you   angry   why   Cain – unto   ihvh   and he said

וְלָמָּה נָפְלוּ פָנֶֽיךָ׃

your face   fell it   and why

6 And the LORD said unto Cain, Why art thou wroth? and why is thy countenance fallen?

הֲלוֹא אִם־תֵּיטִיב שְׂאֵת וְאִם לֹא תֵיטִיב לַפֶּתַח חַטָּאת רֹבֵץ

lieth   sin   to opening   you do good   not   and if   accepted   you do good – if   the it

וְאֵלֶיךָ תְּשׁוּקָתוֹ וְאַתָּה תִּמְשָׁל־בּֽוֹ׃

in him – you will rule   and you   you will be it's impulse   and unto you

7 If thou doest well, shalt thou not be accepted? and if thou doest not well, sin lieth at the door. And unto thee shall be his desire, and thou shalt rule over him.

וַיֹּאמֶר קַיִן אֶל־הֶבֶל אָחִיו

his brother   Able – unto   Cain   and he said

וַיְהִי בִּהְיוֹתָם בַּשָּׂדֶה

in field   in their being   and it was

וַיָּקָם קַיִן אֶל־הֶבֶל אָחִיו וַיַּהַרְגֵֽהוּ׃

and he murdered him   his brother   Abel – unto   Cain   and he rose up

8 And Cain talked with Abel his brother: and it came to pass, when they werein the field, that Cain rose up against Abel his brother, and slew him.

וַיֹּאמֶר יְהֹוָה אֶל־קַיִן אֵי הֶבֶל אָחִיךָ

your brother   Abel   where   Cain – unto   ihvh   and he said

וַיֹּאמֶר לֹא יָדַעְתִּי הֲשֹׁמֵר אָחִי אָנֹֽכִי׃

I am   my brother   the heeder   I know   not   and he said

9 And the LORD said unto Cain, Where is Abel thy brother? And he said, I know not: Am I my brother's keeper.

וַיֹּאמֶר מֶה עָשִׂיתָ

you did   what   and he said

קוֹל דְּמֵי אָחִיךָ צֹעֲקִים אֵלַי מִן־הָאֲדָמָה׃

the ground - from   unto me   crying ones   your brother   bloods   voice

10 And he said, What hast thou done? the voice of thy brother's blood crieth unto me
from the ground.

וְעַתָּה אָרוּר אָתָּה מִן־הָאֲדָמָה

the ground – from   you   cursed   and now

אֲשֶׁר פָּצְתָה אֶת־פִּיהָ לָקַחַת אֶת־דְּמֵי אָחִיךָ מִיָּדֶךָ׃

from your hand   your brother   bloods – that   to take   her mouth – that   opened   which

11 And now art thou cursed from the earth, which hath opened her mouth
to receive thy brother's blood from thy hand;

כִּי תַעֲבֹד אֶת־הָאֲדָמָה לֹא־תֹסֵף תֵּת־כֹּחָהּ לָךְ

to you   its strength - give   continue – not   the ground – that   you work   like

נָע וָנָד תִּהְיֶה בָאָרֶץ׃

in earth   you be   and wondering   restless

12 When thou tillest the ground, it shall not henceforth yield unto thee her strength; a
fugitive and a vagabond shalt thou be in the earth.

וַיֹּאמֶר קַיִן אֶל־יְהֹוָה גָּדוֹל עֲוֹנִי מִנְּשֹׂא׃

from bearing   my inequity   great   ihvh – unto   Cain   and he said

13 And Cain said unto the LORD, My punishment is greater than I can bear.

הֵן גֵּרַשְׁתָּ אֹתִי הַיּוֹם מֵעַל פְּנֵי הָאֲדָמָה וּמִפָּנֶיךָ אֶסָּתֵר

I hide   and from your face   the ground   face   from upon   the day   to me   you drive   here

וְהָיִיתִי נָע וָנָד בָּאָרֶץ וְהָיָה כָל־מֹצְאִי יַהַרְגֵנִי׃

he will murder me   finders of me – all   and it be   in earth   and wondering   restless   and I be

14 Behold, thou hast driven me out this day from the face of the earth; and from thy
face shall I be hid; and I shall be a fugitive and a vagabond in the earth; and it shall
come to pass, that every one that findeth me shall slay me.

וַיֹּאמֶר לוֹ יְהֹוָה לָכֵן כָּל־הֹרֵג קַיִן שִׁבְעָתַיִם יֻקָּם

vengeance   seven ones   Cain   murder – all   to thus   ihvh   to him   and he said

וַיָּשֶׂם יְהֹוָה לְקַיִן אוֹת לְבִלְתִּי הַכּוֹת־אֹתוֹ כָּל־מֹצְאוֹ׃

his finders – all   to him – the kill   to nothing   sign   to Cain   ihvh   and he put

15 And the LORD said unto him, Therefore whosoever slayeth Cain, vengeance shall
be taken on him sevenfold. And the LORD set a mark upon Cain, lest any finding him
should kill him.

וַיֵּצֵא קַיִן מִלִּפְנֵי יְהֹוָה וַיֵּשֶׁב בְּאֶרֶץ־נוֹד קִדְמַת־עֵדֶן׃

Eden – towards east   Nod - in earth   and he dwelled   ihvh   from before   Cain   and he went out

16 And Cain went out from the presence of the LORD, and dwelt in the land of Nod,
on the east of Eden.

וַיֵּ֫דַע   קַ֫יִן   אֶת־אִשְׁתּ֔וֹ   וַתַּ֫הַר   וַתֵּ֫לֶד   אֶת־חֲנ֑וֹךְ
      Enoch – that   and she begat   and she concieved   his wife – that   Cain   and he knew

וַֽיְהִי֙   בֹּ֣נֶה   עִ֔יר   וַיִּקְרָא֙   שֵׁ֣ם   הָעִ֔יר   כְּשֵׁ֖ם   בְּנ֥וֹ   חֲנֽוֹךְ׃
     Enoch   his son   like name   the city   name   and he called   city   builder   and he was

17 And Cain knew his wife; and she conceived, and bare Enoch: and he built a city, and called the name of the city, after the name of his son, Enoch.

וַיִּוָּלֵ֤ד   לַֽחֲנוֹךְ֙   אֶת־עִירָ֔ד   וְעִירָ֕ד   יָלַ֖ד   אֶת־מְחֽוּיָאֵ֑ל
    Mehujael – that   begat   and Irad   Irad – that   to Enoch   and he was born

וּמְחֽיָּאֵ֗ל   יָלַד֙   אֶת־מְת֣וּשָׁאֵ֔ל   וּמְתֽוּשָׁאֵ֖ל   יָלַ֥ד   אֶת־לָֽמֶךְ׃
    Lamech – that   begat   and Methusael   Methusael – that   begat   and Mehujael

18 And unto Enoch was born Irad: and Irad begat Mehujael: and Mehujael begat Methusael: and Methusael begat Lamech.

[חמישי]

וַיִּֽקַּֽח־ל֥וֹ   לֶ֖מֶךְ   שְׁתֵּ֣י   נָשִׁ֑ים
     women   two   Lamech   to him – and he took

שֵׁ֤ם   הָֽאַחַת֙   עָדָ֔ה   וְשֵׁ֥ם   הַשֵּׁנִ֖ית   צִלָּֽה׃
   Zillah   the second   and name   Adah   the one   name

19 And Lamech took unto him two wives: the name of the one was Adah, and the name of the other Zillah.

וַתֵּ֥לֶד   עָדָ֖ה   אֶת־יָבָ֑ל   ה֣וּא   הָיָ֔ה   אֲבִ֕י   יֹשֵׁ֥ב   אֹ֖הֶל   וּמִקְנֶֽה׃
and livestock man   tent   dwelling   father   was   he   Jabel – that   Adah   and begat

20 And Adah bare Jabal: he was the father of such as dwell in tents, and of such as have cattle.

וְשֵׁ֥ם   אָחִ֖יו   יוּבָ֑ל   ה֣וּא   הָיָ֔ה   אֲבִ֕י   כָּל־תֹּפֵ֖שׂ   כִּנּ֥וֹר   וְעוּגָֽב׃
    and flute   harp   playing – all   father   was   he   Jubal   his brother   and name

21 And his brother's name was Jubal: he was the father of all such as handle the harp and organ.

וְצִלָּ֣ה   גַם־הִ֗וא   יָֽלְדָה֙   אֶת־תּ֣וּבַל   קַ֔יִן
      Cain   Tubal – that   begat   she – also   and Zillah

לֹטֵ֕שׁ   כָּל־חֹרֵ֥שׁ   נְחֹ֖שֶׁת   וּבַרְזֶ֑ל
    and iron   bronze   tooling – all   forging

וַֽאֲח֥וֹת   תּֽוּבַל־קַ֖יִן   נַֽעֲמָֽה׃
    Naamah   Cain – Tubal   and sister

22 And Zillah, she also bare Tubal-cain, an instructor of every artificer in brass and iron: and the sister of Tubal-cain wasNaamah.

[שׁשׁי]

וַיֹּאמֶר לֶמֶךְ לְנָשָׁיו עָדָה וְצִלָּה
and Zillah   Adah   to his women   Lamech   and he said

שְׁמַעַן קוֹלִי נְשֵׁי לֶמֶךְ הַאֲזֵנָּה אִמְרָתִי
my word   the ear   Lamech   women   my voice   listen

כִּי אִישׁ הָרַגְתִּי לְפִצְעִי וְיֶלֶד לְחַבֻּרָתִי׃
to my bruise   and boy   to my wound   the I murdered   man   like

23 And Lamech said unto his wives, Adah and Zillah, Hear my voice; ye wives of Lamech, hearken unto my speech: for I have slain a man to my wounding, and a young man to my hurt.

כִּי שִׁבְעָתַיִם יֻקַּם־קָיִן וְלֶמֶךְ שִׁבְעִים וְשִׁבְעָה׃
and seven   seventy   and Lamech   Cain – avenged   seven ones   like

24 If Cain shall be avenged sevenfold, truly Lamech seventy and sevenfold.

וַיֵּדַע אָדָם עוֹד אֶת־אִשְׁתּוֹ וַתֵּלֶד בֵּן
son   and she begat   his wife – that   again   Adam   and he knew

וַתִּקְרָא אֶת־שְׁמוֹ שֵׁת
Seth   his name - that   and she called

כִּי שָׁת־לִי אֱלֹהִים זֶרַע אַחֵר תַּחַת הֶבֶל
Abel   in place of   another   seed   Elohim   to me – he appointed   like

כִּי הֲרָגוֹ קָיִן׃
Cain   his murderer   like

25 And Adam knew his wife again; and she bare a son, and called his name Seth: For God, said she, hath appointed me another seed instead of Abel, whom Cain slew.

וּלְשֵׁת גַּם־הוּא יֻלַּד־בֵּן
son – begat   he – also   and to Seth

וַיִּקְרָא אֶת־שְׁמוֹ אֱנוֹשׁ אָז הוּחַל לִקְרֹא בְּשֵׁם יְהוָה׃
ihvh   in name   to call   he began   then   Enosh   his name – that   he called

26 And to Seth, to him also there was born a son; and he called his name Enos: then began men to call upon the name of the LORD.

CHAPTER 5

ספר בראשית פרק ה

זֶה סֵפֶר תּוֹלְדֹת אָדָם בְּיוֹם בְּרֹא אֱלֹהִים אָדָם
Adam   Elohim   created   in day   Adam   begatings   book   this

בִּדְמוּת אֱלֹהִים עָשָׂה אֹתוֹ׃
to him   made   Elohim   in likeness

1 This is the book of the generations of Adam. In the day that God created man, in the likeness of God made he him;

זָכָר וּנְקֵבָה בְּרָאָם וַיְבָרֶךְ אֹתָם

male   and female   created them   and he blessed   to them

וַיִּקְרָא אֶת־שְׁמָם אָדָם בְּיוֹם הִבָּרְאָם:

and he called   their names - that   Adam   in day   he created them

2 Male and female created he them; and blessed them, and called their name Adam, in the day when they were created.

וַיְחִי אָדָם שְׁלֹשִׁים וּמְאַת שָׁנָה

and lived   Adam   thirty   and one hundred   year

וַיּוֹלֶד בִּדְמוּתוֹ כְּצַלְמוֹ וַיִּקְרָא אֶת־שְׁמוֹ שֵׁת:

and he begat   in his likeness   like his image   and he called   his name – that   Seth

3 And Adam lived an hundred and thirty years, and begat a son in his own likeness, after his image; and called his name Seth:

וַיִּהְיוּ יְמֵי־אָדָם אַחֲרֵי הוֹלִידוֹ אֶת־שֵׁת שְׁמֹנֶה מֵאֹת שָׁנָה

and they were   Adam – days   after   his begatting   Seth – that   eight   hundred   year

וַיּוֹלֶד בָּנִים וּבָנוֹת:

and he begat   sons   and daughters

4 And the days of Adam after he had begotten Seth were eight hundred years: and he begat sons and daughters:

וַיִּהְיוּ כָּל־יְמֵי אָדָם אֲשֶׁר־חַי תְּשַׁע מֵאוֹת שָׁנָה וּשְׁלֹשִׁים

and they were   days – all   Adam   life- which   nine   hundreds   year   and thirty

שָׁנָה וַיָּמֹת:

year   and he died

5 And all the days that Adam lived were nine hundred and thirty years: and he died.

ס

וַיְחִי־שֵׁת חָמֵשׁ שָׁנִים וּמְאַת שָׁנָה

Seth – and he lived   five   years   and hundred   year

וַיּוֹלֶד אֶת־אֱנוֹשׁ:

and he begat   Enosh – that

ס

6 And Seth lived an hundred and five years, and begat Enos:

וַיְחִי־שֵׁת אַחֲרֵי הוֹלִידוֹ אֶת־אֱנוֹשׁ שֶׁבַע שָׁנִים

Seth – and he lived   after   his begetting   Enosh – that   seven   years

וּשְׁמֹנֶה מֵאוֹת שָׁנָה

and eight   hundred   year

וַיּוֹלֶד בָּנִים וּבָנוֹת:

and he begat   sons   and daughters

7 And Seth lived after he begat Enos eight hundred and seven years,
and begat sons and daughters:

וַיִּהְיוּ כָּל־יְמֵי־שֵׁת שְׁתֵּים עֶשְׂרֵה שָׁנָה וּתְשַׁע מֵאוֹת שָׁנָה
and they were — Seth – days – all — twelve — year and nine hundred year

וַיָּמֹת:
and he died

8 And all the days of Seth were nine hundred and twelve years: and he died.

ס

וַיְחִי אֱנוֹשׁ תִּשְׁעִים שָׁנָה וַיּוֹלֶד אֶת־קֵינָן:
and he lived Enosh ninety year and he begat Cainan – that

9 And Enos lived ninety years, and begat Cainan:

וַיְחִי אֱנוֹשׁ אַחֲרֵי הוֹלִידוֹ אֶת־קֵינָן חֲמֵשׁ עֶשְׂרֵה שָׁנָה
and he lived Enosh after his begating Cainan - that — fifteen — year

וּשְׁמֹנֶה מֵאוֹת שָׁנָה
and eight hundreds year

וַיּוֹלֶד בָּנִים וּבָנוֹת:
and he begat sons and daughters

10 And Enos lived after he begat Cainan eight hundred and fifteen years, and begat sons
and daughters:

וַיִּהְיוּ כָּל־יְמֵי אֱנוֹשׁ חָמֵשׁ שָׁנִים וּתְשַׁע מֵאוֹת שָׁנָה
and they were days – all Enosh five years and nine hundred year

וַיָּמֹת:
And he died

11 And all the days of Enos were nine hundred and five years: and he died.

ס

וַיְחִי קֵינָן שִׁבְעִים שָׁנָה וַיּוֹלֶד אֶת־מַהֲלַלְאֵל:
and he lived Cainan seventy year and he begat Mahalaleel – that

12 And Cainan lived seventy years, and begat Mahalaleel:

וַיְחִי קֵינָן אַחֲרֵי הוֹלִידוֹ אֶת־מַהֲלַלְאֵל אַרְבָּעִים שָׁנָה
and he lived Cainan after his begating Mahalaleel – that forty year

וּשְׁמֹנֶה מֵאוֹת שָׁנָה
and eight hundred year

וַיּוֹלֶד בָּנִים וּבָנוֹת:
and he begat sons and daughters

13 And Cainan lived after he begat Mahalaleel eight hundred and forty years, and begat
sons and daughters:

וַיִּהְיוּ כָּל־יְמֵי קֵינָן עֶשֶׂר שָׁנִים וּתְשַׁע מֵאוֹת שָׁנָה
<small>year   hundred   and nine   years   ten   Cainan   days – all   and they were</small>

וַיָּמֹת:
<small>and he died</small>

ס

14 And all the days of Cainan were nine hundred and ten years: and he died.

וַיְחִי מַהֲלַלְאֵל חָמֵשׁ שָׁנִים וְשִׁשִּׁים שָׁנָה
<small>year   and sixty   years   five   Mahalaleel   and he lived</small>

וַיּוֹלֶד אֶת־יָרֶד:
<small>Jared – that   and he begat</small>

15 And Mahalaleel lived sixty and five years, and begat Jared:

ס

וַיְחִי מַהֲלַלְאֵל אַחֲרֵי הוֹלִידוֹ אֶת־יֶרֶד שְׁלֹשִׁים שָׁנָה
<small>year   thirty   Jared- that   his begetting   after   Mahalaleel   and he lived</small>

וּשְׁמֹנֶה מֵאוֹת שָׁנָה
<small>year   hundred   and eight</small>

וַיּוֹלֶד בָּנִים וּבָנוֹת:
<small>and daughters   sons   and he begat</small>

16 And Mahalaleel lived after he begat Jared eight hundred and thirty years, and begat sons and daughters:

וַיִּהְיוּ כָּל־יְמֵי מַהֲלַלְאֵל חָמֵשׁ וְתִשְׁעִים שָׁנָה
<small>year   and ninety   five   Mahalaleel   days- all   and they were</small>

וּשְׁמֹנֶה מֵאוֹת שָׁנָה
<small>year   hundred   and eight</small>

וַיָּמֹת:
<small>and he died</small>

17 And all the days of Mahalaleel were eight hundred ninety and five years: and he died.

ס

וַיְחִי־יֶרֶד שְׁתַּיִם וְשִׁשִּׁים שָׁנָה וּמְאַת שָׁנָה
<small>year   and hundred   year   and sixty   two   Jared – and he lived</small>

וַיּוֹלֶד אֶת־חֲנוֹךְ:
<small>Enoch – that   and he begat</small>

18 And Jared lived an hundred sixty and two years, and he begat Enoch:

וַיְחִי־יֶרֶד אַחֲרֵי הוֹלִידוֹ אֶת־חֲנוֹךְ שְׁמֹנֶה מֵאוֹת שָׁנָה
<small>year   hundred   eight   Enoch – that   his begetting   after   Jarel – and he lived</small>

וַיּוֹלֶד בָּנִים וּבָנוֹת:

and daughters   sons   and he begat

19 And Jared lived after he begat Enoch eight hundred years,
and begat sons and daughters:

וַיִּהְיוּ כָּל־יְמֵי־יֶרֶד שְׁתַּיִם וְשִׁשִּׁים שָׁנָה וּתְשַׁע מֵאוֹת שָׁנָה

year hundred and nine year and sixty two Jared – days – all they were

וַיָּמֹת:

and he died

20 And all the days of Jared were nine hundred sixty and two years: and he died.

ס

וַיְחִי חֲנוֹךְ חָמֵשׁ וְשִׁשִּׁים שָׁנָה

year and sixty five Enoch and he lived

וַיּוֹלֶד אֶת־מְתוּשָׁלַח:

Methuselah – that and he begat

21 And Enoch lived sixty and five years, and begat Methuselah:

וַיִּתְהַלֵּךְ חֲנוֹךְ אֶת־הָאֱלֹהִים אַחֲרֵי הוֹלִידוֹ אֶת־מְתוּשֶׁלַח

Methuselah – that his begating after the Elohim – that Enoch and he walked

שְׁלֹשׁ מֵאוֹת שָׁנָה

year hundred three

וַיּוֹלֶד בָּנִים וּבָנוֹת:

and daughters sons and he begat

22 And Enoch walked with God after he begat Methuselah three hundred years, and
begat sons and daughters:

וַיְהִי כָּל־יְמֵי חֲנוֹךְ חָמֵשׁ וְשִׁשִּׁים שָׁנָה וּשְׁלֹשׁ מֵאוֹת שָׁנָה:

year hundred and three year and sixty five Enoch days – all and he was

23 And all the days of Enoch were three hundred sixty and five years:

וַיִּתְהַלֵּךְ חֲנוֹךְ אֶת־הָאֱלֹהִים

the Elohim – that Enoch and he walked

וְאֵינֶנּוּ כִּי־לָקַח אֹתוֹ אֱלֹהִים:

Elohim to him he took – like and he wasn't

24 And Enoch walked with God: and he was not; for God took him.

ס

[שביעי]

וַיְחִי מְתוּשֶׁלַח שֶׁבַע וּשְׁמֹנִים שָׁנָה וּמְאַת שָׁנָה

year and hundred year and eighty seven Methuselah and he lived

וַיּוֹלֶד אֶת־לָמֶךְ׃

<small>Lamech – that   and he begat</small>

25 And Methuselah lived an hundred eighty and seven years, and begat Lamech:

וַיְחִי מְתוּשֶׁלַח אַחֲרֵי הוֹלִידוֹ אֶת־לֶמֶךְ

<small>Lamech – that   his begating   after   Methuselah   and he lived</small>

שְׁתַּיִם וּשְׁמוֹנִים שָׁנָה וּשְׁבַע מֵאוֹת שָׁנָה

<small>year   hundred   and seven   year   and eighty   two</small>

וַיּוֹלֶד בָּנִים וּבָנוֹת׃

<small>and daughters   sons   and he begat</small>

26 And Methuselah lived after he begat Lamech seven hundred eighty and two years, and begat sons and daughters:

וַיִּהְיוּ כָּל־יְמֵי מְתוּשֶׁלַח תֵּשַׁע וְשִׁשִּׁים שָׁנָה וּתְשַׁע מֵאוֹת

<small>hundred   and nine   year   and sixty   nine   Methuselah   days – all   and they were</small>

שָׁנָה וַיָּמֹת׃

<small>and he died   year</small>

27 And all the days of Methuselah were nine hundred sixty and nine years: and he died.

ס

וַיְחִי־לֶמֶךְ שְׁתַּיִם וּשְׁמֹנִים שָׁנָה וּמְאַת שָׁנָה

<small>year   and hundred   year   and eighty   two   Lamech – and he lived</small>

וַיּוֹלֶד בֵּן׃

<small>son   and he begat</small>

28 And Lamech lived an hundred eighty and two years, and begat a son:

וַיִּקְרָא אֶת־שְׁמוֹ נֹחַ לֵאמֹר זֶה יְנַחֲמֵנוּ מִמַּעֲשֵׂנוּ

<small>from our labors   he will comfort us   this   to say   Noah   his name – that   and he called</small>

וּמֵעִצְּבוֹן יָדֵינוּ מִן־הָאֲדָמָה אֲשֶׁר אֵרְרָהּ יְהוָה׃

<small>ihvh   cursed it   which   the soil – from   our hands   and from toil</small>

29 And he called his name Noah, saying, This same shall comfort us concerning our work and toil of our hands, because of the ground which the LORD hath cursed.

וַיְחִי־לֶמֶךְ אַחֲרֵי הוֹלִידוֹ אֶת־נֹחַ חָמֵשׁ וְתִשְׁעִים שָׁנָה

<small>year   and ninety   five   Noah – that   his begetting   after   Lamech – the lived</small>

וַחֲמֵשׁ מֵאֹת שָׁנָה

<small>year   hundred   and five</small>

וַיּוֹלֶד בָּנִים וּבָנוֹת׃

<small>and daughters   sons   and he begat</small>

30 And Lamech lived after he begat Noah five hundred ninety and five years, and begat sons and daughters:

וַיְהִי֙ כָּל־יְמֵי־לֶ֔מֶךְ שֶׁ֤בַע וְשִׁבְעִים֙ שָׁנָ֔ה וּשְׁבַ֥ע מֵא֖וֹת שָׁנָ֑ה

| year | hundred | and seven | year | and seventy | seven | Lamech – days – all | and he was |

וַיָּמֹֽת׃

| and he died |

31 And all the days of Lamech were seven hundred seventy and seven years: and he died.

ס

וַֽיְהִי־נֹ֕חַ בֶּן־חֲמֵ֥שׁ מֵא֖וֹת שָׁנָ֑ה

| year | hundred | five – age | Noah – and he was |

וַיּ֣וֹלֶד נֹ֔חַ אֶת־שֵׁ֖ם אֶת־חָ֥ם וְאֶת־יָֽפֶת׃

| Jepheth – and that | Ham – that | Shem – that | Noah | and he begat |

32 And Noah was five hundred years old: and Noah begat Shem, Ham, and Japheth.

CHAPTER 6

ספר בראשית פרק ו

וַֽיְהִי֙ כִּֽי־הֵחֵ֣ל הָֽאָדָ֔ם לָרֹ֖ב עַל־פְּנֵ֣י הָֽאֲדָמָ֑ה

| the ground | face – upon | to increase | The Adam | start - like | and it was |

וּבָנ֖וֹת יֻלְּד֥וּ לָהֶֽם׃

| to them | they born | and daughters |

1 And it came to pass, when men began to multiply on the face of the earth, and daughters were born unto them,

וַיִּרְא֤וּ בְנֵי־הָֽאֱלֹהִים֙ אֶת־בְּנ֣וֹת הָֽאָדָ֔ם כִּ֥י טֹבֹ֖ת הֵ֑נָּה

| they | good ones | like | the Adam | daughters – that | the Elohim – sons | and they saw |

וַיִּקְח֤וּ לָהֶם֙ נָשִׁ֔ים מִכֹּ֖ל אֲשֶׁ֥ר בָּחָֽרוּ׃

| they chose | which | from all | women | to them | and they took |

2 That the sons of God saw the daughters of men that they were fair; and they took them wives of all which they chose.

וַיֹּ֣אמֶר יְהֹוָ֗ה לֹֽא־יָד֨וֹן רוּחִ֤י בָֽאָדָם֙ לְעֹלָ֔ם בְּשַׁגַּ֖ם ה֣וּא בָשָׂ֑ר

| flesh | he | in that also | forever | in Adam | my spirit | it adjudicate – not | ihvh | and he said |

וְהָי֣וּ יָמָ֔יו מֵאָ֥ה וְעֶשְׂרִ֖ים שָׁנָֽה׃

| year | and twenty | hundred | his days | and they will be |

3 And the LORD said, My spirit shall not always strive with man, for that he also is flesh: yet his days shall be an hundred and twenty years.

הַנְּפִלִ֞ים הָי֣וּ בָאָרֶץ֮ בַּיָּמִ֣ים הָהֵם֒

| the them | in days | in earth | they were | the fallen ones |

וְגַ֣ם אַֽחֲרֵי־כֵ֗ן אֲשֶׁ֨ר יָבֹ֜אוּ בְּנֵ֤י הָֽאֱלֹהִים֙ אֶל־בְּנ֣וֹת הָֽאָדָ֔ם

| the Adam | daughters – unto | the Elohim | sons | they came | which | thus - after | and also |

וַיֵּלְדוּ   לָהֶם הֵמָּה הַגִּבֹּרִים אֲשֶׁר מֵעוֹלָם אַנְשֵׁי הַשֵּׁם:

the name   men   from forever   which   the great ones   they are   to them   and they begat

4 There were giants in the earth in those days; and also after that, when the sons of God came in unto the daughters of men, and they bare children to them, the same became mighty men which were of old, men of renown.

פ

[מפטיר]

וַיַּרְא יְהוָה כִּי רַבָּה רָעַת הָאָדָם בָּאָרֶץ

in earth   the Adam   bad   many   like   ihvh   and he saw

וְכָל־יֵצֶר   מַחְשְׁבֹת לִבּוֹ רַק רַע כָּל־הַיּוֹם:

the day – all   evil   only   his heart   ideas   came out – and all

5 And God saw that the wickedness of man was great in the earth, and that every imagination of the thoughts of his heart was only evil continually.

וַיִּנָּחֶם   יְהוָה כִּי־עָשָׂה אֶת־הָאָדָם בָּאָרֶץ

in earth   the Adam – that   made – like   ihvh   and he regretted

וַיִּתְעַצֵּב   אֶל־לִבּוֹ:

his heart – unto   and he is grieving

6 And it repented the LORD that he had made man on the earth, and it grieved him at his heart.

וַיֹּאמֶר יְהוָה

ihvh   and he said

אֶמְחֶה   אֶת־הָאָדָם אֲשֶׁר־בָּרָאתִי מֵעַל פְּנֵי הָאֲדָמָה

the ground   face   from upon   I created – which   the Adam – that   I will wipe away

מֵאָדָם עַד־בְּהֵמָה עַד־רֶמֶשׂ וְעַד־עוֹף הַשָּׁמָיִם

the heavens   bird – and till   creeping thing – till   beast – till   from Adam

כִּי נִחַמְתִּי כִּי עֲשִׂיתִם:

I made them   like   I regretted   like

7 And the LORD said, I will destroy man whom I have created from the face of the earth; both man, and beast, and the creeping thing, and the fowls of the air; for it repenteth me that I have made them.

וְנֹחַ מָצָא חֵן בְּעֵינֵי יְהוָה:

ihvh   in eyes   favor   found   and Noah

8 But Noah found grace in the eyes of the LORD.

פ פ פ

2 Noah

Chapter 6 cont

[פרשת נח]

אֵלֶּה תּוֹלְדֹת נֹחַ
these   begattings   Noah

נֹחַ אִישׁ צַדִּיק תָּמִים הָיָה בְּדֹרֹתָיו
Noah   man   righteous   perfect   he was   in his generations

אֶת־הָאֱלֹהִים הִתְהַלֶּךְ־נֹחַ:
that – the Elohim   Noah – walked

9 These are the generations of Noah: Noah was a just man and perfect in his generations, and Noah walked with God.

וַיּוֹלֶד נֹחַ שְׁלֹשָׁה בָנִים אֶת־שֵׁם אֶת־חָם וְאֶת־יָפֶת:
and he begat   Noah   three   sons   that – Shem   that – Ham   and that – Japheth

10 And Noah begat three sons, Shem, Ham, and Japheth.

וַתִּשָּׁחֵת הָאָרֶץ לִפְנֵי הָאֱלֹהִים וַתִּמָּלֵא הָאָרֶץ חָמָס:
and was corrupt   the earth   before   the Elohim   and it was full   the earth   violence

11 The earth also was corrupt before God, and the earth was filled with violence.

וַיַּרְא אֱלֹהִים אֶת־הָאָרֶץ וְהִנֵּה נִשְׁחָתָה
and he saw   Elohim   the earth – that   and here   it corrupt

כִּי־הִשְׁחִית כָּל־בָּשָׂר אֶת־דַּרְכּוֹ עַל־הָאָרֶץ:
like - corrupted   all – flesh   that – his way   upon – the earth

12 And God looked upon the earth, and, behold, it was corrupt; for all flesh had corrupted his way upon the earth.

וַיֹּאמֶר אֱלֹהִים לְנֹחַ קֵץ כָּל־בָּשָׂר בָּא לְפָנַי
and he said   Elohim   to Noah   end   flesh – all   come   before me

כִּי־מָלְאָה הָאָרֶץ חָמָס מִפְּנֵיהֶם
like - filled   the earth   violence   from their face

וְהִנְנִי מַשְׁחִיתָם אֶת־הָאָרֶץ:
and here I   destroy them   the earth – that

13 And God said unto Noah, The end of all flesh is come before me; for the earth is filled with violence through them; and, behold, I will destroy them with the earth.

עֲשֵׂה לְךָ תֵּבַת עֲצֵי־גֹפֶר קִנִּים תַּעֲשֶׂה אֶת־הַתֵּבָה
make   to you   ark   gopher – wood   compartments   you make   the ark - that

וְכָפַרְתָּ אֹתָהּ מִבַּיִת וּמִחוּץ בַּכֹּפֶר:
and you coat   to it   interior   and outside   in pitch

14 Make thee an ark of gopher wood; rooms shalt thou make in the ark, and shalt pitch it within and without with pitch.

וְזֶה אֲשֶׁר תַּעֲשֶׂה אֹתָהּ
    to it   you make   which   and this

שְׁלֹשׁ מֵאוֹת אַמָּה אֹרֶךְ הַתֵּבָה חֲמִשִּׁים אַמָּה רָחְבָּהּ
width   cubit   fifty   the ark   length   cubit   hundreds   three

וּשְׁלֹשִׁים אַמָּה קוֹמָתָהּ:
it's height   cubit   and thirty

15 And this is the fashion which thou shalt make it of: The length of the ark shall be three hundred cubits, the breadth of it fifty cubits, and the height of it thirty cubits.

צֹהַר תַּעֲשֶׂה לַתֵּבָה וְאֶל־אַמָּה תְּכַלֶּנָּה מִלְמַעְלָה
from above   you finish it   cubit – and unto   to ark   you make   window

וּפֶתַח הַתֵּבָה בְּצִדָּהּ תָּשִׂים
you put ones   in it's side   the ark   and opening

תַּחְתִּיִּם שְׁנִיִּם וּשְׁלִשִׁים תַּעֲשֶׂהָ:
you make it   and third ones   second ones   bottom ones

16 A window shalt thou make to the ark, and in a cubit shalt thou finish it above; and the door of the ark shalt thou set in the side thereof; with lower, second, and third stories shalt thou make it.

וַאֲנִי הִנְנִי מֵבִיא אֶת־הַמַּבּוּל מַיִם עַל־הָאָרֶץ
the earth – upon   water   the flood – that   bring   here   and I

לְשַׁחֵת כָּל־בָּשָׂר אֲשֶׁר־בּוֹ רוּחַ חַיִּים מִתַּחַת הַשָּׁמָיִם
the heavens   from under   life   spirit   in it – which   flesh – all   to destroy

כֹּל אֲשֶׁר־בָּאָרֶץ יִגְוָע:
it will expire   in earth – which   all

17 And, behold, I, even I, do bring a flood of waters upon the earth, to destroy all flesh, wherein is the breath of life, from under heaven; and every thing that is in the earth shall die.

וַהֲקִמֹתִי אֶת־בְּרִיתִי אִתָּךְ וּבָאתָ אֶל־הַתֵּבָה אַתָּה וּבָנֶיךָ
and your sons   you   the ark – unto   and you come   with you   covenant – that   and the I will establish

וְאִשְׁתְּךָ וּנְשֵׁי־בָנֶיךָ אִתָּךְ:
with you   your sons – and women   and your wife

18 But with thee will I establish my covenant; and thou shalt come into the ark, thou, and thy sons, and thy wife, and thy sons' wives with thee.

וּמִכָּל־הָחַי מִכָּל־בָּשָׂר שְׁנַיִם מִכֹּל תָּבִיא אֶל־הַתֵּבָה
the ark – unto   you bring   from all   two   flesh – from all   the life – from all

לְהַחֲיֹת   אִתָּךְ   זָכָר   וּנְקֵבָה   יִהְיוּ׃

they be   and female   male   with you   to the sustain life

19 And of every living thing of all flesh, two of every sort shalt thou bring into the ark, to keep them alive with thee; they shall be male and female.

מֵהָעוֹף   לְמִינֵהוּ   וּמִן־הַבְּהֵמָה   לְמִינָהּ

to it's kind   the beast – and from   to it's kind   from the bird

מִכֹּל   רֶמֶשׂ   הָאֲדָמָה   לְמִינֵהוּ

to it's kind   the ground   creeping things   from all

שְׁנַיִם   מִכֹּל   יָבֹאוּ   אֵלֶיךָ   לְהַחֲיוֹת׃

to the sustain life   unto you   they will come   from all   two

20 Of fowls after their kind, and of cattle after their kind, of every creeping thing of the earth after his kind, two of every sort shall come unto thee, to keep them alive.

וְאַתָּה   קַח־לְךָ   מִכָּל־מַאֲכָל   אֲשֶׁר   יֵאָכֵל

it eat   which   food – from all   to you – take   and you

וְאָסַפְתָּ   אֵלֶיךָ   וְהָיָה   לְךָ   וְלָהֶם   לְאָכְלָה׃

to food   and to them   to you   and it will be   unto you   and you gather

21 And take thou unto thee of all food that is eaten, and thou shalt gather it to thee; and it shall be for food for thee, and for them.

וַיַּעַשׂ   נֹחַ   כְּכֹל   אֲשֶׁר   צִוָּה   אֹתוֹ   אֱלֹהִים   כֵּן   עָשָׂה׃

he did   thus   Elohim   to him   commanded   which   like all   Noah   and he did

22 Thus did Noah; according to all that God commanded him, so did he.

CHAPTER 7

ספר בראשית פרק ז

[שני]

וַיֹּאמֶר   יְהֹוָה   לְנֹחַ   בֹּא־אַתָּה   וְכָל־בֵּיתְךָ   אֶל־הַתֵּבָה

the ark – unto   your house – and all   you – come   to Noah   ihvh   and he said

כִּי־אֹתְךָ   רָאִיתִי   צַדִּיק   לְפָנַי   בַּדּוֹר   הַזֶּה׃

the this   in generation   before   righteous   I saw   to you - like

1 And the LORD said unto Noah, Come thou and all thy house into the ark; for thee have I seen righteous before me in this generation.

מִכֹּל   הַבְּהֵמָה   הַטְּהוֹרָה

the clean   the beast   from every

תִּקַּח־לְךָ   שִׁבְעָה   שִׁבְעָה   אִישׁ   וְאִשְׁתּוֹ

and his wife   man   seven   seven   to you – you take

וּמִן־הַבְּהֵמָה   אֲשֶׁר   לֹא   טְהֹרָה   הִוא   שְׁנַיִם   אִישׁ   וְאִשְׁתּוֹ׃

and his wife   man   pair   it   clean   not   which   the beast – and from

2 Of every clean beast thou shalt take to thee by sevens, the male and his female: and of

beasts that are not clean by two, the male and his female.

גַּם מֵעֹוף הַשָּׁמַיִם שִׁבְעָה שִׁבְעָה זָכָר וּנְקֵבָה
and female　male　seven　seven　the heavens　from bird　also

לְחַיֹּות זֶרַע עַל־פְּנֵי כָל־הָאָרֶץ׃
earth – all　face – upon　seed　to sustain life

3 Of fowls also of the air by sevens, the male and the female; to keep seed alive upon the face of all the earth.

כִּי לְיָמִים עֹוד שִׁבְעָה אָנֹכִי מַמְטִיר עַל־הָאָרֶץ
the earth - upon　showering rain　I am　seven　again　to days　like

אַרְבָּעִים יֹום וְאַרְבָּעִים לָיְלָה
nights　and forty　days　forty

וּמָחִיתִי אֶת־כָּל־הַיְקוּם אֲשֶׁר עָשִׂיתִי מֵעַל פְּנֵי הָאֲדָמָה׃
the ground　face　from upon　I made　which　the substance– all - that　and wipe out

4 For yet seven days, and I will cause it to rain upon the earth forty days and forty nights; and every living substance that I have made will I destroy from off the face of the earth.

וַיַּעַשׂ נֹחַ כְּכֹל אֲשֶׁר־צִוָּהוּ יְהוָה׃
ihvh　commanded him – which　like all　Noah　and he did

5 And Noah did according unto all that the LORD commanded him.

וְנֹחַ בֶּן־שֵׁשׁ מֵאֹות שָׁנָה
year　hundred　six – age　Noah

וְהַמַּבּוּל הָיָה מַיִם עַל־הָאָרֶץ׃
earth – upon　water　was　the flood

6 And Noah was six hundred years old when the flood of waters was upon the earth.

וַיָּבֹא נֹחַ וּבָנָיו וְאִשְׁתֹּו
and his wife　and his sons　Noah　and he came

וּנְשֵׁי־בָנָיו אִתֹּו אֶל־הַתֵּבָה מִפְּנֵי מֵי הַמַּבּוּל׃
the flood　waters　from face　the ark – unto　to him　his sons – and women

7 And Noah went in, and his sons, and his wife, and his sons' wives with him, into the ark, because of the waters of the flood.

מִן־הַבְּהֵמָה הַטְּהֹורָה וּמִן־הַבְּהֵמָה אֲשֶׁר אֵינֶנָּה טְהֹרָה
clean　it isn't　which　the beast - and from　the clean　the beast - from

וּמִן־הָעֹוף וְכֹל אֲשֶׁר־רֹמֵשׂ עַל־הָאֲדָמָה׃
the soil – upon　creeps – which　and all　the bird – and from

8 Of clean beasts, and of beasts that are not clean, and of fowls, and of every thing that creepeth upon the earth,

שְׁנַ֤יִם שְׁנַ֙יִם֙ בָּ֤אוּ אֶל־נֹ֙חַ֙ אֶל־הַתֵּבָ֔ה
the ark – unto   Noah – unto   they came   two   two

זָכָ֥ר וּנְקֵבָ֖ה כַּאֲשֶׁ֛ר צִוָּ֥ה אֱלֹהִ֖ים אֶת־נֹֽחַ׃
Noah – that   Elohim   he commanded   when   and female   male

9 There went in two and two unto Noah into the ark, the male and the female, as God had commanded Noah.

וַֽיְהִ֖י לְשִׁבְעַ֣ת הַיָּמִ֑ים וּמֵ֣י הַמַּבּ֔וּל הָי֖וּ עַל־הָאָֽרֶץ׃
the earth – upon   they were   the flood   and water   the days   to seven   and it was

10 And it came to pass after seven days, that the waters of the flood were upon the earth.

בִּשְׁנַ֙ת שֵׁשׁ־מֵא֤וֹת שָׁנָה֙ לְחַיֵּֽי־נֹ֔חַ
Noah – to life   year   hundred – six   in year

בַּחֹ֙דֶשׁ֙ הַשֵּׁנִ֔י בְּשִׁבְעָֽה־עָשָׂ֥ר י֖וֹם לַחֹ֑דֶשׁ
to month   day   -- in seventeen --   the second   in month

בַּיּ֣וֹם הַזֶּ֗ה נִבְקְעוּ֙ כָּל־מַעְיְנֹת֙ תְּה֣וֹם רַבָּ֔ה
many   deep   springs – all   they burst   the this   in day

וַאֲרֻבֹּ֥ת הַשָּׁמַ֖יִם נִפְתָּֽחוּ׃
they opened   the heavens   and windows

11 In the six hundredth year of Noah's life, in the second month, the seventeenth day of the month, the same day were all the fountains of the great deep broken up, and the windows of heaven were opened.

וַֽיְהִ֥י הַגֶּ֖שֶׁם עַל־הָאָ֑רֶץ אַרְבָּעִ֣ים י֔וֹם וְאַרְבָּעִ֖ים לָֽיְלָה׃
night   and forty   day   forty   the earth – upon   the rain   and it was

12 And the rain was upon the earth forty days and forty nights.

בְּעֶ֙צֶם֙ הַיּ֣וֹם הַזֶּ֔ה בָּ֣א נֹ֔חַ וְשֵׁם־וְחָ֥ם וָיֶ֖פֶת בְּנֵי־נֹ֑חַ
Noah – sons   and Japheth   and Ham- and Shem   Noah   came   the this   the day   in selfsame

וְאֵ֣שֶׁת נֹ֗חַ וּשְׁלֹ֧שֶׁת נְשֵֽׁי־בָנָ֛יו אִתָּ֖ם אֶל־הַתֵּבָֽה׃
the ark – unto   with them   his sons - women   and three   Noah   and wife

13 In the selfsame day entered Noah, and Shem, and Ham, and Japheth, the sons of Noah, and Noah's wife, and the three wives of his sons with them, into the ark;

הֵ֜מָּה וְכָל־הַֽחַיָּ֣ה לְמִינָ֗הּ וְכָל־הַבְּהֵמָה֙ לְמִינָ֔הּ
to its kind   the beast – and all   to it's kind   the life – and all   them

וְכָל־הָרֶ֛מֶשׂ הָרֹמֵ֥שׂ עַל־הָאָ֖רֶץ לְמִינֵ֑הוּ
to their kind   the earth – upon   the creeper   the creeping – and all

וְכָל־הָע֣וֹף לְמִינֵ֔הוּ כֹּ֖ל צִפּ֥וֹר כָּל־כָּנָֽף׃
wing – all   bird   all   to their kind   the bird – and all

14 They, and every beast after his kind, and all the cattle after their kind, and every creeping thing that creepeth upon the earth after his kind, and every fowl after his kind,

every bird of every sort.

וַיָּבֹ֨אוּ   אֶל־נֹ֜חַ אֶל־הַתֵּבָ֗ה שְׁנַ֤יִם שְׁנַ֙יִם֙

and they came   Noah - unto   the ark – unto   two   two

מִכָּל־הַבָּשָׂ֔ר אֲשֶׁר־בּ֖וֹ ר֥וּחַ חַיִּֽים׃

the flesh – from all   in him – which   spirit   lives

15 And they went in unto Noah into the ark, two and two of all flesh, wherein is the breath of life.

וְהַבָּאִ֗ים   זָכָ֨ר וּנְקֵבָ֤ה מִכָּל־בָּשָׂר֙ בָּ֔אוּ

and the coming ones   male   and female   flesh – from all   they came

כַּאֲשֶׁ֛ר צִוָּ֥ה   אֹת֖וֹ אֱלֹהִ֑ים וַיִּסְגֹּ֥ר יְהוָ֖ה בַּעֲדֽוֹ׃

when   commanded   to him   Elohim   and he closed   ihvh   in his time

16 And they that went in, went in male and female of all flesh, as God had commanded him: and the LORD shut him in.

[שלישי]

וַֽיְהִ֧י   הַמַּבּ֛וּל אַרְבָּעִ֥ים י֖וֹם עַל־הָאָ֑רֶץ וַיִּרְבּ֣וּ הַמַּ֔יִם

and it came   the flood   forty   day   the earth – upon   they increased   the waters

וַיִּשְׂא֙וּ   אֶת־הַתֵּבָ֔ה וַתָּ֖רָם מֵעַ֥ל הָאָֽרֶץ׃

and they lifted   the ark – that   and it rose up   from upon   the earth

17 And the flood was forty days upon the earth; and the waters increased, and bare up the ark, and it was lift up above the earth.

וַיִּגְבְּר֥וּ   הַמַּ֛יִם וַיִּרְבּ֥וּ מְאֹ֖ד עַל־הָאָ֑רֶץ

and they prevailed   the waters   and they increased   very   the earth – upon

וַתֵּ֥לֶךְ הַתֵּבָ֖ה עַל־פְּנֵ֥י הַמָּֽיִם׃

and it went   the ark   upon – face   the waters

18 And the waters prevailed, and were increased greatly upon the earth; and the ark went upon the face of the waters.

וְהַמַּ֗יִם   גָּ֥ברוּ מְאֹ֛ד מְאֹ֖ד עַל־הָאָ֑רֶץ

and the waters   they prevailed   greatly   greatly   the earth – upon

וַיְכֻסּ֗וּ   כָּל־הֶֽהָרִים֙ הַגְּבֹהִ֔ים אֲשֶׁר־תַּ֖חַת כָּל־הַשָּׁמָֽיִם׃

and they covered   the mountains - all   the high ones   which – under   the heavens – all

19 And the waters prevailed exceedingly upon the earth; and all the high hills, that were under the whole heaven, were covered.

חֲמֵ֨שׁ עֶשְׂרֵ֤ה אַמָּה֙ מִלְמַ֔עְלָה גָּבְר֖וּ הַמָּ֑יִם

-- fifteen --   cubits   upward   they prevailed   the waters

וַיְכֻסּ֖וּ   הֶהָרִֽים׃

and they covered   the mountains

20 Fifteen cubits upward did the waters prevail; and the mountains were covered.

וַיִּגְוַ֞ע   כָּל־בָּשָׂ֣ר ׀ הָרֹמֵ֣שׂ עַל־הָאָ֗רֶץ בָּע֤וֹף וּבַבְּהֵמָ֣ה
and it expired   flesh – all   the creepers   the earth – upon   in bird   and in beasts

וּבַ֣חַיָּ֔ה וּבְכָל־הַשֶּׁ֖רֶץ הַשֹּׁרֵ֣ץ עַל־הָאָ֑רֶץ
and in life   – and in all   the swarming   the swarmer   the earth – upon

וְכֹ֖ל הָאָדָֽם׃
and all   the Adam

21 And all flesh died that moved upon the earth, both of fowl, and of cattle, and of
beast, and of every creeping thing that creepeth upon the earth, and every man:

כֹּ֡ל אֲשֶׁר֩ נִשְׁמַת־ר֨וּחַ חַיִּ֜ים בְּאַפָּ֗יו מִכֹּ֛ל אֲשֶׁ֥ר בֶּחָֽרָבָ֖ה מֵֽתוּ׃
all   which   spirit – high soul   lives   in his nostril   from all   which   in dry land   they died

22 All in whose nostrils was the breath of life, of all that was in the dry land, died.

וַיִּ֜מַח   אֶֽת־כָּל־הַיְק֣וּם ׀ אֲשֶׁ֣ר ׀ עַל־פְּנֵ֣י הָֽאֲדָמָ֗ה
and he wiped out   the it rise - all – that   which   face – upon   the soil

מֵֽאָדָ֤ם עַד־בְּהֵמָה֙ עַד־רֶ֙מֶשׂ֙ וְעַד־ע֣וֹף הַשָּׁמַ֔יִם
from Adam   beasts – till   creeping – till   bird – and till   the heavens

וַיִּמָּח֖וּ   מִן־הָאָ֑רֶץ
and they were wiped out   the earth – from

וַיִשָּׁ֧אֶר אַךְ־נֹ֛חַ וַֽאֲשֶׁ֥ר אִתּ֖וֹ בַּתֵּבָֽה׃
and he remained   Noah – only   and which   with him   in ark

23 And every living substance was destroyed which was upon the face of the ground,
both man, and cattle, and the creeping things, and the fowl of the heaven; and they were
destroyed from the earth: and Noah only remained alive, and they that were with him in
the ark.

וַיִּגְבְּר֥וּ הַמַּ֖יִם עַל־הָאָ֑רֶץ חֲמִשִּׁ֥ים וּמְאַ֖ת יֽוֹם׃
and they prevailed   the waters   the earth – upon   fifty   and hundred   day

24 And the waters prevailed upon the earth an hundred and fifty days.

CHAPTER 8

ספר בראשית פרק ח

וַיִּזְכֹּ֤ר   אֱלֹהִים֙ אֶת־נֹ֔חַ וְאֵ֤ת כָּל־הַֽחַיָּ֔ה
and he remembered   Elohim   Noah – that   and that   the life – all

וְאֶת־כָּל־הַבְּהֵמָ֔ה אֲשֶׁ֥ר אִתּ֖וֹ בַּתֵּבָ֑ה
and that – all – the beasts   which   with him   in ark

וַיַּעֲבֵ֨ר אֱלֹהִ֥ים ר֨וּחַ֙ עַל־הָאָ֔רֶץ וַיָּשֹׁ֖כּוּ הַמָּֽיִם׃
and he passed   Elohim   wind   the earth – upon   and they receded   the waters

1 And God remembered Noah, and every living thing, and all the cattle that was with
him in the ark: and God made a wind to pass over the earth, and the waters asswaged;

וַיִּסָּכְרוּ מַעְיְנֹת תְּהוֹם וַאֲרֻבֹּת הַשָּׁמָיִם
the heavens   and crevices   deep   springs   and they stopped

וַיִּכָּלֵא הַגֶּשֶׁם מִן־הַשָּׁמָיִם:
the heavens – from   the rain   and he restrained

2 The fountains also of the deep and the windows of heaven were stopped, and the rain
from heaven was restrained;

וַיָּשֻׁבוּ הַמַּיִם מֵעַל הָאָרֶץ הָלוֹךְ וָשׁוֹב
and returning   going   the earth   from upon   the waters   and they returned

וַיַּחְסְרוּ הַמַּיִם מִקְצֵה חֲמִשִּׁים וּמְאַת יוֹם:
day   and one hundred   fifty   from end   the waters   and they receded

3 And the waters returned from off the earth continually: and after the end of the
hundred and fifty days the waters were abated.

וַתָּנַח הַתֵּבָה בַּחֹדֶשׁ הַשְּׁבִיעִי בְּשִׁבְעָה־עָשָׂר יוֹם לַחֹדֶשׁ
to month   day   -- in seventeen --   the seventh   in month   the ark   and rested

עַל הָרֵי אֲרָרָט:
Arrat   mountains   upon

4 And the ark rested in the seventh month, on the seventeenth day of the month, upon
the mountains of Ararat.

וְהַמַּיִם הָיוּ הָלוֹךְ
going   they were   and the waters

וְחָסוֹר עַד הַחֹדֶשׁ הָעֲשִׂירִי
the tenth   the month   till   and receding

בָּעֲשִׂירִי בְּאֶחָד לַחֹדֶשׁ נִרְאוּ רָאשֵׁי הֶהָרִים:
the mountains   tops   they appeared   to month   in one   in tenth

5 And the waters decreased continually until the tenth month: in the tenth month, on
the first day of the month, were the tops of the mountains seen.

וַיְהִי מִקֵּץ אַרְבָּעִים יוֹם
day   forty   from end   and it was

וַיִּפְתַּח נֹחַ אֶת־חַלּוֹן הַתֵּבָה אֲשֶׁר עָשָׂה:
he made   which   the ark   window – that   Noah   and he opened

6 And it came to pass at the end of forty days, that Noah opened the window of the ark
which he had made:

וַיְשַׁלַּח אֶת־הָעֹרֵב וַיֵּצֵא יָצוֹא
he went about   and he went out   the raven – that   and he sent

וָשׁוֹב עַד־יְבֹשֶׁת הַמַּיִם מֵעַל הָאָרֶץ:
the earth   from upon   the waters   dryed - till   and returned

7 And he sent forth a raven, which went forth to and fro, until the waters were dried up
from off the earth.

וַיְשַׁלַּח אֶת־הַיּוֹנָה מֵאִתּוֹ

from with him   the dove – that   and he sent

לִרְאוֹת הֲקַלּוּ הַמַּיִם מֵעַל פְּנֵי הָאֲדָמָה:

the ground   face   from upon   the waters   the receded   to seeing

8 Also he sent forth a dove from him, to see if the waters were abated from off the face of the ground;

וְלֹא־מָצְאָה הַיּוֹנָה מָנוֹחַ לְכַף־רַגְלָהּ

her foot – to palm   place   the dove   found - and not

וַתָּשׇׁב אֵלָיו אֶל־הַתֵּבָה כִּי־מַיִם עַל־פְּנֵי כָל־הָאָרֶץ

the earth – all   face – upon   waters – like   the ark – unto   unto him   and she returned

וַיִּשְׁלַח יָדוֹ וַיִּקָּחֶהָ וַיָּבֵא אֹתָהּ אֵלָיו אֶל־הַתֵּבָה:

the ark – unto   unto him   with her   and he came   and took her   his hand   and he sent

9 But the dove found no rest for the sole of her foot, and she returned unto him into the ark, for the waters were on the face of the whole earth: then he put forth his hand, and took her, and pulled her in unto him into the ark.

וַיָּחֶל עוֹד שִׁבְעַת יָמִים אֲחֵרִים

after ones   days   seven   again   and he waited

וַיֹּסֶף שַׁלַּח אֶת־הַיּוֹנָה מִן־הַתֵּבָה:

the ark – from   the dove – that   sent   and he repeated

10 And he stayed yet other seven days; and again he sent forth the dove out of the ark;

וַתָּבֹא אֵלָיו הַיּוֹנָה לְעֵת עֶרֶב

evening   to time   the dove   to him   and she came

וְהִנֵּה עֲלֵה־זַיִת טָרָף בְּפִיהָ

in her mouth   broke off   olive – leaf   and here

וַיֵּדַע נֹחַ כִּי־קַלּוּ הַמַּיִם מֵעַל הָאָרֶץ:

the earth   from upon   the waters   they receded – like   Noah   and he knew

11 And the dove came in to him in the evening; and, lo, in her mouth was an olive leaf plucked off: so Noah knew that the waters were abated from off the earth.

וַיִּיָּחֶל עוֹד שִׁבְעַת יָמִים אֲחֵרִים

after ones   days   seven   again   and he waited

וַיְשַׁלַּח אֶת־הַיּוֹנָה וְלֹא־יָסְפָה שׁוּב־אֵלָיו עוֹד:

again   unto him – return   she repeated – and not   the dove – that   and he sent

12 And he stayed yet other seven days; and sent forth the dove; which returned not again unto him any more.

וַיְהִי בְּאַחַת וְשֵׁשׁ־מֵאוֹת שָׁנָה בָּרִאשׁוֹן בְּאֶחָד לַחֹדֶשׁ

to month   in one   in first   year   one hundred– and six   in one   and it was

חָרְבוּ הַמַּיִם מֵעַל הָאָרֶץ וַיָּסַר נֹחַ אֶת־מִכְסֵה הַתֵּבָה
the ark   covering – that   Noah   and he removed   the earth   from upon   the waters   they dried up

וַיַּרְא וְהִנֵּה חָרְבוּ פְּנֵי הָאֲדָמָה:
the ground   face   it dry   and here   and he looked

13 And it came to pass in the six hundredth and first year, in the first month, the first day of the month, the waters were dried up from off the earth: and Noah removed the covering of the ark, and looked, and, behold, the face of the ground was dry.

וּבַחֹדֶשׁ הַשֵּׁנִי בְּשִׁבְעָה וְעֶשְׂרִים יוֹם לַחֹדֶשׁ יָבְשָׁה הָאָרֶץ:
the earth   it was dry   to month   day   -- in twenty seventh --   the second   and in month

14 And in the second month, on the seven and twentieth day of the month, was the earth dried.

ס

[רביעי]

וַיְדַבֵּר אֱלֹהִים אֶל־נֹחַ לֵאמֹר:
to say   Noah – unto   Elohim   and he spoke

15 And God spake unto Noah, saying,

צֵא מִן־הַתֵּבָה אַתָּה וְאִשְׁתְּךָ וּבָנֶיךָ וּנְשֵׁי־בָנֶיךָ אִתָּךְ:
with you   your sons - and women   and your sons   and your wife   you   the ark – from   come out

16 Go forth of the ark, thou, and thy wife, and thy sons, and thy sons' wives with thee.

כָּל־הַחַיָּה אֲשֶׁר־אִתְּךָ מִכָּל־בָּשָׂר בָּעוֹף וּבַבְּהֵמָה
and in beast   in bird   flesh – from all   with you – which   the life - all

וּבְכָל־הָרֶמֶשׂ הָרֹמֵשׂ עַל־הָאָרֶץ הוֹצֵא [הַיְצֵא] אִתָּךְ
with you   the it come out   the earth – upon   the creeper   the creeping – and in all

וְשָׁרְצוּ בָאָרֶץ וּפָרוּ וְרָבוּ עַל־הָאָרֶץ:
the earth – upon   and you increase   and you fruitful   in earth   and you roam

17 Bring forth with thee every living thing that is with thee, of all flesh, both of fowl, and of cattle, and of every creeping thing that creepeth upon the earth; that they may breed abundantly in the earth, and be fruitful, and multiply upon the earth.

וַיֵּצֵא־נֹחַ וּבָנָיו וְאִשְׁתּוֹ וּנְשֵׁי־בָנָיו אִתּוֹ:
with him   his sons - and women   and his wife   and his sons   Noah – and he came out

18 And Noah went forth, and his sons, and his wife, and his sons' wives with him:

כָּל־הַחַיָּה כָּל־הָרֶמֶשׂ וְכָל־הָעוֹף
the bird – and all   the creeping – all   the life - all

כֹּל רוֹמֵשׂ עַל־הָאָרֶץ לְמִשְׁפְּחֹתֵיהֶם יָצְאוּ מִן־הַתֵּבָה:
the ark – from   they came out   to their families   the earth – upon   creepers   all

19 Every beast, every creeping thing, and every fowl, and whatsoever creepeth upon the earth, after their kinds, went forth out of the ark.

וַיִּבֶן   נֹחַ   מִזְבֵּחַ   לַיהוָה   וַיִּקַּח   מִכֹּל   הַבְּהֵמָה   הַטְּהֹרָה
the clean   the beasts   from all   and he took   to ihvh   altar   Noah   and he built

וּמִכֹּל   הָעוֹף   הַטָּהוֹר   וַיַּעַל   עֹלֹת   בַּמִּזְבֵּחַ:
in altar   burnt offering   and he offered   the clean   the bird   and from all

20 And Noah builded an altar unto the LORD; and took of every clean beast, and of
every clean fowl, and offered burnt offerings on the altar.

וַיָּרַח   יְהוָה   אֶת־רֵיחַ   הַנִּיחֹחַ
the restful fragrance   smell – that   ihvh   and he smelled

וַיֹּאמֶר   יְהוָה   אֶל־לִבּוֹ
his heart – unto   ihvh   and he said

לֹא   אֹסִף   לְקַלֵּל   עוֹד   אֶת־הָאֲדָמָה   בַּעֲבוּר   הָאָדָם
the Adam   in cause   the ground – that   again   to curse   I repeat   not

כִּי   יֵצֶר   לֵב   הָאָדָם   רַע   מִנְּעֻרָיו
from his childhood   bad   the Adam   heart   comes out   like

וְלֹא־אֹסִף   עוֹד   לְהַכּוֹת   אֶת־כָּל־חַי   כַּאֲשֶׁר   עָשִׂיתִי:
I did   when   life – all – that   to smite   again   I repeat - and not

21 And the LORD smelled a sweet savour; and the LORD said in his heart, I will not
again curse the ground any more for man's sake; for the imagination of man's heart
is evil from his youth; neither will I again smite any more every thing living, as I have
done.

עֹד   כָּל־יְמֵי   הָאָרֶץ   זֶרַע   וְקָצִיר   וְקֹר   וָחֹם
and hot   and cold   and harvest   seed   the earth   days – all   again

וְקַיִץ   וָחֹרֶף   וְיוֹם   וָלַיְלָה   לֹא   יִשְׁבֹּתוּ:
they cease   not   and night   and day   and winter   and summer

22 While the earth remaineth, seedtime and harvest, and cold and heat, and summer and
winter, and day and night shall not cease.

CHAPTER 9

ספר בראשית פרק ט

וַיְבָרֶךְ   אֱלֹהִים   אֶת־נֹחַ   וְאֶת־בָּנָיו
his – sons and that   Noah – that   Elohim   and he blessed

וַיֹּאמֶר   לָהֶם   פְּרוּ   וּרְבוּ   וּמִלְאוּ   אֶת־הָאָרֶץ:
the earth – that   and you fill   and you increase   you be fruitful   to them   and he said

1 And God blessed Noah and his sons, and said unto them, Be fruitful, and multiply,
and replenish the earth.

וּמוֹרַאֲכֶם   וְחִתְּכֶם   יִהְיֶה   עַל   כָּל־חַיַּת   הָאָרֶץ
the earth   lives – all   upon   it will be   and dread of you   and fear of you

וְעַל כָּל־עוֹף הַשָּׁמַיִם בְּכֹל אֲשֶׁר תִּרְמֹשׂ הָאֲדָמָה

the soil	it creeps	which	in all	the heavens	bird – all	and upon

וּבְכָל־דְּגֵי הַיָּם בְּיֶדְכֶם נִתָּנוּ׃

given you	in your hand	the sea	fish – and in all

2 And the fear of you and the dread of you shall be upon every beast of the earth, and upon every fowl of the air, upon all that moveth upon the earth, and upon all the fishes of the sea; into your hand are they delivered.

כָּל־רֶמֶשׂ אֲשֶׁר הוּא־חַי לָכֶם יִהְיֶה לְאָכְלָה

to food	it be	to you	lives - it	which	moving - all

כְּיֶרֶק עֵשֶׂב נָתַתִּי לָכֶם אֶת־כֹּל׃

all – that	to you	I give	plant	like green

3 Every moving thing that liveth shall be meat for you; even as the green herb have I given you all things.

אַךְ־בָּשָׂר בְּנַפְשׁוֹ דָמוֹ לֹא תֹאכֵלוּ׃

you eat	not	his blood	in his soul	flesh - then

4 But flesh with the life thereof, which is the blood thereof, shall ye not eat.

וְאַךְ אֶת־דִּמְכֶם לְנַפְשֹׁתֵיכֶם אֶדְרֹשׁ מִיַּד כָּל־חַיָּה אֶדְרְשֶׁנּוּ

I will require it	life – all	from hand	I will require	to your souls	your blood– that	and surely

וּמִיַּד הָאָדָם מִיַּד אִישׁ אָחִיו אֶדְרֹשׁ אֶת־נֶפֶשׁ הָאָדָם׃

the Adam	soul – that	I will require	his brother	man	from hand	the Adam	and from hand

5 And surely your blood of your lives will I require; at the hand of every beast will I require it, and at the hand of man; at the hand of every man's brother will I require the life of man.

שֹׁפֵךְ דַּם הָאָדָם בָּאָדָם דָּמוֹ יִשָּׁפֵךְ

it be shed	his blood	in Adam	the Adam	blood	shedder of

כִּי בְּצֶלֶם אֱלֹהִים עָשָׂה אֶת־הָאָדָם׃

the Adam – that	made	Elohim	in image	like

6 Whoso sheddeth man's blood, by man shall his blood be shed: for in the image of God made he man.

וְאַתֶּם פְּרוּ וּרְבוּ שִׁרְצוּ בָאָרֶץ וּרְבוּ־בָהּ׃

in it – and you increase	in earth	you roam	and you increase	you be fruitful	and you

7 And you, be ye fruitful, and multiply; bring forth abundantly in the earth, and multiply therein.

ס

[חֲמִישִׁי]

וַיֹּאמֶר אֱלֹהִים אֶל־נֹחַ וְאֶל־בָּנָיו אִתּוֹ לֵאמֹר׃

to say	with him	his sons – and unto	Noah – unto	Elohim	and he said

8 And God spake unto Noah, and to his sons with him, saying,

וַאֲנִי הִנְנִי מֵקִים אֶת־בְּרִיתִי אִתְּכֶם וְאֶת־זַרְעֲכֶם אַחֲרֵיכֶם:
after you   your seed– and that   with you   my covenant – that   establish   here   and I

9 And I, behold, I establish my covenant with you, and with your seed after you;

וְאֵת כָּל־נֶפֶשׁ הַחַיָּה אֲשֶׁר אִתְּכֶם בָּעוֹף בַּבְּהֵמָה
in beast   in bird   with you   which   the life   soul – all   and that

וּבְכָל־חַיַּת הָאָרֶץ אִתְּכֶם מִכֹּל יֹצְאֵי הַתֵּבָה
the ark   came out   from all   with you   the earth   lives – and in all

לְכֹל חַיַּת הָאָרֶץ:
the earth   life   to all

10 And with every living creature that is with you, of the fowl, of the cattle, and of every beast of the earth with you; from all that go out of the ark, to every beast of the earth.

וַהֲקִמֹתִי   אֶת־בְּרִיתִי אִתְּכֶם
with you   my covenant – that   and I will the establish

וְלֹא־יִכָּרֵת כָּל־בָּשָׂר עוֹד מִמֵּי הַמַּבּוּל
the flood   from water   again   flesh – all   it cut off – and not

וְלֹא־יִהְיֶה עוֹד מַבּוּל לְשַׁחֵת הָאָרֶץ:
the earth   to destroy   flood   again   it be – and not

11 And I will establish my covenant with you; neither shall all flesh be cut off any more by the waters of a flood; neither shall there any more be a flood to destroy the earth.

וַיֹּאמֶר אֱלֹהִים זֹאת אוֹת־הַבְּרִית אֲשֶׁר־אֲנִי נֹתֵן בֵּינִי וּבֵינֵיכֶם
and between you   between me   give   I – which   the covenant – sign   this   Elohim   and he said

וּבֵין כָּל־נֶפֶשׁ חַיָּה אֲשֶׁר אִתְּכֶם לְדֹרֹת עוֹלָם:
forever   to generations   with you   which   life   soul – all   and between

12 And God said, This is the token of the covenant which I make between me and you and every living creature that is with you, for perpetual generations;

וְהָיָה בְּעַנְנִי עָנָן עַל־הָאָרֶץ וְנִרְאֲתָה הַקֶּשֶׁת בֶּעָנָן:
in cloud   the bow   and it appears   the earth – upon   cloud   in my cloud   and it be

13 I do set my bow in the cloud, and it shall be for a token of a covenant between me and the earth.

אֶת־קַשְׁתִּי נָתַתִּי בֶּעָנָן
in cloud   I give   my bow – that

וְהָיְתָה לְאוֹת בְּרִית בֵּינִי וּבֵין הָאָרֶץ:
the earth   and between   between me   covenant   to sign   and it will be

14 And it shall come to pass, when I bring a cloud over the earth, that the bow shall be seen in the cloud:

וְזָכַרְתִּי אֶת־בְּרִיתִי אֲשֶׁר בֵּינִי וּבֵינֵיכֶם
and between you between me which my covenant – that I will remember

וּבֵין כָּל־נֶפֶשׁ חַיָּה בְּכָל־בָּשָׂר
flesh – in all life soul – all and between

וְלֹא־יִהְיֶה עוֹד הַמַּיִם לְמַבּוּל לְשַׁחֵת כָּל־בָּשָׂר׃
flesh – all to destroy to flood the waters again it be – and not

15 And I will remember my covenant, which is between me and you and every living creature of all flesh; and the waters shall no more become a flood to destroy all flesh.

וְהָיְתָה הַקֶּשֶׁת בֶּעָנָן
in cloud the bow and it will be

וּרְאִיתִיהָ לִזְכֹּר בְּרִית עוֹלָם בֵּין אֱלֹהִים
Elohim between forever covenant to remember and I will see it

וּבֵין כָּל־נֶפֶשׁ חַיָּה בְּכָל־בָּשָׂר אֲשֶׁר עַל־הָאָרֶץ׃
the earth – upon which flesh – in all life soul – all and between

16 And the bow shall be in the cloud; and I will look upon it, that I may remember the everlasting covenant between God and every living creature of all flesh that is upon the earth.

וַיֹּאמֶר אֱלֹהִים אֶל־נֹחַ זֹאת אוֹת־הַבְּרִית אֲשֶׁר הֲקִמֹתִי בֵּינִי
between me I establish which the covenant – sign this Noah – unto Elohim and he said

וּבֵין כָּל־בָּשָׂר אֲשֶׁר עַל־הָאָרֶץ׃
the earth – upon which flesh – all and between

17 And God said unto Noah, This is the token of the covenant, which I have established between me and all flesh that is upon the earth.

פ

[שֹׁשֹׁי]

וַיִּהְיוּ בְנֵי־נֹחַ הַיֹּצְאִים מִן־הַתֵּבָה שֵׁם וְחָם וָיָפֶת
and Japheth and Ham Shem the ark from the coming out ones Noah – sons and they were

וְחָם הוּא אֲבִי כְנָעַן׃
Canaan father he and Ham

18 And the sons of Noah, that went forth of the ark, were Shem, and Ham, and Japheth: and Ham is the father of Canaan.

שְׁלֹשָׁה אֵלֶּה בְּנֵי־נֹחַ וּמֵאֵלֶּה נָפְצָה כָל־הָאָרֶץ׃
the earth – all was populated and from these Noah – sons these three

19 These are the three sons of Noah: and of them was the whole earth overspread.

וַיָּחֶל נֹחַ אִישׁ הָאֲדָמָה וַיִּטַּע כָּרֶם׃
vineyard and he planted the soil man Noah and he started

20 And Noah began to be an husbandman, and he planted a vineyard:

וַיֵּשְׁתְּ מִן־הַיַּיִן וַיִּשְׁכָּר וַיִּתְגַּל בְּתוֹךְ אָהֳלֹה:

tent   amongst   and he uncovered   and he was drunk   the wine – from   and he drank

21 And he drank of the wine, and was drunken; and he was uncovered within his tent.

וַיַּרְא חָם אֲבִי כְנַעַן אֵת עֶרְוַת אָבִיו

his father   nakedness   that   Canaan   father of   Ham   and he saw

וַיַּגֵּד לִשְׁנֵי־אֶחָיו בַּחוּץ:

in outside   his brothers – to two   and he told

22 And Ham, the father of Canaan, saw the nakedness of his father,
and told his two brethren without.

וַיִּקַּח שֵׁם וָיֶפֶת אֶת־הַשִּׂמְלָה

the dress – that   and Japheth   Shem   and he took

וַיָּשִׂימוּ עַל־שְׁכֶם שְׁנֵיהֶם וַיֵּלְכוּ אֲחֹרַנִּית

backwards   and they went   two of them   their shoulders – upon   and they put

וַיְכַסּוּ אֵת עֶרְוַת אֲבִיהֶם וּפְנֵיהֶם אֲחֹרַנִּית

backwards   and their faces   their father   nakedness   that   and they covered

וְעֶרְוַת אֲבִיהֶם לֹא רָאוּ:

they saw   not   their father   and nakedness

23 And Shem and Japheth took a garment, and laid it upon both their shoulders,
and went backward, and covered the nakedness of their father; and their faces were
backward, and they saw not their father's nakedness.

וַיִּיקֶץ נֹחַ מִיֵּינוֹ וַיֵּדַע אֵת אֲשֶׁר־עָשָׂה לוֹ בְּנוֹ הַקָּטָן:

the small   his son   to him   he did – which   that   and he knew   from his wine   Noah   and he awoke

24 And Noah awoke from his wine, and knew what his younger son had done unto him.

וַיֹּאמֶר אָרוּר כְּנַעַן עֶבֶד עֲבָדִים יִהְיֶה לְאֶחָיו:

to his brothers   he be   servant ones   servant   Canaan   cursed   and he said

25 And he said, Cursed be Canaan; a servant of servants shall he be unto his brethren.

וַיֹּאמֶר בָּרוּךְ יְהֹוָה אֱלֹהֵי שֵׁם וִיהִי כְנַעַן עֶבֶד לָמוֹ:

to him   servant   Canaan   and he will be   Shem   Elohim   ihvh   blessed   and he said

26 And he said, Blessed be the LORD God of Shem; and Canaan shall be his servant.

יַפְתְּ אֱלֹהִים לְיֶפֶת וְיִשְׁכֹּן בְּאָהֳלֵי־שֵׁם

Shem – in tent   and he will dwell   to Japheth   Elohim   he will enlarge

וִיהִי כְנַעַן עֶבֶד לָמוֹ:

to him   servant   Canaan   and it be

27 God shall enlarge Japheth, and he shall dwell in the tents of Shem; and Canaan shall
be his servant.

וַיְחִי־נֹחַ אַחַר הַמַּבּוּל שְׁלֹשׁ מֵאוֹת שָׁנָה וַחֲמִשִּׁים שָׁנָה:

year   and fifty   year   hundreds   three   the flood   after   Noah – and lived

28 And Noah lived after the flood three hundred and fifty years.

וַיְהִי כָּל־יְמֵי־נֹחַ תְּשַׁע מֵאוֹת שָׁנָה וַחֲמִשִּׁים שָׁנָה וַיָּמֹת:

and he died   year   and fifty   year   hundred   nine   Noah – days – all   and were

29 And all the days of Noah were nine hundred and fifty years: and he died.

פ

CHAPTER 10

ספר בראשית פרק י

וְאֵלֶּה תּוֹלְדֹת בְּנֵי־נֹחַ שֵׁם חָם וָיָפֶת

and Japheth   Ham   Shem   Noah – sons   begettings   and these

וַיִּוָּלְדוּ לָהֶם בָּנִים אַחַר הַמַּבּוּל:

the flood   after   sons   to them   and they were born

1 Now these are the generations of the sons of Noah, Shem, Ham, and Japheth: and unto them were sons born after the flood.

בְּנֵי יֶפֶת גֹּמֶר וּמָגוֹג וּמָדַי וְיָוָן וְתֻבָל וּמֶשֶׁךְ וְתִירָס:

and Tiras   and Meshech   and Tubal   and Javan   and Madai   and Magog   Gomer   Japheth   sons

2 The sons of Japheth; Gomer, and Magog, and Madai, and Javan, and Tubal, and Meshech, and Tiras.

וּבְנֵי גֹּמֶר אַשְׁכְּנַז וְרִיפַת וְתֹגַרְמָה:

and Togarmah   and Riphath   Ashkenaz   Gomer   and sons

3 And the sons of Gomer; Ashkenaz, and Riphath, and Togarmah.

וּבְנֵי יָוָן אֱלִישָׁה וְתַרְשִׁישׁ כִּתִּים וְדֹדָנִים:

and Dodanim   Kittim   and Tarshish   Elishah   Javan   and sons

4 And the sons of Javan; Elishah, and Tarshish, Kittim, and Dodanim.

מֵאֵלֶּה נִפְרְדוּ אִיֵּי הַגּוֹיִם בְּאַרְצֹתָם

in their lands   the nations   islands   they spread   from these

אִישׁ לִלְשֹׁנוֹ לְמִשְׁפְּחֹתָם בְּגוֹיֵהֶם:

in their nations   to their families   to his tongue   man

5 By these were the isles of the Gentiles divided in their lands; every one after his tongue, after their families, in their nations.

וּבְנֵי חָם כּוּשׁ וּמִצְרַיִם וּפוּט וּכְנָעַן:

and Canaan   and Phut   and Mizraim   Cush   Ham   and sons

6 And the sons of Ham; Cush, and Mizraim, and Phut, and Canaan.

וּבְנֵי כוּשׁ סְבָא וַחֲוִילָה וְסַבְתָּה וְרַעְמָה וְסַבְתְּכָא

and Sabtechah   and Raamah   and Sabtah   and Havilah   Seba   Cush   and sons

וּבְנֵי רַעְמָה שְׁבָא וּדְדָן:

and Dedan   Sheba   Raamah   and sons

7 And the sons of Cush; Seba, and Havilah, and Sabtah, and Raamah, and Sabtechah: and the sons of Raamah; Sheba, and Dedan.

וְכוּשׁ יָלַד אֶת־נִמְרֹד הוּא הֵחֵל לִהְיוֹת גִּבֹּר בָּאָרֶץ׃

in earth   mighty   to being   began   he   Nimrod – that   begat   and Cush

8 And Cush begat Nimrod: he began to be a mighty one in the earth.

הוּא־הָיָה גִבֹּר־צַיִד לִפְנֵי יְהוָה

ihvh   before   hunter – mighty   was - he

עַל־כֵּן יֵאָמַר כְּנִמְרֹד גִּבּוֹר צַיִד לִפְנֵי יְהוָה׃

ihvh   before   hunter   mighty   like Nimrod   it said   thus – upon

9 He was a mighty hunter before the LORD: wherefore it is said, Even as Nimrod the mighty hunter before the LORD.

וַתְּהִי רֵאשִׁית מַמְלַכְתּוֹ בָּבֶל

Babel   from his kingdom   beginning   and it was

וְאֶרֶךְ וְאַכַּד וְכַלְנֵה בְּאֶרֶץ שִׁנְעָר׃

Shinar   in land   and Calneh   and Accad   and Erech

10 And the beginning of his kingdom was Babel, and Erech, and Accad, and Calneh, in the land of Shinar.

מִן־הָאָרֶץ הַהִוא יָצָא אַשּׁוּר

Asshur   went out   the it   the land - from

וַיִּבֶן אֶת־נִינְוֵה וְאֶת־רְחֹבֹת עִיר וְאֶת־כָּלַח׃

Calah – and that   city   Rehoboth – and that   Nineveh – that   and he built

11 Out of that land went forth Asshur, and builded Nineveh, and the city Rehoboth, and Calah,

וְאֶת־רֶסֶן בֵּין נִינְוֵה וּבֵין כָּלַח הִוא הָעִיר הַגְּדֹלָה׃

the great   the city   it   Calah   and between   Nineveh   between   Resen – and that

12 And Resen between Nineveh and Calah: the same is a great city.

וּמִצְרַיִם יָלַד אֶת־לוּדִים וְאֶת־עֲנָמִים

Anamim – and that   Ludim – that   begat   and Mizraim

וְאֶת־לְהָבִים וְאֶת־נַפְתֻּחִים׃

Nephtuhim – and that   Lehabim – and that

13 And Mizraim begat Ludim, and Anamim, and Lehabim, and Naphtuhim,

וְאֶת־פַּתְרֻסִים וְאֶת־כַּסְלֻחִים אֲשֶׁר יָצְאוּ מִשָּׁם פְּלִשְׁתִּים

Philistim   from them   they came out   which   Casluhim – and that   Pathrusim – and that

וְאֶת־כַּפְתֹּרִים׃

Caphtorim – and that

14 And Pathrusim, and Casluhim, (out of whom came Philistim,) and Caphtorim.

ס

וּכְנַעַן יָלַד אֶת־צִידֹן בְּכֹרוֹ וְאֶת־חֵת׃

Heth – and that   his first born   Sidon – that   begat   and Canaan

15 And Canaan begat Sidon his firstborn, and Heth,

וְאֶת־הַיְבוּסִי וְאֶת־הָאֱמֹרִי וְאֵת הַגִּרְגָּשִׁי:

the Girgasite   and that   the Amorite – and that   the Jebusite – and that

16 And the Jebusite, and the Amorite, and the Girgasite,

וְאֶת־הַחִוִּי וְאֶת־הָעַרְקִי וְאֶת־הַסִּינִי:

the Sinite – and that   the Arkite – and that   the Hivite – and that

17 And the Hivite, and the Arkite, and the Sinite,

וְאֶת־הָאַרְוָדִי וְאֶת־הַצְּמָרִי וְאֶת־הַחֲמָתִי

the Hamathite – and that   the Zemarite – and that   the Arvadite – and that

וְאַחַר נָפֹצוּ מִשְׁפְּחוֹת הַכְּנַעֲנִי:

the Canaanites   families   they scattered   and after

18 And the Arvadite, and the Zemarite, and the Hamathite: and afterward were the families of the Canaanites spread abroad.

וַיְהִי גְּבוּל הַכְּנַעֲנִי מִצִּידֹן בֹּאֲכָה גְרָרָה עַד־עַזָּה

Gaza – till   Gerar   towards coming   from Sidon   the Canaanites   border   and it was

בֹּאֲכָה סְדֹמָה וַעֲמֹרָה וְאַדְמָה וּצְבֹיִם עַד־לָשַׁע:

Lasha – till   and Zeboim   and Admah   and Gomorrah   Sodom   towards coming

19 And the border of the Canaanites was from Sidon, as thou comest to Gerar, unto Gaza; as thou goest, unto Sodom, and Gomorrah, and Admah, and Zeboim, even unto Lasha.

אֵלֶּה בְנֵי־חָם לְמִשְׁפְּחֹתָם לִלְשֹׁנֹתָם בְּאַרְצֹתָם בְּגוֹיֵהֶם:

in their nations   in their lands   to their tongues   to their families   Ham – sons   these

20 These are the sons of Ham, after their families, after their tongues, in their countries, and in their nations.

ס

וּלְשֵׁם יֻלַּד גַּם־הוּא אֲבִי כָּל־בְּנֵי־עֵבֶר אֲחִי יֶפֶת הַגָּדוֹל:

the bigger   Japeth   brother of   Eber – sons – all   father of   he – also   begat   and to Shem

21 Unto Shem also, the father of all the children of Eber, the brother of Japheth the elder, even to him were children born.

בְּנֵי שֵׁם עֵילָם וְאַשּׁוּר וְאַרְפַּכְשַׁד וְלוּד וַאֲרָם:

and Aram   and Lud   and Arphaxad   and Asshur   Elam   Shem   sons

22 The children of Shem; Elam, and Asshur, and Arphaxad, and Lud, and Aram.

וּבְנֵי אֲרָם עוּץ וְחוּל וְגֶתֶר וָמַשׁ:

and Mash   and Gether   and Hul   Uz   Aram   and sons of

23 And the children of Aram; Uz, and Hul, and Gether, and Mash.

וְאַרְפַּכְשַׁד יָלַד אֶת־שָׁלַח וְשֶׁלַח יָלַד אֶת־עֵבֶר:

Eber – that   begat   and Salah   Salah – that   begat   and Arphaxad

24 And Arphaxad begat Salah; and Salah begat Eber.

וּלְעֵבֶר יֻלַּד שְׁנֵי בָנִים שֵׁם הָאֶחָד פֶּלֶג
Peleg | the one | name | sons | two | was born | and to Eber

כִּי בְיָמָיו נִפְלְגָה הָאָרֶץ
the earth | was divided | in his days | like

וְשֵׁם אָחִיו יָקְטָן:
Joktan | his brother | and name

25 And unto Eber were born two sons: the name of one was Peleg; for in his days was the earth divided; and his brother's name was Joktan.

וְיָקְטָן יָלַד אֶת־אַלְמוֹדָד וְאֶת־שָׁלֶף וְאֶת־חֲצַרְמָוֶת וְאֶת־יָרַח:
Jerah – and that | Hazarmaveth – and that | Sheleph – and that | Almodad – that | begat | and Joktan

26 And Joktan begat Almodad, and Sheleph, and Hazarmaveth, and Jerah,

וְאֶת־הֲדוֹרָם וְאֶת־אוּזָל וְאֶת־דִּקְלָה:
Diklah – and that | Uzal – and that | Hadoram – and that

27 And Hadoram, and Uzal, and Diklah,

וְאֶת־עוֹבָל וְאֶת־אֲבִימָאֵל וְאֶת־שְׁבָא:
Sheba – and that | Abimael – and that | Obal – and that

28 And Obal, and Abimael, and Sheba,

וְאֶת־אוֹפִר וְאֶת־חֲוִילָה וְאֶת־יוֹבָב כָּל־אֵלֶּה בְּנֵי יָקְטָן:
Joktan | son | these – all | Jobab – and that | Havilah – and that | Ophir – and that

29 And Ophir, and Havilah, and Jobab: all these were the sons of Joktan.

וַיְהִי מוֹשָׁבָם מִמֵּשָׁא בֹּאֲכָה סְפָרָה הַר הַקֶּדֶם:
the east | mountain | towards Sephar | as you come | from Mesha | their dwelling | and it was

30 And their dwelling was from Mesha, as thou goest unto Sephar a mount of the east.

אֵלֶּה בְנֵי־שֵׁם לְמִשְׁפְּחֹתָם לִלְשֹׁנֹתָם בְּאַרְצֹתָם לְגוֹיֵהֶם:
to their nations | in their lands | to their tongues | to their families | Shem – sons | these are

31 These are the sons of Shem, after their families, after their tongues, in their lands, after their nations.

אֵלֶּה מִשְׁפְּחֹת בְּנֵי־נֹחַ לְתוֹלְדֹתָם בְּגוֹיֵהֶם
in their nations | to their begatings | Noah – sons | families | these are

וּמֵאֵלֶּה נִפְרְדוּ הַגּוֹיִם בָּאָרֶץ אַחַר הַמַּבּוּל:
the flood | after | in earth | the nations | they parted | and from these

32 These are the families of the sons of Noah, after their generations, in their nations: and by these were the nations divided in the earth after the flood.

פ

CHAPTER 11

ספר בראשית פרק יא

[שביעי]

וַיְהִי כָל־הָאָרֶץ שָׂפָה אֶחָת וּדְבָרִים אֲחָדִים:

together ones   and speakings   one   language   the earth – all   and it was

1 And the whole earth was of one language, and of one speech.

וַיְהִי בְּנָסְעָם מִקֶּדֶם

from east   in their traveling   and it was

וַיִּמְצְאוּ בִקְעָה בְּאֶרֶץ שִׁנְעָר וַיֵּשְׁבוּ שָׁם:

there   and they dwelt   Shinar   in land   plain   and they found

2 And it came to pass, as they journeyed from the east, that they found a plain in the land of Shinar; and they dwelt there.

וַיֹּאמְרוּ אִישׁ אֶל־רֵעֵהוּ הָבָה נִלְבְּנָה לְבֵנִים

bricks   we "brick"   the in it   neighbor – unto   man   and they said

וְנִשְׂרְפָה לִשְׂרֵפָה וַתְּהִי לָהֶם הַלְּבֵנָה לְאָבֶן

to stone   the brick   to them   and there was   to fire (verb)   and we burn

וְהַחֵמָר הָיָה לָהֶם לַחֹמֶר:

to mortar   to them   it was   and slime

3 And they said one to another, Go to, let us make brick, and burn them thoroughly. And they had brick for stone, and slime had they for mortar.

וַיֹּאמְרוּ הָבָה נִבְנֶה־לָּנוּ עִיר וּמִגְדָּל וְרֹאשׁוֹ בַשָּׁמַיִם

in heavens   and his top   and tower   city   to us – we build   the in it   and they said

וְנַעֲשֶׂה־לָּנוּ שֵׁם פֶּן־נָפוּץ עַל־פְּנֵי כָל־הָאָרֶץ:

the earth – all   face – upon   scattered – lest   name   to us – and we make

4 And they said, Go to, let us build us a city and a tower, whose top may reach unto heaven; and let us make us a name, lest we be scattered abroad upon the face of the whole earth.

וַיֵּרֶד יְהֹוָה לִרְאֹת אֶת־הָעִיר

the city – that   to see   ihvh   and he descended

וְאֶת־הַמִּגְדָּל אֲשֶׁר בָּנוּ בְּנֵי הָאָדָם:

the Adam   sons   they built   which   the tower – and that

5 And the LORD came down to see the city and the tower, which the children of men builded.

וַיֹּאמֶר יְהֹוָה הֵן עַם אֶחָד

one   people   thus   ihvh   and he said

וְשָׂפָה אַחַת לְכֻלָּם וְזֶה הַחִלָּם לַעֲשׂוֹת

to doings   the beginning   and this   to all them   one   and language

וְעַתָּה לֹא־יִבָּצֵר מֵהֶם כֹּל אֲשֶׁר יָזְמוּ לַעֲשֽׂוֹת׃

to doings   they plan   which   all   from them   it will restrain - not   and now

6 And the LORD said, Behold, the people is one, and they have all one language; and this they begin to do: and now nothing will be restrained from them, which they have imagined to do.

הָבָה נֵרְדָה וְנָבְלָה שָׁם שְׂפָתָם

their language   there   and confuse   we descend   the in it

אֲשֶׁר לֹא יִשְׁמְעוּ אִישׁ שְׂפַת רֵעֵהֽוּ׃

neighbor   language   man   they hear   not   which

7 Go to, let us go down, and there confound their language, that they may not understand one another's speech.

וַיָּפֶץ יְהֹוָה אֹתָם מִשָּׁם עַל־פְּנֵי כָל־הָאָרֶץ

the earth – all   face – upon   from there   to them   ihvh   and he scattered

וַיַּחְדְּלוּ לִבְנֹת הָעִיר׃

the city   to building   and they leave off

8 So the LORD scattered them abroad from thence upon the face of all the earth: and they left off to build the city.

עַל־כֵּן קָרָא שְׁמָהּ בָּבֶל כִּי־שָׁם בָּלַל יְהֹוָה שְׂפַת כָּל־הָאָרֶץ

the earth – all   language   ihvh   confused   there – like   Babel   it's name   called   thus - upon

וּמִשָּׁם הֱפִיצָם יְהֹוָה עַל־פְּנֵי כָּל־הָאָרֶץ׃

the earth – all   face – upon   ihvh   the scattering them   and from there

9 Therefore is the name of it called Babel; because the LORD did there confound the language of all the earth: and from thence did the LORD scatter them abroad upon the face of all the earth.

פ

אֵלֶּה תּוֹלְדֹת שֵׁם שֵׁם בֶּן־מְאַת שָׁנָה

year   hundred – age   Shem   Shem   begatings   these are

וַיּוֹלֶד אֶת־אַרְפַּכְשָׁד שְׁנָתַיִם אַחַר הַמַּבּֽוּל׃

the flood   after   two years   Arphaxad – that   and he begat

10 These are the generations of Shem: Shem was an hundred years old, and begat Arphaxad two years after the flood:

וַיְחִי־שֵׁם אַחֲרֵי הוֹלִידוֹ אֶת־אַרְפַּכְשָׁד חֲמֵשׁ מֵאוֹת שָׁנָה

year   hundred   five   Arphaxad – that   his begetting   after   Shem – and lived

וַיּוֹלֶד בָּנִים וּבָנֽוֹת׃

and daughters   sons   and he begat

11 And Shem lived after he begat Arphaxad five hundred years, and begat sons and daughters.

ס

וְאַרְפַּכְשַׁד חַי חָמֵשׁ וּשְׁלשִׁים שָׁנָה וַיּוֹלֶד אֶת־שָׁלַח:

Salah – that   and he begat   year   and thirty   five   life   and Arphaxad

12 And Arphaxad lived five and thirty years, and begat Salah:

וַיְחִי אַרְפַּכְשַׁד אַחֲרֵי הוֹלִידוֹ אֶת־שֶׁלַח

Salah – that   his begetting   after   Arphaxed   and lived

שָׁלֹשׁ שָׁנִים וְאַרְבַּע מֵאוֹת שָׁנָה

year   hundred   and four   years   three

וַיּוֹלֶד בָּנִים וּבָנוֹת:

and daughters   sons   and he begat

13 And Arphaxad lived after he begat Salah four hundred and three years, and begat sons and daughters.

ס

וְשֶׁלַח חַי שְׁלשִׁים שָׁנָה וַיּוֹלֶד אֶת־עֵבֶר:

Eber – that   and he begat   year   thirty   life   and Salah

14 And Salah lived thirty years, and begat Eber:

וַיְחִי־שֶׁלַח אַחֲרֵי הוֹלִידוֹ אֶת־עֵבֶר

Eber – that   his begetting   after   Salah – and lived

שָׁלֹשׁ שָׁנִים וְאַרְבַּע מֵאוֹת שָׁנָה

year   hundreds   and four   years   three

וַיּוֹלֶד בָּנִים וּבָנוֹת:

and daughters   sons   and he begat

15 And Salah lived after he begat Eber four hundred and three years, and begat sons and daughters.

ס

וַיְחִי־עֵבֶר אַרְבַּע וּשְׁלשִׁים שָׁנָה וַיּוֹלֶד אֶת־פָּלֶג:

Peleg – that   and he begat   year   and thirty   four   Eber – and he lived

16 And Eber lived four and thirty years, and begat Peleg:

וַיְחִי־עֵבֶר אַחֲרֵי הוֹלִידוֹ אֶת־פֶּלֶג

Peleg – that   his begetting   after   Eber – and he lived

שְׁלשִׁים שָׁנָה וְאַרְבַּע מֵאוֹת שָׁנָה

year   hundred   and four   year   thirty

וַיּוֹלֶד בָּנִים וּבָנוֹת:

and daughters   sons   and he begat

17 And Eber lived after he begat Peleg four hundred and thirty years, and begat sons and daughters.

ס

וַיְחִי־פֶלֶג שְׁלֹשִׁים שָׁנָה וַיּוֹלֶד אֶת־רְעוּ׃

Reu – that   and he begat   year   thirty   Peleg – and he lived

18 And Peleg lived thirty years, and begat Reu:

וַיְחִי־פֶלֶג אַחֲרֵי הוֹלִידוֹ אֶת־רְעוּ

Reu – that   his begetting   after   Peleg – and he lived

תֵּשַׁע שָׁנִים וּמָאתַיִם שָׁנָה

year   and two hundred   years   nine

וַיּוֹלֶד בָּנִים וּבָנוֹת׃

and daughters   sons   and he begat

19 And Peleg lived after he begat Reu two hundred and nine years, and begat sons and daughters.

ס

וַיְחִי רְעוּ שְׁתַּיִם וּשְׁלֹשִׁים שָׁנָה וַיּוֹלֶד אֶת־שְׂרוּג׃

Serug – that   and he begat   year   and thirty   two   Reu   and he lived

20 And Reu lived two and thirty years, and begat Serug:

וַיְחִי רְעוּ אַחֲרֵי הוֹלִידוֹ אֶת־שְׂרוּג

Serug – that   his begetting   after   Reu   and he lived

שֶׁבַע שָׁנִים וּמָאתַיִם שָׁנָה

year   and two hundred   years   seven

וַיּוֹלֶד בָּנִים וּבָנוֹת׃

and daughters   sons   and he begat

21 And Reu lived after he begat Serug two hundred and seven years, and begat sons and daughters.

ס

וַיְחִי שְׂרוּג שְׁלֹשִׁים שָׁנָה וַיּוֹלֶד אֶת־נָחוֹר׃

Nahor – that   and he begat   year   thirty   Serug   and he lived

22 And Serug lived thirty years, and begat Nahor:

וַיְחִי שְׂרוּג אַחֲרֵי הוֹלִידוֹ אֶת־נָחוֹר מָאתַיִם שָׁנָה

year   two hundred   Nahor – that   his begetting   after   Serug   and he lived

וַיּוֹלֶד בָּנִים וּבָנוֹת׃

daughters   sons   and he begat

23 And Serug lived after he begat Nahor two hundred years, and begat sons and daughters.

ס

וַיְחִי נָחוֹר תֵּשַׁע וְעֶשְׂרִים שָׁנָה
year and twenty nine Nahor and he lived

וַיּוֹלֶד אֶת־תָּרַח:
Terah – that and he begat

24 And Nahor lived nine and twenty years, and begat Terah:

וַיְחִי נָחוֹר אַחֲרֵי הוֹלִידוֹ אֶת־תֶּרַח
Terah – that his begetting after Nahor and he lived

תְּשַׁע־עֶשְׂרֵה שָׁנָה וּמְאַת שָׁנָה
year and hundred year -- nineteen --

וַיּוֹלֶד בָּנִים וּבָנוֹת:
and daughters sons and he bagat

25 And Nahor lived after he begat Terah an hundred and nineteen years, and begat sons and daughters.

ס

וַיְחִי־תֶרַח שִׁבְעִים שָׁנָה
year seventy Terah – and he lived

וַיּוֹלֶד אֶת־אַבְרָם אֶת־נָחוֹר וְאֶת־הָרָן:
Haran – and that Nahor – that Abram – that and he begat

26 And Terah lived seventy years, and begat Abram, Nahor, and Haran.

וְאֵלֶּה תּוֹלְדֹת תֶּרַח
Terah begetting and these

תֶּרַח הוֹלִיד אֶת־אַבְרָם אֶת־נָחוֹר וְאֶת־הָרָן
Haran – and that Nahor – that Abram – that begat Terah

וְהָרָן הוֹלִיד אֶת־לוֹט:
Lot – that begat and Haran

27 Now these are the generations of Terah: Terah begat Abram, Nahor, and Haran; and Haran begat Lot.

וַיָּמָת הָרָן עַל־פְּנֵי תֶּרַח אָבִיו בְּאֶרֶץ מוֹלַדְתּוֹ
his birth in land his father Terah face – upon Haran and he died

בְּאוּר כַּשְׂדִּים:
Chaldees in Ur

28 And Haran died before his father Terah in the land of his nativity, in Ur of the Chaldees.

[מפטיר]

וַיִּקַּח אַבְרָם וְנָחוֹר לָהֶם נָשִׁים שֵׁם אֵשֶׁת־אַבְרָם שָׂרַי

Sarai   Abram – wife   name   women   to them   and Nahor   Abram   and he took

וְשֵׁם אֵשֶׁת־נָחוֹר מִלְכָּה בַּת־הָרָן אֲבִי־מִלְכָּה וַאֲבִי יִסְכָּה:

Iscah   and father of   Milcah - father of   Haran – daughter   Milcah   Nahor – wife   and name

29 And Abram and Nahor took them wives: the name of Abram's wife was Sarai; and the name of Nahor's wife, Milcah, the daughter of Haran, the father of Milcah, and the father of Iscah.

וַתְּהִי שָׂרַי עֲקָרָה אֵין לָהּ וָלָד:

child   to her   isn't   barren   Sarai   and she was

30 But Sarai was barren; she had no child.

וַיִּקַּח תֶּרַח אֶת־אַבְרָם בְּנוֹ וְאֶת־לוֹט בֶּן־הָרָן בֶּן־בְּנוֹ

his son – son   Haran – son   Lot – and that   his son   Abram – that   Terah   and he took

וְאֵת שָׂרַי כַּלָּתוֹ אֵשֶׁת אַבְרָם בְּנוֹ

his son   Abram   wife   his daughter in law   Sarai   and that

וַיֵּצְאוּ אִתָּם מֵאוּר כַּשְׂדִּים לָלֶכֶת אַרְצָה כְּנַעַן

Canaan   land   to go   Chaldees   from Ur   with them   and they went out

וַיָּבֹאוּ עַד־חָרָן וַיֵּשְׁבוּ שָׁם:

there   and they dwelled   Haran – till   and they came

31 And Terah took Abram his son, and Lot the son of Haran his son's son, and Sarai his daughter in law, his son Abram's wife; and they went forth with them from Ur of the Chaldees, to go into the land of Canaan; and they came unto Haran, and dwelt there.

וַיִּהְיוּ יְמֵי־תֶרַח חָמֵשׁ שָׁנִים וּמָאתַיִם שָׁנָה

year   and two hundred   years   five   Terah – days   and they were

וַיָּמָת תֶּרַח בְּחָרָן:

in Haran   Terah   and he died

32 And the days of Terah were two hundred and five years: and Terah died in Haran.

פ פ פ

3 Lech Lecha

[פרשת לך לך]

Chapter 12

ספר בראשית פרק יב

וַיֹּאמֶר יְהֹוָה אֶל־אַבְרָם לֶךְ־לְךָ מֵאַרְצְךָ

from your land   to you – go   Abraham – unto   ihvh   and he said

וּמִמּוֹלַדְתְּךָ וּמִבֵּית אָבִיךָ אֶל־הָאָרֶץ אֲשֶׁר אַרְאֶךָּ:

I show you   which   the land – unto   your father   and from house   and from your kindred

1 Now the LORD had said unto Abram, Get thee out of thy country, and from thy kindred, and from thy father's house, unto a land that I will shew thee:

וְאֶעֶשְׂךָ לְגוֹי גָּדוֹל וַאֲבָרֶכְךָ

and I will bless you   big   to nation   and I will make you

וַאֲגַדְּלָה שְׁמֶךָ וֶהְיֵה בְּרָכָה:

blessing   and you be   your name   and I make great

2 And I will make of thee a great nation, and I will bless thee, and make thy name great; and thou shalt be a blessing:

וַאֲבָרְכָה מְבָרֲכֶיךָ וּמְקַלֶּלְךָ אָאֹר

I curse   and from your cursing   from your blessings   and I will bless

וְנִבְרְכוּ בְךָ כֹּל מִשְׁפְּחֹת הָאֲדָמָה:

the ground   families   all   in you   and they will be blessed

3 And I will bless them that bless thee, and curse him that curseth thee: and in thee shall all families of the earth be blessed.

וַיֵּלֶךְ אַבְרָם כַּאֲשֶׁר דִּבֶּר אֵלָיו יְהֹוָה

ihvh   unto him   spoke   when   Abram   and he went

וַיֵּלֶךְ אִתּוֹ לוֹט

Lot   with him   and he went

וְאַבְרָם בֶּן־חָמֵשׁ שָׁנִים וְשִׁבְעִים שָׁנָה בְּצֵאתוֹ מֵחָרָן:

from Haran   in his going out   year   and seventy   years   five – age   and Abram

4 So Abram departed, as the LORD had spoken unto him; and Lot went with him: and Abram was seventy and five years old when he departed out of Haran.

וַיִּקַּח אַבְרָם אֶת־שָׂרַי אִשְׁתּוֹ

his wife   Sarai - that   Abram   and he took

וְאֶת־לוֹט בֶּן־אָחִיו וְאֶת־כָּל־רְכוּשָׁם אֲשֶׁר רָכָשׁוּ

they possessed   which   their possessions - all - and that   his brother - son   and that Lot

וְאֶת־הַנֶּ֫פֶשׁ אֲשֶׁר־עָשׂ֖וּ בְחָרָ֑ן
in Haran   they made - which   the soul - and that

וַיֵּצְא֗וּ לָלֶ֙כֶת֙ אַ֣רְצָה כְּנַ֔עַן וַיָּבֹ֖אוּ אַ֥רְצָה כְּנָֽעַן:
Canaan   towards land   and they came   Canaan   towards land   to go   and they went out

5 And Abram took Sarai his wife, and Lot his brother's son, and all their substance that
they had gathered, and the souls that they had gotten in Haran; and they went forth to
go into the land of Canaan; and into the land of Canaan they came.

וַיַּעֲבֹ֤ר אַבְרָם֙ בָּאָ֔רֶץ עַ֚ד מְק֣וֹם שְׁכֶ֔ם עַ֖ד אֵל֣וֹן מוֹרֶ֑ה
Moreh   plain   till   Shechem   place   till   in land   Abram   and he passed

וְהַֽכְּנַעֲנִ֖י אָ֥ז בָּאָֽרֶץ:
in land   then   and the Canaanite

6 And Abram passed through the land unto the place of Sichem, unto the plain of
Moreh. And the Canaanite was then in the land.

וַיֵּרָ֤א יְהֹוָה֙ אֶל־אַבְרָ֔ם
Abram - unto   ihvh   and he appeared

וַיֹּ֕אמֶר לְזַ֨רְעֲךָ֔ אֶתֵּ֖ן אֶת־הָאָ֣רֶץ הַזֹּ֑את
the this   the land - that   I give   to your seed   and he said

וַיִּ֣בֶן שָׁ֣ם מִזְבֵּ֔חַ לַיהֹוָ֖ה הַנִּרְאֶ֥ה אֵלָֽיו:
unto him   the appearing one   to ihvh   alter   there   and he built

7 And the LORD appeared unto Abram, and said, Unto thy seed will I give this land:
and there builded he an altar unto the LORD, who appeared unto him.

וַיַּעְתֵּ֤ק מִשָּׁם֙ הָהָ֔רָה מִקֶּ֖דֶם לְבֵֽית־אֵ֑ל
El - to Beth   from east   the mountain   from there   and he shifted

וַיֵּ֣ט אָהֳלֹ֗ה בֵּֽית־אֵ֤ל מִיָּם֙ וְהָעַ֣י מִקֶּ֔דֶם
from East   and Hai   from Sea   El - Beth   his tent   and he pitched

וַיִּֽבֶן־שָׁ֤ם מִזְבֵּ֨חַ֙ לַֽיהֹוָ֔ה וַיִּקְרָ֖א בְּשֵׁ֥ם יְהֹוָֽה:
ihvh   in name   and he called   to ihvh   alter   there - and he built

8 And he removed from thence unto a mountain on the east of Beth-el, and pitched his
tent, having Beth-el on the west, and Hai on the east: and there he builded an altar unto
the LORD, and called upon the name of the LORD.

וַיִּסַּ֣ע אַבְרָ֔ם הָל֥וֹךְ וְנָס֖וֹעַ הַנֶּֽגְבָּה:
the towards Negev   and traveled   going   Abram   and he traveled

9 And Abram journeyed, going on still toward the south.

פ

וַיְהִ֥י רָעָ֖ב בָּאָ֑רֶץ וַיֵּ֨רֶד אַבְרָ֤ם מִצְרַ֨יְמָה֙ לָג֣וּר שָׁ֔ם
there   to reside   towards Egypt   Abram   and he descended   in land   famine   and it was

כִּי־כָבֵד הָרָעָב בָּאָרֶץ:

severe - like   the famine   in land

10 And there was a famine in the land: and Abram went down into Egypt to sojourn there; for the famine was grievous in the land.

וַיְהִי כַּאֲשֶׁר הִקְרִיב לָבוֹא מִצְרָיְמָה

and it was   when   came close   to come   toward Egypt

וַיֹּאמֶר אֶל־שָׂרַי אִשְׁתּוֹ

and he said   Sarai - unto   his wife

הִנֵּה־נָא יָדַעְתִּי כִּי אִשָּׁה יְפַת־מַרְאֶה אָתְּ:

now - here   I know you   like   woman   appearance - beautiful   you

11 And it came to pass, when he was come near to enter into Egypt, that he said unto Sarai his wife, Behold now, I know that thou art a fair woman to look upon:

וְהָיָה כִּי־יִרְאוּ אֹתָךְ הַמִּצְרִים וְאָמְרוּ אִשְׁתּוֹ זֹאת

and it be   to you they see you - like   the Egyptians   and they will say   his wife   this

וְהָרְגוּ אֹתִי וְאֹתָךְ יְחַיּוּ:

and they the kill   to me   and to you   they let live

12 Therefore it shall come to pass, when the Egyptians shall see thee, that they shall say, This is his wife: and they will kill me, but they will save thee alive.

אִמְרִי־נָא אֲחֹתִי אָתְּ לְמַעַן יִיטַב־לִי בַעֲבוּרֵךְ

please - say   my sister   you   to end   it be good - to me   in your service

וְחָיְתָה נַפְשִׁי בִּגְלָלֵךְ:

and it live   my soul   in your account

13 Say, I pray thee, thou art my sister: that it may be well with me for thy sake; and my soul shall live because of thee.

[שני]

וַיְהִי כְּבוֹא אַבְרָם מִצְרָיְמָה

and it was   like he came   Abram   towards Egypt

וַיִּרְאוּ הַמִּצְרִים אֶת־הָאִשָּׁה כִּי־יָפָה הִוא מְאֹד:

and they saw   the Egyptians   the woman - that   beautiful - like   she   very

14 And it came to pass, that, when Abram was come into Egypt, the Egyptians beheld the woman that she was very fair.

וַיִּרְאוּ אֹתָהּ שָׂרֵי פַרְעֹה וַיְהַלְלוּ אֹתָהּ אֶל־פַּרְעֹה

and they saw   to her   officials   Pharaoh   and they praised   to her   Pharaoh - unto

וַתֻּקַּח הָאִשָּׁה בֵּית פַּרְעֹה:

and she was taken   the woman   house   Pharaoh

15 The princes also of Pharaoh saw her, and commended her before Pharaoh: and the woman was taken into Pharaoh's house.

וּלְאַבְרָם הֵיטִיב בַּעֲבוּרָהּ וַיְהִי־לוֹ צֹאן־וּבָקָר וַחֲמֹרִים
and donkeys | and oxen - sheep | to him - and it was | in her service | the it better | and to Abram

וַעֲבָדִים וּשְׁפָחֹת וַאֲתֹנֹת וּגְמַלִּים:
and camels | and female mules | and maids | and men servants

16 And he entreated Abram well for her sake: and he had sheep, and oxen, and he asses, and menservants, and maidservants, and she asses, and camels.

וַיְנַגַּע יְהוָה אֶת־פַּרְעֹה נְגָעִים גְּדֹלִים
big ones | plagues | Pharaoh - that | ihvh | and he plagued

וְאֶת־בֵּיתוֹ עַל־דְּבַר שָׂרַי אֵשֶׁת אַבְרָם:
Abram | wife | Sarai | matter - upon | his house - and that

17 And the LORD plagued Pharaoh and his house with great plagues because of Sarai Abram's wife.

וַיִּקְרָא פַרְעֹה לְאַבְרָם
to Abram | Pharaoh | and he called

וַיֹּאמֶר מַה־זֹּאת עָשִׂיתָ לִּי לָמָּה לֹא־הִגַּדְתָּ לִּי
to me | you tell - not | why | to me | you did | this - what | and he said

כִּי אִשְׁתְּךָ הִוא:
she | your wife | like

18 And Pharaoh called Abram, and said, What is this that thou hast done unto me? why didst thou not tell me that she was thy wife?

לָמָה אָמַרְתָּ אֲחֹתִי הִוא וָאֶקַּח אֹתָהּ לִי לְאִשָּׁה
to wife | to me | to her | and I took | she | sister | you said | why

וְעַתָּה הִנֵּה אִשְׁתְּךָ קַח וָלֵךְ:
and go | take | your wife | here | and now

19 Why saidst thou, She is my sister? so I might have taken her to me to wife: now therefore behold thy wife, take her, and go thy way.

וַיְצַו עָלָיו פַּרְעֹה אֲנָשִׁים
men | Pharaoh | upon him | and he commanded

וַיְשַׁלְּחוּ אֹתוֹ וְאֶת־אִשְׁתּוֹ וְאֶת־כָּל־אֲשֶׁר־לוֹ:
to him – which - all - and that | his wife - and that | to him | and they sent him

20 And Pharaoh commanded his men concerning him: and they sent him away, and his wife, and all that he had.

CHAPTER 13

ספר בראשית פרק יג

וַיַּעַל אַבְרָם מִמִּצְרַיִם הוּא וְאִשְׁתּוֹ
and his wife | he | from Egypt | Abram | and he ascended

וְכָל־אֲשֶׁר־לוֹ וְלוֹט עִמּוֹ הַנֶּגְבָּה:

the towards Negev   with him   and Lot   to him – which - and all

1 And Abram went up out of Egypt, he, and his wife, and all that he had, and Lot with him, into the south.

וְאַבְרָם כָּבֵד מְאֹד בַּמִּקְנֶה בַּכֶּסֶף וּבַזָּהָב:

and in gold   in silver   in livestock   very   heavy   and Abram

2 And Abram was very rich in cattle, in silver, and in gold.

וַיֵּלֶךְ לְמַסָּעָיו מִנֶּגֶב

from Negev   to his journey   and he went

וְעַד־בֵּית־אֵל עַד־הַמָּקוֹם אֲשֶׁר־הָיָה שָׁם אָהֳלֹה בַּתְּחִלָּה

in start   his tent   there   he was – which   the place - till   El – Beth – and till

בֵּין בֵּית־אֵל וּבֵין הָעָי:

the Hai   and between   El – Beth   between

3 And he went on his journeys from the south even to Beth-el, unto the place where his tent had been at the beginning, between Beth-el and Hai;

אֶל־מְקוֹם הַמִּזְבֵּחַ אֲשֶׁר־עָשָׂה שָׁם בָּרִאשֹׁנָה

in first   there   made – which   the altar   place - unto

וַיִּקְרָא שָׁם אַבְרָם בְּשֵׁם יְהֹוָה:

ihvh   in name   Abram   there   and he called

4 Unto the place of the altar, which he had made there at the first: and there Abram called on the name of the LORD.

[שְׁלִישִׁי]

וְגַם־לְלוֹט הַהֹלֵךְ אֶת־אַבְרָם הָיָה צֹאן־וּבָקָר וְאֹהָלִים:

and tents   and cattle – sheep   it was   Abram – that   the going   to Lot – and also

5 And Lot also, which went with Abram, had flocks, and herds, and tents.

וְלֹא־נָשָׂא אֹתָם הָאָרֶץ לָשֶׁבֶת יַחְדָּו כִּי־הָיָה רְכוּשָׁם רָב

great   their possessions   it was – like   together   to dwell   the earth   to them   bear – and not

וְלֹא יָכְלוּ לָשֶׁבֶת יַחְדָּו:

together   to dwell   they able   and not

6 And the land was not able to bear them, that they might dwell together: for their substance was great, so that they could not dwell together.

וַיְהִי־רִיב בֵּין רֹעֵי מִקְנֵה־אַבְרָם וּבֵין רֹעֵי מִקְנֵה־לוֹט

Lot – cattle   shepherds   and between   Abram – cattle   shepherds   between   quarrel – and it was

וְהַכְּנַעֲנִי וְהַפְּרִזִּי אָז יֹשֵׁב בָּאָרֶץ:

in land   dwelled   then   and Perizzite   and the Canaanite

7 And there was a strife between the herdmen of Abram's cattle and the herdmen of Lot's cattle: and the Canaanite and the Perizzite dwelled then in the land.

וַיֹּאמֶר אַבְרָם אֶל־לוֹט אַל־נָא תְהִי מְרִיבָה בֵּינִי וּבֵינֶךָ

and between you   between me   strife   there be   now – don't   Lot – unto   Abram   and he said

וּבֵין רֹעַי וּבֵין רֹעֶיךָ כִּי־אֲנָשִׁים אַחִים אֲנָחְנוּ׃

we   brothers   men – like   your shepherds   and between   my shepherds   and between

8 And Abram said unto Lot, Let there be no strife, I pray thee, between me and thee, and between my herdmen and thy herdmen; for we be brethren.

הֲלֹא כָל־הָאָרֶץ לְפָנֶיךָ הִפָּרֶד נָא מֵעָלָי

from upon me   now   cause to separate   before you   the land – all   the not

אִם־הַשְּׂמֹאל וְאֵימִנָה

and I towards right   the left – if

וְאִם־הַיָּמִין וְאַשְׂמְאִילָה׃

and I towards left   the right – and if

9 Is not the whole land before thee? separate thyself, I pray thee, from me: if thou wilt take the left hand, then I will go to the right; or if thou depart to the right hand, then I will go to the left.

וַיִּשָּׂא־לוֹט אֶת־עֵינָיו וַיַּרְא אֶת־כָּל־כִּכַּר הַיַּרְדֵּן

the Jordan   plain – all – that   and he saw   his eyes – that   Lot – he lifted

כִּי כֻלָּהּ מַשְׁקֶה לִפְנֵי שַׁחֵת יְהוָה אֶת־סְדֹם וְאֶת־עֲמֹרָה

Gomorrah - and that   Sodom – that   ihvh   destroyed   before   well watered   all of her   like

כְּגַן־יְהוָה כְּאֶרֶץ מִצְרַיִם בֹּאֲכָה צֹעַר׃

Zoar   in coming   Egypt   like land   ihvh – like garden

10 And Lot lifted up his eyes, and beheld all the plain of Jordan, that it was well watered every where, before the LORD destroyed Sodom and Gomorrah, even as the garden of the LORD, like the land of Egypt, as thou comest unto Zoar.

וַיִּבְחַר־לוֹ לוֹט אֵת כָּל־כִּכַּר הַיַּרְדֵּן

the Jordan   plain – all   that   Lot   to him – and he chose

וַיִּסַּע לוֹט מִקֶּדֶם וַיִּפָּרְדוּ אִישׁ מֵעַל אָחִיו׃

his brother   from upon   man   and they parted   from east   Lot   and he set out

11 Then Lot chose him all the plain of Jordan; and Lot journeyed east: and they separated themselves the one from the other.

אַבְרָם יָשַׁב בְּאֶרֶץ־כְּנָעַן

Canaan – in land   dwelled   Abram

וְלוֹט יָשַׁב בְּעָרֵי הַכִּכָּר וַיֶּאֱהַל עַד־סְדֹם׃

Sodom – till   and he tented   the plain   in cities   he dwelled   and Lot

12 Abram dwelled in the land of Canaan, and Lot dwelled in the cities of the plain, and pitched his tent toward Sodom.

וְאַנְשֵׁי סְדֹם רָעִים וְחַטָּאִים לַיהוָה מְאֹד׃

greatly   to ihvh   and sinners ones   wicked ones   Sodom   and men

13 But the men of Sodom were wicked and sinners before the LORD exceedingly.

וַיהוָה אָמַר אֶל־אַבְרָם אַחֲרֵי הִפָּרֶד־לוֹט מֵעִמּוֹ

from with him   Lot - separated   after   Abram - unto   said   and ihvh

שָׂא־נָא עֵינֶיךָ וּרְאֵה מִן־הַמָּקוֹם אֲשֶׁר־אַתָּה שָׁם

there   you - which   the place - from   and see   your eyes   now - lift

צָפֹנָה וָנֶגְבָּה וָקֵדְמָה וָיָמָּה׃

and towards sea   and towards east   and toward south   towards north

14 And the LORD said unto Abram, after that Lot was separated from him, Lift up now thine eyes, and look from the place where thou art northward, and southward, and eastward, and westward:

כִּי אֶת־כָּל־הָאָרֶץ אֲשֶׁר־אַתָּה רֹאֶה

see   you - which   the land - all - that   like

לְךָ אֶתְּנֶנָּה וּלְזַרְעֲךָ עַד־עוֹלָם׃

forever - till   and to your seed   I will give it   to you

15 For all the land which thou seest, to thee will I give it, and to thy seed for ever.

וְשַׂמְתִּי אֶת־זַרְעֲךָ כַּעֲפַר הָאָרֶץ

the earth   like dust   your seed - that   and I will put

אֲשֶׁר אִם־יוּכַל אִישׁ לִמְנוֹת אֶת־עֲפַר הָאָרֶץ גַּם־זַרְעֲךָ יִמָּנֶה׃

it counted   your seed also   the earth   your dust - that   to account   man   able - if   which

16 And I will make thy seed as the dust of the earth: so that if a man can number the dust of the earth, then shall thy seed also be numbered.

קוּם הִתְהַלֵּךְ בָּאָרֶץ לְאָרְכָּהּ וּלְרָחְבָּהּ כִּי לְךָ אֶתְּנֶנָּה׃

I will give you   to you   like   and to it's breadth   to it's length   in the land   walk   rise

17 Arise, walk through the land in the length of it and in the breadth of it; for I will give it unto thee.

וַיֶּאֱהַל אַבְרָם וַיָּבֹא

and he came   Abram   and he tented

וַיֵּשֶׁב בְּאֵלֹנֵי מַמְרֵא אֲשֶׁר בְּחֶבְרוֹן וַיִּבֶן־שָׁם מִזְבֵּחַ לַיהוָה׃

to ihvh   altar   there – and he built   in Hebron   when   Mamre   in plain   and he dwelt

18 Then Abram removed his tent, and came and dwelt in the plain of Mamre, which is in Hebron, and built there an altar unto the LORD.

פ

CHAPTER 14

ספר בראשית פרק יד

[רביעי]

וַיְהִי֙ בִּימֵ֣י אַמְרָפֶ֣ל מֶֽלֶךְ־שִׁנְעָ֔ר
Shinar - king   Amraphel   in days   and it was

אַרְי֖וֹךְ מֶ֣לֶךְ אֶלָּסָ֑ר כְּדָרְלָעֹ֙מֶר֙ מֶ֣לֶךְ עֵילָ֔ם
Elam   king   Chedorlaomer   Ellasar   king   Arioch

וְתִדְעָ֖ל מֶ֥לֶךְ גּוֹיִֽם:
nations   king   and Tidal

1 And it came to pass in the days of Amraphel king of Shinar, Arioch king of Ellasar, Chedorlaomer king of Elam, and Tidal king of nations;

עָשׂ֣וּ מִלְחָמָ֔ה אֶת־בֶּ֖רַע מֶ֣לֶךְ סְדֹ֑ם
Sodom   king   Bera - that   war   they made

וְאֶת־בִּרְשַׁ֖ע מֶ֣לֶךְ עֲמֹרָ֑ה שִׁנְאָ֣ב ׀ מֶ֣לֶךְ אַדְמָ֗ה
Admah   king   Shinab   Gomorrah   king   Birsha - and that

וְשֶׁמְאֵ֙בֶר֙ מֶ֣לֶךְ צְבֹייִ֔ם [צְבוֹיִ֔ם]
Zeboiim   king   and Shemeber

וּמֶ֥לֶךְ בֶּ֖לַע הִיא־צֹֽעַר:
Zoar - he   Bela   and king

2 That these made war with Bera king of Sodom, and with Birsha king of Gomorrah, Shinab king of Admah, and Shemeber king of Zeboiim, and the king of Bela, which is Zoar.

כָּל־אֵ֙לֶּה֙ חָֽבְר֔וּ אֶל־עֵ֖מֶק הַשִּׂדִּ֑ים ה֖וּא יָ֥ם הַמֶּֽלַח:
the salt   sea   it   the Siddim   valley - unto   they joined   these - all

3 All these were joined together in the vale of Siddim, which is the salt sea.

שְׁתֵּ֤ים עֶשְׂרֵה֙ שָׁנָ֔ה עָֽבְד֖וּ אֶת־כְּדָרְלָעֹ֑מֶר
Chedorlaomer - that   they served   year   -------- 12 -------

וּשְׁלֹשׁ־עֶשְׂרֵ֥ה שָׁנָ֖ה מָרָֽדוּ:
they rebelled   year   and-------- 13-------

4 Twelve years they served Chedorlaomer, and in the thirteenth year they rebelled.

וּבְאַרְבַּע֩ עֶשְׂרֵ֨ה שָׁנָ֜ה בָּ֣א כְדָרְלָעֹ֗מֶר וְהַמְּלָכִים֙ אֲשֶׁ֣ר אִתּ֔וֹ
with him   which   and the kings   Chedorlaomer   came   year   and in-------------14 -------

וַיַּכּ֤וּ אֶת־רְפָאִים֙ בְּעַשְׁתְּרֹ֣ת קַרְנַ֔יִם
Karnaim   in Ashteroth   Rephaims - that   and they smote

וְאֶת־הַזּוּזִ֖ים בְּהָ֑ם וְאֵת֙ הָֽאֵימִ֔ים בְּשָׁוֵ֖ה קִרְיָתָֽיִם:
Kiriathaim   in Shaveh   the Emims   and that   in Ham   the Zuzims - and that

5 And in the fourteenth year came Chedorlaomer, and the kings that were with him, and smote the Rephaims in Ashteroth Karnaim, and the Zuzims in Ham, and the Emims in Shaveh Kiriathaim,

וְאֶת־הַחֹרִי   בְּהַרְרָם   שֵׂעִיר   עַד   אֵיל   פָּארָן   אֲשֶׁר   עַל־הַמִּדְבָּר׃
the wilderness - upon   which   paran - El   till   Seir   in their mount   the Horites - and that

6 And the Horites in their mount Seir, unto El-paran, which is by the wilderness.

וַיָּשֻׁבוּ   וַיָּבֹאוּ אֶל־עֵין מִשְׁפָּט הִוא קָדֵשׁ
Kadesh   it   mishpat - En – unto   and they came   and they returned

וַיַּכּוּ   אֶת־כָּל־שְׂדֵה הָעֲמָלֵקִי
the Amalekites   field - all - that   and they smote

וְגַם   אֶת־הָאֱמֹרִי הַיֹּשֵׁב בְּחַצְצֹן תָּמָר׃
tamar - in Hazezon   the dwellers   the Amorites - that   and also

7 And they returned, and came to En-mishpat, which is Kadesh, and smote all the country of the Amalekites, and also the Amorites, that dwelt in Hazezon-tamar.

וַיֵּצֵא   מֶלֶךְ־סְדֹם וּמֶלֶךְ עֲמֹרָה וּמֶלֶךְ אַדְמָה
Admah   and king   Gomorrah   and king   Sodom - King   and he went out

וּמֶלֶךְ צְבֹיִים [צְבוֹיִם] וּמֶלֶךְ בֶּלַע הוא־צֹעַר
Zoar – it   Bela   and King   Zeboiim   and King

וַיַּעַרְכוּ אִתָּם מִלְחָמָה בְּעֵמֶק הַשִּׂדִּים׃
the Siddim   in Valley   war   with them   and he joined

8 And there went out the king of Sodom, and the king of Gomorrah, and the king of Admah, and the king of Zeboiim, and the king of Bela (the same is Zoar;) and they joined battle with them in the vale of Siddim;

אֵת כְּדָרְלָעֹמֶר מֶלֶךְ עֵילָם
Elam   king   Chedorlaomer   that

וְתִדְעָל מֶלֶךְ גּוֹיִם וְאַמְרָפֶל מֶלֶךְ שִׁנְעָר
Shinar   king   and Amraphel   nations   king   and Tidal

וְאַרְיוֹךְ מֶלֶךְ אֶלָּסָר אַרְבָּעָה מְלָכִים אֶת־הַחֲמִשָּׁה׃
the five – that   kings   four   Ellasar   king   and Arioch

9 With Chedorlaomer the king of Elam, and with Tidal king of nations, and Amraphel king of Shinar, and Arioch king of Ellasar; four kings with five.

וְעֵמֶק הַשִּׂדִּים בֶּאֱרֹת בֶּאֱרֹת חֵמָר
tar   wells   wells   the Siddim   and valley

וַיָּנֻסוּ מֶלֶךְ־סְדֹם וַעֲמֹרָה
and Gomorrah   Sodom - king   and they fled

וַיִּפְּלוּ־שָׁמָּה וְהַנִּשְׁאָרִים הֶרָה נָסוּ׃
they fled   towards mountain   and the remaining ones   there - and they fell

10 And the vale of Siddim was full of slimepits; and the kings of Sodom and
Gomorrah fled, and fell there; and they that remained fled to the mountain.

וַיִּקְחוּ אֶת־כָּל־רְכֻשׁ סְדֹם וַעֲמֹרָה וְאֶת־כָּל־אָכְלָם וַיֵּלֵכוּ׃

and they went   their food - all - and that   and Gomorrah   Sodom   possessions - all - that   and they took

11 And they took all the goods of Sodom and Gomorrah, and all their victuals, and
went their way.

וַיִּקְחוּ אֶת־לוֹט וְאֶת־רְכֻשׁוֹ בֶּן־אֲחִי אַבְרָם וַיֵּלֵכוּ

and they went   Abram   brother – son   his possessions - and that   Lot - that   and they took

וְהוּא יֹשֵׁב בִּסְדֹם׃

in Sodom   dwelled   and he

12 And they took Lot, Abram's brother's son, who dwelt in Sodom, and his goods, and
departed.

וַיָּבֹא הַפָּלִיט וַיַּגֵּד לְאַבְרָם הָעִבְרִי

the Hebrew   to Abram   and he told   the escaped   and he came

וְהוּא שֹׁכֵן בְּאֵלֹנֵי מַמְרֵא הָאֱמֹרִי אֲחִי אֶשְׁכֹּל וַאֲחִי עָנֵר

Aner   and brother   Eschcol   brother   the Amorite   Mamre   in plains   dwelt   and he

וְהֵם בַּעֲלֵי בְרִית־אַבְרָם׃

Abram – covenant   masters   and them

13 And there came one that had escaped, and told Abram the Hebrew; for he dwelt in
the plain of Mamre the Amorite, brother of Eshcol, and brother of Aner: and these
were confederate with Abram.

וַיִּשְׁמַע אַבְרָם כִּי נִשְׁבָּה אָחִיו

his brother   captive   like   Abram   and he heard

וַיָּרֶק אֶת־חֲנִיכָיו יְלִידֵי בֵיתוֹ שְׁמֹנָה עָשָׂר וּשְׁלֹשׁ מֵאוֹת

hundreds   and three   -----18---------   his house   born ones   his trained men – that   and he armed

וַיִּרְדֹּף עַד־דָּן׃

Dan - till   and he pursued

14 And when Abram heard that his brother was taken captive, he armed his trained
servants, born in his own house, three hundred and eighteen, and pursued them unto
Dan.

וַיֵּחָלֵק עֲלֵיהֶם לַיְלָה הוּא וַעֲבָדָיו

and his servants   he   night   upon them   and he divided

וַיַּכֵּם וַיִּרְדְּפֵם עַד־חוֹבָה אֲשֶׁר מִשְּׂמֹאל לְדַמָּשֶׂק׃

to Damascus   from left   which   Hobah - till   and he pursued them   and he smote them

15 And he divided himself against them, he and his servants, by night, and smote them,
and pursued them unto Hobah, which is on the left hand of Damascus.

וַיָּשֶׁב אֵת כָּל־הָרְכֻשׁ וְגַם אֶת־לוֹט אָחִיו

his brother   Lot - that   and also   the possession - all   that   and he returned

וּרְכֻשׁוֹ   הֵשִׁיב   וְגַם אֶת־הַנָּשִׁים וְאֶת־הָעָם:
and his possession   the returned   and also   the women - that   the people - and that

16 And he brought back all the goods, and also brought again his brother Lot, and his goods, and the women also, and the people.

וַיֵּצֵא   מֶלֶךְ־סְדֹם   לִקְרָאתוֹ
and he came out   Sodom - king   to his meet

אַחֲרֵי שׁוּבוֹ מֵהַכּוֹת אֶת־כְּדָרְלָעֹמֶר וְאֶת־הַמְּלָכִים אֲשֶׁר אִתּוֹ
after   which   kings – and that   Chedorlaomer - that   from smiting   his return   with him

אֶל־עֵמֶק שָׁוֵה הוּא עֵמֶק הַמֶּלֶךְ:
valley - unto   Shaveh   it   valley   the king

17 And the king of Sodom went out to meet him after his return from the slaughter of Chedorlaomer, and of the kings that were with him, at the valley of Shaveh, which is the king's dale.

וּמַלְכִּי־צֶדֶק מֶלֶךְ שָׁלֵם הוֹצִיא לֶחֶם וָיָיִן
Melchi - tzedek   King   Salem   brought out   bread   and wine

וְהוּא כֹהֵן לְאֵל עֶלְיוֹן:
and he   high priest   to El   most high

18 And Melchizedek king of Salem brought forth bread and wine: and he was the priest of the most high God.

וַיְבָרְכֵהוּ וַיֹּאמַר בָּרוּךְ אַבְרָם לְאֵל עֶלְיוֹן קֹנֵה שָׁמַיִם וָאָרֶץ:
and he blessed him   and he said   blessed   Abram   to El   most high   possessor   heaven   and earth

19 And he blessed him, and said, Blessed be Abram of the most high God, possessor of heaven and earth:

וּבָרוּךְ אֵל עֶלְיוֹן אֲשֶׁר־מִגֵּן צָרֶיךָ בְּיָדֶךָ
and blessed   El   most high   which - awarded   your adversaries   in your hand

וַיִּתֶּן־לוֹ   מַעֲשֵׂר מִכֹּל:
to him - and he gave   from tenth   from all

20 And blessed be the most high God, which hath delivered thine enemies into thy hand. And he gave him tithes of all.

[חמישי]

וַיֹּאמֶר מֶלֶךְ־סְדֹם אֶל־אַבְרָם תֶּן־לִי הַנָּפֶשׁ
and he said   Sodom - king   Abram - unto   give - to me   the soul

וְהָרְכֻשׁ   קַח־לָךְ:
and the possessions   take - to you

21 And the king of Sodom said unto Abram, Give me the persons, and take the goods to thyself.

וַיֹּאמֶר אַבְרָם אֶל־מֶלֶךְ סְדֹם
and he said   Abram   king - unto   Sodom

הֲרִמֹתִי יָדִי אֶל־יְהוָֹה אֵל עֶלְיוֹן קֹנֵה שָׁמַיִם וָאָרֶץ:

| and earth | heaven | possessor | most high | El | ihvh - unto | my hand | I raised high |

22 And Abram said to the king of Sodom, I have lift up mine hand unto the LORD, the most high God, the possessor of heaven and earth,

אִם־מִחוּט וְעַד שְׂרוֹךְ־נַעַל וְאִם־אֶקַּח מִכָּל־אֲשֶׁר־לָךְ

| to you - which - from all | I take - and if | shoe - thong | and till | thread -with |

וְלֹא תֹאמַר אֲנִי הֶעֱשַׁרְתִּי אֶת־אַבְרָם:

| Abram - that | I made rich | I | you say | and not |

23 That I will not take from a thread even to a shoelatchet, and that I will not take any thing that is thine, lest thou shouldest say, I have made Abram rich:

בִּלְעָדַי רַק אֲשֶׁר אָכְלוּ הַנְּעָרִים

| the young ones | they ate | which | only | nothing to me |

וְחֵלֶק הָאֲנָשִׁים אֲשֶׁר הָלְכוּ אִתִּי עָנֵר אֶשְׁכֹּל וּמַמְרֵא

| and Mamre | Eschol | Aner | with me | they went | which | the men | and portion |

הֵם יִקְחוּ חֶלְקָם:

| their portion | they take | them |

24 Save only that which the young men have eaten, and the portion of the men which went with me, Aner, Eshcol, and Mamre; let them take their portion.

ס

CHAPTER 15

ספר בראשית פרק טו

אַחַר הַדְּבָרִים הָאֵלֶּה הָיָה דְבַר־יְהוָֹה אֶל־אַבְרָם בַּמַּחֲזֶה

| in vision | Abram – unto | ihvh – speak | it was | the these | the matters | after |

לֵאמֹר אַל־תִּירָא אַבְרָם

| Abram | you fear - don't | to say |

אָנֹכִי מָגֵן לָךְ שְׂכָרְךָ הַרְבֵּה מְאֹד:

| great | the much | your reward | to you | shield | I am |

1 After these things the word of the LORD came unto Abram in a vision, saying, Fear not, Abram: I am thy shield, and thy exceeding great reward.

וַיֹּאמֶר אַבְרָם אֲדֹנָי יֱהוִֹה מַה־תִּתֶּן־לִי

| to me - you give - what | ihvh | Adoni | Abram | and he said |

וְאָנֹכִי הוֹלֵךְ עֲרִירִי

| childless | going | I am |

וּבֶן־מֶשֶׁק בֵּיתִי הוּא דַּמֶּשֶׂק אֱלִיעֶזֶר:

| Eliezer | Damascus | he | my house | steward - and son |

2 And Abram said, Lord GOD, what wilt thou give me, seeing I go childless, and the steward of my house is this Eliezer of Damascus?

וַיֹּאמֶר אַבְרָם הֵן לִי לֹא נָתַתָּה זָרַע
and he said   Abram   thus   to me   not   you gave   seed

וְהִנֵּה בֶן־בֵּיתִי יוֹרֵשׁ אֹתִי׃
and here   my house – son   heir   to me

3 And Abram said, Behold, to me thou hast given no seed: and, lo, one born in my house is mine heir.

וְהִנֵּה דְבַר־יְהֹוָה אֵלָיו לֵאמֹר לֹא יִירָשְׁךָ זֶה
and here   ihvh – speech   unto him   to say   not   he will be your heir   this

כִּי־אִם אֲשֶׁר יֵצֵא מִמֵּעֶיךָ הוּא יִירָשֶׁךָ׃
with - like   which   he come out   from your being   he   he will be your heir

4 And, behold, the word of the LORD came unto him, saying, This shall not be thine heir; but he that shall come forth out of thine own bowels shall be thine heir.

וַיּוֹצֵא אֹתוֹ הַחוּצָה וַיֹּאמֶר הַבֶּט־נָא הַשָּׁמַיְמָה
and he came out   to him   the outside   and he said   please - look   the towards heaven

וּסְפֹר הַכּוֹכָבִים אִם־תּוּכַל לִסְפֹּר אֹתָם
and number   the stars   you able - if   to number   to them

וַיֹּאמֶר לוֹ כֹּה יִהְיֶה זַרְעֶךָ׃
and he said   to him   thus   it will be   your seed

5 And he brought him forth abroad, and said, Look now toward heaven, and tell the stars, if thou be able to number them: and he said unto him, So shall thy seed be.

וְהֶאֱמִן בַּיהֹוָה וַיַּחְשְׁבֶהָ לּוֹ צְדָקָה׃
and he believed   in ihvh   and he credited it   to him   righteousness

6 And he believed in the LORD; and he counted it to him for righteousness.

[שׁשׁי]

וַיֹּאמֶר אֵלָיו אֲנִי יְהֹוָה אֲשֶׁר הוֹצֵאתִיךָ מֵאוּר כַּשְׂדִּים
and he said   unto him   I   ihvh   which   brought you out   from Ur   Chaldees

לָתֵת לְךָ אֶת־הָאָרֶץ הַזֹּאת לְרִשְׁתָּהּ׃
to give   to you   the land - that   the this   to inherit it

7 And he said unto him, I am the LORD that brought thee out of Ur of the Chaldees, to give thee this land to inherit it.

וַיֹּאמַר אֲדֹנָי יֱהֹוִה בַּמָּה אֵדַע כִּי אִירָשֶׁנָּה׃
and he said   Adoni   ihvh   in what   I know   like   I will inherit it

8 And he said, Lord GOD, whereby shall I know that I shall inherit it?

וַיֹּאמֶר אֵלָיו קְחָה לִי עֶגְלָה מְשֻׁלֶּשֶׁת
and he said   unto him   take   to me   heifer   from three [years]

וְעֵז מְשֻׁלֶּשֶׁת וְאַיִל מְשֻׁלָּשׁ וְתֹר וְגוֹזָל׃
and goat   from three [years]   and ram   from three [years]   and dove   and Pigeon

9 And he said unto him, Take me an heifer of three years old, and a she goat of three years old, and a ram of three years old, and a turtledove, and a young pigeon.

וַיִּקַּח־לֹו   אֶת־כָּל־אֵלֶּה וַיְבַתֵּר אֹתָם בַּתָּוֶךְ

in midst   to them   and he divided   these - all - that   to him - and he took

וַיִּתֵּן   אִישׁ־בִּתְרֹו לִקְרַאת רֵעֵהוּ

his neighbor   to meet   his half - piece   and he gave

וְאֶת־הַצִּפֹּר לֹא בָתָר:

divided   not   the bird - and that

10 And he took unto him all these, and divided them in the midst, and laid each piece one against another: but the birds divided he not.

וַיֵּרֶד   הָעַיִט עַל־הַפְּגָרִים וַיַּשֵּׁב אֹתָם אַבְרָם:

Abram   to them and he made return   the carcasses – upon   the bird prey   and he descended

11 And when the fowls came down upon the carcases, Abram drove them away.

וַיְהִי הַשֶּׁמֶשׁ לָבֹוא וְתַרְדֵּמָה נָפְלָה עַל־אַבְרָם

Abram – upon   fell   and deep sleep   to come   the sun   and he was

וְהִנֵּה אֵימָה חֲשֵׁכָה גְדֹלָה נֹפֶלֶת עָלָיו:

upon him   fell   great   darkness   horror   and here

12 And when the sun was going down, a deep sleep fell upon Abram; and, lo, an horror of great darkness fell upon him.

וַיֹּאמֶר לְאַבְרָם יָדֹעַ תֵּדַע

you know   knower   to Abram   and he said

כִּי־גֵר יִהְיֶה זַרְעֲךָ בְּאֶרֶץ לֹא לָהֶם

to them   not   in land   your seed   it be   stranger - like

וַעֲבָדוּם   וְעִנּוּ אֹתָם אַרְבַּע מֵאֹות שָׁנָה:

year   hundreds   four   to them   and they afflict   and they serve them

13 And he said unto Abram, Know of a surety that thy seed shall be a stranger in a land that is not theirs, and shall serve them; and they shall afflict them four hundred years;

וְגַם אֶת־הַגֹּוי אֲשֶׁר יַעֲבֹדוּ דָּן אָנֹכִי

I am   judge   they serve   which   the nation - that   and also

וְאַחֲרֵי־כֵן יֵצְאוּ בִּרְכֻשׁ גָּדֹול:

great   in possession   they come out   thus - and after

14 And also that nation, whom they shall serve, will I judge: and afterward shall they come out with great substance.

וְאַתָּה תָּבֹוא אֶל־אֲבֹתֶיךָ בְּשָׁלֹום תִּקָּבֵר בְּשֵׂיבָה טֹובָה:

good   in old age   you be buried   in peace   your fathers - unto   you come   and you

15 And thou shalt go to thy fathers in peace; thou shalt be buried in a good old age.

וְדוֹר   רְבִיעִי   יָשׁוּבוּ   הֵנָּה
here   they will return   fourth   and generation

כִּי לֹא־שָׁלֵם עֲוֹן הָאֱמֹרִי עַד־הֵנָּה:
here - till   the Amorite   sin   full - not   like

16 But in the fourth generation they shall come hither again: for the iniquity of the
Amorites is not yet full.

וַיְהִי הַשֶּׁמֶשׁ בָּאָה וַעֲלָטָה הָיָה
was   and twilight   came   the sun   and was

וְהִנֵּה תַנּוּר עָשָׁן
smoke   furnace   and here

וְלַפִּיד אֵשׁ אֲשֶׁר עָבַר בֵּין הַגְּזָרִים הָאֵלֶּה:
the these   the pieces   between   passed   which   fire   and torch

17 And it came to pass, that, when the sun went down, and it was dark, behold a
smoking furnace, and a burning lamp that passed between those pieces.

בַּיּוֹם הַהוּא כָּרַת יְהֹוָה
ihvh   cut   the it   in day

אֶת־אַבְרָם בְּרִית לֵאמֹר
to say   covenant   Abram - that

לְזַרְעֲךָ נָתַתִּי אֶת־הָאָרֶץ הַזֹּאת
the this   the land – that   I have given   to your seed

מִנְּהַר מִצְרַיִם עַד־הַנָּהָר הַגָּדֹל נְהַר־פְּרָת:
Parat - river   the great   the river - till   Egyptians   from river

18 In the same day the LORD made a covenant with Abram, saying, Unto thy seed have
I given this land, from the river of Egypt unto the great river, the river Euphrates:

אֶת־הַקֵּינִי וְאֶת־הַקְּנִזִּי וְאֵת הַקַּדְמֹנִי:
the Kadmonites   and that   the Kenizzites - and that   the Kenites - that

19 The Kenites, and the Kenizzites, and the Kadmonites,

וְאֶת־הַחִתִּי וְאֶת־הַפְּרִזִּי וְאֶת־הָרְפָאִים:
the Rephaims - and that   the Perizzites - and that   the Hittites - and that

20 And the Hittites, and the Perizzites, and the Rephaims,

וְאֶת־הָאֱמֹרִי וְאֶת־הַכְּנַעֲנִי וְאֶת־הַגִּרְגָּשִׁי וְאֶת־הַיְבוּסִי:
the Jebusites - and that   the Girgashites and that   the Canaanites - and that   the Amorites - and that

21 And the Amorites, and the Canaanites, and the Girgashites, and the Jebusites.

CHAPTER 16

ספר בראשית פרק טז

וְשָׂרַי אֵשֶׁת אַבְרָם לֹא יָלְדָה לוֹ
to him   she bore   not   Abram   wife   and Sarai

וְלָהּ שִׁפְחָה מִצְרִית וּשְׁמָהּ הָגָר:
Hagar   and her name   Egyptian   maidservant   and to her

1 Now Sarai Abram's wife bare him no children: and she had an handmaid, an Egyptian, whose name was Hagar.

וַתֹּאמֶר שָׂרַי אֶל־אַבְרָם
Abram - unto   Sarai   and she said

הִנֵּה־נָא עֲצָרַנִי יְהוָֹה מִלֶּדֶת
from bearing   ihvh   he restrained me   now - here

בֹּא־נָא אֶל־שִׁפְחָתִי אוּלַי אִבָּנֶה מִמֶּנָּה
from her   I build   perhaps   my maidservant - unto   please - come

וַיִּשְׁמַע אַבְרָם לְקוֹל שָׂרָי:
Sarai   to voice   Abram   and he listened

2 And Sarai said unto Abram, Behold now, the LORD hath restrained me from bearing: I pray thee, go in unto my maid; it may be that I may obtain children by her. And Abram hearkened to the voice of Sarai.

וַתִּקַּח שָׂרַי אֵשֶׁת אַבְרָם אֶת־הָגָר הַמִּצְרִית שִׁפְחָתָהּ
her maidservant   the Egyptian   Hagar - that   Abram   wife   Sarai   and she took

מִקֵּץ עֶשֶׂר שָׁנִים לְשֶׁבֶת אַבְרָם בְּאֶרֶץ כְּנָעַן
Canaan   in land   Abram   to dwell   years   ten   from very end

וַתִּתֵּן אֹתָהּ לְאַבְרָם אִישָׁהּ לוֹ לְאִשָּׁה:
to wife   to him   her husband   to Abram   to her   and she gave

3 And Sarai Abram's wife took Hagar her maid the Egyptian, after Abram had dwelt ten years in the land of Canaan, and gave her to her husband Abram to be his wife.

וַיָּבֹא אֶל־הָגָר וַתַּהַר וַתֵּרֶא כִּי הָרָתָה
she was pregnant   like   and she saw   and she conceived   Hagar - unto   and he came

וַתֵּקַל גְּבִרְתָּהּ בְּעֵינֶיהָ:
in her eyes   her lady   and she despised

4 And he went in unto Hagar, and she conceived: and when she saw that she had conceived, her mistress was despised in her eyes.

וַתֹּאמֶר שָׂרַי אֶל־אַבְרָם חֲמָסִי עָלֶיךָ
upon you   my violence   Abram - unto   Sarai   and she said

אָנֹכִי נָתַתִּי שִׁפְחָתִי בְּחֵיקֶךָ וַתֵּרֶא כִּי הָרָתָה
she pregnant   like   and she saw   in your bosom   my maidservant   I gave   I am

וָאֵקַל בְּעֵינֶיהָ יִשְׁפֹּט יְהוָֹה בֵּינִי וּבֵינֶיךָ:
and between you   between me   ihvh   he judge   in her eyes   and I despised

5 And Sarai said unto Abram, My wrong be upon thee: I have given my maid into thy bosom; and when she saw that she had conceived, I was despised in her eyes: the LORD judge between me and thee.

וַיֹּאמֶר אַבְרָם אֶל־שָׂרַי
Sarai - unto   Abram   and he said

הִנֵּה שִׁפְחָתֵךְ בְּיָדֵךְ עֲשִׂי־לָהּ הַטּוֹב בְּעֵינָיִךְ
in your eyes   the good   to her - do   in your hands   your maidservant   here

וַתְּעַנֶּהָ שָׂרַי וַתִּבְרַח מִפָּנֶיהָ׃
from her face   and she fled   Sarai   and she afflicted her

6 But Abram said unto Sarai, Behold, thy maid is in thy hand; do to her as it pleaseth thee. And when Sarai dealt hardly with her, she fled from her face.

וַיִּמְצָאָהּ מַלְאַךְ יְהֹוָה עַל־עֵין הַמַּיִם בַּמִּדְבָּר
in wilderness   the water   spring – upon   ihvh   angel   and he found

עַל־הָעַיִן בְּדֶרֶךְ שׁוּר׃
Shur   in way   the spring - upon

7 And the angel of the LORD found her by a fountain of water in the wilderness, by the fountain in the way to Shur.

וַיֹּאמַר הָגָר שִׁפְחַת שָׂרַי אֵי־מִזֶּה בָאת וְאָנָה תֵלֵכִי
you go   and to where   you came   from this - where   Sarai   maidservant   Hagar   and he said

וַתֹּאמֶר מִפְּנֵי שָׂרַי גְּבִרְתִּי אָנֹכִי בֹּרַחַת׃
fleeing   I am   my lady   Sarai   from face   and she said

8 And he said, Hagar, Sarai's maid, whence camest thou? and whither wilt thou go? And she said, I flee from the face of my mistress Sarai.

וַיֹּאמֶר לָהּ מַלְאַךְ יְהֹוָה שׁוּבִי אֶל־גְּבִרְתֵּךְ
your lady - unto   you return   ihvh   angel   to her   and he said

וְהִתְעַנִּי תַּחַת יָדֶיהָ׃
her hand   under   and be afflicted

9 And the angel of the LORD said unto her, Return to thy mistress, and submit thyself under her hands.

וַיֹּאמֶר לָהּ מַלְאַךְ יְהֹוָה הַרְבָּה אַרְבֶּה אֶת־זַרְעֵךְ
your seed - that   I increase   the increase   ihvh   angel   to her   and he said

וְלֹא יִסָּפֵר מֵרֹב׃
from many   it be numbered   and not

10 And the angel of the LORD said unto her, I will multiply thy seed exceedingly, that it shall not be numbered for multitude.

וַיֹּאמֶר לָהּ מַלְאַךְ יְהֹוָה הִנָּךְ הָרָה
pregnant   here you   ihvh   angel   to her   and he said

וְיֹלַדְתְּ בֵּן וְקָרָאת שְׁמוֹ יִשְׁמָעֵאל
Ishmael   his name   and you call   son   and you will beget

כִּי־שָׁמַע יְהֹוָה אֶל־עָנְיֵךְ:

your affliction - unto   ihvh   heard - like

11 And the angel of the LORD said unto her, Behold, thou art with child, and shalt
bear a son, and shalt call his name Ishmael; because the LORD hath heard thy affliction.

וְהוּא יִהְיֶה פֶּרֶא אָדָם יָדוֹ בַכֹּל

in all   his hand   Adam   wild donkey   will be   and he

וְיַד כֹּל בּוֹ וְעַל־פְּנֵי כָל־אֶחָיו יִשְׁכֹּן:

he will dwell   his brothers – all   face - and upon   in him   all   and hand

12 And he will be a wild man; his hand will be against every man, and every man's hand
against him; and he shall dwell in the presence of all his brethren.

וַתִּקְרָא שֵׁם־יְהֹוָה הַדֹּבֵר אֵלֶיהָ אַתָּה אֵל רֳאִי

my seeing   El   you   unto her   the speaker   ihvh - name   and she called

כִּי אָמְרָה הֲגַם הֲלֹם רָאִיתִי אַחֲרֵי רֹאִי:

my seer   after   I saw   dream   the also   she said   like

13 And she called the name of the LORD that spake unto her, Thou God seest me: for
she said, Have I also here looked after him that seeth me?

עַל־כֵּן קָרָא לַבְּאֵר בְּאֵר לַחַי רֹאִי

Roi   Lahai   Beer   to [the] well   called   thus - upon

הִנֵּה בֵין־קָדֵשׁ וּבֵין בָּרֶד:

Bered   and between   Kadesh - between   here

14 Wherefore the well was called Beer-lahai-roi; behold, it is between Kadesh and
Bered.

וַתֵּלֶד הָגָר לְאַבְרָם בֵּן

son   to Abram   Hagar   and she begat

וַיִּקְרָא אַבְרָם שֶׁם־בְּנוֹ אֲשֶׁר־יָלְדָה הָגָר יִשְׁמָעֵאל:

Ishmael   Hagar   begat - which   his son - name   Abram   and he called

15 And Hagar bare Abram a son: and Abram called his son's name, which Hagar bare,
Ishmael.

וְאַבְרָם בֶּן־שְׁמֹנִים שָׁנָה וְשֵׁשׁ שָׁנִים

years   and six   year   eighty - age   and Abram

בְּלֶדֶת־הָגָר אֶת־יִשְׁמָעֵאל לְאַבְרָם:

to Abram   Ishmael - that   Hagar - to beget

16 And Abram was fourscore and six years old, when Hagar bare Ishmael to Abram.

ס

CHAPTER 17

ספר בראשית פרק יז

וַיְהִי אַבְרָם בֶּן־תִּשְׁעִים שָׁנָה וְתֵשַׁע שָׁנִים
<small>years   and nine   year   ninety – age   Abram   and he was</small>

וַיֵּרָא יְהֹוָה אֶל־אַבְרָם
<small>Abram - unto   ihvh   and appeared</small>

וַיֹּאמֶר אֵלָיו אֲנִי־אֵל שַׁדַּי הִתְהַלֵּךְ לְפָנַי
<small>before me   cause to walk   Shadi   El - I   to him   and he said</small>

וֶהְיֵה תָמִים:
<small>perfect   and you be</small>

1 And when Abram was ninety years old and nine, the LORD appeared to Abram, and said unto him, I am the Almighty God; walk before me, and be thou perfect.

וְאֶתְּנָה בְרִיתִי בֵּינִי וּבֵינֶךָ
<small>and between you   between me   my covenant   and I will give</small>

וְאַרְבֶּה אוֹתְךָ בִּמְאֹד מְאֹד:
<small>greatly   in greatly   to you   and I increase</small>

2 And I will make my covenant between me and thee, and will multiply thee exceedingly.

וַיִּפֹּל אַבְרָם עַל־פָּנָיו וַיְדַבֵּר אִתּוֹ אֱלֹהִים לֵאמֹר:
<small>to say   Elohim   to him   and he spoke   his face - upon   Abram   and he fell</small>

3 And Abram fell on his face: and God talked with him, saying,

אֲנִי הִנֵּה בְרִיתִי אִתָּךְ וְהָיִיתָ לְאַב הֲמוֹן גּוֹיִם:
<small>nations   throng   to father   and you will be   with you   my covenant   here   I</small>

4 As for me, behold, my covenant is with thee, and thou shalt be a father of many nations.

וְלֹא־יִקָּרֵא עוֹד אֶת־שִׁמְךָ אַבְרָם
<small>Abram   your name - that   again   it will call - and not</small>

וְהָיָה שִׁמְךָ אַבְרָהָם כִּי אַב־הֲמוֹן גּוֹיִם נְתַתִּיךָ:
<small>I give you   nations   throng - father   like   for Abram   your name   and it will be</small>

5 Neither shall thy name any more be called Abram, but thy name shall be Abraham; for a father of many nations have I made thee.

וְהִפְרֵתִי אֹתְךָ בִּמְאֹד מְאֹד
<small>greatly   in greatly   to you   and I will make fruitful</small>

וּנְתַתִּיךָ לְגוֹיִם וּמְלָכִים מִמְּךָ יֵצֵאוּ:
<small>they come out   from you   and kings   to nations   and I will give you</small>

6 And I will make thee exceeding fruitful, and I will make nations of thee, and kings shall come out of thee.

[שביעי]

וַהֲקִמֹתִי אֶת־בְּרִיתִי בֵּינִי וּבֵינֶךָ
and between you   between me   my covenant - that   and I will establish

וּבֵין זַרְעֲךָ אַחֲרֶיךָ לְדֹרֹתָם לִבְרִית עוֹלָם
forever   to covenant   to their generations   after you   your seed   and between

לִהְיוֹת לְךָ לֵאלֹהִים וּלְזַרְעֲךָ אַחֲרֶיךָ:
after you   and to your seed   to Elohim   to you   to be

7 And I will establish my covenant between me and thee and thy seed after thee in their generations for an everlasting covenant, to be a God unto thee, and to thy seed after thee.

וְנָתַתִּי לְךָ וּלְזַרְעֲךָ אַחֲרֶיךָ אֵת אֶרֶץ מְגֻרֶיךָ
from your sojourning   land   that   after you   and to your seed   to you   and I give

אֵת כָּל־אֶרֶץ כְּנַעַן לַאֲחֻזַּת עוֹלָם
forever   to possession   Canaan   land - all   that

וְהָיִיתִי לָהֶם לֵאלֹהִים:
to Elohim   to them   and I will be

8 And I will give unto thee, and to thy seed after thee, the land wherein thou art a stranger, all the land of Canaan, for an everlasting possession; and I will be their God.

וַיֹּאמֶר אֱלֹהִים אֶל־אַבְרָהָם
Abraham - unto   Elohim   and he said

וְאַתָּה אֶת־בְּרִיתִי תִשְׁמֹר אַתָּה וְזַרְעֲךָ אַחֲרֶיךָ לְדֹרֹתָם:
to their generations   after you   and your seed   you   you heed   my covenant - that   and you

9 And God said unto Abraham, Thou shalt keep my covenant therefore, thou, and thy seed after thee in their generations.

זֹאת בְּרִיתִי אֲשֶׁר תִּשְׁמְרוּ בֵּינִי וּבֵינֵיכֶם
and between you   between me   you heed   which   my covenant   this

וּבֵין זַרְעֲךָ אַחֲרֶיךָ הִמּוֹל לָכֶם כָּל־זָכָר:
male - all   to you   circumcise   after you   your seed   and between

10 This is my covenant, which ye shall keep, between me and you and thy seed after thee; Every man child among you shall be circumcised.

וּנְמַלְתֶּם אֵת בְּשַׂר עָרְלַתְכֶם
your foreskin   flesh   that   and you will circumcise

וְהָיָה לְאוֹת בְּרִית בֵּינִי וּבֵינֵיכֶם:
and between you   between me   covenant   to sign   and it will be

11 And ye shall circumcise the flesh of your foreskin; and it shall be a token of the covenant betwixt me and you.

וּבֶן־שְׁמֹנַת יָמִים יִמּוֹל לָכֶם
to you   he will be circumcised   days   eight -- and age

כָּל־זָכָר לְדֹרֹתֵיכֶם יְלִיד בָּיִת
house   born   to your generations   male - all

וּמִקְנַת־כֶּסֶף מִכֹּל בֶּן־נֵכָר אֲשֶׁר לֹא מִזַּרְעֲךָ הוּא:
he   from your seed   not   who   foreigner - son   from all   silver – and from bought

12 And he that is eight days old shall be circumcised among you, every man child in your generations, he that is born in the house, or bought with money of any stranger, which is not of thy seed.

הִמּוֹל יִמּוֹל יְלִיד בֵּיתְךָ וּמִקְנַת כַּסְפֶּךָ
your silver   and from bought   your house   born   he be circumcised   circumcise

וְהָיְתָה בְרִיתִי בִּבְשַׂרְכֶם לִבְרִית עוֹלָם:
forever   to covenant   in your flesh   my covenant   and it be

13 He that is born in thy house, and he that is bought with thy money, must needs be circumcised: and my covenant shall be in your flesh for an everlasting covenant.

וְעָרֵל זָכָר אֲשֶׁר לֹא־יִמּוֹל אֶת־בְּשַׂר עָרְלָתוֹ
his foreskin   flesh - that   circumcised - not   which   male   and foreskin

וְנִכְרְתָה הַנֶּפֶשׁ הַהִוא מֵעַמֶּיהָ אֶת־בְּרִיתִי הֵפַר:
broke   my covenant - that   from his people   the it   the soul   and will be cut off

ס

14 And the uncircumcised man child whose flesh of his foreskin is not circumcised, that soul shall be cut off from his people; he hath broken my covenant.

וַיֹּאמֶר אֱלֹהִים אֶל־אַבְרָהָם
Abraham -unto   Elohim   and he said

שָׂרַי אִשְׁתְּךָ לֹא־תִקְרָא אֶת־שְׁמָהּ שָׂרָי
Sarai   her name - that   you will call - not   your wife   Sarai

כִּי שָׂרָה שְׁמָהּ:
her name   Sarah   like

15 And God said unto Abraham, As for Sarai thy wife, thou shalt not call her name Sarai, but Sarah shall her name be.

וּבֵרַכְתִּי אֹתָהּ וְגַם נָתַתִּי מִמֶּנָּה לְךָ בֵּן
son   to you   from her   I give   and also   you   and I will bless

וּבֵרַכְתִּיהָ וְהָיְתָה לְגוֹיִם מַלְכֵי עַמִּים מִמֶּנָּה יִהְיוּ:
they will be   from her   peoples   kings   to nations   and she be   and I will bless her

16 And I will bless her, and give thee a son also of her: yea, I will bless her, and she shall be a mother of nations; kings of people shall be of her.

וַיִּפֹּל אַבְרָהָם עַל־פָּנָיו וַיִּצְחָק

and he laughed   his face - upon   Abraham   and he fell

וַיֹּאמֶר בְּלִבּוֹ הַלְּבֶן מֵאָה־שָׁנָה יִוָּלֵד

he be born   year – hundred   the to age   in his heart   and he said

וְאִם־שָׂרָה הֲבַת־תִּשְׁעִים שָׁנָה תֵּלֵד:

she will bear   year   ninety – the age   Sarah - and with

17 Then Abraham fell upon his face, and laughed, and said in his heart, Shall a child
be born unto him that is an hundred years old? and shall Sarah, that is ninety years old,
bear?

וַיֹּאמֶר אַבְרָהָם אֶל־הָאֱלֹהִים לוּ יִשְׁמָעֵאל יִחְיֶה לְפָנֶיךָ:

before you   he live   Ishmael   only   the Elohim – unto   Abraham   and he said

18 And Abraham said unto God, O that Ishmael might live before thee!

וַיֹּאמֶר אֱלֹהִים אֲבָל שָׂרָה אִשְׁתְּךָ יֹלֶדֶת לְךָ בֵּן

son   to you   will bear   your wife   Sarah   but   Elohim   and he said

וְקָרָאתָ אֶת־שְׁמוֹ יִצְחָק

Isaac   his name - that   and you will call

וַהֲקִמֹתִי אֶת־בְּרִיתִי אִתּוֹ לִבְרִית עוֹלָם לְזַרְעוֹ אַחֲרָיו:

after him   to his seed   forever   to covenant   with him   my covenant - that   and I will establish

19 And God said, Sarah thy wife shall bear thee a son indeed; and thou shalt call his
name Isaac: and I will establish my covenant with him for an everlasting covenant, and
with his seed after him.

וּלְיִשְׁמָעֵאל שְׁמַעְתִּיךָ הִנֵּה בֵּרַכְתִּי אֹתוֹ

to him   I blessed   here   I heard you   and to Ishmael

וְהִפְרֵיתִי אֹתוֹ וְהִרְבֵּיתִי אֹתוֹ בִּמְאֹד מְאֹד

greatly   in greatly   to him   and I will increase   to him   and I will make fruitful

שְׁנֵים־עָשָׂר נְשִׂיאִם יוֹלִיד וּנְתַתִּיו לְגוֹי גָּדוֹל:

great   to nations   and I give him   he will beget   princes   ---- twelve ----

20 And as for Ishmael, I have heard thee: Behold, I have blessed him, and will make him
fruitful, and will multiply him exceedingly; twelve princes shall he beget, and I will make
him a great nation.

וְאֶת־בְּרִיתִי אָקִים אֶת־יִצְחָק

Issac - that   I establish   my covenant - and that

אֲשֶׁר תֵּלֵד לְךָ שָׂרָה לַמּוֹעֵד הַזֶּה בַּשָּׁנָה הָאַחֶרֶת:

the following   in year   the this   to set time   Sarah   to you   she befot   which

21 But my covenant will I establish with Isaac, which Sarah shall bear unto thee at this
set time in the next year.

וַיְכַל לְדַבֵּר אִתּוֹ וַיַּעַל אֱלֹהִים מֵעַל אַבְרָהָם:

Abraham   from upon   Elohim   and he ascended   with him   to speak   and he finished

22 And he left off talking with him, and God went up from Abraham.

וַיִּקַּח אַבְרָהָם אֶת־יִשְׁמָעֵאל בְּנוֹ
his son   Ishmael - that   Abraham   and he took

וְאֵת כָּל־יְלִידֵי בֵיתוֹ
his house   born ones - all   and that

וְאֵת כָּל־מִקְנַת כַּסְפּוֹ כָּל־זָכָר בְּאַנְשֵׁי בֵּית אַבְרָהָם
Abraham   house   in men   male - every   his silver   from bought - all   and that

וַיָּמָל אֶת־בְּשַׂר עָרְלָתָם בְּעֶצֶם הַיּוֹם הַזֶּה
the this   the day   in exactly   their foreskin   flesh - that   and he circumcised

כַּאֲשֶׁר דִּבֶּר אִתּוֹ אֱלֹהִים׃
Elohim   to him   spoke   when

23 And Abraham took Ishmael his son, and all that were born in his house, and all that were bought with his money, every male among the men of Abraham's house; and circumcised the flesh of their foreskin in the selfsame day, as God had said unto him.

[מפטיר]

וְאַבְרָהָם בֶּן־תִּשְׁעִים וָתֵשַׁע שָׁנָה
year   and nine   ninety – age   and Abraham

בְּהִמֹּלוֹ בְּשַׂר עָרְלָתוֹ׃
his foreskin   flesh   in his circumcised

24 And Abraham was ninety years old and nine, when he was circumcised in the flesh of his foreskin.

וְיִשְׁמָעֵאל בְּנוֹ בֶּן־שָׁלֹשׁ עֶשְׂרֵה שָׁנָה
year   ---thirteen---   - age   his son   and Ishmael

בְּהִמֹּלוֹ אֵת בְּשַׂר עָרְלָתוֹ׃
his foreskin   flesh   that   in his circumcised

25 And Ishmael his son was thirteen years old, when he was circumcised in the flesh of his foreskin.

בְּעֶצֶם הַיּוֹם הַזֶּה נִמּוֹל אַבְרָהָם
Abraham   was circumcised   the this   the day   in exactly

וְיִשְׁמָעֵאל בְּנוֹ׃
his son   and Ishmael

26 In the selfsame day was Abraham circumcised, and Ishmael his son.

וְכָל־אַנְשֵׁי בֵיתוֹ יְלִיד בַּיִת
house   born   his house   men - and all

וּמִקְנַת־כֶּסֶף מֵאֵת בֶּן־נֵכָר נִמֹּלוּ אִתּוֹ׃
with him   they were circumcised   foreigner - son   from that   silver - and from bought

27 And all the men of his house, born in the house, and bought with money of the

stranger, were circumcised with him.

פ פ פ

4 VAIERA

CHAPTER 18

ספר בראשית פרק יח

וַיֵּרָא֩   אֵלָ֨יו יְהֹוָ֜ה בְּאֵלֹנֵ֣י מַמְרֵ֗א
<small>Mamre   in plain   ihvh   unto him   and he appeared</small>

וְה֛וּא יֹשֵׁ֥ב פֶּֽתַח־הָאֹ֖הֶל כְּחֹ֥ם הַיּֽוֹם׃
<small>the day   like heat   the tent - entrance   sat   and he</small>

1 And the LORD appeared unto him in the plains of Mamre: and he sat in the tent door in the heat of the day;

וַיִּשָּׂ֤א   עֵינָיו֙ וַיַּ֔רְא וְהִנֵּה֙ שְׁלֹשָׁ֣ה אֲנָשִׁ֔ים נִצָּבִ֖ים עָלָ֑יו
<small>upon him   standing ones   men   three   and here   and he saw   his eyes   and he lifted</small>

וַיַּ֗רְא   וַיָּ֤רָץ לִקְרָאתָם֙ מִפֶּ֣תַח הָאֹ֔הֶל וַיִּשְׁתַּ֖חוּ אָֽרְצָה׃
<small>towards earth   and he bowed   the tent   from opening   to meet them   and he ran   and he saw</small>

2 And he lift up his eyes and looked, and, lo, three men stood by him: and when he saw them, he ran to meet them from the tent door, and bowed himself toward the ground,

וַיֹּאמַ֑ר אֲדֹנָ֗י אִם־נָ֨א מָצָ֤אתִי חֵן֙ בְּעֵינֶ֔יךָ
<small>in your eyes   favor   I found   please - if   Adoni   and he said</small>

אַל־נָ֥א תַעֲבֹ֖ר מֵעַ֥ל עַבְדֶּֽךָ׃
<small>your servant   from upon   you pass   please – don't</small>

3 And said, My Lord, if now I have found favour in thy sight, pass not away, I pray thee, from thy servant:

יֻקַּֽח־נָ֣א מְעַט־מַ֔יִם וְרַחֲצ֖וּ רַגְלֵיכֶ֑ם
<small>your feet   and you wash   water - little   please - it take</small>

וְהִֽשָּׁעֲנ֖וּ תַּ֥חַת הָעֵֽץ׃
<small>the tree   under   and you lean back</small>

4 Let a little water, I pray you, be fetched, and wash your feet, and rest yourselves under the tree:

וְאֶקְחָ֨ה פַת־לֶ֜חֶם וְסַעֲד֤וּ לִבְּכֶם֙ אַחַ֣ר תַּעֲבֹ֔רוּ
<small>you pass it   afterward   your hearts   and you refresh   bread - piece   and I will take</small>

כִּֽי־עַל־כֵּ֥ן עֲבַרְתֶּ֖ם עַֽל־עַבְדְּכֶ֑ם
<small>your servant - upon   you pass   thus - upon - like</small>

וַיֹּ֣אמְר֔וּ כֵּ֥ן תַּעֲשֶׂ֖ה כַּאֲשֶׁ֥ר דִּבַּֽרְתָּ׃
<small>you spoke   when   you do   thus   and they said</small>

5 And I will fetch a morsel of bread, and comfort ye your hearts; after that ye shall pass on: for therefore are ye come to your servant. And they said, So do, as thou hast said.

וַיְמַהֵר אַבְרָהָם הָאֹהֱלָה אֶל־שָׂרָה

Sarah - unto　　toward the tent　　Abraham　　and he hurried

וַיֹּאמֶר מַהֲרִי שְׁלֹשׁ סְאִים קֶמַח סֹלֶת לוּשִׁי וַעֲשִׂי עֻגוֹת:

cakes　and make it　kneed it　fine　flour　measures　three　quickly　and he said

6 And Abraham hastened into the tent unto Sarah, and said, Make ready quickly three
measures of fine meal, knead it, and make cakes upon the hearth.

וְאֶל־הַבָּקָר רָץ אַבְרָהָם וַיִּקַּח בֶּן־בָּקָר רַךְ וָטוֹב

and good　soft　cattle - son　and he took　Abraham　ran　the cattle - and unto

וַיִּתֵּן אֶל־הַנַּעַר וַיְמַהֵר לַעֲשׂוֹת אֹתוֹ:

to it　to do　and he hurried　the boy - unto　and he gave

7 And Abraham ran unto the herd, and fetched a calf tender and good, and gave it unto
a young man; and he hasted to dress it.

וַיִּקַּח חֶמְאָה וְחָלָב וּבֶן־הַבָּקָר אֲשֶׁר עָשָׂה

he made　which　the cattle - and son　and milk　butter　and he took

וַיִּתֵּן לִפְנֵיהֶם וְהוּא עֹמֵד עֲלֵיהֶם תַּחַת הָעֵץ וַיֹּאכֵלוּ:

and they ate　the tree　under　upon them　stood　and it　before them　and he gave

8 And he took butter, and milk, and the calf which he had dressed, and set it before
them; and he stood by them under the tree, and they did eat.

וַיֹּאמְרוּ אֵלָיו אַיֵּה שָׂרָה אִשְׁתֶּךָ וַיֹּאמֶר הִנֵּה בָאֹהֶל:

in tent　here　and he said　your wife　Sarah　where　unto him　and they said

9 And they said unto him, Where is Sarah thy wife? And he said, Behold, in the tent.

וַיֹּאמֶר שׁוֹב אָשׁוּב אֵלֶיךָ כָּעֵת חַיָּה

life　like [the] time　unto you　I will return　returner　and he said

וְהִנֵּה־בֵן לְשָׂרָה אִשְׁתֶּךָ

your wife　to Sarah　son - and here

וְשָׂרָה שֹׁמַעַת פֶּתַח הָאֹהֶל וְהוּא אַחֲרָיו:

behind him　and it　the tent　opening　listening　and Sarah

10 And he said, I will certainly return unto thee according to the time of life; and, lo,
Sarah thy wife shall have a son. And Sarah heard it in the tent door, which was behind
him.

וְאַבְרָהָם וְשָׂרָה זְקֵנִים בָּאִים בַּיָּמִים

in days　coming　old ones　and Sarah　and Abraham

חָדַל לִהְיוֹת לְשָׂרָה אֹרַח כַּנָּשִׁים:

like women　road　to Sarah　to be　ceased

11 Now Abraham and Sarah were old and well stricken in age; and it ceased to be with
Sarah after the manner of women.

וַתִּצְחַק שָׂרָה בְּקִרְבָּהּ לֵאמֹר אַחֲרֵי בְלֹתִי הָיְתָה־לִּי עֶדְנָה

pleasure　to me - it be　nothing me　after　to say　in her closeness　Sarah　and she laughed

וַאדֹנִי זָקֵן:
<small>old and my master</small>

12 Therefore Sarah laughed within herself, saying, After I am waxed old shall I have pleasure, my lord being old also?

וַיֹּאמֶר יְהֹוָה אֶל־אַבְרָהָם לָמָּה זֶּה צָחֲקָה שָׂרָה
<small>Sarah she laughed this why Abraham - unto ihvh and he said</small>

לֵאמֹר הַאַף אֻמְנָם אֵלֵד וַאֲנִי זָקַנְתִּי:
<small>my old and I child I will bear the then to say</small>

13 And the LORD said unto Abraham, Wherefore did Sarah laugh, saying, Shall I of a surety bear a child, which am old?

הֲיִפָּלֵא מֵיהֹוָה דָּבָר לַמּוֹעֵד אָשׁוּב אֵלֶיךָ כָּעֵת חַיָּה
<small>life like time unto you I will return to appointed time matter from ihvh the it work</small>

וּלְשָׂרָה בֵן:
<small>son and to Sarah</small>

14 Is any thing too hard for the LORD? At the time appointed I will return unto thee, according to the time of life, and Sarah shall have a son.

[שני]

וַתְּכַחֵשׁ שָׂרָה לֵאמֹר לֹא צָחַקְתִּי כִּי יָרֵאָה
<small>she was afraid like I laughed not to say Sarah and she denied</small>

וַיֹּאמֶר לֹא כִּי צָחָקְתְּ:
<small>you laughed like not and he said</small>

15 Then Sarah denied, saying, I laughed not; for she was afraid. And he said, Nay; but thou didst laugh.

וַיָּקֻמוּ מִשָּׁם הָאֲנָשִׁים וַיַּשְׁקִפוּ עַל־פְּנֵי סְדֹם
<small>Sodom face - upon and they gazed the men from there and they got up</small>

וְאַבְרָהָם הֹלֵךְ עִמָּם לְשַׁלְּחָם:
<small>to send off them with them walked and Abraham</small>

16 And the men rose up from thence, and looked toward Sodom: and Abraham went with them to bring them on the way.

וַיהֹוָה אָמָר הַמֲכַסֶּה אֲנִי מֵאַבְרָהָם אֲשֶׁר אֲנִי עֹשֶׂה:
<small>do I which from Abraham I the covering said and ihvh</small>

17 And the LORD said, Shall I hide from Abraham that thing which I do;

וְאַבְרָהָם הָיוֹ יִהְיֶה לְגוֹי גָּדוֹל
<small>great to nation he will be his be and Abraham</small>

וְעָצוּם וְנִבְרְכוּ־בוֹ כֹּל גּוֹיֵי הָאָרֶץ:
<small>the earth nations all in him - and they be blessed and powerful</small>

18 Seeing that Abraham shall surely become a great and mighty nation, and all the nations of the earth shall be blessed in him?

כִּי יְדַעְתִּיו לְמַעַן אֲשֶׁר יְצַוֶּה אֶת־בָּנָיו וְאֶת־בֵּיתוֹ אַחֲרָיו
after him   his house - and that   his son - that   he will command   which   to end   I know him   like

וְשָׁמְרוּ דֶּרֶךְ יְהוָה לַעֲשׂוֹת צְדָקָה וּמִשְׁפָּט
and judgment   righteousness   to doings   ihvh   way   and they will heed

לְמַעַן הָבִיא יְהוָה עַל־אַבְרָהָם אֵת אֲשֶׁר־דִּבֶּר עָלָיו׃
upon him   spoken - which   that   Abraham – upon   ihvh   the bring   to end

19 For I know him, that he will command his children and his household after him, and they shall keep the way of the LORD, to do justice and judgment; that the LORD may bring upon Abraham that which he hath spoken of him.

וַיֹּאמֶר יְהוָה זַעֲקַת סְדֹם וַעֲמֹרָה כִּי־רָבָּה
much - like   and Gomorrah   Sodom   help cry   ihvh   and he said

וְחַטָּאתָם כִּי כָבְדָה מְאֹד׃
very   it heavy   like   and their sin

20 And the LORD said, Because the cry of Sodom and Gomorrah is great, and because their sin is very grievous;

אֵרֲדָה־נָּא וְאֶרְאֶה הַכְּצַעֲקָתָהּ הַבָּאָה אֵלַי עָשׂוּ כָּלָה
toward all   they did   unto me   the come   the it's cry out   and I see   now - I will descend

וְאִם־לֹא אֵדָעָה׃
I will know   not - and if

21 I will go down now, and see whether they have done altogether according to the cry of it, which is come unto me; and if not, I will know.

וַיִּפְנוּ מִשָּׁם הָאֲנָשִׁים
the men   from there   and they turned

וַיֵּלְכוּ סְדֹמָה וְאַבְרָהָם עוֹדֶנּוּ עֹמֵד לִפְנֵי יְהוָה׃
ihvh   before   standing   remained   and Abraham   toward Sodom   and they went

22 And the men turned their faces from thence, and went toward Sodom: but Abraham stood yet before the LORD.

וַיִּגַּשׁ אַבְרָהָם וַיֹּאמַר הַאַף תִּסְפֶּה צַדִּיק עִם־רָשָׁע׃
wicked – with   righteous   you sweep up   the surely   and he said   Abraham   and he drew near

23 And Abraham drew near, and said, Wilt thou also destroy the righteous with the wicked?

אוּלַי יֵשׁ חֲמִשִּׁים צַדִּיקִם בְּתוֹךְ הָעִיר
the city   inside   righteous ones   fifty   there are   perhaps

הַאַף תִּסְפֶּה וְלֹא־תִשָּׂא לַמָּקוֹם
to place   you lift - and not   you sweep uo   the surely

לְמַעַן חֲמִשִּׁים הַצַּדִּיקִם אֲשֶׁר בְּקִרְבָּהּ׃
in close   which   the righteous ones   fifty   to end

24 Peradventure there be fifty righteous within the city: wilt thou also destroy and not

spare the place for the fifty righteous that are therein?

חָלִלָה לְּךָ מֵעֲשֹׂת כַּדָּבָר הַזֶּה לְהָמִית צַדִּיק עִם־רָשָׁע
wicked – with righteous to the kill the this like matter from doings to you far be it

וְהָיָה כַצַּדִּיק כָּרָשָׁע חָלִלָה לְּךָ
to you far be it like wicked like righteous and it be

הֲשֹׁפֵט כָּל־הָאָרֶץ לֹא יַעֲשֶׂה מִשְׁפָּט׃
judgement he do not earth - all the judger

25 That be far from thee to do after this manner, to slay the righteous with the wicked:
and that the righteous should be as the wicked, that be far from thee: Shall not the
Judge of all the earth do right?

וַיֹּאמֶר יְהוָה אִם־אֶמְצָא בִסְדֹם חֲמִשִּׁים צַדִּיקִם בְּתוֹךְ הָעִיר
the city inside righteous ones fifty in Sodom I find – if ihvh and he said

וְנָשָׂאתִי לְכָל־הַמָּקוֹם בַּעֲבוּרָם׃
in their sake the place - to all and I will lift

26 And the LORD said, If I find in Sodom fifty righteous within the city, then I will
spare all the place for their sakes.

וַיַּעַן אַבְרָהָם
Abraham and he answered

וַיֹּאמֶר הִנֵּה־נָא הוֹאַלְתִּי לְדַבֵּר אֶל־אֲדֹנָי
Adoni - unto to speak I I am disposed now - here and he said

וְאָנֹכִי עָפָר וָאֵפֶר׃
and ash dust and I am

27 And Abraham answered and said, Behold now, I have taken upon me to speak unto
the Lord, which am but dust and ashes:

אוּלַי יַחְסְרוּן חֲמִשִּׁים הַצַּדִּיקִם חֲמִשָּׁה
five the righteous ones fifty they will lack perhaps

הֲתַשְׁחִית בַּחֲמִשָּׁה אֶת־כָּל־הָעִיר
the city - all - that in five the you will destroy

וַיֹּאמֶר לֹא אַשְׁחִית אִם־אֶמְצָא שָׁם אַרְבָּעִים וַחֲמִשָּׁה׃
and five forty there I find - if I will destroy not and he said

28 Peradventure there shall lack five of the fifty righteous: wilt thou destroy all the city
for lack of five? And he said, If I find there forty and five, I will not destroy it.

וַיֹּסֶף עוֹד לְדַבֵּר אֵלָיו
unto him to speak again and he repeated

וַיֹּאמֶר אוּלַי יִמָּצְאוּן שָׁם אַרְבָּעִים
forty there he will find perhaps and he said

וַיֹּאמֶר לֹא אֶעֱשֶׂה בַּעֲבוּר הָאַרְבָּעִים:
the forty · in sake · I will do · not · and he said

29 And he spake unto him yet again, and said, Peradventure there shall be forty found there. And he said, I will not do it for forty's sake.

וַיֹּאמֶר אַל־נָא יִחַר לַאדֹנָי וַאֲדַבֵּרָה
and I will speak · to Adoni · it anger · please – don't · and he said

אוּלַי יִמָּצְאוּן שָׁם שְׁלֹשִׁים
thirty · there · he will find · perhaps

וַיֹּאמֶר לֹא אֶעֱשֶׂה אִם־אֶמְצָא שָׁם שְׁלֹשִׁים:
thirty · there · I find - if · I will do · not · and he said

30 And he said unto him, Oh let not the Lord be angry, and I will speak: Peradventure there shall thirty be found there. And he said, I will not do it, if I find thirty there.

וַיֹּאמֶר הִנֵּה־נָא הוֹאַלְתִּי לְדַבֵּר אֶל־אֲדֹנָי
Adoni - unto · to speak · I bold · please – here · and he said

אוּלַי יִמָּצְאוּן שָׁם עֶשְׂרִים
twenty · there · he will find · perhaps

וַיֹּאמֶר לֹא אַשְׁחִית בַּעֲבוּר הָעֶשְׂרִים:
the twenty · in sake · I will destroyed · not · and he said

31 And he said, Behold now, I have taken upon me to speak unto the Lord: Peradventure there shall be twenty found there. And he said, I will not destroy it for twenty's sake.

וַיֹּאמֶר אַל־נָא יִחַר לַאדֹנָי וַאֲדַבְּרָה אַךְ־הַפַּעַם
the once - just · and I will speak · to Adoni · it anger · please - don't · and he said

אוּלַי יִמָּצְאוּן שָׁם עֲשָׂרָה
ten · there · he will find · perhaps

וַיֹּאמֶר לֹא אַשְׁחִית בַּעֲבוּר הָעֲשָׂרָה:
the ten · in sake · I will destroy · not · and he said

32 And he said, Oh let not the Lord be angry, and I will speak yet but this once: Peradventure ten shall be found there. And he said, I will not destroy it for ten's sake.

וַיֵּלֶךְ יְהוָֹה כַּאֲשֶׁר כִּלָּה לְדַבֵּר אֶל־אַבְרָהָם
Abraham - unto · to speak · he finished · when · ihvh · and he went

וְאַבְרָהָם שָׁב לִמְקֹמוֹ:
to his place · returned · and Abraham

33 And the LORD went his way, as soon as he had left communing with Abraham: and Abraham returned unto his place.

Chapter 19

ספר בראשית פרק יט

[שלישי]

וַיָּבֹאוּ שְׁנֵי הַמַּלְאָכִים סְדֹמָה בָּעֶרֶב
in evening   towards Sodom   the angels   two   and they came

וְלוֹט יֹשֵׁב בְּשַׁעַר־סְדֹם
Sodom - in gate   he sat   and Lot

וַיַּרְא־לוֹט וַיָּקָם לִקְרָאתָם וַיִּשְׁתַּחוּ אַפַּיִם אָרְצָה:
towards ground   faces   and he bowed   to meet them   and he arose   Lot - and he saw

1 And there came two angels to Sodom at even; and Lot sat in the gate of Sodom: and Lot seeing them rose up to meet them; and he bowed himself with his face toward the ground;

וַיֹּאמֶר הִנֶּה נָּא־אֲדֹנַי סוּרוּ נָא אֶל־בֵּית עַבְדְּכֶם
your servant   house - unto   please you turn   my Adoni - please   here   and he said

וְלִינוּ וְרַחֲצוּ רַגְלֵיכֶם וְהִשְׁכַּמְתֶּם וַהֲלַכְתֶּם לְדַרְכְּכֶם
to your way   and you go   and you rise early   your feet   and you wash   and you spend night

וַיֹּאמְרוּ לֹּא כִּי בָרְחוֹב נָלִין:
we will spend night   in road   like   not   and they said

2 And he said, Behold now, my lords, turn in, I pray you, into your servant's house, and tarry all night, and wash your feet, and ye shall rise up early, and go on your ways. And they said, Nay; but we will abide in the street all night.

וַיִּפְצַר־בָּם מְאֹד וַיָּסֻרוּ אֵלָיו וַיָּבֹאוּ אֶל־בֵּיתוֹ
his house – unto   and they came   unto him   and they turned   greatly   in them - and he persisted

וַיַּעַשׂ לָהֶם מִשְׁתֶּה וּמַצּוֹת אָפָה וַיֹּאכֵלוּ:
and they ate   baked   and unleavened bread   feast   to them   and he made

3 And he pressed upon them greatly; and they turned in unto him, and entered into his house; and he made them a feast, and did bake unleavened bread, and they did eat.

טֶרֶם יִשְׁכָּבוּ
they lied down   before

וְאַנְשֵׁי הָעִיר אַנְשֵׁי סְדֹם נָסַבּוּ עַל־הַבַּיִת
the house – upon   they surrounded   Sodom   men   the city   and men

מִנַּעַר וְעַד־זָקֵן כָּל־הָעָם מִקָּצֶה:
from quarter   the people - all   old - and till   from young

4 But before they lay down, the men of the city, even the men of Sodom, compassed the house round, both old and young, all the people from every quarter:

וַיִּקְרְאוּ אֶל־לוֹט וַיֹּאמְרוּ לוֹ
to him   and they said   Lot - unto   and they called

אַיֵּה הָאֲנָשִׁים אֲשֶׁר־בָּאוּ אֵלֶיךָ הַלָּיְלָה
the night — unto you — they came - which — the men — where

הוֹצִיאֵם אֵלֵינוּ וְנֵדְעָה אֹתָם:
to them — and we know — unto us — bring out them

5 And they called unto Lot, and said unto him, Where are the men which came in to thee this night? bring them out unto us, that we may know them.

וַיֵּצֵא אֲלֵהֶם לוֹט הַפֶּתְחָה וְהַדֶּלֶת סָגַר אַחֲרָיו:
after him — shut — and the door — the opening — Lot — unto them — and he went out

6 And Lot went out at the door unto them, and shut the door after him,

וַיֹּאמַר אַל־נָא אַחַי תָּרֵעוּ:
you be evil — my brothers — please – don't — and he said

7 And said, I pray you, brethren, do not so wickedly.

הִנֵּה־נָא לִי שְׁתֵּי בָנוֹת אֲשֶׁר לֹא־יָדְעוּ אִישׁ
man — they knew - not — which — daughters — two — to me — please - here

אוֹצִיאָה־נָּא אֶתְהֶן אֲלֵיכֶם וַעֲשׂוּ לָהֶן כַּטּוֹב בְּעֵינֵיכֶם
in your eyes — like good — to them — and you do — unto you — that them — now – I bringer out

רַק לָאֲנָשִׁים הָאֵל אַל־תַּעֲשׂוּ דָבָר
matter — you do – don't — the El — to men — only

כִּי־עַל־כֵּן בָּאוּ בְּצֵל קֹרָתִי:
my roof — in shade — they came — thus - upon - like

8 Behold now, I have two daughters which have not known man; let me, I pray you, bring them out unto you, and do ye to them as is good in your eyes: only unto these men do nothing; for therefore came they under the shadow of my roof.

וַיֹּאמְרוּ גֶּשׁ־הָלְאָה וַיֹּאמְרוּ הָאֶחָד בָּא־לָגוּר
to sojourn - came — the one — and they said — yonder - come close — and they said

וַיִּשְׁפֹּט שָׁפוֹט עַתָּה נָרַע לְךָ מֵהֶם
from them — to you — we be bad — now — judges — and he judger

וַיִּפְצְרוּ בָאִישׁ בְּלוֹט מְאֹד וַיִּגְּשׁוּ לִשְׁבֹּר הַדָּלֶת:
the door — to break — and they touched — greatly — in Lot — in man — and they pressed

9 And they said, Stand back. And they said again, This one fellow came in to sojourn, and he will needs be a judge: now will we deal worse with thee, than with them. And they pressed sore upon the man, even Lot, and came near to break the door.

וַיִּשְׁלְחוּ הָאֲנָשִׁים אֶת־יָדָם
their hand - that — the men — and they sent out

וַיָּבִיאוּ אֶת־לוֹט אֲלֵיהֶם הַבָּיְתָה וְאֶת־הַדֶּלֶת סָגָרוּ:
they closed — the door - and that — the towards house — unto them — Lot - that — and they brought

10 But the men put forth their hand, and pulled Lot into the house to them, and shut to the door.

וְאֶת־הָאֲנָשִׁים אֲשֶׁר־פֶּתַח הַבַּיִת הִכּוּ בַּסַּנְוֵרִים

in blindnesses   they smote   the house   opening - which   the men - and that

מִקָּטֹן וְעַד־גָּדוֹל

big - and till   from small

וַיִּלְאוּ לִמְצֹא הַפָּתַח׃

the opening   to find   and they wearied

11 And they smote the men that were at the door of the house with blindness, both small and great: so that they wearied themselves to find the door.

וַיֹּאמְרוּ הָאֲנָשִׁים אֶל־לוֹט עֹד מִי־לְךָ פֹה

here   to you - who   still   Lot - unto   the men   and they said

חָתָן וּבָנֶיךָ וּבְנֹתֶיךָ וְכֹל אֲשֶׁר־לְךָ בָּעִיר

in city   to you - which   and all   and your daughters   and your sons   son-in-law

הוֹצֵא מִן־הַמָּקוֹם׃

the place – from   bring out

12 And the men said unto Lot, Hast thou here any besides? son in law, and thy sons, and thy daughters, and whatsoever thou hast in the city, bring them out of this place:

כִּי־מַשְׁחִתִים אֲנַחְנוּ אֶת־הַמָּקוֹם הַזֶּה

the this   the place - that   we   destroying ones - like

כִּי־גָדְלָה צַעֲקָתָם אֶת־פְּנֵי יְהוָה

ihvh   face - that   their cry   great - like

וַיְשַׁלְּחֵנוּ יְהוָה לְשַׁחֲתָהּ׃

to destroy it   ihvh   and he send us

13 For we will destroy this place, because the cry of them is waxen great before the face of the LORD; and the LORD hath sent us to destroy it.

וַיֵּצֵא לוֹט וַיְדַבֵּר אֶל־חֲתָנָיו לֹקְחֵי בְנֹתָיו

his daughters   takers   his son in law - unto   and he spoke   Lot   and he went out

וַיֹּאמֶר קוּמוּ צְּאוּ מִן־הַמָּקוֹם הַזֶּה

the this   the place - from   you get out   you rise   and he said

כִּי־מַשְׁחִית יְהוָה אֶת־הָעִיר

the city - that   ihvh   will destroy - like

וַיְהִי כִמְצַחֵק בְּעֵינֵי חֲתָנָיו׃

his sons in law   in eyes   like joking   and he was

14 And Lot went out, and spake unto his sons in law, which married his daughters, and said, Up, get you out of this place; for the LORD will destroy this city. But he seemed as one that mocked unto his sons in law.

וּכְמוֹ הַשַּׁחַר עָלָה וַיָּאִיצוּ הַמַּלְאָכִים בְּלוֹט לֵאמֹר

to say   in Lot   the angels   and they urged   rose up   the dawn   and like when

קוּם קַח אֶת־אִשְׁתְּךָ וְאֶת־שְׁתֵּי בְנֹתֶיךָ הַנִּמְצָאֹת
the found ones   your daughters   two - and that   your wife - that   take   rise

פֶּן־תִּסָּפֶה בַּעֲוֹן הָעִיר:
the city   in iniquity   you consumed - lest

15 And when the morning arose, then the angels hastened Lot, saying, Arise, take thy
wife, and thy two daughters, which are here; lest thou be consumed in the iniquity of
the city.

וַיִּתְמַהְמָהּ וַיַּחֲזִיקוּ הָאֲנָשִׁים בְּיָדוֹ
in his hand   the men   and they grasped   and he lingered

וּבְיַד־אִשְׁתּוֹ וּבְיַד שְׁתֵּי בְנֹתָיו בְּחֶמְלַת יְהוָה עָלָיו
upon him   ihvh   in merciful   his daughters   two   and hand   his wife - and hand

וַיֹּצִאֻהוּ וַיַּנִּחֻהוּ מִחוּץ לָעִיר:
to city   from outside   and they put him at rest   and they brought him out

16 And while he lingered, the men laid hold upon his hand, and upon the hand of his
wife, and upon the hand of his two daughters; the LORD being merciful unto him: and
they brought him forth, and set him without the city.

וַיְהִי כְהוֹצִיאָם אֹתָם הַחוּצָה
the outside   to them   like bring out them   and it was

וַיֹּאמֶר הִמָּלֵט עַל־נַפְשֶׁךָ אַל־תַּבִּיט אַחֲרֶיךָ
behind you   you look - don't   your soul - upon   escape   and he said

וְאַל־תַּעֲמֹד בְּכָל־הַכִּכָּר הָהָרָה הִמָּלֵט פֶּן־תִּסָּפֶה:
you consumed - lest   escape   the towards mountain   the plane - in all   you stand - and not

17 And it came to pass, when they had brought them forth abroad, that he said,
Escape for thy life; look not behind thee, neither stay thou in all the plain; escape to the
mountain, lest thou be consumed.

וַיֹּאמֶר לוֹט אֲלֵהֶם אַל־נָא אֲדֹנָי:
Adoni   now - don't   unto them   Lot   and he said

18 And Lot said unto them, Oh, not so, my Lord:

הִנֵּה־נָא מָצָא עַבְדְּךָ חֵן בְּעֵינֶיךָ
in your eyes   favor   your servant   he found   now - here

וַתַּגְדֵּל חַסְדְּךָ אֲשֶׁר עָשִׂיתָ עִמָּדִי לְהַחֲיוֹת אֶת־נַפְשִׁי
my soul – that   to the living   to me   you did   which   your kindness   and you great

וְאָנֹכִי לֹא אוּכַל לְהִמָּלֵט הָהָרָה
to the mountain   to escape   I able   not   and I am

פֶּן־תִּדְבָּקַנִי הָרָעָה וָמַתִּי:
and I die   the evil   it clings me - lest

19 Behold now, thy servant hath found grace in thy sight, and thou hast magnified thy
mercy, which thou hast shewed unto me in saving my life; and I cannot escape to the

mountain, lest some evil take me, and I die:

הִנֵּה־נָא הָעִיר הַזֹּאת קְרֹבָה לָנוּס שָׁמָּה

towards there   to travel   near   the this   the city   now - here

וְהִוא מִצְעָר אִמָּלְטָה נָּא שָׁמָּה הֲלֹא מִצְעָר הִוא

it   interior   the not   towards there   now   I escape   interior   and it

וּתְחִי נַפְשִׁי:

my soul   and it live

20 Behold now, this city is near to flee unto, and it is a little one: Oh, let me escape thither, (is it not a little one?) and my soul shall live.

[רביעי]

וַיֹּאמֶר אֵלָיו הִנֵּה נָשָׂאתִי פָנֶיךָ

your face   I accepted   here   unto him   and he said

גַּם לַדָּבָר הַזֶּה לְבִלְתִּי הָפְכִּי אֶת־הָעִיר אֲשֶׁר דִּבַּרְתָּ:

you spoke   which   the city – that   overthrow   to not do   the this   to matter   also

21 And he said unto him, See, I have accepted thee concerning this thing also, that I will not overthrow this city, for the which thou hast spoken.

מַהֵר הִמָּלֵט שָׁמָּה לֹא אוּכַל לַעֲשׂוֹת דָּבָר עַד־בֹּאֲךָ שָׁמָּה

to there   your coming - until   matter   to do   I can   not   to there   escape   hurry

עַל־כֵּן קָרָא שֵׁם־הָעִיר צוֹעַר:

Zoar   the city - name   called   thus - upon

22 Haste thee, escape thither; for I cannot do any thing till thou be come thither. Therefore the name of the city was called Zoar.

הַשֶּׁמֶשׁ יָצָא עַל־הָאָרֶץ וְלוֹט בָּא צֹעֲרָה:

to Zoar   came   and Lot   the land - upon   came out   the sun

23 The sun was risen upon the earth when Lot entered into Zoar.

וַיהוָה הִמְטִיר עַל־סְדֹם וְעַל־עֲמֹרָה גָּפְרִית וָאֵשׁ

and fire   brimstone   Gomorrah - and upon   Sodom - upon   rained   and ihvh

מֵאֵת יְהוָה מִן־הַשָּׁמָיִם:

the heaven - from   ihvh   from that

24 Then the LORD rained upon Sodom and upon Gomorrah brimstone and fire from the LORD out of heaven;

וַיַּהֲפֹךְ אֶת־הֶעָרִים הָאֵל וְאֵת כָּל־הַכִּכָּר

the plain - all   and that   the these   the cities - that   and he overthrew

וְאֵת כָּל־יֹשְׁבֵי הֶעָרִים וְצֶמַח הָאֲדָמָה:

the ground   and vegetation   the cities   dwelling - all   and that

25 And he overthrew those cities, and all the plain, and all the inhabitants of the cities, and that which grew upon the ground.

וַתַּבֵּט אִשְׁתּוֹ מֵאַחֲרָיו וַתְּהִי נְצִיב מֶלַח:
salt pillar and she became from his after his wife and she looked

26 But his wife looked back from behind him, and she became a pillar of salt.

וַיַּשְׁכֵּם אַבְרָהָם בַּבֹּקֶר אֶל־הַמָּקוֹם
the place - unto in morning Abraham and he arose early

אֲשֶׁר־עָמַד שָׁם אֶת־פְּנֵי יְהֹוָה:
ihvh before - that there stood - which

27 And Abraham got up early in the morning to the place where he stood before the
LORD:

וַיַּשְׁקֵף עַל־פְּנֵי סְדֹם וַעֲמֹרָה
and Gomorrah Sodom face - upon and he gazed

וְעַל כָּל־פְּנֵי אֶרֶץ הַכִּכָּר
the plain land face - all and upon

וַיַּרְא וְהִנֵּה עָלָה קִיטֹר הָאָרֶץ כְּקִיטֹר הַכִּבְשָׁן:
the furnace like smoke the land smoke arose and here and he saw

28 And he looked toward Sodom and Gomorrah, and toward all the land of the plain,
and beheld, and, lo, the smoke of the country went up as the smoke of a furnace.

וַיְהִי בְּשַׁחֵת אֱלֹהִים אֶת־עָרֵי הַכִּכָּר
the plain cities - that Elohim in destroyed and it was

וַיִּזְכֹּר אֱלֹהִים אֶת־אַבְרָהָם
Abraham - that Elohim and he remembered

וַיְשַׁלַּח אֶת־לוֹט מִתּוֹךְ הַהֲפֵכָה בַּהֲפֹךְ אֶת־הֶעָרִים
the cities – that in overthrow the overthrow from among Lot - that and he sent

אֲשֶׁר־יָשַׁב בָּהֵן לוֹט:
Lot in them he dwelled - which

29 And it came to pass, when God destroyed the cities of the plain, that God
remembered Abraham, and sent Lot out of the midst of the overthrow, when he
overthrew the cities in the which Lot dwelt.

וַיַּעַל לוֹט מִצּוֹעַר וַיֵּשֶׁב בָּהָר
in mountain and he dwelled from Zoar Lot and he ascended

וּשְׁתֵּי בְנֹתָיו עִמּוֹ כִּי יָרֵא לָשֶׁבֶת בְּצוֹעַר
in Zoar to dwell he was afraid like with him his daughters and two

וַיֵּשֶׁב בַּמְּעָרָה הוּא וּשְׁתֵּי בְנֹתָיו:
his daughters and two he in cave and he dwelled

30 And Lot went up out of Zoar, and dwelt in the mountain, and his two daughters
with him; for he feared to dwell in Zoar: and he dwelt in a cave, he and his two
daughters.

וַתֹּאמֶר הַבְּכִירָה אֶל־הַצְּעִירָה אָבִינוּ זָקֵן
<small>old   our father   the younger – unto   the firstborn   and she said</small>

וְאִישׁ אֵין בָּאָרֶץ לָבוֹא עָלֵינוּ כְּדֶרֶךְ כָּל־הָאָרֶץ׃
<small>the earth - all   like way   upon us   to come   in earth   isn't   and man</small>

31 And the firstborn said unto the younger, Our father is old, and there is not a man in the earth to come in unto us after the manner of all the earth:

לְכָה נַשְׁקֶה אֶת־אָבִינוּ יָיִן
<small>wine   our father - that   we libate   let's go</small>

וְנִשְׁכְּבָה עִמּוֹ וּנְחַיֶּה מֵאָבִינוּ זָרַע׃
<small>seed   from our father   and we preserve   with him   and we lie</small>

32 Come, let us make our father drink wine, and we will lie with him, that we may preserve seed of our father.

וַתַּשְׁקֶיןָ אֶת־אֲבִיהֶן יַיִן בַּלַּיְלָה הוּא
<small>it   in night   wine   their father - that   and they gave drink</small>

וַתָּבֹא הַבְּכִירָה וַתִּשְׁכַּב אֶת־אָבִיהָ
<small>her father – that   and she lay   the older   and she came</small>

וְלֹא־יָדַע בְּשִׁכְבָהּ וּבְקוּמָהּ׃
<small>and in her rising   in her lying down   he knew - and not</small>

33 And they made their father drink wine that night: and the firstborn went in, and lay with her father; and he perceived not when she lay down, nor when she arose.

וַיְהִי מִמָּחֳרָת וַתֹּאמֶר הַבְּכִירָה אֶל־הַצְּעִירָה
<small>the younger - unto   the older   that she said   from next day   and it was</small>

הֵן־שָׁכַבְתִּי אֶמֶשׁ אֶת־אָבִי נַשְׁקֶנּוּ יַיִן גַּם־הַלַּיְלָה
<small>the night - also   wine   let us libate   my father - that   last night   I lay - thus</small>

וּבֹאִי שִׁכְבִי עִמּוֹ
<small>with him   and I preserve   and I come</small>

וּנְחַיֶּה מֵאָבִינוּ זָרַע׃
<small>seed   from our father   and we preserve</small>

34 And it came to pass on the morrow, that the firstborn said unto the younger, Behold, I lay yesternight with my father: let us make him drink wine this night also; and go thou in, and lie with him, that we may preserve seed of our father.

וַתַּשְׁקֶיןָ גַּם בַּלַּיְלָה הַהוּא אֶת־אֲבִיהֶן יָיִן
<small>wine   their father - that   the it   in night   also   and it they libated</small>

וַתָּקָם הַצְּעִירָה וַתִּשְׁכַּב עִמּוֹ וְלֹא־יָדַע בְּשִׁכְבָהּ וּבְקֻמָהּ׃
<small>and in her rising   in her lying   he knew - and not   with him   and she lay   the younger   and she got up</small>

35 And they made their father drink wine that night also: and the younger arose, and lay with him; and he perceived not when she lay down, nor when she arose.

וַתַּהֲרֶ֛ין שְׁתֵּ֥י בְנֽוֹת־ל֖וֹט מֵאֲבִיהֶֽן׃

from their father   Lot - daughters   two   and pregnant

36 Thus were both the daughters of Lot with child by their father.

וַתֵּ֥לֶד הַבְּכִירָ֖ה בֵּ֑ן

son   the first born   and she bore

וַתִּקְרָ֤א שְׁמוֹ֙ מוֹאָ֔ב ה֥וּא אֲבִֽי־מוֹאָ֖ב עַד־הַיּֽוֹם׃

the day - till   Moab – fathers   he   Moab   his name   and she called

37 And the firstborn bare a son, and called his name Moab: the same is the father of the Moabites unto this day.

וְהַצְּעִירָ֤ה גַם־הִוא֙ יָ֣לְדָה בֵּ֑ן

son   bore   she – also   and the younger

וַתִּקְרָ֥א שְׁמ֖וֹ בֶּן־עַמִּ֑י

(my father – son) Ami – Ben   his name   and she called

ה֛וּא אֲבִ֥י בְנֵֽי־עַמּ֖וֹן עַד־הַיּֽוֹם׃

the day – till   Ammon - sons   my father   he

38 And the younger, she also bare a son, and called his name Benammi: the same [is] the father of the children of Ammon unto this day.

ס

Chapter 20

ספר בראשית פרק כ

וַיִּסַּ֨ע מִשָּׁ֜ם אַבְרָהָם֙ אַ֣רְצָה הַנֶּ֔גֶב

the Negev   towards land   Abraham   from there   he journeyed

וַיֵּ֥שֶׁב בֵּין־קָדֵ֖שׁ וּבֵ֣ין שׁ֑וּר וַיָּ֖גָר בִּגְרָֽר׃

in Gerar   and he lived   Shur   and between   Kadesh - between   and he dwelled

1 And Abraham journeyed from thence toward the south country, and dwelled between Kadesh and Shur, and sojourned in Gerar.

וַיֹּ֧אמֶר אַבְרָהָ֛ם אֶל־שָׂרָ֥ה אִשְׁתּ֖וֹ אֲחֹ֣תִי הִ֑וא

she   my sister   his wife   Sarah - unto   Abraham   and he said

וַיִּשְׁלַ֗ח אֲבִימֶ֙לֶךְ֙ מֶ֣לֶךְ גְּרָ֔ר וַיִּקַּ֖ח אֶת־שָׂרָֽה׃

Sarah - that   and he took   Gerar   King   Abimelech   and he sent

2 And Abraham said of Sarah his wife, She is my sister: and Abimelech king of Gerar sent, and took Sarah.

וַיָּבֹ֧א אֱלֹהִ֛ים אֶל־אֲבִימֶ֖לֶךְ בַּחֲל֣וֹם הַלָּ֑יְלָה

the night   in dream   Abimelech - unto   Elohim   and he came

וַיֹּ֣אמֶר ל֗וֹ הִנְּךָ֥ מֵת֙ עַל־הָאִשָּׁ֣ה אֲשֶׁר־לָקַ֔חְתָּ

you took - which   the woman - upon   dead   here you   to him   and he said

וְהִוא בְּעֻלַת בָּעַל:

husband   wife   and she

3 But God came to Abimelech in a dream by night, and said to him, Behold, thou art but a dead man, for the woman which thou hast taken; for she is a man's wife.

וַאֲבִימֶלֶךְ לֹא קָרַב אֵלֶיהָ

unto her   near   not   Abimelech

וַיֹּאמַר אֲדֹנָי הֲגוֹי גַּם־צַדִּיק תַּהֲרֹג:

you slay   righteous one - also   the nation   Adoni   and he said

4 But Abimelech had not come near her: and he said, Lord, wilt thou slay also a righteous nation?

הֲלֹא הוּא אָמַר־לִי אֲחֹתִי הִוא

she   my sister   to me - he said   he   the not

וְהִיא־גַם־הִוא אָמְרָה אָחִי הוּא בְּתָם־לְבָבִי

my heart - integrity   he   my brother   she said   she - also - and she

וּבְנִקְיֹן כַּפַּי עָשִׂיתִי זֹאת:

this   I did   my palms   and in innocent

5 Said he not unto me, She is my sister? and she, even she herself said, He is my brother: in the integrity of my heart and innocency of my hands have I done this.

וַיֹּאמֶר אֵלָיו הָאֱלֹהִים בַּחֲלֹם

in dream   the Elohim   unto him   and he said

גַּם אָנֹכִי יָדַעְתִּי כִּי בְתָם־לְבָבְךָ עָשִׂיתָ זֹּאת

this   you did   your heart – in integrity   like   I know   I am   also

וָאֶחְשֹׂךְ גַּם־אָנֹכִי אוֹתְךָ מֵחֲטוֹ־לִי

to me - from his sin   to you   I am - also   and I withheld

עַל־כֵּן לֹא־נְתַתִּיךָ לִנְגֹּעַ אֵלֶיהָ:

unto her   to touch   give you - not   thus - upon

6 And God said unto him in a dream, Yea, I know that thou didst this in the integrity of thy heart; for I also withheld thee from sinning against me: therefore suffered I thee not to touch her.

וְעַתָּה הָשֵׁב אֵשֶׁת־הָאִישׁ כִּי־נָבִיא הוּא

he   prophet - like   the man - wife   the return   and now

וְיִתְפַּלֵּל בַּעַדְךָ וֶחְיֵה

and you live   in your behalf   and he will pray

וְאִם־אֵינְךָ מֵשִׁיב דַּע כִּי־מוֹת תָּמוּת אַתָּה וְכָל־אֲשֶׁר־לָךְ:

to you - which - and all   you   you die   die - like   know   restoring   isn't you - and if

7 Now therefore restore the man his wife; for he is a prophet, and he shall pray for thee, and thou shalt live: and if thou restore her not, know thou that thou shalt surely die, thou, and all that are thine.

וַיַּשְׁכֵּם אֲבִימֶלֶךְ בַּבֹּקֶר וַיִּקְרָא לְכָל־עֲבָדָיו
servants - to all   and he called   in morning   Abimelech   and he rose

וַיְדַבֵּר אֶת־כָּל־הַדְּבָרִים הָאֵלֶּה בְּאָזְנֵיהֶם
in their ears   the these   the matters - all - that   and he spoke

וַיִּירְאוּ הָאֲנָשִׁים מְאֹד:
greatly   the men   and they were afraid

8 Therefore Abimelech rose early in the morning, and called all his servants, and told all these things in their ears: and the men were sore afraid.

וַיִּקְרָא אֲבִימֶלֶךְ לְאַבְרָהָם
to Abraham   Abimelech   and he called

וַיֹּאמֶר לוֹ מֶה־עָשִׂיתָ לָּנוּ
to us   you did - what   to him   and he said

וּמֶה־חָטָאתִי לָךְ כִּי־הֵבֵאתָ עָלַי
upon me   you brought - like   to you   my sin - and how

וְעַל־מַמְלַכְתִּי חֲטָאָה גְדֹלָה
great   sin   my kingdom - and upon

מַעֲשִׂים אֲשֶׁר לֹא־יֵעָשׂוּ עָשִׂיתָ עִמָּדִי:
with me   you did   they do – not   which   deeds

9 Then Abimelech called Abraham, and said unto him, What hast thou done unto us? and what have I offended thee, that thou hast brought on me and on my kingdom a great sin? thou hast done deeds unto me that ought not to be done.

וַיֹּאמֶר אֲבִימֶלֶךְ אֶל־אַבְרָהָם
Abraham – unto   Abimelech   and he said

מָה רָאִיתָ כִּי עָשִׂיתָ אֶת־הַדָּבָר הַזֶּה:
the this   the matter - that   you did   like   you saw   what

10 And Abimelech said unto Abraham, What sawest thou, that thou hast done this thing?

וַיֹּאמֶר אַבְרָהָם כִּי אָמַרְתִּי
I said   like   Abraham   and he said

רַק אֵין־יִרְאַת אֱלֹהִים בַּמָּקוֹם הַזֶּה
the this   in place   Elohim   fear - isn't   only

וַהֲרָגוּנִי עַל־דְּבַר אִשְׁתִּי:
my wife   matter - upon   and they will kill me

11 And Abraham said, Because I thought, Surely the fear of God is not in this place; and they will slay me for my wife's sake.

וְגַם־אָמְנָה אֲחֹתִי בַת־אָבִי הִוא אַךְ לֹא בַת־אִמִּי
my mother - daughter   not   so   she   my father - daughter   my sister   indeed - and also

וַתְּהִי־לִי לְאִשָּֽׁה׃
to wife   to me - she became

12 And yet indeed she is my sister; she is the daughter of my father, but not the daughter of my mother; and she became my wife.

וַיְהִי כַּאֲשֶׁר הִתְעוּ אֹתִי אֱלֹהִים מִבֵּית אָבִי
my father   from house   Elohim   to me   wander   when   and it was

וָאֹמַר לָהּ זֶה חַסְדֵּךְ אֲשֶׁר תַּעֲשִׂי עִמָּדִי אֶל כָּל־הַמָּקוֹם
the place - all   unto   with me   you do   which   your mercy   this   to her   and I said

אֲשֶׁר נָבוֹא שָׁמָּה אִמְרִי־לִי אָחִי הֽוּא׃
he   my brother   to me - saying   there   we came   which

13 And it came to pass, when God caused me to wander from my father's house, that I said unto her, This is thy kindness which thou shalt shew unto me; at every place whither we shall come, say of me, He is my brother.

וַיִּקַּח אֲבִימֶלֶךְ צֹאן וּבָקָר
and cattle   sheep   Abimelech   and he took

וַעֲבָדִים וּשְׁפָחֹת וַיִּתֵּן לְאַבְרָהָם
to Abraham   and he gave   and maids   and servants

וַיָּשֶׁב לוֹ אֵת שָׂרָה אִשְׁתּֽוֹ׃
his wife   Sarah   that   to him   and he returned

14 And Abimelech took sheep, and oxen, and menservants, and women servants, and gave them unto Abraham, and restored him Sarah his wife.

וַיֹּאמֶר אֲבִימֶלֶךְ הִנֵּה אַרְצִי לְפָנֶיךָ בַּטּוֹב בְּעֵינֶיךָ שֵֽׁב׃
dwell   in your eyes   in good   before you   my land   here   Abimelech   and he said

15 And Abimelech said, Behold, my land is before thee: dwell where it pleaseth thee.

וּלְשָׂרָה אָמַר
he said   and to Sarah

הִנֵּה נָתַתִּי אֶלֶף כֶּסֶף לְאָחִיךְ
to your brother   silver   thousand   I give   here

הִנֵּה הוּא־לָךְ כְּסוּת עֵינַיִם לְכֹל אֲשֶׁר אִתָּךְ וְאֶת־כֹּל
all – and that   with you   which   to all   eyes   cover   to you - he   here

וְנֹכָֽחַת׃
and vindicated

16 And unto Sarah he said, Behold, I have given thy brother a thousand pieces of silver: behold, he is to thee a covering of the eyes, unto all that are with thee, and with all other: thus she was reproved.

וַיִּתְפַּלֵּל אַבְרָהָם אֶל־הָאֱלֹהִים וַיִּרְפָּא אֱלֹהִים אֶת־אֲבִימֶלֶךְ
Abimelech - that   Elohim   and he healed   the Elohim - unto   Abraham   and he prayed

וְאֶת־אִשְׁתּוֹ וְאַמְהֹתָיו וַיֵּלֵדוּ׃

and they begat   and his maids   his wife - and that

17 So Abraham prayed unto God: and God healed Abimelech, and his wife, and his maidservants; and they bare children.

כִּי־עָצֹר עָצַר יְהֹוָה בְּעַד כָּל־רֶחֶם לְבֵית אֲבִימֶלֶךְ

Abimelech   to house   womb - all   in being   ihvh   he closed   closer - like

עַל־דְּבַר שָׂרָה אֵשֶׁת אַבְרָהָם׃

Abraham   wife   Sarah   matter - upon

18 For the LORD had fast closed up all the wombs of the house of Abimelech, because of Sarah Abraham's wife.

CHAPTER 21

ספר בראשית פרק כא

וַיהֹוָה פָּקַד אֶת־שָׂרָה כַּאֲשֶׁר אָמָר

he said   when   Sarah - that   visited   and ihvh

וַיַּעַשׂ יְהֹוָה לְשָׂרָה כַּאֲשֶׁר דִּבֵּר׃

he spoke   when   to Sarah   ihvh   and he did

1 And the LORD visited Sarah as he had said, and the LORD did unto Sarah as he had spoken.

וַתַּהַר וַתֵּלֶד שָׂרָה לְאַבְרָהָם בֵּן לִזְקֻנָיו

in his old age   son   to Abraham   Sarah   and she bore   and she pregnant

לַמּוֹעֵד אֲשֶׁר־דִּבֶּר אֹתוֹ אֱלֹהִים׃

Elohim   to him   he spoke - which   to set time

2 For Sarah conceived, and bare Abraham a son in his old age, at the set time of which God had spoken to him.

וַיִּקְרָא אַבְרָהָם אֶת־שֶׁם־בְּנוֹ הַנּוֹלַד־לוֹ

to him - the born one   his son - name - that   Abraham   and he called

אֲשֶׁר־יָלְדָה־לּוֹ שָׂרָה יִצְחָק׃

Isaac   Sarah   to him - she begat - which

3 And Abraham called the name of his son that was born unto him, whom Sarah bare to him, Isaac.

וַיָּמָל אַבְרָהָם אֶת־יִצְחָק בְּנוֹ בֶּן־שְׁמֹנַת יָמִים

days   eight - son   his son   Isaac - that   Abraham   and he circumcised

כַּאֲשֶׁר צִוָּה אֹתוֹ אֱלֹהִים׃

Elohim   to him   he commanded   when

4 And Abraham circumcised his son Isaac being eight days old, as God had commanded him.

וְאַבְרָהָם בֶּן־מְאַת שָׁנָה בְּהִוָּלֶד לוֹ אֵת יִצְחָק בְּנוֹ:

his son	Isaac	that	to him	in being born	year	hundreds - age	and Abraham

5 And Abraham was an hundred years old, when his son Isaac was born unto him.

וַתֹּאמֶר שָׂרָה צְחֹק עָשָׂה לִי אֱלֹהִים כָּל־הַשֹּׁמֵעַ יִצְחַק־לִי:

to me - he will laugh	the hearers - all	Elohim	to me	did	laughter	Sarah	and she said

6 And Sarah said, God hath made me to laugh, so that all that hear will laugh with me.

וַתֹּאמֶר מִי מִלֵּל לְאַבְרָהָם הֵינִיקָה בָנִים שָׂרָה

Sarah	sons	the she nurse	to Abraham	declared	who	and she said

כִּי־יָלַדְתִּי בֵן לִזְקֻנָיו:

to his old age	son	I bore - like

7 And she said, Who would have said unto Abraham, that Sarah should have given children suck? for I have born him a son in his old age.

וַיִּגְדַּל הַיֶּלֶד וַיִּגָּמַל

and he was circumcised	the child	and he grew

וַיַּעַשׂ אַבְרָהָם מִשְׁתֶּה גָדוֹל בְּיוֹם הִגָּמֵל אֶת־יִצְחָק:

Isaac - that	circumcised	in day	great	feast	Abraham	and he did

8 And the child grew, and was weaned: and Abraham made a great feast the same day that Isaac was weaned.

וַתֵּרֶא שָׂרָה אֶת־בֶּן־הָגָר הַמִּצְרִית

the Egyptian	Hagar - son - that	Sarah	and she saw

אֲשֶׁר־יָלְדָה לְאַבְרָהָם מְצַחֵק:

mocking	to Abraham	she bore - which

9 And Sarah saw the son of Hagar the Egyptian, which she had born unto Abraham, mocking.

וַתֹּאמֶר לְאַבְרָהָם גָּרֵשׁ הָאָמָה הַזֹּאת וְאֶת־בְּנָהּ

her son - and that	the this	the slave woman	cast away	to Abraham	and she said

כִּי לֹא יִירַשׁ בֶּן־הָאָמָה הַזֹּאת עִם־בְּנִי עִם־יִצְחָק:

Isaac - with	my son - with	the this	the slave woman - son	he will inherit	not	like

10 Wherefore she said unto Abraham, Cast out this bondwoman and her son: for the son of this bondwoman shall not be heir with my son, even with Isaac.

וַיֵּרַע הַדָּבָר מְאֹד בְּעֵינֵי אַבְרָהָם עַל אוֹדֹת בְּנוֹ:

his son	cases	upon	Abraham	in eyes	greatly	the matter	and it bad

11 And the thing was very grievous in Abraham's sight because of his son.

וַיֹּאמֶר אֱלֹהִים אֶל־אַבְרָהָם אַל־יֵרַע בְּעֵינֶיךָ עַל־הַנַּעַר

the boy - upon	in your eyes	it be bad – don't	Abraham - unto	Elohim	and he said

וְעַל־אֲמָתֶךְ   כֹּל אֲשֶׁר תֹּאמַר אֵלֶיךָ שָׂרָה שְׁמַע בְּקֹלָהּ

in her voice   hear   Sarah   unto you   she says   which   all   your slave woman - and upon

כִּי בְיִצְחָק יִקָּרֵא לְךָ זָרַע׃

seed   to you   he be called   in Isaac   like

12 And God said unto Abraham, Let it not be grievous in thy sight because of the lad, and because of thy bondwoman; in all that Sarah hath said unto thee, hearken unto her voice; for in Isaac shall thy seed be called.

וְגַם   אֶת־בֶּן־הָאָמָה   לְגוֹי אֲשִׂימֶנּוּ כִּי זַרְעֲךָ הוּא׃

he   your seed   like   I will do   to nation   the slave woman - son - that   and also

13 And also of the son of the bondwoman will I make a nation, because he is thy seed.

וַיַּשְׁכֵּם   אַבְרָהָם בַּבֹּקֶר וַיִּקַּח־לֶחֶם וְחֵמַת מַיִם

water and skin bottle bread - and he took in morning   Abraham   and he rose early

וַיִּתֵּן   אֶל־הָגָר שָׂם עַל־שִׁכְמָהּ וְאֶת־הַיֶּלֶד וַיְשַׁלְּחֶהָ

and he sent her   the boy – and that   her shoulder - upon   put   Hagar- unto   and he gave

וַתֵּלֶךְ   וַתֵּתַע   בְּמִדְבַּר בְּאֵר שָׁבַע׃

Sheba   Beer   in wilderness   and she wandered   and she went

14 And Abraham rose up early in the morning, and took bread, and a bottle of water, and gave it unto Hagar, putting it on her shoulder, and the child, and sent her away: and she departed, and wandered in the wilderness of Beer-sheba.

וַיִּכְלוּ   הַמַּיִם מִן־הַחֵמֶת

the skin bottle - from   the waters   and they finished

וַתַּשְׁלֵךְ אֶת־הַיֶּלֶד תַּחַת אַחַד הַשִּׂיחִם׃

the bushes   one   under   the child – that   and she flung

15 And the water was spent in the bottle, and she cast the child under one of the shrubs.

וַתֵּלֶךְ   וַתֵּשֶׁב לָהּ מִנֶּגֶד הַרְחֵק כִּמְטַחֲוֵי קֶשֶׁת

bow   like one shooting   the far away   from front   to her   and she sat   and she went

כִּי אָמְרָה אַל־אֶרְאֶה בְּמוֹת הַיָּלֶד וַתֵּשֶׁב מִנֶּגֶד

from front   and she sat   the boy   in death   I look - don't   she said   like

וַתִּשָּׂא   אֶת־קֹלָהּ וַתֵּבְךְּ׃

and she wept   her voice - that   and she lifted

16 And she went, and sat her down over against him a good way off, as it were a bowshot: for she said, Let me not see the death of the child. And she sat over against him, and lift up her voice, and wept.

וַיִּשְׁמַע אֱלֹהִים אֶת־קוֹל הַנַּעַר

the boy   voice - that   Elohim   and he heard

וַיִּקְרָא מַלְאַךְ אֱלֹהִים אֶל־הָגָר מִן־הַשָּׁמַיִם

the heavens - from   Hagar - unto   Elohim   angel   and he called

וַיֹּאמֶר לָהּ מַה־לָּךְ הָגָר אַל־תִּירְאִי
you be afraid - don't   Hagar   to you - what   to her   and he said

כִּי־שָׁמַע אֱלֹהִים אֶל־קוֹל הַנַּעַר בַּאֲשֶׁר הוּא־שָׁם:
there - he   in which   the boy   voice – unto   Elohim   heard - like

17 And God heard the voice of the lad; and the angel of God called to Hagar out of heaven, and said unto her, What aileth thee, Hagar? fear not; for God hath heard the voice of the lad where he is.

קוּמִי שְׂאִי אֶת־הַנַּעַר
the boy - that   lift   arise

וְהַחֲזִיקִי אֶת־יָדֵךְ בּוֹ כִּי־לְגוֹי גָּדוֹל אֲשִׂימֶנּוּ:
I will make him   great   nation - like   in him   your hand - that   and the hold

18 Arise, lift up the lad, and hold him in thine hand; for I will make him a great nation.

וַיִּפְקַח אֱלֹהִים אֶת־עֵינֶיהָ וַתֵּרֶא בְּאֵר מָיִם
waters   well   and she saw   her eyes - that   Elohim   and he opened

וַתֵּלֶךְ וַתְּמַלֵּא אֶת־הַחֵמֶת מַיִם וַתַּשְׁקְ אֶת־הַנָּעַר:
the boy - that   and she let drink   water   the skin bottle - that   and she filled   and she went

19 And God opened her eyes, and she saw a well of water; and she went, and filled the bottle with water, and gave the lad drink.

וַיְהִי אֱלֹהִים אֶת־הַנַּעַר
the boy - that   Elohim   and it be

וַיִּגְדָּל וַיֵּשֶׁב בַּמִּדְבָּר וַיְהִי רֹבֶה קַשָּׁת:
bow   shooter   and he became   in the wilderness   and he dwelled   and he grew

20 And God was with the lad; and he grew, and dwelt in the wilderness, and became an archer.

וַיֵּשֶׁב בְּמִדְבַּר פָּארָן
Paran   in wilderness   and he dwelled

וַתִּקַּח־לוֹ אִמּוֹ אִשָּׁה מֵאֶרֶץ מִצְרָיִם:
Egypt   from land   wife   his mother   to him - and she took

21 And he dwelt in the wilderness of Paran: and his mother took him a wife out of the land of Egypt.

פ

[שׁשׁי]

וַיְהִי בָּעֵת הַהִוא וַיֹּאמֶר אֲבִימֶלֶךְ
Abimelech   and he said   the it   in time   and it be

וּפִיכֹל שַׂר־צְבָאוֹ אֶל־אַבְרָהָם לֵאמֹר
to say   Abraham - unto   his force – prince   and Phicol

אֱלֹהִים עִמְּךָ בְּכֹל אֲשֶׁר־אַתָּה עֹשֶׂה:

do   you - which   in all   with you   Elohim

22 And it came to pass at that time, that Abimelech and Phichol the chief captain of his host spake unto Abraham, saying, God is with thee in all that thou doest:

וְעַתָּה הִשָּׁבְעָה לִּי בֵאלֹהִים הֵנָּה אִם־תִּשְׁקֹר לִי

to me   you deal falsely - if   here   in Elohim   to me   swear   and now

וּלְנִינִי   וּלְנֶכְדִּי   כַּחֶסֶד אֲשֶׁר־עָשִׂיתִי עִמְּךָ תַּעֲשֶׂה עִמָּדִי

with me   you do   with you   I did – which   like kindness   and my grandson   and to my son

וְעִם־הָאָרֶץ אֲשֶׁר־גַּרְתָּה בָּהּ:

in it   you live - which   the earth - and with

23 Now therefore swear unto me here by God that thou wilt not deal falsely with me, nor with my son, nor with my son's son: but according to the kindness that I have done unto thee, thou shalt do unto me, and to the land wherein thou hast sojourned.

וַיֹּאמֶר אַבְרָהָם אָנֹכִי אִשָּׁבֵעַ:

I swear   I am   Abraham   and he said

24 And Abraham said, I will swear.

וְהוֹכִחַ אַבְרָהָם אֶת־אֲבִימֶלֶךְ עַל־אֹדוֹת בְּאֵר הַמַּיִם

the water   well   concerns - upon   Abimelech - that   Abraham   and he reproved

אֲשֶׁר גָּזְלוּ עַבְדֵי אֲבִימֶלֶךְ:

Abimelech   servants   they seized   which

25 And Abraham reproved Abimelech because of a well of water, which Abimelech's servants had violently taken away.

וַיֹּאמֶר אֲבִימֶלֶךְ לֹא יָדַעְתִּי מִי עָשָׂה אֶת־הַדָּבָר הַזֶּה

the this   the matter - that   did   who   I know   not   Abimelech   and he said

וְגַם־אַתָּה לֹא־הִגַּדְתָּ לִּי

to me   you told - not   you - and also

וְגַם אָנֹכִי לֹא שָׁמַעְתִּי בִּלְתִּי הַיּוֹם:

the day   nothing   I heard   not   I am   and also

26 And Abimelech said, I wot not who hath done this thing: neither didst thou tell me, neither yet heard I of it, but to day.

וַיִּקַּח אַבְרָהָם צֹאן וּבָקָר וַיִּתֵּן לַאֲבִימֶלֶךְ

to Abimelech   and he gave   and cattle   sheep   Abraham   and he took

וַיִּכְרְתוּ שְׁנֵיהֶם בְּרִית:

covenant   two of them   and they cut

27 And Abraham took sheep and oxen, and gave them unto Abimelech; and both of them made a covenant.

וַיַּצֵּב אַבְרָהָם אֶת־שֶׁבַע כִּבְשֹׂת הַצֹּאן לְבַדְּהֶן:

them alone   the flock   female lambs   seven - that   Abraham   and he set out

28 And Abraham set seven ewe lambs of the flock by themselves.

וַיֹּאמֶר אֲבִימֶלֶךְ אֶל־אַבְרָהָם

Abraham - unto   Abimelech   and he said

מָה הֵנָּה שֶׁבַע כְּבָשֹׂת הָאֵלֶּה אֲשֶׁר הִצַּבְתָּ לְבַדָּנָה:

towards alone   you set out   which   the these   female lambs   seven   here   what

29 And Abimelech said unto Abraham, What mean these seven ewe lambs which thou hast set by themselves?

וַיֹּאמֶר כִּי אֶת־שֶׁבַע כְּבָשֹׂת תִּקַּח מִיָּדִי

from my hand   you take   female lambs   seven - that   like   and he said

בַּעֲבוּר תִּהְיֶה־לִּי לְעֵדָה

to witness   to me – it be   in order

כִּי חָפַרְתִּי אֶת־הַבְּאֵר הַזֹּאת:

the this   the well - that   I dug   like

30 And he said, For these seven ewe lambs shalt thou take of my hand, that they may be a witness unto me, that I have digged this well.

עַל־כֵּן קָרָא לַמָּקוֹם הַהוּא בְּאֵר שָׁבַע

Sheba   Beer   the it   to place   he called   thus - upon

כִּי שָׁם נִשְׁבְּעוּ שְׁנֵיהֶם:

two of them   they swore   there   like

31 Wherefore he called that place Beer-sheba; because there they sware both of them.

וַיִּכְרְתוּ בְרִית בִּבְאֵר שָׁבַע

Sheba   in Beer   covenant   and they cut

וַיָּקָם אֲבִימֶלֶךְ וּפִיכֹל שַׂר־צְבָאוֹ

his forces – prince   and Phichol   Abimelech   and he rose

וַיָּשֻׁבוּ אֶל־אֶרֶץ פְּלִשְׁתִּים:

Philistines   land - unto   and they returned

32 Thus they made a covenant at Beer-sheba: then Abimelech rose up, and Phichol the chief captain of his host, and they returned into the land of the Philistines.

וַיִּטַּע אֵשֶׁל בִּבְאֵר שָׁבַע

Sheba   in Beer   tamarisk tree   and he planted

וַיִּקְרָא־שָׁם בְּשֵׁם יְהֹוָה אֵל עוֹלָם:

forever   El   ihvh   in name   there - and he called

33 And Abraham planted a grove in Beer-sheba, and called there on the name of the LORD, the everlasting God.

וַיָּגָר אַבְרָהָם בְּאֶרֶץ פְּלִשְׁתִּים יָמִים רַבִּים:

many   days   Philistines   in land   Abraham   and he lived

34 And Abraham sojourned in the Philistines' land many days.

פ

CHAPTER 22

ספר בראשית פרק כב

[שביעי]

וַיְהִי אַחַר הַדְּבָרִים הָאֵלֶּה
the these   the matters   after   and it was

וְהָאֱלֹהִים נִסָּה אֶת־אַבְרָהָם
Abraham - that   probed   and the Elohim

וַיֹּאמֶר אֵלָיו אַבְרָהָם וַיֹּאמֶר הִנֵּנִי׃
here I am   and he said   Abraham   unto him   and he said

1 And it came to pass after these things, that God did tempt Abraham, and said unto him, Abraham: and he said, Behold, here I am.

וַיֹּאמֶר קַח־נָא אֶת־בִּנְךָ אֶת־יְחִידְךָ אֲשֶׁר־אָהַבְתָּ אֶת־יִצְחָק
Isaac - that   you love - which   your only - that   your son - that   now - take   and he said

וְלֶךְ־לְךָ אֶל־אֶרֶץ הַמֹּרִיָּה
the Moriah   land - unto   to you - and go

וְהַעֲלֵהוּ שָׁם לְעֹלָה עַל אַחַד הֶהָרִים אֲשֶׁר אֹמַר אֵלֶיךָ׃
unto you   I say   which   the mountains   one   upon   to burnt offering   there   and the offer him

2 And he said, Take now thy son, thine only son Isaac, whom thou lovest, and get thee into the land of Moriah; and offer him there for a burnt offering upon one of the mountains which I will tell thee of.

וַיַּשְׁכֵּם אַבְרָהָם בַּבֹּקֶר וַיַּחֲבֹשׁ אֶת־חֲמֹרוֹ
his donkey - that   and he saddled   in morning   Abraham   and he rose early

וַיִּקַּח אֶת־שְׁנֵי נְעָרָיו אִתּוֹ וְאֵת יִצְחָק בְּנוֹ
his son   Isaac   and that   with him   his boys   two - that   and he took

וַיְבַקַּע עֲצֵי עֹלָה
burnt offering   wood   and he bundled

וַיָּקָם וַיֵּלֶךְ אֶל־הַמָּקוֹם אֲשֶׁר־אָמַר־לוֹ הָאֱלֹהִים׃
the Elohim   to him - said - which   the place – unto   and he went   and he rose up

3 And Abraham rose up early in the morning, and saddled his ass, and took two of his young men with him, and Isaac his son, and clave the wood for the burnt offering, and rose up, and went unto the place of which God had told him.

בַּיּוֹם הַשְּׁלִישִׁי וַיִּשָּׂא אַבְרָהָם אֶת־עֵינָיו
his eyes - that   Abraham   and he lifted   the third   in day

וַיַּרְא אֶת־הַמָּקוֹם מֵרָחֹק׃
from far   the place - that   and he saw

4 Then on the third day Abraham lifted up his eyes, and saw the place afar off.

וַיֹּאמֶר אַבְרָהָם אֶל־נְעָרָיו שְׁבוּ־לָכֶם פֹּה עִם־הַחֲמוֹר
and he said Abraham unto - his boys you dwell – to you here with - the donkey

וַאֲנִי וְהַנַּעַר נֵלְכָה עַד־כֹּה וְנִשְׁתַּחֲוֶה וְנָשׁוּבָה אֲלֵיכֶם:
and I and the boy we go till – there and we worship and we return unto you

5 And Abraham said unto his young men, Abide ye here with the ass; and I and the lad
will go yonder and worship, and come again to you.

וַיִּקַּח אַבְרָהָם אֶת־עֲצֵי הָעֹלָה וַיָּשֶׂם עַל־יִצְחָק בְּנוֹ
and he took Abraham that - wood the burnt offering and he placed upon - Isaac his son

וַיִּקַּח בְּיָדוֹ אֶת־הָאֵשׁ וְאֶת־הַמַּאֲכֶלֶת וַיֵּלְכוּ שְׁנֵיהֶם יַחְדָּו:
and he took in his hand that - the fire and that - the knife and they went two them together

6 And Abraham took the wood of the burnt offering, and laid it upon Isaac his son;
and he took the fire in his hand, and a knife; and they went both of them together.

וַיֹּאמֶר יִצְחָק אֶל־אַבְרָהָם אָבִיו וַיֹּאמֶר אָבִי
and he said Issac Abraham - unto his father and he said my father

וַיֹּאמֶר הִנֶּנִּי בְנִי
and he said here I am my son

וַיֹּאמֶר הִנֵּה הָאֵשׁ וְהָעֵצִים וְאַיֵּה הַשֶּׂה לְעֹלָה:
and he said here the fire and the wood and where the lamb to burnt offering

7 And Isaac spake unto Abraham his father, and said, My father: and he said, Here am
I, my son. And he said, Behold the fire and the wood: but where is the lamb for a burnt
offering?

וַיֹּאמֶר אַבְרָהָם אֱלֹהִים יִרְאֶה־לּוֹ הַשֶּׂה לְעֹלָה בְּנִי
and he said Abraham Elohim he sees – to it the lamb to burnt offering my son

וַיֵּלְכוּ שְׁנֵיהֶם יַחְדָּו:
and they went two them together

8 And Abraham said, My son, God will provide himself a lamb for a burnt offering: so
they went both of them together.

וַיָּבֹאוּ אֶל־הַמָּקוֹם אֲשֶׁר אָמַר־לוֹ הָאֱלֹהִים
and they came unto - the place which he said - to him the Elohim

וַיִּבֶן שָׁם אַבְרָהָם אֶת־הַמִּזְבֵּחַ
and he built there Abraham that - the altar

וַיַּעֲרֹךְ אֶת־הָעֵצִים וַיַּעֲקֹד אֶת־יִצְחָק בְּנוֹ
and he arranging that - the wood and he bound that - Isaac his son

וַיָּשֶׂם אֹתוֹ עַל־הַמִּזְבֵּחַ מִמַּעַל לָעֵצִים:
and he put to him upon – the altar from on top to wood

9 And they came to the place which God had told him of; and Abraham built an altar

there, and laid the wood in order, and bound Isaac his son, and laid him on the altar
upon the wood.

וַיִּשְׁלַח אַבְרָהָם אֶת־יָדוֹ

his hand - that   Abraham   and he sent

וַיִּקַּח אֶת־הַמַּאֲכֶלֶת לִשְׁחֹט אֶת־בְּנוֹ:

his son - that   to slay   the kinfe - that   and he took

10 And Abraham stretched forth his hand, and took the knife to slay his son.

וַיִּקְרָא אֵלָיו מַלְאַךְ יְהֹוָה מִן־הַשָּׁמַיִם

the heavens - from   ihvh   angel   unto him   and he called

וַיֹּאמֶר אַבְרָהָם אַבְרָהָם וַיֹּאמֶר הִנֵּנִי:

here I am   and he said   Abraham   Abraham   and he said

11 And the angel of the LORD called unto him out of heaven, and said, Abraham,
Abraham: and he said, Here am I.

וַיֹּאמֶר אַל־תִּשְׁלַח יָדְךָ אֶל־הַנַּעַר

the boy - unto   your hand   you sent - don't   and he said

וְאַל־תַּעַשׂ לוֹ מְאוּמָה כִּי עַתָּה יָדַעְתִּי כִּי־יְרֵא אֱלֹהִים אַתָּה

you   Elohim   you fear - like   I know   now   like   from speck   to him   you do   and don't

וְלֹא חָשַׂכְתָּ אֶת־בִּנְךָ אֶת־יְחִידְךָ מִמֶּנִּי:

from me   your only - that   your son - that   you withheld   and not

12 And he said, Lay not thine hand upon the lad, neither do thou any thing unto him:
for now I know that thou fearest God, seeing thou hast not withheld thy son, thine only
son from me.

וַיִּשָּׂא אַבְרָהָם אֶת־עֵינָיו וַיַּרְא

and he saw   his eyes - that   Abraham   and he lifted

וְהִנֵּה־אַיִל אַחַר נֶאֱחַז בַּסְּבַךְ בְּקַרְנָיו

in his horns   in thicket   being caught   behind   ram - and here

וַיֵּלֶךְ אַבְרָהָם וַיִּקַּח אֶת־הָאַיִל וַיַּעֲלֵהוּ לְעֹלָה תַּחַת בְּנוֹ:

his son   instead   to burnt offering   and they offered it   the ram - that   and he took   Abraham   and he went

13 And Abraham lifted up his eyes, and looked, and behold behind him a ram caught in
a thicket by his horns: and Abraham went and took the ram, and offered him up for a
burnt offering in the stead of his son.

וַיִּקְרָא אַבְרָהָם שֵׁם־הַמָּקוֹם הַהוּא יְהֹוָה יִרְאֶה

he sees   ihvh   the it   the place - name   Abraham   and he called

אֲשֶׁר יֵאָמֵר הַיּוֹם בְּהַר יְהֹוָה יֵרָאֶה:

he sees   ihvh   in mountain   the day   he said   which

14 And Abraham called the name of that place Jehovah-jireh: as it is said to this day, In
the mount of the LORD it shall be seen.

וַיִּקְרָא מַלְאַךְ יְהוָה אֶל־אַבְרָהָם שֵׁנִית מִן־הַשָּׁמָיִם׃

the heavens – from   second one   Abraham – unto   ihvh   angel   and he called

15 And the angel of the LORD called unto Abraham out of heaven the second time,

וַיֹּאמֶר בִּי נִשְׁבַּעְתִּי נְאֻם־יְהוָה

ihvh - affirmation   I swear   in me   and he said

כִּי יַעַן אֲשֶׁר עָשִׂיתָ אֶת־הַדָּבָר הַזֶּה

the this   the matter - that   you did   which   answer   like

וְלֹא חָשַׂכְתָּ אֶת־בִּנְךָ אֶת־יְחִידֶךָ׃

your only - that   your son - that   you withheld   and not

16 And said, By myself have I sworn, saith the LORD, for because thou hast done this thing, and hast not withheld thy son, thine only son:

כִּי־בָרֵךְ אֲבָרֶכְךָ

I will bless you   bless - like

וְהַרְבָּה אַרְבֶּה אֶת־זַרְעֲךָ כְּכוֹכְבֵי הַשָּׁמַיִם

the heavens   like stars   your seed - that   I will increase   and the increase

וְכַחוֹל אֲשֶׁר עַל־שְׂפַת הַיָּם

the sea   shore - upon   which   and like sand

וְיִרַשׁ זַרְעֲךָ אֵת שַׁעַר אֹיְבָיו׃

it's enemies   gate   that   your seed   and it will possess

17 That in blessing I will bless thee, and in multiplying I will multiply thy seed as the stars of the heaven, and as the sand which is upon the sea shore; and thy seed shall possess the gate of his enemies;

וְהִתְבָּרֲכוּ בְזַרְעֲךָ כֹּל גּוֹיֵי הָאָרֶץ עֵקֶב

very end   the earth   nations   all   in your seed   and they will be blessed

אֲשֶׁר שָׁמַעְתָּ בְּקֹלִי׃

in my voice   you heard   which

18 And in thy seed shall all the nations of the earth be blessed; because thou hast obeyed my voice.

וַיָּשָׁב אַבְרָהָם אֶל־נְעָרָיו וַיָּקֻמוּ

and they rose up   his boys - unto   Abraham   and he returned

וַיֵּלְכוּ יַחְדָּו אֶל־בְּאֵר שָׁבַע

sheba   Beer - unto   together   and they went

וַיֵּשֶׁב אַבְרָהָם בִּבְאֵר שָׁבַע׃

sheba   in Beer   Abraham   and he dwelled

19 So Abraham returned unto his young men, and they rose up and went together to Beer-sheba; and Abraham dwelt at Beer-sheba.

פ

וַיְהִי אַחֲרֵי הַדְּבָרִים הָאֵלֶּה
the these   the matters   after   and he was

וַיֻּגַּד לְאַבְרָהָם לֵאמֹר הִנֵּה יָלְדָה מִלְכָּה
Milcah   she bore   here   to say   to Abraham   he told

גַּם־הִוא בָּנִים לְנָחוֹר אָחִיךָ:
your brother   to Nahor   sons   she - also

20 And it came to pass after these things, that it was told Abraham, saying, Behold, Milcah, she hath also born children unto thy brother Nahor;

אֶת־עוּץ בְּכֹרוֹ וְאֶת־בּוּז אָחִיו
his brother   Buz – and that   in his firstborn   Huz - that

וְאֶת־קְמוּאֵל אֲבִי אֲרָם:
Aram   father   Kemuel - and that

21 Huz his firstborn, and Buz his brother, and Kemuel the father of Aram,

וְאֶת־כֶּשֶׂד וְאֶת־חֲזוֹ וְאֶת־פִּלְדָּשׁ
and Pildash - and that   Hazo - and that   Chesed - and that

וְאֶת־יִדְלָף וְאֵת בְּתוּאֵל:
Bethuel   and that   Jidlaph - and that

22 And Chesed, and Hazo, and Pildash, and Jidlaph, and Bethuel.

וּבְתוּאֵל יָלַד אֶת־רִבְקָה
Rebekah - that   he begat   and Bethuel

שְׁמֹנָה אֵלֶּה יָלְדָה מִלְכָּה לְנָחוֹר אֲחִי אַבְרָהָם:
Abraham   brother   to Nahor   Milcah   she bore   these   eight

23 And Bethuel begat Rebekah: these eight Milcah did bear to Nahor, Abraham's brother.

וּפִילַגְשׁוֹ וּשְׁמָהּ רְאוּמָה
Reumah   and her name   and his concubine

וַתֵּלֶד גַּם־הִוא אֶת־טֶבַח וְאֶת־גַּחַם
Gaham - and that   Tebah - that   she - also   and she bore

וְאֶת־תַּחַשׁ וְאֶת־מַעֲכָה:
Maachah - and that   Thahash - and that

24 And his concubine, whose name was Reumah, she bare also Tebah, and Gaham, and Thahash, and Maachah.

פ פ פ

5 CHAI SARA

CHAPTER 23

ספר בראשית פרק כג

וַיִּהְיוּ חַיֵּי שָׂרָה מֵאָה שָׁנָה וְעֶשְׂרִים שָׁנָה וְשֶׁבַע שָׁנִים
years   and seven   year   and twenty   year   hundred   Sarah   life   and they were

שְׁנֵי חַיֵּי שָׂרָה:
Sarah   life   years

1 And Sarah was an hundred and seven and twenty years old: these were the years of the life of Sarah.

וַתָּמָת שָׂרָה בְּקִרְיַת אַרְבַּע הִוא חֶבְרוֹן בְּאֶרֶץ כְּנָעַן
Canaan   in land   Hebron   it   arba   in Kirjath   Sarah   and she died

וַיָּבֹא אַבְרָהָם לִסְפֹּד לְשָׂרָה וְלִבְכֹּתָהּ:
and to weep for her   to Sarah   to mourn   Abraham   and he came

2 And Sarah died in Kirjath-arba; the same is Hebron in the land of Canaan: and Abraham came to mourn for Sarah, and to weep for her.

וַיָּקָם אַבְרָהָם מֵעַל פְּנֵי מֵתוֹ
his dead   face   from upon   Abraham   and he rose up

וַיְדַבֵּר אֶל־בְּנֵי־חֵת לֵאמֹר:
to say   Heth - sons – unto   and he spoke

3 And Abraham stood up from before his dead, and spake unto the sons of Heth, saying,

גֵּר־וְתוֹשָׁב אָנֹכִי עִמָּכֶם
among you   I am   and sojourner – stranger

תְּנוּ לִי אֲחֻזַּת־קֶבֶר עִמָּכֶם
among you   burial - possession   to me   you give

וְאֶקְבְּרָה מֵתִי מִלְּפָנָי:
from before me   my dead   and I will bury

4 I am a stranger and a sojourner with you: give me a possession of a burying place with you, that I may bury my dead out of my sight.

וַיַּעֲנוּ בְּנֵי־חֵת אֶת־אַבְרָהָם לֵאמֹר לוֹ:
to him   to say   Abraham - that   Heth - sons   and they answered

5 And the children of Heth answered Abraham, saying unto him,

שְׁמָעֵנוּ אֲדֹנִי נְשִׂיא אֱלֹהִים אַתָּה בְּתוֹכֵנוּ:
among us   you   Elohim   prince   my lord   listen to us

בְּמִבְחַר קְבָרֵינוּ קְבֹר אֶת־מֵתֶךָ
your dead - that　bury　our tombs　in choice

אִישׁ מִמֶּנּוּ אֶת־קִבְרוֹ לֹא־יִכְלֶה מִמְּךָ מִקְּבֹר מֵתֶךָ:
your dead　from bury　from you　he refuse - not　his tomb - that　from us　man

6 Hear us, my lord: thou art a mighty prince among us: in the choice of our sepulchres bury thy dead; none of us shall withhold from thee his sepulchre, but that thou mayest bury thy dead.

וַיָּקָם אַבְרָהָם וַיִּשְׁתַּחוּ לְעַם־הָאָרֶץ לִבְנֵי־חֵת:
Heth - to sons　the land – to people　and he bowed　Abraham　and he rose up

7 And Abraham stood up, and bowed himself to the people of the land, even to the children of Heth.

וַיְדַבֵּר אִתָּם לֵאמֹר
to say　with them　and he spoke

אִם־יֵשׁ אֶת־נַפְשְׁכֶם לִקְבֹּר אֶת־מֵתִי מִלְּפָנַי
from before me　my dead – that　to bury　souls of you – that　it is - if

שְׁמָעוּנִי וּפִגְעוּ־לִי בְּעֶפְרוֹן בֶּן־צֹחַר:
Zohar - son　in Ephron　to me - and you entreat　you listen to me

8 And he communed with them, saying, If it be your mind that I should bury my dead out of my sight; hear me, and entreat for me to Ephron the son of Zohar,

וְיִתֶּן־לִי אֶת־מְעָרַת הַמַּכְפֵּלָה
the Machpelah　cave of - that　to me - and he gives

אֲשֶׁר־לוֹ אֲשֶׁר בִּקְצֵה שָׂדֵהוּ
his field　in end　which　to him - which

בְּכֶסֶף מָלֵא יִתְּנֶנָּה לִי בְּתוֹכְכֶם לַאֲחֻזַּת־קָבֶר:
burial - to possession　among you　to me　he give it　full　in silver

9 That he may give me the cave of Machpelah, which he hath, which is in the end of his field; for as much money as it is worth he shall give it me for a possession of a burying place amongst you.

וְעֶפְרוֹן יֹשֵׁב בְּתוֹךְ בְּנֵי־חֵת
Heth - sons　among　dwelt　and Ephron

וַיַּעַן עֶפְרוֹן הַחִתִּי אֶת־אַבְרָהָם בְּאָזְנֵי בְנֵי־חֵת
Heth - sons　in ears　Abraham - that　the Hittile　Ephron　and he answered

לְכֹל בָּאֵי שַׁעַר־עִירוֹ לֵאמֹר:
to say　his city - gate　coming ones　to all

10 And Ephron dwelt among the children of Heth: and Ephron the Hittite answered Abraham in the audience of the children of Heth, even of all that went in at the gate of his city, saying,

לֹא־אֲדֹנִי שְׁמָעֵנִי הַשָּׂדֶה נָתַתִּי לָךְ
to you | I give | the field | listen me | my lord - not

וְהַמְּעָרָה אֲשֶׁר־בּוֹ לְךָ נְתַתִּיהָ לְעֵינֵי בְנֵי־עַמִּי
my people - sons | to eyes | I give it | to you | in it - which | and the cave

נְתַתִּיהָ לָּךְ קְבֹר מֵתֶךָ׃
your dead | you bury | to you | I give it

11 Nay, my lord, hear me: the field give I thee, and the cave that is therein, I give it thee;
in the presence of the sons of my people give I it thee: bury thy dead.

וַיִּשְׁתַּחוּ אַבְרָהָם לִפְנֵי עַם־הָאָרֶץ׃
the land - people | before | Abraham | and he bowed

12 And Abraham bowed down himself before the people of the land.

וַיְדַבֵּר אֶל־עֶפְרוֹן בְּאָזְנֵי עַם־הָאָרֶץ לֵאמֹר
to say | the land - people | in ears | Ephron – unto | and he spoke

אַךְ אִם־אַתָּה לוּ שְׁמָעֵנִי נָתַתִּי כֶּסֶף הַשָּׂדֶה קַח מִמֶּנִּי
from me | take | the field | silver | I give | hear me | perhaps | you - with | only

וְאֶקְבְּרָה אֶת־מֵתִי שָׁמָּה׃
there | my dead - that | and will I bury

13 And he spake unto Ephron in the audience of the people of the land, saying, But if
thou wilt give it, I pray thee, hear me: I will give thee money for the field; take it of me,
and I will bury my dead there.

וַיַּעַן עֶפְרוֹן אֶת־אַבְרָהָם לֵאמֹר לוֹ׃
to him | to say | Abraham - that | Ephron | and he answered

14 And Ephron answered Abraham, saying unto him,

אֲדֹנִי שְׁמָעֵנִי אֶרֶץ אַרְבַּע מֵאֹת שֶׁקֶל־כֶּסֶף
silver - shekel | hundreds | four | land | hear me | my lord

בֵּינִי וּבֵינְךָ מַה־הִוא
it - what | and between you | between me

וְאֶת־מֵתְךָ קְבֹר׃
bury | your dead – and that

15 My lord, hearken unto me: the land is worth four hundred shekels of silver; what is
that betwixt me and thee? bury therefore thy dead.

וַיִּשְׁמַע אַבְרָהָם אֶל־עֶפְרוֹן
Ephron – unto | Abraham | and he heard

וַיִּשְׁקֹל אַבְרָהָם לְעֶפְרֹן אֶת־הַכֶּסֶף
the silver - that | to Ephron | Abraham | and he weighed

אֲשֶׁר דִּבֶּר בְּאָזְנֵי בְנֵי־חֵת
Heth - sons | in ears | he spoke | which

אַרְבַּע מֵאוֹת שֶׁקֶל כֶּסֶף עֹבֵר לַסֹּחֵר:

to merchant	passing	silver	shekel	hundreds	four

16 And Abraham hearkened unto Ephron; and Abraham weighed to Ephron the silver, which he had named in the audience of the sons of Heth, four hundred shekels of silver, current money with the merchant.

[שני]

וַיָּקָם שְׂדֵה עֶפְרוֹן אֲשֶׁר בַּמַּכְפֵּלָה

in Machpelah	which	Ephron	field	and he established

אֲשֶׁר לִפְנֵי מַמְרֵא הַשָּׂדֶה וְהַמְּעָרָה אֲשֶׁר־בּוֹ

in it - which	and the cave	the field	Mamre	before	which

וְכָל־הָעֵץ אֲשֶׁר בַּשָּׂדֶה אֲשֶׁר בְּכָל־גְּבֻלוֹ סָבִיב:

around	his border - in all	which	in field	which	the tree - and all

17 And the field of Ephron, which was in Machpelah, which was before Mamre, the field, and the cave which was therein, and all the trees that were in the field, that were in all the borders round about, were made sure

לְאַבְרָהָם לְמִקְנָה לְעֵינֵי בְנֵי־חֵת בְּכֹל בָּאֵי שַׁעַר־עִירוֹ:

his city - gate	coming ones	in all	Heth - sons	to eyes	to acquisition	to Abraham

18 Unto Abraham for a possession in the presence of the children of Heth, before all that went in at the gate of his city.

וְאַחֲרֵי־כֵן קָבַר אַבְרָהָם אֶת־שָׂרָה אִשְׁתּוֹ אֶל־מְעָרַת

cave – unto	his wife	Sarah - that	Abraham	buried	thus - and after

שְׂדֵה הַמַּכְפֵּלָה

the Machpelah	field

עַל־פְּנֵי מַמְרֵא הִוא חֶבְרוֹן בְּאֶרֶץ כְּנָעַן:

Canaan	in land	Hebron	it	Mamre	face - upon

19 And after this, Abraham buried Sarah his wife in the cave of the field of Machpelah before Mamre: the same is Hebron in the land of Canaan.

וַיָּקָם הַשָּׂדֶה וְהַמְּעָרָה אֲשֶׁר־בּוֹ לְאַבְרָהָם לַאֲחֻזַּת־קָבֶר

burial - to possession	to Abraham	in it - which	and the cave	the field	and he established

מֵאֵת בְּנֵי־חֵת:

Heth - sons	from that

20 And the field, and the cave that is therein, were made sure unto Abraham for a possession of a burying place by the sons of Heth.

ס

CHAPTER 24

ספר בראשית פרק כד

וְאַבְרָהָם זָקֵן בָּא בַּיָּמִים וַיהוָה בֵּרַךְ אֶת־אַבְרָהָם בַּכֹּל:

| in all | Abraham - that | blessed | and ihvh | in days | come | old | and Abraham |

1 And Abraham was old, and well stricken in age: and the LORD had blessed Abraham in all things.

וַיֹּאמֶר אַבְרָהָם אֶל־עַבְדּוֹ זְקַן בֵּיתוֹ הַמֹּשֵׁל בְּכָל־אֲשֶׁר־לוֹ

| to him - which - in all | the ruler | his house | old | his servant - unto | Abraham | and he said |

שִׂים־נָא יָדְךָ תַּחַת יְרֵכִי:

| my thigh | under | your hand | please - put |

2 And Abraham said unto his eldest servant of his house, that ruled over all that he had, Put, I pray thee, thy hand under my thigh:

וְאַשְׁבִּיעֲךָ בַּיהוָה אֱלֹהֵי הַשָּׁמַיִם וֵאלֹהֵי הָאָרֶץ

| the earth | and Elohim | the heavens | Elohim | in ihvh | and I will swear you |

אֲשֶׁר לֹא־תִקַּח אִשָּׁה לִבְנִי מִבְּנוֹת הַכְּנַעֲנִי

| the Canaanite | from daughters | to my son | wife | you take - not | which |

אֲשֶׁר אָנֹכִי יוֹשֵׁב בְּקִרְבּוֹ:

| in his midst | dwelling | I am | which |

3 And I will make thee swear by the LORD, the God of heaven, and the God of the earth, that thou shalt not take a wife unto my son of the daughters of the Canaanites, among whom I dwell:

כִּי אֶל־אַרְצִי וְאֶל־מוֹלַדְתִּי תֵּלֵךְ

| you go | my relatives - and unto | my country – unto | like |

וְלָקַחְתָּ אִשָּׁה לִבְנִי לְיִצְחָק:

| to Isaac | to my son | wife | and you will take |

4 But thou shalt go unto my country, and to my kindred, and take a wife unto my son Isaac.

וַיֹּאמֶר אֵלָיו הָעֶבֶד

| the servant | unto him | and he said |

אוּלַי לֹא־תֹאבֶה הָאִשָּׁה לָלֶכֶת אַחֲרַי אֶל־הָאָרֶץ הַזֹּאת

| the this | the land - unto | after me | to go | the woman | she will come - not | perhaps |

הֶהָשֵׁב אָשִׁיב אֶת־בִּנְךָ אֶל־הָאָרֶץ אֲשֶׁר־יָצָאתָ מִשָּׁם:

| from there | you came out - which | the land - unto | your son - that | I return | the return |

5 And the servant said unto him, Peradventure the woman will not be willing to follow me unto this land: must I needs bring thy son again unto the land from whence thou camest?

וַיֹּאמֶר אֵלָיו אַבְרָהָם הִשָּׁמֶר לְךָ פֶּן־תָּשִׁיב אֶת־בְּנִי שָׁמָּה:

towards there   my son - that   you return – lest   to you   heed   Abraham   unto him   and he said

6 And Abraham said unto him, Beware thou that thou bring not my son thither again.

יְהוָה אֱלֹהֵי הַשָּׁמַיִם אֲשֶׁר לְקָחַנִי מִבֵּית אָבִי

my father   from house   he took me   which   the heavens   Elohim   ihvh

וּמֵאֶרֶץ מוֹלַדְתִּי וַאֲשֶׁר דִּבֶּר־לִי וַאֲשֶׁר נִשְׁבַּע־לִי

to me - he swore   and which   to me - he spoke   and which   my relatives   and from land

לֵאמֹר לְזַרְעֲךָ אֶתֵּן אֶת־הָאָרֶץ הַזֹּאת

the this   the land - that   I will give   to your seed   to say

הוּא יִשְׁלַח מַלְאָכוֹ לְפָנֶיךָ

before you   his angel   he will send   he

וְלָקַחְתָּ אִשָּׁה לִבְנִי מִשָּׁם:

from there   to my son   wife   and you will take her

7 The LORD God of heaven, which took me from my father's house, and from the land of my kindred, and which spake unto me, and that sware unto me, saying, Unto thy seed will I give this land; he shall send his angel before thee, and thou shalt take a wife unto my son from thence.

וְאִם־לֹא תֹאבֶה הָאִשָּׁה לָלֶכֶת אַחֲרֶיךָ

after you   to go   the woman   she will come   not - and if

וְנִקִּיתָ מִשְּׁבֻעָתִי זֹאת רַק אֶת־בְּנִי לֹא תָשֵׁב שָׁמָּה:

towards there   you return   not   my son - that   only   this   from my oath   and you will be free

8 And if the woman will not be willing to follow thee, then thou shalt be clear from this my oath: only bring not my son thither again.

וַיָּשֶׂם הָעֶבֶד אֶת־יָדוֹ תַּחַת יֶרֶךְ אַבְרָהָם אֲדֹנָיו

his master   Abraham   thigh   under   his hand - that   the servant   and he put

וַיִּשָּׁבַע לוֹ עַל־הַדָּבָר הַזֶּה:

the this   the matter - upon   to him   and he swore

9 And the servant put his hand under the thigh of Abraham his master, and sware to him concerning that matter.

[שְׁלִישִׁי]

וַיִּקַּח הָעֶבֶד עֲשָׂרָה גְמַלִּים מִגְּמַלֵּי אֲדֹנָיו וַיֵּלֶךְ

and he went   his master   from camels   camels   ten   the servant   and he took

וְכָל־טוּב אֲדֹנָיו בְּיָדוֹ וַיָּקָם וַיֵּלֶךְ אֶל־אֲרַם נַהֲרַיִם

Naharaim   Aram – unto   and he went   and he rose   in his hand   his master   good - and all

אֶל־עִיר נָחוֹר:

Nahor   city - unto

10 And the servant took ten camels of the camels of his master, and departed; for all

the goods of his master were in his hand: and he arose, and went to Mesopotamia, unto the city of Nahor.

וַיַּבְרֵךְ הַגְּמַלִּים מִחוּץ לָעִיר אֶל־בְּאֵר הַמָּיִם
the waters   well – unto   to city   from outside   the camels   and he kneeled

לְעֵת עֶרֶב לְעֵת צֵאת הַשֹּׁאֲבֹת׃
the water drawers   go out   to time   evening   to time

11 And he made his camels to kneel down without the city by a well of water at the time of the evening, even the time that women go out to draw water.

וַיֹּאמַר יְהוָֹה אֱלֹהֵי אֲדֹנִי אַבְרָהָם הַקְרֵה־נָא לְפָנַי הַיּוֹם
the day   before   please – the meet   Abraham   my master   Elohim   ihvh   and he said

וַעֲשֵׂה־חֶסֶד עִם אֲדֹנִי אַבְרָהָם׃
Abraham   my master   with   kindness - and do

12 And he said, O LORD God of my master Abraham, I pray thee, send me good speed this day, and shew kindness unto my master Abraham.

הִנֵּה אָנֹכִי נִצָּב עַל־עֵין הַמָּיִם
the waters   spring – upon   fixed   I am   here

וּבְנוֹת אַנְשֵׁי הָעִיר יֹצְאֹת לִשְׁאֹב מָיִם׃
waters   to draw   coming outs   the city   men   and daughters

13 Behold, I stand here by the well of water; and the daughters of the men of the city come out to draw water:

וְהָיָה הַנַּעֲרָ אֲשֶׁר אֹמַר אֵלֶיהָ הַטִּי־נָא כַדֵּךְ וְאֶשְׁתֶּה
and I drink   your jar   now - let down   unto her   I say   which   the girl   and it be

וְאָמְרָה שְׁתֵה וְגַם־גְּמַלֶּיךָ אַשְׁקֶה
I water   your camels - and also   drink   and she says

אֹתָהּ הֹכַחְתָּ לְעַבְדְּךָ לְיִצְחָק
to Isaac   to your servant   you appointed   to her

וּבָהּ אֵדַע כִּי־עָשִׂיתָ חֶסֶד עִם־אֲדֹנִי׃
my master – with   kindness   you did - like   I will know   and in her

14 And let it come to pass, that the damsel to whom I shall say, Let down thy pitcher, I pray thee, that I may drink; and she shall say, Drink, and I will give thy camels drink also: let the same be she that thou hast appointed for thy servant Isaac; and thereby shall I know that thou hast shewed kindness unto my master.

וַיְהִי־הוּא טֶרֶם כִּלָּה לְדַבֵּר
to speak   he finished   before   she – and it was

וְהִנֵּה רִבְקָה יֹצֵאת אֲשֶׁר יֻלְּדָה לִבְתוּאֵל בֶּן־מִלְכָּה
Milcah - son   to Bethuel   she born   which   coming out   Rebekah   and here

אֵשֶׁת נָחֹור אֲחִי אַבְרָהָם

Abraham   brother   Nahor   wife

וְכַדָּהּ עַל־שִׁכְמָהּ:

her shoulder – upon   and jar

15 And it came to pass, before he had done speaking, that, behold, Rebekah came out, who was born to Bethuel, son of Milcah, the wife of Nahor, Abraham's brother, with her pitcher upon her shoulder.

וְהַנַּעֲרָ טֹבַת מַרְאֶה מְאֹד בְּתוּלָה

virgin   greatly   appearance   good   and the young girl

וְאִישׁ לֹא יְדָעָהּ וַתֵּרֶד הָעַיְנָה וַתְּמַלֵּא כַדָּהּ וַתָּעַל:

and she ascended   her jar   and she filled   the spring   and she descended   he know her   not   and man

16 And the damsel was very fair to look upon, a virgin, neither had any man known her: and she went down to the well, and filled her pitcher, and came up.

וַיָּרָץ הָעֶבֶד לִקְרָאתָהּ

to meet her   the servant   and he ran

וַיֹּאמֶר הַגְמִיאִינִי נָא מְעַט־מַיִם מִכַּדֵּךְ:

from your jar   water - little   now   the please me   and he said

17 And the servant ran to meet her, and said, Let me, I pray thee, drink a little water of thy pitcher.

וַתֹּאמֶר שְׁתֵה אֲדֹנִי וַתְּמַהֵר

and she hurried   my lord   drink   and she said

וַתֹּרֶד כַּדָּהּ עַל־יָדָהּ וַתַּשְׁקֵהוּ:

and she gave him drink   her hand – upon   her jar   and she lowered

18 And she said, Drink, my lord: and she hasted, and let down her pitcher upon her hand, and gave him drink.

וַתְּכַל לְהַשְׁקֹתוֹ

to give his drink   and she finished

וַתֹּאמֶר גַּם לִגְמַלֶּיךָ אֶשְׁאָב עַד אִם־כִּלּוּ לִשְׁתֹּת:

to drink   they finish – if   till   I will bail   to your camels   also   and she said

19 And when she had done giving him drink, she said, I will draw water for thy camels also, until they have done drinking.

וַתְּמַהֵר וַתְּעַר כַּדָּהּ אֶל־הַשֹּׁקֶת

the trough - unto   her jar   and she emptied   and she hurried

וַתָּרָץ עֹוד אֶל־הַבְּאֵר לִשְׁאֹב וַתִּשְׁאַב לְכָל־גְּמַלָּיו:

his camels – to all   and she drew   to draw   the well – unto   again   and she ran

20 And she hasted, and emptied her pitcher into the trough, and ran again unto the well to draw water, and drew for all his camels.

וְהָאִישׁ מִשְׁתָּאֵה לָהּ מַחֲרִישׁ
became silent   to her   agitated   and the man

לָדַעַת הַהִצְלִיחַ יְהֹוָה דַּרְכּוֹ אִם־לֹא:
not – if   his way   ihvh   the success   to know

21 And the man wondering at her held his peace, to wit whether the LORD had made his journey prosperous or not.

וַיְהִי כַּאֲשֶׁר כִּלּוּ הַגְּמַלִּים לִשְׁתּוֹת
to drinking   the camels   they finished   when   and it was

וַיִּקַּח הָאִישׁ נֶזֶם זָהָב בֶּקַע מִשְׁקָלוֹ
it's weight   beka   gold   nose ring   the man   and he took

וּשְׁנֵי צְמִידִים עַל־יָדֶיהָ עֲשָׂרָה זָהָב מִשְׁקָלָם:
their weight (in shekels)   gold   ten   her hand – upon   bracelets   and two

22 And it came to pass, as the camels had done drinking, that the man took a golden earring of half a shekel weight, and two bracelets for her hands of ten shekels weight of gold;

וַיֹּאמֶר בַּת־מִי אַתְּ הַגִּידִי נָא לִי
to me   please   the tell me   you   who – daughter   and he said

הֲיֵשׁ בֵּית־אָבִיךְ מָקוֹם לָנוּ לָלִין:
to spend night   to us   place   your father – house   the there is

23 And said, Whose daughter art thou? tell me, I pray thee: is there room in thy father's house for us to lodge in?

וַתֹּאמֶר אֵלָיו
unto him   and she said

בַּת־בְּתוּאֵל אָנֹכִי בֶּן־מִלְכָּה אֲשֶׁר יָלְדָה לְנָחוֹר:
to Nahor   she was bore   which   Milcah – son   I am   Bethuel – daughter

24 And she said unto him, I am the daughter of Bethuel the son of Milcah, which she bare unto Nahor.

וַתֹּאמֶר אֵלָיו גַּם־תֶּבֶן גַּם־מִסְפּוֹא רַב עִמָּנוּ גַּם־מָקוֹם לָלוּן:
to spend night   place – also   with us   much   fodder - also   straw – also   unto him   and she said

25 She said moreover unto him, We have both straw and provender enough, and room to lodge in.

וַיִּקֹּד הָאִישׁ וַיִּשְׁתַּחוּ לַיהֹוָה:
to ihvh   and he worshiped   the man   and he bowed head

26 And the man bowed down his head, and worshipped the LORD.

[רביעי]

וַיֹּאמֶר בָּרוּךְ יְהֹוָה אֱלֹהֵי אֲדֹנִי אַבְרָהָם
Abraham   my master   Elohim   ihvh   blessed   and he said

אֲשֶׁר לֹא־עָזַב חַסְדּוֹ
his kindness   forsook – not   which

וַאֲמִתּוֹ   מֵעִם   אֲדֹנִי   אָנֹכִי בַּדֶּרֶךְ
in way   I am   my lord   from with   and his faithfulness

נָחַנִי יְהוָה בֵּית אֲחֵי אֲדֹנִי:
my master   my brother   house   ihvh   led me

27 And he said, Blessed be the LORD God of my master Abraham, who hath not left destitute my master of his mercy and his truth: I being in the way, the LORD led me to the house of my master's brethren.

וַתָּרָץ הַנַּעֲרָ וַתַּגֵּד לְבֵית אִמָּהּ כַּדְּבָרִים הָאֵלֶּה:
the these   like matters   her mother   to house   and she told   the girl   and she ran

28 And the damsel ran, and told them of her mother's house these things.

וּלְרִבְקָה אָח וּשְׁמוֹ לָבָן
Laban   and his name   brother   and to Rebekah

וַיָּרָץ לָבָן אֶל־הָאִישׁ הַחוּצָה אֶל־הָעָיִן:
the spring – unto   the outside   the man – unto   Laban   and he ran

29 And Rebekah had a brother, and his name was Laban: and Laban ran out unto the man, unto the well.

וַיְהִי כִּרְאֹת אֶת־הַנֶּזֶם
the nose ring – that   like seeing   and it was

וְאֶת־הַצְּמִדִים עַל־יְדֵי אֲחֹתוֹ
his sister   hands – upon   the bracelets – and that

וּכְשָׁמְעוֹ אֶת־דִּבְרֵי רִבְקָה אֲחֹתוֹ לֵאמֹר
to say   his sister   Rebekah   speaking – that   and like his hearing

כֹּה־דִבֶּר אֵלַי הָאִישׁ
the man   unto me   spoke – thus

וַיָּבֹא אֶל־הָאִישׁ
the man – unto   and he came

וְהִנֵּה עֹמֵד עַל־הַגְּמַלִּים עַל־הָעָיִן:
the spring – upon   the camels – upon   standing   and here

30 And it came to pass, when he saw the earring and bracelets upon his sister's hands, and when he heard the words of Rebekah his sister, saying, Thus spake the man unto me; that he came unto the man; and, behold, he stood by the camels at the well.

וַיֹּאמֶר בּוֹא בְּרוּךְ יְהוָה לָמָּה תַעֲמֹד בַּחוּץ
outside   you stand   why   ihvh   blessed   come   and he said

וְאָנֹכִי פִּנִּיתִי הַבַּיִת וּמָקוֹם לַגְּמַלִּים:
to camels   and place   the house   I prepared   and I am

31 And he said, Come in, thou blessed of the LORD; wherefore standest thou without? for I have prepared the house, and room for the camels.

וַיָּבֹא הָאִישׁ הַבַּיְתָה וַיְפַתַּח הַגְּמַלִּים
the camels   and he opened   the house   the man   and he came

וַיִּתֵּן תֶּבֶן וּמִסְפּוֹא לַגְּמַלִּים וּמַיִם לִרְחֹץ רַגְלָיו
his feet   to wash   and water   to camels   and fodder   straw   and he gave

וְרַגְלֵי הָאֲנָשִׁים אֲשֶׁר אִתּוֹ׃
with him   which   the men   and feet

32 And the man came into the house: and he ungirded his camels, and gave straw and provender for the camels, and water to wash his feet, and the men's feet that were with him.

וַיִּישֶׂם [וַיּוּשַׂם] לְפָנָיו לֶאֱכֹל
to eat   before him   and it was set

וַיֹּאמֶר לֹא אֹכַל עַד אִם־דִּבַּרְתִּי דְּבָרָי וַיֹּאמֶר דַּבֵּר׃
speak   and he said   my matter   I speak - with   till   I will eat   not   and he said

33 And there was set meat before him to eat: but he said, I will not eat, until I have told mine errand. And he said, Speak on.

וַיֹּאמַר עֶבֶד אַבְרָהָם אָנֹכִי׃
I am   Abraham   servant   and he said

34 And he said, I am Abraham's servant.

וַיהוָה בֵּרַךְ אֶת־אֲדֹנִי מְאֹד וַיִּגְדָּל וַיִּתֶּן־לוֹ צֹאן וּבָקָר
and cattle sheep to him - and he gave and he mighty greatly my master - that he blessed and ihvh

וְכֶסֶף וְזָהָב וַעֲבָדִם וּשְׁפָחֹת וּגְמַלִּים וַחֲמֹרִים׃
and donkeys   and camels   and maidservants   and menservants   and gold   and silver

35 And the LORD hath blessed my master greatly; and he is become great: and he hath given him flocks, and herds, and silver, and gold, and menservants, and maidservants, and camels, and asses.

וַתֵּלֶד שָׂרָה אֵשֶׁת אֲדֹנִי בֵן לַאדֹנִי אַחֲרֵי זִקְנָתָהּ
her old age   after   my master   son   my master   wife   Sarah   and she bore

וַיִּתֶּן־לוֹ אֶת־כָּל־אֲשֶׁר־לוֹ׃
to him - which - all - that   to him - and he gave

36 And Sarah my master's wife bare a son to my master when she was old: and unto him hath he given all that he hath.

וַיַּשְׁבִּעֵנִי אֲדֹנִי לֵאמֹר
to say   my master   and he made me swear

לֹא־תִקַּח אִשָּׁה לִבְנִי מִבְּנוֹת הַכְּנַעֲנִי
the Canaanites   from daughters   to my son   wife   you take - not

אֲשֶׁר אָנֹכִי יֹשֵׁב בְּאַרְצוֹ:
in his land   dwelling   I am   which

37 And my master made me swear, saying, Thou shalt not take a wife to my son of the daughters of the Canaanites, in whose land I dwell:

אִם־לֹא אֶל־בֵּית־אָבִי תֵּלֵךְ וְאֶל־מִשְׁפַּחְתִּי
my family - and unto   you go   my father - house – unto   not - with

וְלָקַחְתָּ אִשָּׁה לִבְנִי:
to my son   wife   and to you take

38 But thou shalt go unto my father's house, and to my kindred, and take a wife unto my son.

וָאֹמַר אֶל־אֲדֹנִי אֻלַי לֹא־תֵלֵךְ הָאִשָּׁה אַחֲרָי:
after me   the woman   she goes - not   perhaps   my master - unto   and I said

39 And I said unto my master, Peradventure the woman will not follow me.

וַיֹּאמֶר אֵלַי יְהֹוָה אֲשֶׁר־הִתְהַלַּכְתִּי לְפָנָיו יִשְׁלַח מַלְאָכוֹ אִתָּךְ
with you   his angel   he will send   before him   walks with me - which   ihvh   unto me   and he said

וְהִצְלִיחַ דַּרְכֶּךָ
your way   and he causes succeed

וְלָקַחְתָּ אִשָּׁה לִבְנִי מִמִּשְׁפַּחְתִּי וּמִבֵּית אָבִי:
my father   and from house   from my family   to my son   wife   and you will take

40 And he said unto me, The LORD, before whom I walk, will send his angel with thee, and prosper thy way; and thou shalt take a wife for my son of my kindred, and of my father's house:

אָז תִּנָּקֶה מֵאָלָתִי כִּי תָבוֹא אֶל־מִשְׁפַּחְתִּי
my family - unto   you come   like   from my oath   you be free   then

וְאִם־לֹא יִתְּנוּ לָךְ וְהָיִיתָ נָקִי מֵאָלָתִי:
from my oath   clean   and you will be   to you   they give   not – and if

41 Then shalt thou be clear from this my oath, when thou comest to my kindred; and if they give not thee one, thou shalt be clear from my oath.

וָאָבֹא הַיּוֹם אֶל־הָעָיִן וָאֹמַר יְהֹוָה אֱלֹהֵי אֲדֹנִי אַבְרָהָם
Abraham   my master   Elohim   ihvh   and I said   the spring – unto   the day   and I came

אִם־יֶשְׁךָ־נָּא מַצְלִיחַ דַּרְכִּי אֲשֶׁר אָנֹכִי הֹלֵךְ עָלֶיהָ:
upon it   going   I am   which   my way   make success   now – you do - if

42 And I came this day unto the well, and said, O LORD God of my master Abraham, if now thou do prosper my way which I go:

הִנֵּה אָנֹכִי נִצָּב עַל־עֵין הַמָּיִם
the water   spring - upon   standing   I am   here

וְהָיָה הָעַלְמָה הַיֹּצֵאת לִשְׁאֹב
to draw   the one coming out   the maiden   and it be

וְאָמַרְתִּי אֵלֶיהָ הַשְׁקִינִי־נָא
please – the my drink   unto her   and I say

מְעַט־מַיִם מִכַּדֵּךְ:
from your jar   water - little

43 Behold, I stand by the well of water; and it shall come to pass, that when the virgin cometh forth to draw water, and I say to her, Give me, I pray thee, a little water of thy pitcher to drink;

וְאָמְרָה אֵלַי גַּם־אַתָּה שְׁתֵה
drink   you – also   unto me   and she says

וְגַם לִגְמַלֶּיךָ אֶשְׁאָב
I draw   to your camels   and also

הִוא הָאִשָּׁה אֲשֶׁר־הֹכִיחַ יְהֹוָה לְבֶן־אֲדֹנִי:
my master - to son   ihvh   appointed - which   the woman   she

44 And she say to me, Both drink thou, and I will also draw for thy camels: let the same be the woman whom the LORD hath appointed out for my master's son.

אֲנִי טֶרֶם אֲכַלֶּה לְדַבֵּר אֶל־לִבִּי וְהִנֵּה רִבְקָה יֹצֵאת
coming out   Rebekah   and here   my heart - unto   to speak   finished   before   I

וְכַדָּהּ עַל־שִׁכְמָהּ וַתֵּרֶד הָעַיְנָה וַתִּשְׁאָב
and she drew   the towards spring   and she descended   her shoulder - upon   and her jar

וָאֹמַר אֵלֶיהָ הַשְׁקִינִי נָא:
please   the give me drink   unto her   and I said

45 And before I had done speaking in mine heart, behold, Rebekah came forth with her pitcher on her shoulder; and she went down unto the well, and drew water: and I said unto her, Let me drink, I pray thee.

וַתְּמַהֵר וַתּוֹרֶד כַּדָּהּ מֵעָלֶיהָ וַתֹּאמֶר שְׁתֵה
drink   and she said   from upon her   her jar   and she lowered   and she hurried

וְגַם־גְּמַלֶּיךָ אַשְׁקֶה
I make drink   your camels - and also

וָאֵשְׁתְּ וְגַם הַגְּמַלִּים הִשְׁקָתָה:
she made to drink   the camels   and also   and I drank

46 And she made haste, and let down her pitcher from her shoulder, and said, Drink, and I will give thy camels drink also: so I drank, and she made the camels drink also.

וָאֶשְׁאַל אֹתָהּ וָאֹמַר בַּת־מִי אַתְּ
you   who - daughter   and I said   to her   and I asked

וַתֹּאמֶר בַּת־בְּתוּאֵל בֶּן־נָחוֹר אֲשֶׁר יָלְדָה־לּוֹ מִלְכָּה
Milcah   to him - she bore   which   Nahor - son   Bethuel - daughter   and she said

וָאָשִׂם הַנֶּזֶם עַל־אַפָּהּ וְהַצְּמִידִים עַל־יָדֶיהָ:

her hands - upon	and the bracelets	nose - upon	the ring	and I put

47 And I asked her, and said, Whose daughter art thou? And she said, The daughter of
Bethuel, Nahor's son, whom Milcah bare unto him: and I put the earring upon her face,
and the bracelets upon her hands.

וָאֶקֹּד וָאֶשְׁתַּחֲוֶה לַיהֹוָה

to ihvh	and I worshiped	and I bowed

וָאֲבָרֵךְ אֶת־יְהֹוָה אֱלֹהֵי אֲדֹנִי אַבְרָהָם

Abraham	my master	Elohim	ihvh - that	and I blessed

אֲשֶׁר הִנְחַנִי בְּדֶרֶךְ אֱמֶת

truth	in road	led me	which

לָקַחַת אֶת־בַּת־אֲחִי אֲדֹנִי לִבְנוֹ:

to his son	my master	my brother - daughter - that	to take

48 And I bowed down my head, and worshipped the LORD, and blessed the LORD
God of my master Abraham, which had led me in the right way to take my master's
brother's daughter unto his son.

וְעַתָּה אִם־יֶשְׁכֶם עֹשִׂים חֶסֶד

kindness	doings	you deal - if	and now

וֶאֱמֶת אֶת־אֲדֹנִי הַגִּידוּ לִי וְאִם־לֹא הַגִּידוּ לִי

to me	the tell you	not - and if	to me	the you tell	my master - that	and truth

וְאֶפְנֶה עַל־יָמִין אוֹ עַל־שְׂמֹאל:

left - upon	or	right - upon	and turn

49 Now if you will deal kindly and truly with my master, tell me. And if not, tell me,
that I may turn to the right hand or to the left."

וַיַּעַן לָבָן וּבְתוּאֵל וַיֹּאמְרוּ מֵיהֹוָה יָצָא הַדָּבָר

the matter	it comes out	from ihvh	and they said	and Bethuel	Laban	and he answered

לֹא נוּכַל דַּבֵּר אֵלֶיךָ רַע אוֹ־טוֹב:

good - or	bad	unto you	speak	we able	not

50 Then Laban and Bethuel answered and said, The thing proceedeth from the LORD:
we cannot speak unto thee bad or good.

הִנֵּה־רִבְקָה לְפָנֶיךָ קַח וָלֵךְ

and go	take	before you	Rebekah - here

וּתְהִי אִשָּׁה לְבֶן־אֲדֹנֶיךָ כַּאֲשֶׁר דִּבֶּר יְהֹוָה:

ihvh	spoke	when	your master - to son	wife	and let her be

51 Behold, Rebekah is before thee, take her, and go, and let her be thy master's son's
wife, as the LORD hath spoken.

וַיְהִי כַּאֲשֶׁר שָׁמַע עֶבֶד אַבְרָהָם אֶת־דִּבְרֵיהֶם

their speaking - that	Abraham	servant	he heard	when	and it was

וַיִּשְׁתַּ֥חוּ אַ֖רְצָה לַֽיהוָֽה׃

to ihvh   towards ground   and he bowed

52 And it came to pass, that, when Abraham's servant heard their words, he worshipped the LORD, bowing himself to the earth.

[חמישי]

וּבְגָדִ֗ים זָהָ֜ב וּכְלֵ֨י כְּלֵי־כֶ֠סֶף הָעֶ֡בֶד וַיּוֹצֵ֣א

and clothing   gold   and jewelry   silver - jewelry   the servant   and he brought out

וּלְאִמָּֽהּ׃ לְאָחִ֥יהָ נָתַ֛ן וּמִ֨גְדָּנֹ֔ת לְרִבְקָ֑ה וַיִּתֵּ֣ן

and to her mother   to her brother   he gave   and precious things   to Rebekah   and he gave

53 And the servant brought forth jewels of silver, and jewels of gold, and raiment, and gave them to Rebekah: he gave also to her brother and to her mother precious things.

אֲשֶׁר־עִמּ֖וֹ וְהָאֲנָשִׁ֥ים ה֛וּא וַיִּשְׁתּ֗וּ וַיֹּאכְל֣וּ

with him - which   and the men   he   and they drank   and they ate

לַֽאדֹנִֽי׃ שַׁלְּחֻ֣נִי וַיֹּ֕אמֶר בַבֹּ֔קֶר וַיָּק֣וּמוּ וַיָּלִ֑ינוּ

to my master   send me   and he said   in morning   and they rose   and they spent night

54 And they did eat and drink, he and the men that werewith him, and tarried all night; and they rose up in the morning, and he said, Send me away unto my master.

וְאִמָּ֔הּ אָחִ֣יהָ וַיֹּ֤אמֶר

and her mother   her brother   and he replied

תֵּלֵֽךְ׃ אַחַ֥ר ע֑שׂוֹר א֣וֹ יָמִ֖ים אִתָּ֛נוּ הַֽנַּעֲרָ֧ תֵּשֵׁ֨ב

she will go   afterwards   ten   or   days   with us   the girl   she dwell

55 And her brother and her mother said, Let the damsel abide with us a few days, at the least ten; after that she shall go.

אֹתִ֑י אַל־תְּאַחֲר֖וּ אֲלֵהֶ֔ם וַיֹּ֣אמֶר

to me   you delay it - don't   to them   and he said

לַֽאדֹנִֽי׃ וְאֵלְכָ֖ה שַׁלְּח֔וּנִי דַּרְכִּ֑י הִצְלִ֣יחַ וַֽיהוָ֖ה

to my master   and I go   send me   my way   caused to succeed   and ihvh

56 And he said unto them, Hinder me not, seeing the LORD hath prospered my way; send me away that I may go to my master.

אֶת־פִּֽיהָ׃ וְנִֽשְׁאֲלָ֖ה לַֽנַּעֲרָ֑ נִקְרָ֣א וַיֹּאמְר֖וּ

her mouth - that   and we ask her   to girl   let us call   and they said

57 And they said, We will call the damsel, and inquire at her mouth.

לְרִבְקָ֗ה וַיִּקְרְא֣וּ

to Rebekah   and they called

הַזֶּ֑ה עִם־הָאִ֣ישׁ הֲתֵלְכִ֖י אֵלֶ֔יהָ וַיֹּאמְר֣וּ

the this   the man - with   the you go   unto her   and they said

וַתֹּאמֶר אֵלֵךְ:

I go   and she said

58 And they called Rebekah, and said unto her, Wilt thou go with this man? And she said, I will go.

וַיְשַׁלְּחוּ אֶת־רִבְקָה אֲחֹתָם וְאֶת־מֵנִקְתָּהּ

and her nurse - and that   their sister   Rebekah - that   and they sent

וְאֶת־עֶבֶד אַבְרָהָם וְאֶת־אֲנָשָׁיו:

his men - and that   Abraham   servant – and that

59 And they sent away Rebekah their sister, and her nurse, and Abraham's servant, and his men.

וַיְבָרֲכוּ אֶת־רִבְקָה וַיֹּאמְרוּ לָהּ

to her   and they said   Rebekah - that   and they blessed

אֲחֹתֵנוּ אַתְּ הֲיִי לְאַלְפֵי רְבָבָה

many   to thousand   you be   you   our sister

וְיִירַשׁ זַרְעֵךְ אֵת שַׁעַר שֹׂנְאָיו:

his haters   gate   that   your seed   and he possess

60 And they blessed Rebekah, and said unto her, Thou art our sister, be thou the mother of thousands of millions, and let thy seed possess the gate of those which hate them.

וַתָּקָם רִבְקָה וְנַעֲרֹתֶיהָ

and her young girls   Rebekah   and she rose

וַתִּרְכַּבְנָה עַל־הַגְּמַלִּים וַתֵּלַכְנָה אַחֲרֵי הָאִישׁ

the man   after   and she went   the camels – upon   and they mounted

וַיִּקַּח הָעֶבֶד אֶת־רִבְקָה וַיֵּלַךְ:

and he went   Rebekah - that   the servant   and he took

61 And Rebekah arose, and her damsels, and they rode upon the camels, and followed the man: and the servant took Rebekah, and went his way.

וְיִצְחָק בָּא מִבּוֹא בְּאֵר לַחַי רֹאִי

Roi   Lahai   Beer   from coming   came   and Isaac

וְהוּא יוֹשֵׁב בְּאֶרֶץ הַנֶּגֶב:

the Negev   in land   he dwelt   and he

62 And Isaac came from the way of the well Lahai-roi; for he dwelt in the south country.

וַיֵּצֵא יִצְחָק לָשׂוּחַ בַּשָּׂדֶה לִפְנוֹת עָרֶב וַיִּשָּׂא עֵינָיו

his eyes   and he lifted   evening   before   in field   to meditate   Isaac   and he went out

וַיַּרְא וְהִנֵּה גְמַלִּים בָּאִים:

coming ones   camels   and here   and he saw

63 And Isaac went out to meditate in the field at the eventide: and he lifted up his eyes,

and saw, and, behold, the camels were coming.

וַתִּשָּׂא רִבְקָה אֶת־עֵינֶיהָ
and she lifted | Rebekah | that - her eyes

וַתֵּרֶא אֶת־יִצְחָק וַתִּפֹּל מֵעַל הַגָּמָל:
and she saw | that - Isaac | and she fell | from upon | the camel

64 And Rebekah lifted up her eyes, and when she saw Isaac, she lighted off the camel.

וַתֹּאמֶר אֶל־הָעֶבֶד מִי־הָאִישׁ הַלָּזֶה הַהֹלֵךְ בַּשָּׂדֶה לִקְרָאתֵנוּ
and she said | unto- the servant | who - the man | the to this | the going | in field | to meet us

וַיֹּאמֶר הָעֶבֶד הוּא אֲדֹנִי
and he said | the servant | he | my master

וַתִּקַּח הַצָּעִיף וַתִּתְכָּס:
and she took | the veil | and she covered

65 For she had said unto the servant, What man is this that walketh in the field to meet us? And the servant had said, It is my master: therefore she took a veil, and covered herself.

וַיְסַפֵּר הָעֶבֶד לְיִצְחָק אֵת כָּל־הַדְּבָרִים אֲשֶׁר עָשָׂה:
and he storied | the servant | to Isaac | that | all the matters - | which | he did

66 And the servant told Isaac all things that he had done.

וַיְבִאֶהָ יִצְחָק הָאֹהֱלָה שָׂרָה אִמּוֹ
and he brought her | Isaac | towards the tent | Sarah | his mother

וַיִּקַּח אֶת־רִבְקָה וַתְּהִי־לוֹ לְאִשָּׁה
and he took | that - Rebekah | and she became - to him | to wife

וַיֶּאֱהָבֶהָ וַיִּנָּחֵם יִצְחָק אַחֲרֵי אִמּוֹ:
and he loved her | and he was comforted | Isaac | after | his mother

67 And Isaac brought her into his mother Sarah's tent, and took Rebekah, and she became his wife; and he loved her: and Isaac was comforted after his mother's death.

פ

CHAPTER 25

ספר בראשית פרק כה

[ששי]

וַיֹּסֶף אַבְרָהָם וַיִּקַּח אִשָּׁה וּשְׁמָהּ קְטוּרָה:
and he added | Abraham | and he took | wife | and her name | Keturah

1 Then again Abraham took a wife, and her name was Keturah.

וַתֵּלֶד לוֹ אֶת־זִמְרָן וְאֶת־יָקְשָׁן
and she bore | to him | that - Zimran | and that - Jokshan

וְאֶת־מְדָן וְאֶת־מִדְיָן וְאֶת־יִשְׁבָּק וְאֶת־שׁוּחַ:

Shuah - and that   Ishbak – and that   Midian – and that   Medan – and that

2 And she bare him Zimran, and Jokshan, and Medan, and Midian, and Ishbak, and Shuah.

וְיָקְשָׁן יָלַד אֶת־שְׁבָא וְאֶת־דְּדָן

Dedan - and that   Sheba - that   begat   and Jokshan

וּבְנֵי דְדָן הָיוּ אַשּׁוּרִם וּלְטוּשִׁם וּלְאֻמִּים:

and Leummim   and Letushim   Asshurim   they were   Dedan   and sons

3 And Jokshan begat Sheba, and Dedan. And the sons of Dedan were Asshurim, and Letushim, and Leummim.

וּבְנֵי מִדְיָן עֵיפָה וָעֵפֶר וַחֲנֹךְ וַאֲבִידָע וְאֶלְדָּעָה

and Eldaah   and Abidah   and Hanoch   and Epher   Ephah   Midian   and sons

כָּל־אֵלֶּה בְּנֵי קְטוּרָה:

Keturah   sons   these - all

4 And the sons of Midian; Ephah, and Epher, and Hanoch, and Abidah, and Eldaah. All these were the children of Keturah.

וַיִּתֵּן אַבְרָהָם אֶת־כָּל־אֲשֶׁר־לוֹ לְיִצְחָק:

to Isaac   to him - which - all - that   Abraham   and he gave

5 And Abraham gave all that he had unto Isaac.

וְלִבְנֵי הַפִּילַגְשִׁים אֲשֶׁר לְאַבְרָהָם נָתַן אַבְרָהָם מַתָּנֹת

gifts   Abraham   he gave   to Abraham   which   the concubines   and to sons

וַיְשַׁלְּחֵם מֵעַל יִצְחָק בְּנוֹ בְּעוֹדֶנּוּ חַי קֵדְמָה

towards east   alive   in still   his son   Isaac   from upon   and he sent them

אֶל־אֶרֶץ קֶדֶם:

east country   land – unto

6 But unto the sons of the concubines, which Abraham had, Abraham gave gifts, and sent them away from Isaac his son, while he yet lived, eastward, unto the east country.

וְאֵלֶּה יְמֵי שְׁנֵי־חַיֵּי אַבְרָהָם אֲשֶׁר־חָי

life - which   Abraham   lives - years   days   and these

מְאַת שָׁנָה וְשִׁבְעִים שָׁנָה וְחָמֵשׁ שָׁנִים:

years   and five   year   and seventy   year   hundred

7 And these are the days of the years of Abraham's life which he lived, an hundred threescore and fifteen years.

וַיִּגְוַע וַיָּמָת אַבְרָהָם בְּשֵׂיבָה טוֹבָה זָקֵן וְשָׂבֵעַ

and full   old   good   in full   Abraham   and he died   and he expired

וַיֵּאָסֶף אֶל־עַמָּיו:

his people - unto   and he gathered

8 Then Abraham gave up the ghost, and died in a good old age, an old man, and full of

years; and was gathered to his people.

וַיִּקְבְּרוּ אֹתוֹ יִצְחָק וְיִשְׁמָעֵאל בָּנָיו
his sons   and Ishmael   Isaac   that him   and they buried

אֶל־מְעָרַת הַמַּכְפֵּלָה אֶל־שְׂדֵה עֶפְרֹן
Ephron   field – unto   the Machpelah   cave - unto

בֶּן־צֹחַר הַחִתִּי אֲשֶׁר עַל־פְּנֵי מַמְרֵא׃
Mamre   face – upon   which   the Hittite   Zohar - son

9 And his sons Isaac and Ishmael buried him in the cave of Machpelah, in the field of
Ephron the son of Zohar the Hittite, which is before Mamre;

הַשָּׂדֶה אֲשֶׁר־קָנָה אַבְרָהָם מֵאֵת בְּנֵי־חֵת
Heth - sons   from that   Abraham   bought - which   the field

שָׁמָּה קֻבַּר אַבְרָהָם וְשָׂרָה אִשְׁתּוֹ׃
his wife   and Sarah   Abraham   was buried   at there

10 The field which Abraham purchased of the sons of Heth: there was Abraham
buried, and Sarah his wife.

וַיְהִי אַחֲרֵי מוֹת אַבְרָהָם וַיְבָרֶךְ אֱלֹהִים אֶת־יִצְחָק בְּנוֹ
his son   Isaac - that   Elohim   and he blessed   Abraham   death   after   and it was

וַיֵּשֶׁב יִצְחָק עִם־בְּאֵר לַחַי רֹאִי׃
Roi   Lahai   well – with   Isaac   and he lived

11 And it came to pass after the death of Abraham, that God blessed his son Isaac; and
Isaac dwelt by the well Lahai-roi.

פ

[שביעי]

וְאֵלֶּה תֹּלְדֹת יִשְׁמָעֵאל בֶּן־אַבְרָהָם
Abraham - son   Ishmael   begettings   and these

אֲשֶׁר יָלְדָה הָגָר הַמִּצְרִית שִׁפְחַת שָׂרָה לְאַבְרָהָם׃
to Abraham   Sarah   maid   the Egyptian   Hagar   she bore   which

12 Now these are the generations of Ishmael, Abraham's son, whom Hagar the
Egyptian, Sarah's handmaid, bare unto Abraham:

וְאֵלֶּה שְׁמוֹת בְּנֵי יִשְׁמָעֵאל בִּשְׁמֹתָם לְתוֹלְדֹתָם
to their begettings   in their names   Ishmael   sons   names   and these

בְּכֹר יִשְׁמָעֵאל נְבָיֹת וְקֵדָר וְאַדְבְּאֵל וּמִבְשָׂם׃
and Mibsam   and Adbeel   and Kedar   Nebajoth   Ishmael   firstborn

13 And these are the names of the sons of Ishmael, by their names, according to their
generations: the firstborn of Ishmael, Nebajoth; and Kedar, and Adbeel, and Mibsam,

וּמִשְׁמָע וְדוּמָה וּמַשָּׂא׃
and Massa   and Dumah   and Mishma

14 And Mishma, and Dumah, and Massa,

וְקֵדְמָה: נָפִישׁ יְטוּר וְתֵימָא חֲדַד
and Kedemah Naphish Jetur and Tema Hadad

15 Hadar, and Tema, Jetur, Naphish, and Kedemah:

[מפטיר]

אֵלֶּה הֵם בְּנֵי יִשְׁמָעֵאל וְאֵלֶּה שְׁמֹתָם
their names and these Ishmael sons them these

לְאֻמֹּתָם: נְשִׂיאִם שְׁנֵים־עָשָׂר וּבְטִירֹתָם בְּחַצְרֵיהֶם
to their peoples men - twelve - and in their castles in their settlements

16 These are the sons of Ishmael, and these are their names, by their towns, and by their castles; twelve princes according to their nations.

וְאֵלֶּה שְׁנֵי חַיֵּי יִשְׁמָעֵאל
Ishmael life years and these

מְאַת שָׁנָה וּשְׁלֹשִׁים שָׁנָה וְשֶׁבַע שָׁנִים
years and seven year and thirty years hundred

וַיִּגְוַע וַיָּמָת וַיֵּאָסֶף אֶל־עַמָּיו:
his people – unto and he gathered and he died and he expired

17 And these are the years of the life of Ishmael, an hundred and thirty and seven years: and he gave up the ghost and died; and was gathered unto his people.

וַיִּשְׁכְּנוּ מֵחֲוִילָה עַד־שׁוּר
Shur - till from Havilah and they dwelt

אַשּׁוּרָה בֹּאֲכָה מִצְרַיִם עַל־פְּנֵי אֲשֶׁר
towards Assyria towards coming Egypt face - upon which

עַל־פְּנֵי כָל־אֶחָיו נָפָל:
he fell his brothers - all face - upon

18 And they dwelt from Havilah unto Shur, that is before Egypt, as thou goest toward Assyria: and he died in the presence of all his brethren.

פ פ פ

6 TOLEDOT

CHAPTER 25 CONT

[פרשת תולדות]

וְאֵלֶּה תּוֹלְדֹת יִצְחָק בֶּן־אַבְרָהָם
and these   begeting lines   Isaac   Abraham – son

אַבְרָהָם הוֹלִיד אֶת־יִצְחָק:
Abraham   begot   Isaac - that

19 And these are the generations of Isaac, Abraham's son: Abraham begat Isaac:

וַיְהִי יִצְחָק בֶּן־אַרְבָּעִים שָׁנָה בְּקַחְתּוֹ אֶת־רִבְקָה
and he was   Isaac   forty - age   year   in his taking   Rebekah - that

בַּת־בְּתוּאֵל הָאֲרַמִּי מִפַּדַּן אֲרָם
Bethuel - daughter   the Aramean   from Paddan   Aram

אֲחוֹת לָבָן הָאֲרַמִּי לוֹ לְאִשָּׁה:
sister   Laban   the Aramean   to him   to wife

20 And Isaac was forty years old when he took Rebekah to wife, the daughter of Bethuel the Syrian of Padan-aram, the sister to Laban the Syrian.

וַיֶּעְתַּר יִצְחָק לַיהוָה לְנֹכַח אִשְׁתּוֹ כִּי עֲקָרָה הִוא
and he entreated   Isaac   to ihvh   to ahead   his wife   like   barren   she

וַיֵּעָתֶר לוֹ יְהוָה וַתַּהַר רִבְקָה אִשְׁתּוֹ:
and he entreated   to him   ihvh   and she conceived   Rebekah   his wife

21 And Isaac entreated the LORD for his wife, because she was barren: and the LORD was entreated of him, and Rebekah his wife conceived.

וַיִּתְרֹצֲצוּ הַבָּנִים בְּקִרְבָּהּ
and they jostled   the sons   in her close

וַתֹּאמֶר אִם־כֵּן לָמָּה זֶּה אָנֹכִי וַתֵּלֶךְ לִדְרֹשׁ אֶת־יְהוָה:
and she said   so - if   why   this   I am   and she went   to inquire   ihvh - that

22 And the children struggled together within her; and she said, If it be so, why am I thus? And she went to inquire of the LORD.

וַיֹּאמֶר יְהוָה לָהּ שְׁנֵי גיים [גוֹיִם] בְּבִטְנֵךְ
and he said   ihvh   to her   two   rulers of nations   in your belly

וּשְׁנֵי לְאֻמִּים מִמֵּעַיִךְ יִפָּרֵדוּ
and two   peoples   from within you   they will separate

וּלְאֹם מִלְאֹם יֶאֱמָץ
and to people   from people stems   he be stronger

וְרַב יַעֲבֹד צָעִיר:

younger   he serves   and greater

23 And the LORD said unto her, Two nations are in thy womb, and two manner of people shall be separated from thy bowels; and the one people shall be stronger than the other people; and the elder shall serve the younger.

וַיִּמְלְאוּ יָמֶיהָ לָלֶדֶת וְהִנֵּה תוֹמִם בְּבִטְנָהּ:

in her belly   twin boys   and here   to beget   her days   and they were filled

24 And when her days to be delivered were fulfilled, behold, there were twins in her womb.

וַיֵּצֵא הָרִאשׁוֹן אַדְמוֹנִי כֻּלּוֹ כְּאַדֶּרֶת שֵׂעָר

hair   like garment   his all   reddish   the first   and he came out

וַיִּקְרְאוּ שְׁמוֹ עֵשָׂו:

Esau   his name   and they called

25 And the first came out red, all over like an hairy garment; and they called his name Esau.

וְאַחֲרֵי־כֵן יָצָא אָחִיו וְיָדוֹ אֹחֶזֶת בַּעֲקֵב עֵשָׂו

Esau   in heel   grasping   and his hand   his brother   he came out   thus - and after

וַיִּקְרָא שְׁמוֹ יַעֲקֹב

Jacob   his name   and he called

וְיִצְחָק בֶּן־שִׁשִּׁים שָׁנָה בְּלֶדֶת אֹתָם:

to them   in begetting   year   sixty - age   and Isaac

26 And after that came his brother out, and his hand took hold on Esau's heel; and his name was called Jacob: and Isaac was threescore years old when she bare them.

וַיִּגְדְּלוּ הַנְּעָרִים וַיְהִי עֵשָׂו אִישׁ יֹדֵעַ צַיִד אִישׁ שָׂדֶה

field   man   hunting   knower   man   Esau   and he was   the boys   and they grew big

וְיַעֲקֹב אִישׁ תָּם יֹשֵׁב אֹהָלִים:

tents   dwelling   perfect   man   and Jacob

27 And the boys grew: and Esau was a cunning hunter, a man of the field; and Jacob was a plain man, dwelling in tents.

וַיֶּאֱהַב יִצְחָק אֶת־עֵשָׂו כִּי־צַיִד בְּפִיו

in his mouth   game - like   Esau - that   Isaac   and he loved

וְרִבְקָה אֹהֶבֶת אֶת־יַעֲקֹב:

Jacob - that   loved   and Rebekah

28 And Isaac loved Esau, because he did eat of his venison: but Rebekah loved Jacob.

וַיָּזֶד יַעֲקֹב נָזִיד

stew   Jacob   and he cooked mix

וַיָּבֹא עֵשָׂו מִן־הַשָּׂדֶה וְהוּא עָיֵף:

tired   and he   the field - from   Esau   and he came

29 And Jacob sod pottage: and Esau came from the field, and he was faint:

וַיֹּאמֶר עֵשָׂו אֶל־יַעֲקֹב הַלְעִיטֵנִי נָא מִן־הָאָדֹם הָאָדֹם הַזֶּה

the this   the red   the red - from   now   the to gluten me   Jacob - unto   Esau   and he said

כִּי עָיֵף אָנֹכִי

I am   tired   like

עַל־כֵּן קָרָא־שְׁמוֹ אֱדוֹם׃

Edom   name his - he called   thus - upon

30 And Esau said to Jacob, Feed me, I pray thee, with that same red pottage; for I am faint: therefore was his name called Edom.

וַיֹּאמֶר יַעֲקֹב מִכְרָה כַיּוֹם אֶת־בְּכֹרָתְךָ לִי׃

to me   birthright your - that   like day   sell   Jacob   and he said

31 And Jacob said, Sell me this day thy birthright.

וַיֹּאמֶר עֵשָׂו הִנֵּה אָנֹכִי הוֹלֵךְ לָמוּת

to die   I go   I am   here   Esau   and he said

וְלָמָּה־זֶּה לִי בְּכֹרָה׃

birthright   to me   this – and why

32 And Esau said, Behold, I am at the point to die: and what profit shall this birthright do to me?

וַיֹּאמֶר יַעֲקֹב הִשָּׁבְעָה לִּי כַּיּוֹם

like day   to me   cause to swear   Jacob   and he said

וַיִּשָּׁבַע לוֹ וַיִּמְכֹּר אֶת־בְּכֹרָתוֹ לְיַעֲקֹב׃

to Jacob   his birthright - that   and he sold   to him   and he swore

33 And Jacob said, Swear to me this day; and he sware unto him: and he sold his birthright unto Jacob.

וְיַעֲקֹב נָתַן לְעֵשָׂו לֶחֶם וּנְזִיד עֲדָשִׁים

lentils   and stew   bread   to Esau   he gave   and Jacob

וַיֹּאכַל וַיֵּשְׁתְּ וַיָּקָם וַיֵּלַךְ

and he went   and he got up   and he drank   and he ate

וַיִּבֶז עֵשָׂו אֶת־הַבְּכֹרָה׃

the birthright - that   Esau   and he despising

34 Then Jacob gave Esau bread and pottage of lentiles; and he did eat and drink, and rose up, and went his way: thus Esau despised his birthright.

פ

CHAPTER 26

ספר בראשית פרק כו

וַיְהִי רָעָב בָּאָרֶץ
in land   hunger   and it was

מִלְּבַד הָרָעָב הָרִאשׁוֹן אֲשֶׁר הָיָה בִּימֵי אַבְרָהָם
Abraham   in days   it was   which   the first   the hunger   besides

וַיֵּלֶךְ יִצְחָק אֶל־אֲבִימֶלֶךְ מֶלֶךְ־פְּלִשְׁתִּים גְּרָרָה:
towards Gerar   Philistines - king   Abimelech - unto   Isaac   and he went

1 And there was a famine in the land, beside the first famine that was in the days of Abraham. And Isaac went unto Abimelech king of the Philistines unto Gerar.

וַיֵּרָא אֵלָיו יְהֹוָה
ihvh   to him   and he appeared

וַיֹּאמֶר אַל־תֵּרֵד מִצְרָיְמָה שְׁכֹן בָּאָרֶץ אֲשֶׁר אֹמַר אֵלֶיךָ:
unto you   I say   which   in land   dwell   towards Egypt   you go down - don't   and he said

2 And the LORD appeared unto him, and said, Go not down into Egypt; dwell in the land which I shall tell thee of:

גּוּר בָּאָרֶץ הַזֹּאת וְאֶהְיֶה עִמְּךָ וַאֲבָרֲכֶךָּ
and I will bless you   with you   and I be   the this   in land   sojourn

כִּי־לְךָ וּלְזַרְעֲךָ אֶתֵּן אֶת־כָּל־הָאֲרָצֹת הָאֵל
the these   the lands - all - that   I give   and to your seed   to you - like

וַהֲקִמֹתִי אֶת־הַשְּׁבֻעָה אֲשֶׁר נִשְׁבַּעְתִּי לְאַבְרָהָם אָבִיךָ:
your father   to Abraham   I swore   which   the oath - that   and the I will perform

3 Sojourn in this land, and I will be with thee, and will bless thee; for unto thee, and unto thy seed, I will give all these countries, and I will perform the oath which I sware unto Abraham thy father;

וְהִרְבֵּיתִי אֶת־זַרְעֲךָ כְּכוֹכְבֵי הַשָּׁמַיִם
the heavens   like stars   seed your - that   and I will increase

וְנָתַתִּי לְזַרְעֲךָ אֵת כָּל־הָאֲרָצֹת הָאֵל
the these   the lands - all   that   to your seed   and I give

וְהִתְבָּרֲכוּ בְזַרְעֲךָ כֹּל גּוֹיֵי הָאָרֶץ:
the earth   nations   all   in your seed   and will be blessed it

4 And I will make thy seed to multiply as the stars of heaven, and will give unto thy seed all these countries; and in thy seed shall all the nations of the earth be blessed;

עֵקֶב אֲשֶׁר־שָׁמַע אַבְרָהָם בְּקֹלִי
in my voice   Abraham   heard - which   because

וַיִּשְׁמֹר מִשְׁמַרְתִּי מִצְוֹתַי חֻקּוֹתַי וְתוֹרֹתָי:
and laws   my decrees   my commandments   my requirements   and he heeded

5 Because that Abraham obeyed my voice, and kept my charge, my commandments, my statutes, and my laws.

[שני]

וַיֵּשֶׁב   יִצְחָק   בִּגְרָר׃
and he dwelled   Isaac   in Gerar

6 And Isaac dwelt in Gerar:

וַיִּשְׁאֲלוּ אַנְשֵׁי הַמָּקוֹם לְאִשְׁתּוֹ
and they asked   men   the place   to his wife

וַיֹּאמֶר אֲחֹתִי הִוא כִּי יָרֵא לֵאמֹר אִשְׁתִּי
and he said   my sister   she   like   he afraid   to say   my wife

פֶּן־יַהַרְגֻנִי אַנְשֵׁי הַמָּקוֹם עַל־רִבְקָה
they kill me - lest   men   the place   Rebekah - upon

כִּי־טוֹבַת מַרְאֶה הִוא׃
good - like   sight   she

7 And the men of the place asked him of his wife; and he said, She is my sister: for he feared to say, She is my wife; lest, said he, the men of the place should kill me for Rebekah; because she was fair to look upon.

וַיְהִי   כִּי־אָרְכוּ־לוֹ שָׁם הַיָּמִים
and it was   to him – length it - like   there   the days

וַיַּשְׁקֵף   אֲבִימֶלֶךְ מֶלֶךְ פְּלִשְׁתִּים בְּעַד הַחַלּוֹן וַיַּרְא
and he saw   the window   in till   Philistines   king   Abimelech   and he looked out

וְהִנֵּה יִצְחָק מְצַחֵק אֵת רִבְקָה אִשְׁתּוֹ׃
and here   Isaac   playing   that   Rebekah   his wife

8 And it came to pass, when he had been there a long time, that Abimelech king of the Philistines looked out at a window, and saw, and, behold, Isaac was sporting with Rebekah his wife.

וַיִּקְרָא אֲבִימֶלֶךְ לְיִצְחָק וַיֹּאמֶר אַךְ הִנֵּה אִשְׁתְּךָ הִוא
and he called   Abimelech   to Isaac   and he said   surely   here   wife your   she

וְאֵיךְ אָמַרְתָּ אֲחֹתִי הִוא
and how   you said   my sister   she

וַיֹּאמֶר   אֵלָיו יִצְחָק כִּי אָמַרְתִּי פֶּן־אָמוּת עָלֶיהָ׃
and he answered   unto him   Isaac   like   I said   I die - lest   upon her

9 And Abimelech called Isaac, and said, Behold, of a surety she is thy wife: and how saidst thou, She is my sister? And Isaac said unto him, Because I said, Lest I die for her.

וַיֹּאמֶר אֲבִימֶלֶךְ מַה־זֹּאת עָשִׂיתָ לָּנוּ
and he said   Abimelech   what - this   you did   to us

כְּמְעַט שָׁכַב אַחַד הָעָם אֶת־אִשְׁתְּךָ וְהֵבֵאתָ עָלֵינוּ אָשָׁם׃

| guiltiness | upon us | and the you bring | your wife - that | the people | one | lay | like little |

10 And Abimelech said, What is this thou hast done unto us? one of the people might lightly have lien with thy wife, and thou shouldest have brought guiltiness upon us.

וַיְצַו אֲבִימֶלֶךְ אֶת־כָּל־הָעָם לֵאמֹר

| to say | the people - all - that | Abimelech | and he commanded |

הַנֹּגֵעַ בָּאִישׁ הַזֶּה וּבְאִשְׁתּוֹ מוֹת יוּמָת׃

| he be dead | death | and in his wife | the this | in man | the one touching |

11 And Abimelech charged all his people, saying, He that toucheth this man or his wife shall surely be put to death.

וַיִּזְרַע יִצְחָק בָּאָרֶץ הַהִוא

| the it | in land | Isaac | he planted seed |

וַיִּמְצָא בַּשָּׁנָה הַהִוא מֵאָה שְׁעָרִים וַיְבָרְכֵהוּ יְהֹוָה׃

| ihvh | and he blessed him | gates | hundred | the it | in year | and he finding |

12 Then Isaac sowed in that land, and received in the same year a hundredfold: and the LORD blessed him.

[שְׁלִישִׁי]

וַיִּגְדַּל הָאִישׁ וַיֵּלֶךְ הָלוֹךְ

| walking | and he went | the man | and he became great |

וְגָדֵל עַד כִּי־גָדַל מְאֹד׃

| very | great - like | until | and he grew |

13 And the man waxed great, and went forward, and grew until he became very great:

וַיְהִי־לוֹ מִקְנֵה־צֹאן וּמִקְנֵה בָקָר וַעֲבֻדָּה רַבָּה

| many | and services | cattle | and possession | sheep - possession | to him - and it was |

וַיְקַנְאוּ אֹתוֹ פְּלִשְׁתִּים׃

| Philistines | to him | and they envied |

14 For he had possession of flocks, and possession of herds, and great store of servants: and the Philistines envied him.

וְכָל־הַבְּאֵרֹת אֲשֶׁר חָפְרוּ עַבְדֵי אָבִיו בִּימֵי אַבְרָהָם אָבִיו

| his father | Abraham | in days | his father | servants | they dug | which | the wells - and all |

סִתְּמוּם פְּלִשְׁתִּים וַיְמַלְאוּם עָפָר׃

| dust | and they filled them | Phillistins | stopped up them |

15 For all the wells which his father's servants had digged in the days of Abraham his father, the Philistines had stopped them, and filled them with earth.

וַיֹּאמֶר אֲבִימֶלֶךְ אֶל־יִצְחָק לֵךְ מֵעִמָּנוּ

| from with us | go | Isaac - unto | Abimelech | and he said |

כִּי־עָצַמְתָּ מִמֶּנּוּ מְאֹד׃
greatly   from us   you powerful - like

16 And Abimelech said unto Isaac, Go from us; for thou art much mightier than we.

וַיֵּלֶךְ מִשָּׁם יִצְחָק
Isaac   from there   and he went

וַיִּחַן בְּנַחַל־גְּרָר וַיֵּשֶׁב שָׁם׃
there   and he dwelled   Garar - in valley   and he camped

17 And Isaac departed thence, and pitched his tent in the valley of Gerar, and dwelt there.

וַיָּשָׁב יִצְחָק
Isaac   and he returned

וַיַּחְפֹּר אֶת־בְּאֵרֹת הַמַּיִם אֲשֶׁר חָפְרוּ בִּימֵי אַבְרָהָם אָבִיו
his father   Abraham   in days   they dug   which   the water   wells - that   and he dug

וַיְסַתְּמוּם פְּלִשְׁתִּים אַחֲרֵי מוֹת אַבְרָהָם
Abraham   death   after   Philistines   and they stopped up them

וַיִּקְרָא לָהֶן שֵׁמוֹת כַּשֵּׁמֹת אֲשֶׁר־קָרָא לָהֶן אָבִיו׃
his father   to them   he called - which   like names   names   to them   and he called

18 And Isaac digged again the wells of water, which they had digged in the days of Abraham his father; for the Philistines had stopped them after the death of Abraham: and he called their names after the names by which his father had called them.

וַיַּחְפְּרוּ עַבְדֵי־יִצְחָק בַּנָּחַל
in valley   Isaac - servants   and they dug

וַיִּמְצְאוּ־שָׁם בְּאֵר מַיִם חַיִּים׃
life   water   well   there - and they found

19 And Isaac's servants digged in the valley, and found there a well of springing water.

וַיָּרִיבוּ רֹעֵי גְרָר עִם־רֹעֵי יִצְחָק לֵאמֹר לָנוּ הַמָּיִם
the water   to us   to say   Isaac   shepherds - with   Gerar   shepherds   and they quarreled

וַיִּקְרָא שֵׁם־הַבְּאֵר עֵשֶׂק כִּי הִתְעַשְּׂקוּ עִמּוֹ׃
with him   they caused to dispute   like   Esek   the well - name   and he called

20 And the herdmen of Gerar did strive with Isaac's herdmen, saying, The water is ours: and he called the name of the well Esek; because they strove with him.

וַיַּחְפְּרוּ בְּאֵר אַחֶרֶת
another   well   and they dug

וַיָּרִיבוּ גַּם־עָלֶיהָ וַיִּקְרָא שְׁמָהּ שִׂטְנָה׃
Sitnah   it's name   and he called   over it – also   and they quarreled

21 And they digged another well, and strove for that also: and he called the name of it Sitnah.

וַיַּעְתֵּק   מִשָּׁם   וַיַּחְפֹּר   בְּאֵר   אַחֶרֶת
                                                                                                    another   well   and digged   from there   and he shifting

וְלֹא   רָבוּ   עָלֶיהָ   וַיִּקְרָא   שְׁמָהּ   רְחֹבוֹת
                                        Rehoboth   it's name   and he called   over it   they quarreled   and not

וַיֹּאמֶר   כִּי־עַתָּה   הִרְחִיב   יְהוָה   לָנוּ   וּפָרִינוּ   בָאָרֶץ:
                    in land   and we will be fruitful   to us   ihvh   made room   now - like   and he said

22 And he removed from thence, and digged another well; and for that they strove not:
and he called the name of it Rehoboth; and he said, For now the LORD hath made
room for us, and we shall be fruitful in the land.

[רביעי]

וַיַּעַל   מִשָּׁם   בְּאֵר   שָׁבַע:
                                    Sheba   Beer   from there   and he ascended

23 And he went up from thence to Beer-sheba.

וַיֵּרָא   אֵלָיו   יְהוָה   בַּלַּיְלָה   הַהוּא
                                the it   in night   ihvh   unto him   and he saw

וַיֹּאמֶר   אָנֹכִי   אֱלֹהֵי   אַבְרָהָם   אָבִיךָ   אַל־תִּירָא   כִּי־אִתְּךָ   אָנֹכִי
        I am   with you - like   you fear - don't   your father   Abraham   Elohim   I am   and he said

וּבֵרַכְתִּיךָ   וְהִרְבֵּיתִי   אֶת־זַרְעֲךָ   בַּעֲבוּר   אַבְרָהָם   עַבְדִּי:
        my servant   Abraham   in sake   your seed – that   and will increase   and I will bless you

24 And the LORD appeared unto him the same night, and said, I am the God of
Abraham thy father: fear not, for I am with thee, and will bless thee, and multiply thy
seed for my servant Abraham's sake.

וַיִּבֶן   שָׁם   מִזְבֵּחַ
                        altar   there   and he built

וַיִּקְרָא   בְּשֵׁם   יְהוָה   וַיֶּט־שָׁם   אָהֳלוֹ
        his tent   there - and he pitched   ihvh   in name   and he called

וַיִּכְרוּ־שָׁם   עַבְדֵי־יִצְחָק   בְּאֵר:
                        well   Isaac - servants   there - and they dug

25 And he builded an altar there, and called upon the name of the LORD, and pitched
his tent there: and there Isaac's servants digged a well.

וַאֲבִימֶלֶךְ   הָלַךְ   אֵלָיו   מִגְּרָר
            from Gerar   unto him   he went   and Abimelech

וַאֲחֻזַּת   מֵרֵעֵהוּ   וּפִיכֹל   שַׂר־צְבָאוֹ:
                his force - commander   and Phicol   his neighbor friend   and Ahuzzath

26 Then Abimelech went to him from Gerar, and Ahuzzath one of his friends, and
Phichol the chief captain of his army.

וַיֹּאמֶר אֲלֵהֶם יִצְחָק מַדּוּעַ בָּאתֶם אֵלָי
and he asked   unto them   Isaac   why   you come   unto me

וְאַתֶּם שְׂנֵאתֶם אֹתִי וַתְּשַׁלְּחוּנִי מֵאִתְּכֶם:
and you   you hate   to me   and you sent me   from with you

27 And Isaac said unto them, Wherefore come ye to me, seeing ye hate me, and have sent me away from you?

וַיֹּאמְרוּ רָאוֹ רָאִינוּ כִּי־הָיָה יְהוָֹה עִמָּךְ
and they answered   his seeing   we saw   he was - like   ihvh   with you

וַנֹּאמֶר תְּהִי נָא אָלָה בֵּינוֹתֵינוּ בֵּינֵינוּ וּבֵינֶךְ
and we said   let it be   now   oath   between we   between us   and between you

וְנִכְרְתָה בְרִית עִמָּךְ:
and we cut   covenant   with you

28 And they said, We saw certainly that the LORD was with thee: and we said, Let there be now an oath betwixt us, even betwixt us and thee, and let us make a covenant with thee;

אִם־תַּעֲשֵׂה עִמָּנוּ רָעָה כַּאֲשֶׁר לֹא נְגַעֲנוּךְ
if - you do   to us   evil   when   not   we touched you

וְכַאֲשֶׁר עָשִׂינוּ עִמְּךָ רַק־טוֹב
and when   we did   with you   good - only

וַנְּשַׁלֵּחֲךָ בְּשָׁלוֹם אַתָּה עַתָּה בְּרוּךְ יְהוָֹה:
and we sent you   in peace   you   now   blessed   ihvh

29 That thou wilt do us no hurt, as we have not touched thee, and as we have done unto thee nothing but good, and have sent thee away in peace: thou art now the blessed of the LORD.

[חמישי]

וַיַּעַשׂ לָהֶם מִשְׁתֶּה וַיֹּאכְלוּ וַיִּשְׁתּוּ:
and he made   to them   feast   and they ate   and they drank

30 And he made them a feast, and they did eat and drink.

וַיַּשְׁכִּימוּ בַבֹּקֶר וַיִּשָּׁבְעוּ אִישׁ לְאָחִיו
and they arose   in morning   and they swore   man   to his brother

וַיְשַׁלְּחֵם יִצְחָק וַיֵּלְכוּ מֵאִתּוֹ בְּשָׁלוֹם:
and he sent them   Isaac   and they went   from with him   in peace

31 And they rose up betimes in the morning, and sware one to another: and Isaac sent them away, and they departed from him in peace.

וַיְהִי בַּיּוֹם הַהוּא וַיָּבֹאוּ עַבְדֵי יִצְחָק
and it was   in day   the it   and they came   servants   Isaac

וַיַּגִּדוּ לוֹ עַל־אֹדוֹת הַבְּאֵר אֲשֶׁר חָפָרוּ
they dug   which   the well   matter – upon   to him   and they told

וַיֹּאמְרוּ לוֹ מָצָאנוּ מָיִם:
water   we found   to him   and they said

32 And it came to pass the same day, that Isaac's servants came, and told him
concerning the well which they had digged, and said unto him, We have found water.

וַיִּקְרָא אֹתָהּ שִׁבְעָה
Shebah   to it   and he called

עַל־כֵּן שֵׁם־הָעִיר בְּאֵר שֶׁבַע עַד הַיּוֹם הַזֶּה:
the this   the day   till   Seba   Beer   the city - name   this - upon

33 And he called it Shebah: therefore the name of the city is Beer-sheba unto this day.

ס

וַיְהִי עֵשָׂו בֶּן־אַרְבָּעִים שָׁנָה
year   forty - age   Essau   and it was

וַיִּקַּח אִשָּׁה אֶת־יְהוּדִית בַּת־בְּאֵרִי הַחִתִּי
the Hittite   Beeri - daughter   Judith - that   wife   and he took

וְאֶת־בָּשְׂמַת בַּת־אֵילֹן הַחִתִּי:
the Hittite   Elon - daughter   Bashemath - and that

34 And Esau was forty years old when he took to wife Judith the daughter of Beeri the
Hittite, and Bashemath the daughter of Elon the Hittite:

וַתִּהְיֶיןָ מֹרַת רוּחַ לְיִצְחָק וּלְרִבְקָה:
and to Rebakah   to Isaac   spirit   grief   and they were

35 Which were a grief of mind unto Isaac and to Rebekah.

ס

CHAPTER 27

ספר בראשית פרק כז

וַיְהִי כִּי־זָקֵן יִצְחָק וַתִּכְהֶיןָ עֵינָיו מֵרְאֹת
from seeing   his eyes   and dim them   Isaac   old - like   and he was

וַיִּקְרָא אֶת־עֵשָׂו בְּנוֹ הַגָּדֹל
the big   his son   Esau - that   and he called

וַיֹּאמֶר אֵלָיו בְּנִי וַיֹּאמֶר אֵלָיו הִנֵּנִי:
here I am   unto him   and he said   son my   unto him   and he said

1 And it came to pass, that when Isaac was old, and his eyes were dim, so that he could
not see, he called Esau his eldest son, and said unto him, My son: and he said unto him,
Behold, here am I.

וַיֹּאמֶר הִנֵּה־נָא זָקַנְתִּי לֹא יָדַעְתִּי יוֹם מוֹתִי:
my death   day   I know   not   I old   now – here   and he said

2 And he said, Behold now, I am old, I know not the day of my death:

וְעַתָּה שָׂא־נָא כֵלֶיךָ תֶּלְיְךָ וְקַשְׁתֶּךָ
and your bow   your quiver   your weapons   now - put   and now

וְצֵא הַשָּׂדֶה וְצוּדָה לִי צֵידָה [צָיִד] :
game   to me   and hunt   the field   and go out

3 Now therefore take, I pray thee, thy weapons, thy quiver and thy bow, and go out to the field, and take me some venison;

וַעֲשֵׂה־לִי מַטְעַמִּים כַּאֲשֶׁר אָהַבְתִּי וְהָבִיאָה לִי
to me   and the bring   I love   when   tasty meats   to me - and make

וְאֹכֵלָה בַּעֲבוּר תְּבָרֶכְךָ נַפְשִׁי בְּטֶרֶם אָמוּת:
I die   before   my soul   I bless you   in sake   and I eat

4 And make me savoury meat, such as I love, and bring it to me, that I may eat; that my soul may bless thee before I die.

וְרִבְקָה שֹׁמַעַת בְּדַבֵּר יִצְחָק אֶל־עֵשָׂו בְּנוֹ
his son   Esau - unto   Isaac   in speak   listening   and Rebekah

וַיֵּלֶךְ עֵשָׂו הַשָּׂדֶה לָצוּד צַיִד לְהָבִיא:
to the bring   game   to hunt   the field   Esau   and he went

5 And Rebekah heard when Isaac spake to Esau his son. And Esau went to the field to hunt for venison, and to bring it.

וְרִבְקָה אָמְרָה אֶל־יַעֲקֹב בְּנָהּ לֵאמֹר
to say   her son   Jacob - unto   she said   and Rebekah

הִנֵּה שָׁמַעְתִּי אֶת־אָבִיךָ מְדַבֵּר אֶל־עֵשָׂו אָחִיךָ לֵאמֹר:
to say   your brother   Esau - unto   speaking   your father - that   I heard   here

6 And Rebekah spake unto Jacob her son, saying, Behold, I heard thy father speak unto Esau thy brother, saying,

הָבִיאָה לִי צַיִד
game   to me   the bring

וַעֲשֵׂה־לִי מַטְעַמִּים וְאֹכֵלָה
and I eat   tasty meats   to me - and make

וַאֲבָרֶכְכָה לִפְנֵי יְהוָה לִפְנֵי מוֹתִי:
my death   before   ihvh   before   and I bless you

7 Bring me venison, and make me savoury meat, that I may eat, and bless thee before the LORD before my death.

וְעַתָּה בְנִי שְׁמַע בְּקֹלִי לַאֲשֶׁר אֲנִי מְצַוָּה אֹתָךְ:
to you   command   I   to which   in my voice   hear   my son   and now

8 Now therefore, my son, obey my voice according to that which I command thee.

לֶךְ־נָא אֶל־הַצֹּאן וְקַח־לִי מִשָּׁם שְׁנֵי גְּדָיֵי עִזִּים טֹבִים
good ones   goats   kids   two   from there   to me - and take   the flock - unto   now - go

וְאֶעֱשֶׂה אֹתָם מַטְעַמִּים לְאָבִיךָ כַּאֲשֶׁר אָהֵב:
he loves   when   to your father   tasty meats   to them   and I make

9 Go now to the flock, and fetch me from thence two good kids of the goats; and I will make them savoury meat for thy father, such as he loveth:

וְהֵבֵאתָ לְאָבִיךָ וְאָכָל בַּעֲבֻר אֲשֶׁר יְבָרֶכְךָ לִפְנֵי מוֹתוֹ:
his death   before   he bless you   which   in sake   and he eat   to your father   and you the bring

10 And thou shalt bring it to thy father, that he may eat, and that he may bless thee before his death.

וַיֹּאמֶר יַעֲקֹב אֶל־רִבְקָה אִמּוֹ הֵן עֵשָׂו אָחִי אִישׁ שָׂעִר
hair   man   my brother   Esau   thus   his mother   Rebekah - unto   Jacob   and he said

וְאָנֹכִי אִישׁ חָלָק:
smooth   man   and I am

11 And Jacob said to Rebekah his mother, Behold, Esau my brother is a hairy man, and I am a smooth man:

אוּלַי יְמֻשֵּׁנִי אָבִי וְהָיִיתִי בְעֵינָיו כִּמְתַעְתֵּעַ
like tricking   in his eyes   and it be   my father   he feels me   perhaps

וְהֵבֵאתִי עָלַי קְלָלָה וְלֹא בְרָכָה:
blessing   and not   curse   upon me   and I the bring

12 My father peradventure will feel me, and I shall seem to him as a deceiver; and I shall bring a curse upon me, and not a blessing.

וַתֹּאמֶר לוֹ אִמּוֹ עָלַי קִלְלָתְךָ בְּנִי
my son   curse your   upon me   his mother   to him   and she said

אַךְ שְׁמַע בְּקֹלִי וְלֵךְ קַח־לִי:
to me - take   and go   in my voice   hear   only

13 And his mother said unto him, Upon me be thy curse, my son: only obey my voice, and go fetch me them.

וַיֵּלֶךְ וַיִּקַּח וַיָּבֵא לְאִמּוֹ
to his mother   and he brought   and he took   and he went

וַתַּעַשׂ אִמּוֹ מַטְעַמִּים כַּאֲשֶׁר אָהֵב אָבִיו:
his father   he loved   when   tasty meats   his mother   and she made

14 And he went, and fetched, and brought them to his mother: and his mother made savoury meat, such as his father loved.

וַתִּקַּח רִבְקָה אֶת־בִּגְדֵי עֵשָׂו בְּנָהּ הַגָּדֹל
the big   her son   Esau   clothes - that   Rebekah   and she took

הַחֲמֻדֹת אֲשֶׁר אִתָּהּ בַּבָּיִת
in house   to her   which   the coats

וַתַּלְבֵּשׁ אֶת־יַעֲקֹב בְּנָהּ הַקָּטָן׃

| the small | her son | Jacob - that | and she dressed |

15 And Rebekah took goodly raiment of her eldest son Esau, which were with her in the house, and put them upon Jacob her younger son:

וְאֵת עֹרֹת גְּדָיֵי הָעִזִּים הִלְבִּישָׁה עַל־יָדָיו

| his hands - upon | she dressed | the goats | kids | skins | and that |

וְעַל חֶלְקַת צַוָּארָיו׃

| his neck | smooth | and upon |

16 And she put the skins of the kids of the goats upon his hands, and upon the smooth of his neck:

וַתִּתֵּן אֶת־הַמַּטְעַמִּים

| the tasty meats - that | and she gave |

וְאֶת־הַלֶּחֶם אֲשֶׁר עָשָׂתָה בְּיַד יַעֲקֹב בְּנָהּ׃

| son her | Jacob | in hand | she made | which | the bread - and that |

17 And she gave the savoury meat and the bread, which she had prepared, into the hand of her son Jacob.

וַיָּבֹא אֶל־אָבִיו

| father his- unto | and he came |

וַיֹּאמֶר אָבִי וַיֹּאמֶר הִנֶּנִּי מִי אַתָּה בְּנִי׃

| my son | you | who | here I | and he answered | my father | and he said |

18 And he came unto his father, and said, My father: and he said, Here am I; who art thou, my son?

וַיֹּאמֶר יַעֲקֹב אֶל־אָבִיו אָנֹכִי עֵשָׂו בְּכֹרֶךָ

| your firstborn | Esau | I am | father his - unto | Jacob | and he said |

עָשִׂיתִי כַּאֲשֶׁר דִּבַּרְתָּ אֵלָי קוּם־נָא שְׁבָה

| sit | now - rise | unto me | you spoke | when | I did |

וְאָכְלָה מִצֵּידִי בַּעֲבוּר תְּבָרֲכַנִּי נַפְשֶׁךָ׃

| your soul | you bless me | in sake | from my game | and eat |

19 And Jacob said unto his father, I am Esau thy firstborn; I have done according as thou badest me: arise, I pray thee, sit and eat of my venison, that thy soul may bless me.

וַיֹּאמֶר יִצְחָק אֶל־בְּנוֹ מַה־זֶּה מִהַרְתָּ לִמְצֹא בְּנִי

| my son | to find | you quick | this - how | his son - unto | Isaac | and he said |

וַיֹּאמֶר כִּי הִקְרָה יְהוָה אֱלֹהֶיךָ לְפָנָי׃

| before me | your Elohim | ihvh | caused to happen | like | and he said |

20 And Isaac said unto his son, How is it that thou hast found it so quickly, my son? And he said, Because the LORD thy God brought it to me.

וַיֹּאמֶר יִצְחָק אֶל־יַעֲקֹב גְּשָׁה־נָּא

| now - come close | Jacob - unto | Isaac | and he said |

וָאֲמֻשְׁךָ֔ בְּנִ֥י הַאַתָּ֨ה זֶ֥ה בְּנִ֖י עֵשָׂ֥ו אִם־לֹֽא׃

not - if   Esau   my son   this   the you   my son   and I feel you

21 And Isaac said unto Jacob, Come near, I pray thee, that I may feel thee, my son, whether thou be my very son Esau or not.

וַיִּגַּ֧שׁ יַעֲקֹ֛ב אֶל־יִצְחָ֥ק אָבִ֖יו וַיְמֻשֵּׁ֑הוּ

and he felt him   his father   Isaac - unto   Jacob   and he went close

וַיֹּ֗אמֶר הַקֹּל֙ ק֣וֹל יַעֲקֹ֔ב וְהַיָּדַ֖יִם יְדֵ֥י עֵשָֽׂו׃

Esau   hands   and the hands   Jacob   voice   the voice   and he said

22 And Jacob went near unto Isaac his father; and he felt him, and said, The voice is Jacob's voice, but the hands are the hands of Esau.

וְלֹ֣א הִכִּיר֔וֹ כִּֽי־הָי֣וּ יָדָ֗יו כִּידֵ֛י עֵשָׂ֥ו אָחִ֖יו שְׂעִרֹ֑ת

hairy ones   his brother   Esau   like hands   his hands   they were - like   his recognizing   and not

וַֽיְבָרְכֵֽהוּ׃

and he blessed him

23 And he discerned him not, because his hands were hairy, as his brother Esau's hands: so he blessed him.

וַיֹּ֗אמֶר אַתָּ֥ה זֶ֖ה בְּנִ֣י עֵשָׂ֑ו וַיֹּ֖אמֶר אָֽנִי׃

I   and he replied   Esau   my son   this   you   and he said

24 And he said, Art thou my very son Esau? And he said, I am.

וַיֹּ֗אמֶר הַגִּ֤שָׁה לִּ֨י

to me   the come close   and he said

וְאֹֽכְלָה֙ מִצֵּ֣יד בְּנִ֔י לְמַ֖עַן תְּבָרֶכְךָ֣ נַפְשִׁ֑י

my soul   it bless you   to end   my son   from game   and I eat

וַיַּגֶּשׁ־לוֹ֙ וַיֹּאכַ֔ל וַיָּ֧בֵא ל֛וֹ יַ֖יִן וַיֵּֽשְׁתְּ׃

and he drank   wine   to him   and he brought   and he ate   to him - and he came close

25 And he said, Bring it near to me, and I will eat of my son's venison, that my soul may bless thee. And he brought it near to him, and he did eat: and he brought him wine, and he drank.

וַיֹּ֥אמֶר אֵלָ֖יו יִצְחָ֣ק אָבִ֑יו גְּשָׁה־נָּ֥א

now - come close   his father   Isaac   unto him   and he said

וּשְׁקָה־לִּ֖י בְּנִֽי׃

my son   to me - and kiss

26 And his father Isaac said unto him, Come near now, and kiss me, my son.

וַיִּגַּשׁ֙ וַיִּשַּׁק־ל֔וֹ וַיָּ֛רַח אֶת־רֵ֥יחַ בְּגָדָ֖יו

his clothes   odor - that   and he smelled   to him - and he kissed   and he came close

וַֽיְבָרְכֵ֖הוּ וַיֹּ֑אמֶר

and he said   and he blessed him

רְאֵה רֵיחַ בְּנִי כְּרֵיחַ שָׂדֶה אֲשֶׁר בֵּרְכוֹ יְהוָֹה׃

ihvh	his blessed	which	field	like odor	my son	smell	see

27 And he came near, and kissed him: and he smelled the smell of his raiment, and blessed him, and said, See, the smell of my son is as the smell of a field which the LORD hath blessed:

[ששי]

וְיִתֶּן־לְךָ הָאֱלֹהִים מִטַּל הַשָּׁמַיִם

the heavens	from dew	the Elohim	to you - and he gives

וּמִשְׁמַנֵּי הָאָרֶץ וְרֹב דָּגָן וְתִירֹשׁ׃

and grape juice	grain	and much	the earth	and from fatness

28 Therefore God give thee of the dew of heaven, and the fatness of the earth, and plenty of corn and wine:

יַעַבְדוּךָ עַמִּים

peoples	they serve you

וְיִשְׁתַּחֲוֻ [וְיִשְׁתַּחֲווּ] לְךָ לְאֻמִּים הֱוֵה גְבִיר לְאַחֶיךָ

to your brothers	mighty	be you	to peoples	to you	and they bow down

וְיִשְׁתַּחֲווּ לְךָ בְּנֵי אִמֶּךָ

your mother	your sons	to you	and they bow down

אֹרְרֶיךָ אָרוּר וּמְבָרְכֶיךָ בָּרוּךְ׃

blessed	and from your blesses	cursed	your cursing ones

29 Let people serve thee, and nations bow down to thee: be lord over thy brethren, and let thy mother's sons bow down to thee: cursed be every one that curseth thee, and blessed be he that blesseth thee.

וַיְהִי כַּאֲשֶׁר כִּלָּה יִצְחָק לְבָרֵךְ אֶת־יַעֲקֹב

Jacob - that	to bless	Isaac	he finished	when	and he was

וַיְהִי אַךְ יָצֹא יָצָא יַעֲקֹב מֵאֵת פְּנֵי יִצְחָק אָבִיו

his father	Isaac	face	from that	Jacob	he goes out	he goer out	only	and it was

וְעֵשָׂו אָחִיו בָּא מִצֵּידוֹ׃

from his hunt	he came	his brother	and Esau

30 And it came to pass, as soon as Isaac had made an end of blessing Jacob, and Jacob was yet scarce gone out from the presence of Isaac his father, that Esau his brother came in from his hunting.

וַיַּעַשׂ גַּם־הוּא מַטְעַמִּים

tasty meats	he – also	and he made

וַיָּבֵא לְאָבִיו וַיֹּאמֶר לְאָבִיו יָקֻם אָבִי

my father	he rise	to his father	and he said	to his father	and he brought

וַיֹּאכַל מִצַּיִד בְּנוֹ בַּעֲבֻר תְּבָרֲכַנִּי נַפְשֶׁךָ׃

your soul   you bless me   in sake   his son   from game   and he eat

31 And he also had made savoury meat, and brought it unto his father, and said unto his father, Let my father arise, and eat of his son's venison, that thy soul may bless me.

וַיֹּאמֶר לוֹ יִצְחָק אָבִיו מִי־אָתָּה

you - who   his father   Isaac   to him   and he said

וַיֹּאמֶר אֲנִי בִּנְךָ בְכֹרְךָ עֵשָׂו׃

Esau   your firstborn   your son   I   and he said

32 And Isaac his father said unto him, Who art thou? And he said, I am thy son, thy firstborn Esau.

וַיֶּחֱרַד יִצְחָק חֲרָדָה גְדֹלָה עַד־מְאֹד

greatly - till   big   towards tremble   Isaac   and he trembled

וַיֹּאמֶר מִי־אֵפוֹא הוּא הַצָּד־צַיִד וַיָּבֵא לִי

to me   and he brought   game - the hunter   he   possible - who   and he said

וָאֹכַל מִכֹּל בְּטֶרֶם תָּבוֹא וָאֲבָרֲכֵהוּ גַּם־בָּרוּךְ יִהְיֶה׃

he will be   blessed - also   and I blessed him   you came   in before   from all   and I ate

33 And Isaac trembled very exceedingly, and said, Who? where is he that hath taken venison, and brought it me, and I have eaten of all before thou camest, and have blessed him? yea, and he shall be blessed.

כִּשְׁמֹעַ עֵשָׂו אֶת־דִּבְרֵי אָבִיו

his father   speakings - that   Esau   like heard

וַיִּצְעַק צְעָקָה גְדֹלָה וּמָרָה עַד־מְאֹד

greatly - till   and bitter   big   cry   and he cried

וַיֹּאמֶר לְאָבִיו בָּרֲכֵנִי גַם־אָנִי אָבִי׃

my father   me - also   bless me   to his father   and he said

34 And when Esau heard the words of his father, he cried with a great and exceeding bitter cry, and said unto his father, Bless me, even me also, O my father.

וַיֹּאמֶר בָּא אָחִיךָ בְּמִרְמָה וַיִּקַּח בִּרְכָתֶךָ׃

your blessing   and he took   in deceit   your brother   came   and he said

35 And he said, Thy brother came with subtlety, and hath taken away thy blessing.

וַיֹּאמֶר הֲכִי קָרָא שְׁמוֹ יַעֲקֹב

Jacob   his name   he called   the like   and he said

וַיַּעְקְבֵנִי זֶה פַעֲמַיִם אֶת־בְּכֹרָתִי לָקָח

took   my birthright - that   two times   this   and he deceived me

וְהִנֵּה עַתָּה לָקַח בִּרְכָתִי

my blessing   he took   now   and here

וַיֹּאמֶר הֲלֹא־אָצַלְתָּ לִּי בְּרָכָה׃
blessing	to me	you reserved – the not	and he said

36 And he said, Is not he rightly named Jacob? for he hath supplanted me these two
times: he took away my birthright; and, behold, now he hath taken away my blessing.
And he said, Hast thou not reserved a blessing for me?

וַיַּעַן		יִצְחָק וַיֹּאמֶר לְעֵשָׂו
to Esau	and he said	Isaac	and he answered

הֵן גְּבִיר שַׂמְתִּיו לָךְ
to you	I put his	mighty	thus

וְאֶת־כָּל־אֶחָיו נָתַתִּי לוֹ לַעֲבָדִים וְדָגָן וְתִירֹשׁ סְמַכְתִּיו
his sustenance	and grape juice	and grain	to servant ones	to him	I gave	his brothers - all - and that

וּלְכָה אֵפוֹא מָה אֶעֱשֶׂה בְּנִי׃
my son	I do	what	how	and to thus

37 And Isaac answered and said unto Esau, Behold, I have made him thy lord, and all
his brethren have I given to him for servants; and with corn and wine have I sustained
him: and what shall I do now unto thee, my son?

וַיֹּאמֶר עֵשָׂו אֶל־אָבִיו
his father - unto	Esau	and he said

הַבְרָכָה אַחַת הִוא־לְךָ אָבִי בָּרֲכֵנִי גַם־אָנִי אָבִי
my father	I - also	bless me	my father	to you - it	one	the blessing

וַיִּשָּׂא עֵשָׂו קֹלוֹ וַיֵּבְךְּ׃
and he wept	his voice	Esau	and he lifted

38 And Esau said unto his father, Hast thou but one blessing, my father? bless me, even
me also, O my father. And Esau lifted up his voice, and wept.

וַיַּעַן		יִצְחָק אָבִיו
his father	Isaac	and he answered

וַיֹּאמֶר אֵלָיו הִנֵּה מִשְׁמַנֵּי הָאָרֶץ יִהְיֶה מוֹשָׁבֶךָ
your dwelling	it be	the earth	from oils	here	unto him	and he said

וּמִטַּל הַשָּׁמַיִם מֵעָל׃
from above	the heavens	and dew

39 And Isaac his father answered and said unto him, Behold, thy dwelling shall be the
fatness of the earth, and of the dew of heaven from above;

וְעַל־חַרְבְּךָ תִחְיֶה וְאֶת־אָחִיךָ תַּעֲבֹד
you will serve	your brother - and that	you will live	your sword - and upon

וְהָיָה כַּאֲשֶׁר תָּרִיד וּפָרַקְתָּ עֻלּוֹ מֵעַל צַוָּארֶךָ׃
your neck	from upon	his yoke	and you will break off	you will dominate	when	and it be

40 And by thy sword shalt thou live, and shalt serve thy brother; and it shall come to
pass when thou shalt have the dominion, that thou shalt break his yoke from off thy

neck.

וַיִּשְׂטֹם   עֵשָׂו   אֶת־יַעֲקֹב   עַל־הַבְּרָכָה   אֲשֶׁר   בֵּרֲכוֹ   אָבִיו
his father   his blessing   which   the blessing - upon   Jacob - that   Esau   and he held grudge

וַיֹּאמֶר   עֵשָׂו   בְּלִבּוֹ   יִקְרְבוּ   יְמֵי   אֵבֶל   אָבִי
my father   mourning   days   they approaching   in his heart   Esau   and he said

וְאַהַרְגָה   אֶת־יַעֲקֹב   אָחִי׃
my brother   Jacob - that   and I the kill

41 And Esau hated Jacob because of the blessing wherewith his father blessed him: and Esau said in his heart, The days of mourning for my father are at hand; then will I slay my brother Jacob.

וַיֻּגַּד   לְרִבְקָה   אֶת־דִּבְרֵי   עֵשָׂו   בְּנָהּ   הַגָּדֹל
the big   her son   Esau   speakings - that   to Rebekah   and he was told

וַתִּשְׁלַח   וַתִּקְרָא   לְיַעֲקֹב   בְּנָהּ   הַקָּטָן
the small   her son   to Jacob   and she called   and she sent

וַתֹּאמֶר   אֵלָיו   הִנֵּה   עֵשָׂו   אָחִיךָ   מִתְנַחֵם   לְךָ   לְהָרְגֶךָ׃
to the your killer   to you   consoling himself   your brother   Esau   here   unto him   and she said

42 And these words of Esau her elder son were told to Rebekah: and she sent and called Jacob her younger son, and said unto him, Behold, thy brother Esau, as touching thee, doth comfort himself, purposing to kill thee.

וְעַתָּה   בְנִי   שְׁמַע   בְּקֹלִי
in my voice   hear   my son   and now

וְקוּם   בְּרַח־לְךָ   אֶל־לָבָן   אָחִי   חָרָנָה׃
towards Haran   my brother   Laban - unto   to you - flee   and rise

43 Now therefore, my son, obey my voice; and arise, flee thou to Laban my brother to Haran;

וְיָשַׁבְתָּ   עִמּוֹ   יָמִים   אֲחָדִים   עַד   אֲשֶׁר־תָּשׁוּב   חֲמַת   אָחִיךָ׃
your brother   violence   you turn - which   until   several ones   days   with him   and you dwell

44 And tarry with him a few days, until thy brother's fury turn away;

עַד־שׁוּב   אַף־אָחִיךָ   מִמְּךָ
from you   your brother - anger   turn - till

וְשָׁכַח   אֵת   אֲשֶׁר־עָשִׂיתָ   לּוֹ
to him   you did - which   that   and he forgets

וְשָׁלַחְתִּי   וּלְקַחְתִּיךָ   מִשָּׁם   לָמָה   אֶשְׁכַּל   גַּם־שְׁנֵיכֶם   יוֹם   אֶחָד׃
one   day   two of you - also   I lose   why   from there   and I take you   and I will send

45 Until thy brother's anger turn away from thee, and he forget that which thou hast done to him: then I will send, and fetch thee from thence: why should I be deprived also of you both in one day?

וַתֹּאמֶר רִבְקָה אֶל־יִצְחָק קַצְתִּי בְחַיַּי מִפְּנֵי בְּנוֹת חֵת

Heth   daughters   from face   in my life   I disgusted   Isaac - unto   Rebecca   and she said

אִם־לֹקֵחַ יַעֲקֹב אִשָּׁה מִבְּנוֹת־חֵת כָּאֵלֶּה מִבְּנוֹת הָאָרֶץ

the earth   from daughters   like these   Heth - from daughters   wife   Jacob   to taker - if

לָמָּה לִּי חַיִּים:

life   to me   to what

46 And Rebekah said to Isaac, I am weary of my life because of the daughters of Heth: if Jacob take a wife of the daughters of Heth, such as these which are of the daughters of the land, what good shall my life do.

CHAPTER 28

ספר בראשית פרק כח

וַיִּקְרָא יִצְחָק אֶל־יַעֲקֹב וַיְבָרֶךְ אֹתוֹ

to him   and he blessed   Jacob - unto   Isaac   and he called

וַיְצַוֵּהוּ וַיֹּאמֶר לוֹ לֹא־תִקַּח אִשָּׁה מִבְּנוֹת כְּנָעַן:

Canaan   from daughters   wife   you take - not   to him   and he said   and he commanded him

1 And Isaac called Jacob, and blessed him, and charged him, and said unto him, Thou shalt not take a wife of the daughters of Canaan.

קוּם לֵךְ פַּדֶּנָה אֲרָם בֵּיתָה בְתוּאֵל אֲבִי אִמֶּךְ

your mother   father   Bethuel   house   aram   Padan   go   rise

וְקַח־לְךָ מִשָּׁם אִשָּׁה מִבְּנוֹת לָבָן אֲחִי אִמֶּךְ:

your mother   brother   Laban   from daughters   wife   from there   to you - and take

2 Arise, go to Padan-aram, to the house of Bethuel thy mother's father; and take thee a wife from thence of the daughters of Laban thy mother's brother.

וְאֵל שַׁדַּי יְבָרֵךְ אֹתְךָ

to you   he blesses you   Shaddai   and El

וְיַפְרְךָ וְיַרְבֶּךָ וְהָיִיתָ לִקְהַל עַמִּים:

peoples   to assembly   and you be   and he increases you   and he fruitful you

3 And God Almighty bless thee, and make thee fruitful, and multiply thee, that thou mayest be a multitude of people;

וְיִתֶּן־לְךָ אֶת־בִּרְכַּת אַבְרָהָם לְךָ

to you   Abraham   blessing - that   to you - and he gives

וּלְזַרְעֲךָ אִתָּךְ לְרִשְׁתְּךָ אֶת־אֶרֶץ מְגֻרֶיךָ

from your soujourns   land - that   to you inheriting   with you   and to your seed

אֲשֶׁר־נָתַן אֱלֹהִים לְאַבְרָהָם:

to Abraham   Elohim   he gave – which

4 And give thee the blessing of Abraham, to thee, and to thy seed with thee; that thou mayest inherit the land wherein thou art a stranger, which God gave unto Abraham.

[שביעי]

וַיִּשְׁלַח יִצְחָק אֶת־יַעֲקֹב וַיֵּלֶךְ פַּדֶּנָה אֲרָם אֶל־לָבָן
Laban - unto   aram   Padan   and he went   Jacob - that   Issac   and he sent

בֶּן־בְּתוּאֵל הָאֲרַמִּי אֲחִי רִבְקָה אֵם יַעֲקֹב וְעֵשָׂו׃
and Esau   Jacob   mother   Rebekah   brother   the Aramean   Bethuel - son

5 And Isaac sent away Jacob: and he went to Padan-aram unto Laban, son of Bethuel the Syrian, the brother of Rebekah, Jacob's and Esau's mother.

וַיַּרְא עֵשָׂו כִּי־בֵרַךְ יִצְחָק אֶת־יַעֲקֹב
Jacob - that   Isaac   he blessed – like   Esau   and he saw

וְשִׁלַּח אֹתוֹ פַּדֶּנָה אֲרָם
aram   Padan   to him   and he sent

לָקַחַת־לוֹ מִשָּׁם אִשָּׁה בְּבָרֲכוֹ אֹתוֹ
to him   in his blessing   wife   from there   to him - to take

וַיְצַו עָלָיו לֵאמֹר לֹא־תִקַּח אִשָּׁה מִבְּנוֹת כְּנָעַן׃
Canaan   from daughters   wife   you take - not   to say   upon him   and he commanded

6 When Esau saw that Isaac had blessed Jacob, and sent him away to Padan-aram, to take him a wife from thence; and that as he blessed him he gave him a charge, saying, Thou shalt not take a wife of the daughters of Canaan;

[מפטיר]

וַיִּשְׁמַע יַעֲקֹב אֶל־אָבִיו וְאֶל־אִמּוֹ
his mother - and unto   his father - unto   Jacob   and he heard

וַיֵּלֶךְ פַּדֶּנָה אֲרָם׃
aram   Padan   and he went

7 And that Jacob obeyed his father and his mother, and was gone to Padan-aram;

וַיַּרְא עֵשָׂו
Esau   and he saw

כִּי רָעוֹת בְּנוֹת כְּנָעַן בְּעֵינֵי יִצְחָק אָבִיו׃
his father   Isaac   in eyes   Canaan   daughters   bad ones   like

8 And Esau seeing that the daughters of Canaan pleased not Isaac his father;

וַיֵּלֶךְ עֵשָׂו אֶל־יִשְׁמָעֵאל
Ishmael - unto   Esau   and he went

וַיִּקַּח אֶת־מַחֲלַת בַּת־יִשְׁמָעֵאל בֶּן־אַבְרָהָם אֲחוֹת נְבָיוֹת
Nebajoth   sister   Abraham - son   Ishmael - daughter   Mahalath - that   and he took

עַל־נָשָׁיו לוֹ לְאִשָּׁה׃
to wife   to him   his women - upon

9 Then went Esau unto Ishmael, and took unto the wives which he had Mahalath the daughter of Ishmael Abraham's son, the sister of Nebajoth, to be his wife.

ס ס ס

7 Vᴀʏᴇɪᴛᴢᴇɪ

[פרשת ויצא]

Cʜᴀᴘᴛᴇʀ 28 ᴄᴏɴᴛ

וַיֵּצֵא יַעֲקֹב מִבְּאֵר שָׁבַע וַיֵּלֶךְ חָרָנָה:

toward Haran   and he went   Sheba   from Beer   Jacob   and he went out

10 And Jacob went out from Beer-sheba, and went toward Haran.

וַיִּפְגַּע בַּמָּקוֹם וַיָּלֶן שָׁם כִּי־בָא הַשֶּׁמֶשׁ

the sun   came – like   there   and he spent night   in place   and he touched

וַיִּקַּח מֵאַבְנֵי הַמָּקוֹם

the place   from stones   and he took

וַיָּשֶׂם מְרַאֲשֹׁתָיו וַיִּשְׁכַּב בַּמָּקוֹם הַהוּא:

the it   in place   and he lay down   from his pillow   and he put them

11 And he lighted upon a certain place, and tarried there all night, because the sun was set; and he took of the stones of that place, and put *them for* his pillows, and lay down in that place to sleep.

וַיַּחֲלֹם וְהִנֵּה סֻלָּם מֻצָּב אַרְצָה

towards earth   set up   ladder   and here   and he dreamed

וְרֹאשׁוֹ מַגִּיעַ הַשָּׁמַיְמָה וְהִנֵּה מַלְאֲכֵי אֱלֹהִים עֹלִים

ascending ones   Elohim   angels   and here   towards the heavens   touching   and it's top

וְיֹרְדִים בּוֹ:

in it   and descending ones

12 And he dreamed, and behold a ladder set up on the earth, and the top of it reached to heaven: and behold the angels of God ascending and descending on it.

וְהִנֵּה יְהֹוָה נִצָּב עָלָיו

upon him   stood   ihvh   and here

וַיֹּאמַר אֲנִי יְהֹוָה אֱלֹהֵי אַבְרָהָם אָבִיךָ וֵאלֹהֵי יִצְחָק

Issac   and Elohim   your father   Abraham   Elohim   ihvh   I   and he said

הָאָרֶץ אֲשֶׁר אַתָּה שֹׁכֵב עָלֶיהָ

upon it   you lye   you   which   the earth

לְךָ אֶתְּנֶנָּה וּלְזַרְעֶךָ:

and to your seed   I will give it   to you

13 And, behold, the LORD stood above it, and said, I *am*the LORD God of Abraham thy father, and the God of Isaac: the land whereon thou liest, to thee will I give it, and to thy seed;

וְהָיָה זַרְעֲךָ כַּעֲפַר הָאָרֶץ

the earth   like dust   your seed   and it will be

וּפָרַצְתָּ֙   יָ֣מָּה   וָקֵ֧דְמָה   וְצָפֹ֛נָה   וָנֶ֑גְבָּה
and you will spread   towards right   and towards east   and towards north   and towards south

וְנִבְרְכ֥וּ   בְךָ֛   כָּל־מִשְׁפְּחֹ֥ת   הָאֲדָמָ֖ה   וּבְזַרְעֶֽךָ׃
and they will be blessed   in it   families – all   the soil   and in your seed

14 And thy seed shall be as the dust of the earth, and thou shalt spread abroad to the
west, and to the east, and to the north, and to the south: and in thee and in thy seed
shall all the families of the earth be blessed.

וְהִנֵּ֨ה   אָנֹכִ֜י   עִמָּ֗ךְ   וּשְׁמַרְתִּ֙יךָ֙   בְּכֹ֣ל   אֲשֶׁר־תֵּלֵ֔ךְ
and here   I am   with you   and will be your heeder   in all   you go – which

וַהֲשִׁ֣בֹתִ֔יךָ   אֶל־הָאֲדָמָ֖ה   הַזֹּ֑את
and the you will return   the soil – unto   the this

כִּ֚י   לֹ֣א   אֶֽעֱזָבְךָ֔
like   not   I will leave you

עַ֚ד   אֲשֶׁ֣ר   אִם־עָשִׂ֔יתִי   אֵ֥ת   אֲשֶׁר־דִּבַּ֖רְתִּי   לָֽךְ׃
till   which   I did – with   that   I spoke – which   to you

15 And, behold, I am with thee, and will keep thee in all places whither thou goest, and
will bring thee again into this land; for I will not leave thee, until I have done that which
I have spoken to thee of.

וַיִּיקַ֣ץ   יַעֲקֹב֮   מִשְּׁנָתוֹ֒
and he awoke   Jacob   from his sleep

וַיֹּ֕אמֶר   אָכֵן֙   יֵ֣שׁ   יְהוָ֔ה   בַּמָּק֖וֹם   הַזֶּ֑ה
and he said   surely   this is   ihvh   in place   the this

וְאָנֹכִ֖י   לֹ֥א   יָדָֽעְתִּי׃
and I am   not   I knew

16 And Jacob awaked out of his sleep, and he said, Surely the LORD is in this place;
and I knew it not.

וַיִּירָא֙   וַיֹּאמַ֔ר   מַה־נּוֹרָ֖א   הַמָּק֣וֹם
and he was afraid   and he said   awesome – what   the place

הַזֶּ֑ה   אֵ֣ין   זֶ֗ה   כִּ֚י   אִם־בֵּ֣ית   אֱלֹהִ֔ים
the this   isn't   this   like   house – with   Elohim

וְזֶ֖ה   שַׁ֥עַר   הַשָּׁמָֽיִם׃
and this   gate   the heavens

17 And he was afraid, and said, How dreadful is this place! this is none other but the
house of God, and this is the gate of heaven.

וַיַּשְׁכֵּ֨ם   יַעֲקֹ֜ב   בַּבֹּ֗קֶר
and he rose up   Jacob   in mourning

וַיִּקַּח אֶת־הָאֶבֶן אֲשֶׁר־שָׂם מְרַאֲשֹׁתָיו

from his pillow   put – which   the stone – that   and he took

וַיָּשֶׂם אֹתָהּ מַצֵּבָה וַיִּצֹק שֶׁמֶן עַל־רֹאשָׁהּ:

towards top – upon   oil   and he poured   pillar   to it   and he set

18 And Jacob rose up early in the morning, and took the stone that he had put for his
pillows, and set it up for a pillar, and poured oil upon the top of it.

וַיִּקְרָא אֶת־שֵׁם־הַמָּקוֹם הַהוּא בֵּית־אֵל

El – house   the it   the place – name – that   and he called

וְאוּלָם לוּז שֵׁם־הָעִיר לָרִאשֹׁנָה:

to first   the city – name   Luz   and although

19 And he called the name of that place Beth-el: but the name of that city was called
Luz at the first.

וַיִּדַּר יַעֲקֹב נֶדֶר לֵאמֹר אִם־יִהְיֶה אֱלֹהִים עִמָּדִי

with me   Elohim   it will be – with   to say   vow   Jacob   and he vowed

וּשְׁמָרַנִי בַּדֶּרֶךְ הַזֶּה אֲשֶׁר אָנֹכִי הוֹלֵךְ

walk   I am   which   the this   in way   and will heed me

וְנָתַן־לִי לֶחֶם לֶאֱכֹל וּבֶגֶד לִלְבֹּשׁ:

to dress up   and clothes   to eat   bread   to me – and will give

20 And Jacob vowed a vow, saying, If God will be with me, and will keep me in this way
that I go, and will give me bread to eat, and raiment to put on,

וְשַׁבְתִּי בְשָׁלוֹם אֶל־בֵּית אָבִי וְהָיָה יְהֹוָה לִי לֵאלֹהִים:

to Elohim   to me   ihvh   and it will be   my father   house - unto   in peace   and my returning

21 So that I come again to my father's house in peace; then shall the LORD be my God:

וְהָאֶבֶן הַזֹּאת אֲשֶׁר־שַׂמְתִּי מַצֵּבָה יִהְיֶה בֵּית אֱלֹהִים

Elohim   house   it will be   pillar   I put – which   the this   and the stone

וְכֹל אֲשֶׁר תִּתֶּן־לִי עַשֵּׂר אֲעַשְּׂרֶנּוּ לָךְ:

to you   I will tenth   ten   to me – it will give   which   and all

22 And this stone, which I have set for a pillar, shall be God's house: and of all that
thou shalt give me I will surely give the tenth unto thee.

CHAPTER 29

ספר בראשית פרק כט

[שני]

וַיִּשָּׂא יַעֲקֹב רַגְלָיו וַיֵּלֶךְ אַרְצָה בְנֵי־קֶדֶם:

east – sons   towards land   and he went   his feet   Jacob   and he lifted

1 Then Jacob went on his journey, and came into the land of the people of the east.

וַיַּרְא וְהִנֵּה בְאֵר בַּשָּׂדֶה

in field   well   and here   and he saw

וְהִנֵּה־שָׁם שְׁלֹשָׁה עֶדְרֵי־צֹאן רֹבְצִים עָלֶיהָ
upon it   lying   sheep – flocks   three   there – and here

כִּי מִן־הַבְּאֵר הַהִוא יַשְׁקוּ הָעֲדָרִים
the flocks   they watered   the it   the well – from   like

וְהָאֶבֶן גְּדֹלָה עַל־פִּי הַבְּאֵר:
the well   mouth – upon   great   and the stone

2 And he looked, and behold a well in the field, and, lo, there were three flocks of sheep lying by it; for out of that well they watered the flocks: and a great stone was upon the well's mouth.

וְנֶאֶסְפוּ־שָׁמָּה כָּל־הָעֲדָרִים
flocks – all   towards there – and they gathered

וְגָלְלוּ אֶת־הָאֶבֶן מֵעַל פִּי הַבְּאֵר
the well   mouth   from upon   the stone – that   and they rolled it

וְהִשְׁקוּ אֶת־הַצֹּאן
the sheep – that   and they watered

וְהֵשִׁיבוּ אֶת־הָאֶבֶן עַל־פִּי הַבְּאֵר לִמְקֹמָהּ:
to its place   the well   mouth – upon   the stone – that   and they returned

3 And thither were all the flocks gathered: and they rolled the stone from the well's mouth, and watered the sheep, and put the stone again upon the well's mouth in his place.

וַיֹּאמֶר לָהֶם יַעֲקֹב אַחַי מֵאַיִן אַתֶּם
you   from where   my brothers   Jacob   to them   and he said

וַיֹּאמְרוּ מֵחָרָן אֲנָחְנוּ:
we   from Haran   and they said

4 And Jacob said unto them, My brethren, whence be ye? And they said, Of Haran are we.

וַיֹּאמֶר לָהֶם הַיְדַעְתֶּם אֶת־לָבָן בֶּן־נָחוֹר
Nahor - son   Laben – that   the know you   to them   and he said

וַיֹּאמְרוּ יָדָעְנוּ:
we know   and they said

5 And he said unto them, Know ye Laban the son of Nahor? And they said, We know him.

וַיֹּאמֶר לָהֶם הֲשָׁלוֹם לוֹ וַיֹּאמְרוּ שָׁלוֹם
peace   and they said   to him   the peace   to them   and he said

וְהִנֵּה רָחֵל בִּתּוֹ בָּאָה עִם־הַצֹּאן:
the sheep – with   she comes   his daughter   Rachel   and here

6 And he said unto them, Is he well? And they said, He is well: and, behold, Rachel his daughter cometh with the sheep.

וַיֹּאמֶר הֵן עוֹד הַיּוֹם גָּדוֹל
and he said   thus   still   the day   great

לֹא־עֵת הֵאָסֵף הַמִּקְנֶה
time – not   the gather   the cattle

הַשְׁקוּ הַצֹּאן וּלְכוּ רְעוּ:
the water it   the sheep   and go   shepherding

7 And he said, Lo, it is yet high day, neither is it time that the cattle should be gathered together: water ye the sheep, and go and feed them.

וַיֹּאמְרוּ לֹא נוּכַל עַד אֲשֶׁר יֵאָסְפוּ כָּל־הָעֲדָרִים
and they said   not   we able   till   which   they gather   the flocks – all

וְגָלֲלוּ אֶת־הָאֶבֶן מֵעַל פִּי הַבְּאֵר וְהִשְׁקִינוּ הַצֹּאן:
and they roll   the stone – that   from upon   mouth   the well   and we water   the sheep

8 And they said, We cannot, until all the flocks be gathered together, and till they roll the stone from the well's mouth; then we water the sheep.

עוֹדֶנּוּ מְדַבֵּר עִמָּם
still   speaking   with them

וְרָחֵל בָּאָה עִם־הַצֹּאן אֲשֶׁר לְאָבִיהָ
and Rachel   came   the sheep – with   which   to her father

כִּי רֹעָה הִוא:
like   shepherd   she

9 And while he yet spake with them, Rachel came with her father's sheep: for she kept them.

וַיְהִי כַּאֲשֶׁר רָאָה יַעֲקֹב אֶת־רָחֵל בַּת־לָבָן אֲחִי אִמּוֹ
and it was   when   she saw   Jacob   Rachel – that   Laban – daughter   brother   his mother

וְאֶת־צֹאן לָבָן אֲחִי אִמּוֹ
sheep – and that   Laban   brother   his mother

וַיִּגַּשׁ יַעֲקֹב וַיָּגֶל אֶת־הָאֶבֶן מֵעַל פִּי הַבְּאֵר
and he touched   Jacob   and he rolled   the stone – that   from upon   mouth   the well

וַיַּשְׁקְ אֶת־צֹאן לָבָן אֲחִי אִמּוֹ:
and he watered   sheep – that   Laban   brother   his mother

10 And it came to pass, when Jacob saw Rachel the daughter of Laban his mother's brother, and the sheep of Laban his mother's brother, that Jacob went near, and rolled the stone from the well's mouth, and watered the flock of Laban his mother's brother.

וַיִּשַּׁק יַעֲקֹב לְרָחֵל וַיִּשָּׂא אֶת־קֹלוֹ וַיֵּבְךְּ:
and he kissed   Jacob   to Rachel   and he lifted   his voice – that   and he wept

11 And Jacob kissed Rachel, and lifted up his voice, and wept.

וַיַּגֵּד יַעֲקֹב לְרָחֵל כִּי אֲחִי אָבִיהָ הוּא

he   her father   brother   like   to Rachel   Jacob   and he told

וְכִי בֶן־רִבְקָה הוּא

he   Rebeka – son   and like

וַתָּרָץ וַתַּגֵּד לְאָבִיהָ:

to her father   and she told   and she ran

12 And Jacob told Rachel that he was her father's brother, and that he was Rebekah's son: and she ran and told her father.

וַיְהִי כִשְׁמֹעַ לָבָן אֶת־שֵׁמַע יַעֲקֹב בֶּן־אֲחֹתוֹ

his sister – son   Jacob   hearing – that   Laban   like heard   and it was

וַיָּרָץ לִקְרָאתוֹ וַיְחַבֶּק־לוֹ

to him - and he embraced   to his meeting   and he ran

וַיְנַשֶּׁק־לוֹ וַיְבִיאֵהוּ אֶל־בֵּיתוֹ

his house – unto   and he brought him   to him – and he kissed

וַיְסַפֵּר לְלָבָן אֵת כָּל־הַדְּבָרִים הָאֵלֶּה:

the these   the speakings – all   that   to Laban   and he storied

13 And it came to pass, when Laban heard the tidings of Jacob his sister's son, that he ran to meet him, and embraced him, and kissed him, and brought him to his house. And he told Laban all these things.

וַיֹּאמֶר לוֹ לָבָן אַךְ עַצְמִי וּבְשָׂרִי אָתָּה

you   and my flesh   my bone   surely   Laban   to him   and he said

וַיֵּשֶׁב עִמּוֹ חֹדֶשׁ יָמִים:

days   month   with him   and he dwelled

14 And Laban said to him, Surely thou art my bone and my flesh. And he abode with him the space of a month.

וַיֹּאמֶר לָבָן לְיַעֲקֹב הֲכִי־אָחִי אַתָּה

you   my brother – the like   to Jacob   Laban   and he said

וַעֲבַדְתַּנִי חִנָּם הַגִּידָה לִּי מַה־מַּשְׂכֻּרְתֶּךָ:

your wages – what   to me   the tell   without cause   and you serve me

15 And Laban said unto Jacob, Because thou art my brother, shouldest thou therefore serve me for nought? tell me, what shall thy wages be?

וּלְלָבָן שְׁתֵּי בָנוֹת שֵׁם הַגְּדֹלָה לֵאָה

Lea   the big   name   daughter   two   and to Laban

וְשֵׁם הַקְּטַנָּה רָחֵל:

Rachel   the small   and name

16 And Laban had two daughters: the name of the elder was Leah, and the name of the younger was Rachel.

וְעֵינֵי לֵאָה רַכּוֹת

tender   Lea   and eyes

וְרָחֵל הָיְתָה יְפַת־תֹּאַר וִיפַת מַרְאֶה:

appearance   and beautiful   countenance - beautiful   she was   and Rachel

17 Leah was tender eyed; but Rachel was beautiful and well favoured.

[שלישי]

וַיֶּאֱהַב יַעֲקֹב אֶת־רָחֵל

Rachel – that   Jacob   and he loved

וַיֹּאמֶר אֶעֱבָדְךָ שֶׁבַע שָׁנִים בְּרָחֵל בִּתְּךָ הַקְּטַנָּה:

the small   your daughter   in Rachel   years   seven   I will serve you   and he said

18 And Jacob loved Rachel; and said, I will serve thee seven years for Rachel thy younger daughter.

וַיֹּאמֶר לָבָן טוֹב תִּתִּי אֹתָהּ לָךְ

to you   her   I give   good   Laban   and he said

מִתִּתִּי אֹתָהּ לְאִישׁ אַחֵר שְׁבָה עִמָּדִי:

with me   sit   another   to man   her   from my giving

19 And Laban said, It is better that I give her to thee, than that I should give her to another man: abide with me.

וַיַּעֲבֹד יַעֲקֹב בְּרָחֵל שֶׁבַע שָׁנִים

years   seven   in Rachel   Jacob   and he served

וַיִּהְיוּ בְעֵינָיו כְּיָמִים אֲחָדִים בְּאַהֲבָתוֹ אֹתָהּ:

to her   in his love   few ones   like days   in his eyes   and they were

20 And Jacob served seven years for Rachel; and they seemed unto him but a few days, for the love he had to her.

וַיֹּאמֶר יַעֲקֹב אֶל־לָבָן הָבָה אֶת־אִשְׁתִּי

my wife – that   the come   Laban – unto   Jacob   and he said

כִּי מָלְאוּ יָמָי וְאָבוֹאָה אֵלֶיהָ:

unto her   and I come   days   they filled   like

21 And Jacob said unto Laban, Give me my wife, for my days are fulfilled, that I may go in unto her.

וַיֶּאֱסֹף לָבָן אֶת־כָּל־אַנְשֵׁי הַמָּקוֹם וַיַּעַשׂ מִשְׁתֶּה:

feast   and he did   the place   men – all – that   Laban   and he gathered

22 And Laban gathered together all the men of the place, and made a feast.

וַיְהִי בָעֶרֶב וַיִּקַּח אֶת־לֵאָה בִתּוֹ

his daughter   Lea – that   and he took   in evening   and it was

וַיָּבֵא אֹתָהּ אֵלָיו וַיָּבֹא אֵלֶיהָ:

unto her   and he came   unto him   to her   and he brought

23 And it came to pass in the evening, that he took Leah his daughter, and brought her to him; and he went in unto her.

וַיִּתֵּן לָבָן לָהּ אֶת־זִלְפָּה שִׁפְחָתוֹ לְלֵאָה בִתּוֹ שִׁפְחָה׃

| maid | his daughter | to Lea | his maid | Zilpah – that | to her | Laban | and he gave |

24 And Laban gave unto his daughter Leah Zilpah his maid for an handmaid.

וַיְהִי בַבֹּקֶר וְהִנֵּה־הִוא לֵאָה

| Lea | she – and here | in morning | and it was |

וַיֹּאמֶר אֶל־לָבָן מַה־זֹּאת עָשִׂיתָ לִּי

| to me | you did | this – what | Laban – unto | and he said |

הֲלֹא בְרָחֵל עָבַדְתִּי עִמָּךְ

| with you | I served | in Rachel | the not |

וְלָמָּה רִמִּיתָנִי׃

| you tricked me | and why |

25 And it came to pass, that in the morning, behold, it was Leah: and he said to Laban, What is this thou hast done unto me? did not I serve with thee for Rachel? wherefore then hast thou beguiled me?

וַיֹּאמֶר לָבָן לֹא־יֵעָשֶׂה כֵן בִּמְקוֹמֵנוּ

| in our place | thus | it done – not | Laban | and he said |

לָתֵת הַצְּעִירָה לִפְנֵי הַבְּכִירָה׃

| the first born | before | younger | to give |

26 And Laban said, It must not be so done in our country, to give the younger before the firstborn.

מַלֵּא שְׁבֻעַ זֹאת

| this | week | fill |

וְנִתְּנָה לְךָ גַּם־אֶת־זֹאת בַּעֲבֹדָה

| in service | this – that – also | to you | and we give |

אֲשֶׁר תַּעֲבֹד עִמָּדִי עוֹד שֶׁבַע־שָׁנִים אֲחֵרוֹת׃

| other ones | years – seven | again | with me | you serve | which |

27 Fulfil her week, and we will give thee this also for the service which thou shalt serve with me yet seven other years.

וַיַּעַשׂ יַעֲקֹב כֵּן וַיְמַלֵּא שְׁבֻעַ זֹאת

| this | week | and he filled | thus | Jacob | and he did |

וַיִּתֶּן־לוֹ אֶת־רָחֵל בִּתּוֹ לוֹ לְאִשָּׁה׃

| to wife | to him | his daughter | Rachel – that | to him - and he gave |

28 And Jacob did so, and fulfilled her week: and he gave him Rachel his daughter to wife also.

וַיִּתֵּן לָבָן לְרָחֵל בִּתּוֹ אֶת־בִּלְהָה שִׁפְחָתוֹ לָהּ לְשִׁפְחָה:

| to maid | to her | his handmaid | Bilhah – that | his daughter | to Rachel | Laban | and he gave |

29 And Laban gave to Rachel his daughter Bilhah his handmaid to be her maid.

וַיָּבֹא גַּם אֶל־רָחֵל וַיֶּאֱהַב גַּם־אֶת־רָחֵל מִלֵּאָה

| from Leah | Rachel – that – also | and he loved | Rachel – unto | also | and he came |

וַיַּעֲבֹד עִמּוֹ עוֹד שֶׁבַע־שָׁנִים אֲחֵרוֹת:

| other ones | years – seven | again | with him | and he served |

30 And he went in also unto Rachel, and he loved also Rachel more than Leah, and served with him yet seven other years.

וַיַּרְא יְהֹוָה כִּי־שְׂנוּאָה לֵאָה

| Lea | hated – like | ihvh | and he saw |

וַיִּפְתַּח אֶת־רַחְמָהּ

| womb – that | and he opened |

וְרָחֵל עֲקָרָה:

| barren | and Rachel |

31 And when the LORD saw that Leah was hated, he opened her womb: but Rachel was barren.

וַתַּהַר לֵאָה וַתֵּלֶד בֵּן וַתִּקְרָא שְׁמוֹ רְאוּבֵן

| Ruben | his name | and she called | son | and she begat | Lea | and she conceived |

כִּי אָמְרָה כִּי־רָאָה יְהֹוָה בְּעָנְיִי

| in my affliction | ihvh | saw – like | she said | like |

כִּי עַתָּה יֶאֱהָבַנִי אִישִׁי:

| my man | he will love me | now | like |

32 And Leah conceived, and bare a son, and she called his name Reuben: for she said, Surely the LORD hath looked upon my affliction; now therefore my husband will love me.

וַתַּהַר עוֹד וַתֵּלֶד בֵּן

| son | and begot | again | and conceived |

וַתֹּאמֶר כִּי־שָׁמַע יְהֹוָה כִּי־שְׂנוּאָה אָנֹכִי

| I am | hated – like | ihvh | heard – like | and she said |

וַיִּתֶּן־לִי גַּם־אֶת־זֶה וַתִּקְרָא שְׁמוֹ שִׁמְעוֹן:

| Simeon | his name | and she called | this – that – also | to me – and he gave |

33 And she conceived again, and bare a son; and said, Because the LORD hath heard that I was hated, he hath therefore given me this son also: and she called his name Simeon.

וַתַּהַר עוֹד וַתֵּלֶד בֵּן

| son | and she begat | again | and she conceived |

אֵלַי אִישִׁי יִלָּוֶה הַפַּעַם עַתָּה וַתֹּאמֶר

unto me	my man	he obligated	the again time	now	and she said

בָּנִים שְׁלֹשָׁה לוֹ כִּי־יָלַדְתִּי

sons	three	to him	I begot – like

לֵוִי׃ קָרָא־שְׁמוֹ עַל־כֵּן

Levi	his name – she called	thus – upon

34 And she conceived again, and bare a son; and said, Now this time will my husband
be joined unto me, because I have born him three sons: therefore was his name called
Levi.

בֵּן וַתֵּלֶד עוֹד וַתַּהַר

son	and she begot	again	and she conceived

אֶת־יְהֹוָה אוֹדֶה הַפַּעַם וַתֹּאמֶר

ihvh – that	I will thank	the once again	and she said

מִלֶּדֶת׃ וַתַּעֲמֹד יְהוּדָה שְׁמוֹ קָרְאָה עַל־כֵּן

from birthing	and she stopped	Judah	his name	she called	thus - upon

35 And she conceived again, and bare a son: and she said, Now will I praise the LORD:
therefore she called his name Judah; and left bearing.

CHAPTER 30

ספר בראשית פרק ל

לְיַעֲקֹב יָלְדָה לֹא כִּי רָחֵל וַתֵּרֶא

to Jacob	beget	not	like	Rachel	and she saw

בַּאֲחֹתָהּ רָחֵל וַתְּקַנֵּא

in her sister	Rachel	and she envied

בָנִים הָבָה־לִּי אֶל־יַעֲקֹב וַתֹּאמֶר

sons	to me – the in it	Jacob – unto	and she said

אָנֹכִי׃ מֵתָה וְאִם־אַיִן

I am	death	isn't – and if

1 And when Rachel saw that she bare Jacob no children, Rachel envied her sister; and
said unto Jacob, Give me children, or else I die.

בְּרָחֵל יַעֲקֹב וַיִּחַר־אַף

in Rachel	Jacob	anger – and he kindled

פְּרִי־בָטֶן׃ מִמֵּךְ אֲשֶׁר־מָנַע אָנֹכִי אֱלֹהִים הֲתַחַת וַיֹּאמֶר

belly – fruit	from me	portion – which	I am	Elohim	the instead	and she said

2 And Jacob's anger was kindled against Rachel: and he said, Am I in God's stead, who
hath withheld from thee the fruit of the womb?

וַתֹּאמֶר הִנֵּה אֲמָתִי בִלְהָה בֹּא אֵלֶיהָ וְתֵלֵד עַל־בִּרְכָּי
and she said   here   my maid   Bilhah   come   unto her   and she beget   my knees – upon

וְאִבָּנֶה גַם־אָנֹכִי מִמֶּנָּה:
and I build   I am – also   from her

3 And she said, Behold my maid Bilhah, go in unto her; and she shall bear upon my knees, that I may also have children by her.

וַתִּתֶּן־לוֹ אֶת־בִּלְהָה שִׁפְחָתָהּ לְאִשָּׁה
and she gave – to him   Bilhah – that   her maid   to wife

וַיָּבֹא אֵלֶיהָ יַעֲקֹב:
and he came   unto her   Jacob

4 And she gave him Bilhah her handmaid to wife: and Jacob went in unto her.

וַתַּהַר בִּלְהָה וַתֵּלֶד לְיַעֲקֹב בֵּן:
and she conceived   Bilhah   and begot   to Jacob   son

5 And Bilhah conceived, and bare Jacob a son.

וַתֹּאמֶר רָחֵל דָּנַנִּי אֱלֹהִים וְגַם שָׁמַע בְּקֹלִי
and she said   Rachel   judged me   Elohim   and also   heard   in my voice

וַיִּתֶּן־לִי בֵּן עַל־כֵּן קָרְאָה שְׁמוֹ דָּן:
to me – and he gave   son   upon – thus   I called   his name   Dan

6 And Rachel said, God hath judged me, and hath also heard my voice, and hath given me a son: therefore called she his name Dan.

וַתַּהַר עוֹד וַתֵּלֶד בִּלְהָה שִׁפְחַת רָחֵל בֵּן שֵׁנִי לְיַעֲקֹב:
and conceived   again   and she begat   Bilhah   maid   Rachel   son   second   to Jacob

7 And Bilhah Rachel's maid conceived again, and bare Jacob a second son.

וַתֹּאמֶר רָחֵל נַפְתּוּלֵי אֱלֹהִים
and she said   Rachel   wrestling   Elohim

נִפְתַּלְתִּי עִם־אֲחֹתִי גַּם־יָכֹלְתִּי
I wrestled   my sister – with   I finished – also

וַתִּקְרָא שְׁמוֹ נַפְתָּלִי:
and she called   his name   Napphtali

8 And Rachel said, With great wrestlings have I wrestled with my sister, and I have prevailed: and she called his name Naphtali.

וַתֵּרֶא לֵאָה כִּי עָמְדָה מִלֶּדֶת
and she saw   Leah   like   she stood   from begetting

וַתִּקַּח אֶת־זִלְפָּה שִׁפְחָתָהּ
and she took   Zilpah – that   her maid

וַתִּתֵּן אֹתָהּ לְיַעֲקֹב לְאִשָּׁה:
and she gave   to her   to Jacob   to wife

9 When Leah saw that she had left bearing, she took Zilpah her maid, and gave her
Jacob to wife.

וַתֵּלֶד   זִלְפָּה שִׁפְחַת לֵאָה לְיַעֲקֹב בֵּן׃
and she conceived   Ziilpah   maid   Lea   to Jacob   son

10 And Zilpah Leah's maid bare Jacob a son.

וַתֹּאמֶר לֵאָה בָּגָד [בָּא גָד]
and she said   Lea   troop come

וַתִּקְרָא אֶת־שְׁמוֹ גָּד׃
and she called   that – his name   Gad

11 And Leah said, A troop cometh: and she called his name Gad.

וַתֵּלֶד   זִלְפָּה שִׁפְחַת לֵאָה בֵּן שֵׁנִי לְיַעֲקֹב׃
and she begot   Zilpah   maid   Lea   son   second   to Jacob

12 And Zilpah Leah's maid bare Jacob a second son.

וַתֹּאמֶר לֵאָה בְּאָשְׁרִי כִּי אִשְּׁרוּנִי בָּנוֹת
and she said   Lea   in happiness   like   I will be happy   daughters

וַתִּקְרָא אֶת־שְׁמוֹ אָשֵׁר׃
and she called   that – his name   Asher

13 And Leah said, Happy am I, for the daughters will call me blessed: and she called his
name Asher.

[רביעי]

וַיֵּלֶךְ רְאוּבֵן בִּימֵי קְצִיר־חִטִּים
and he went   Ruben   in days   harvest - wheat

וַיִּמְצָא דוּדָאִים בַּשָּׂדֶה וַיָּבֵא אֹתָם אֶל־לֵאָה אִמּוֹ
and he found   mandrakes   in field   and he brought   them   unto – Lea   his mother

וַתֹּאמֶר רָחֵל אֶל־לֵאָה תְּנִי־נָא לִי מִדּוּדָאֵי בְּנֵךְ׃
and she said   Rachel   unto – Leah   give – now   to me   mandrakes   your son's

14 And Reuben went in the days of wheat harvest, and found mandrakes in the field,
and brought them unto his mother Leah. Then Rachel said to Leah, Give me, I pray
thee, of thy son's mandrakes.

וַתֹּאמֶר לָהּ הַמְעַט קַחְתֵּךְ אֶת־אִישִׁי
and she said   to her   the little   your taking   that – my man

וְלָקַחַת גַּם אֶת־דּוּדָאֵי בְּנִי
and to take   also   that – mandrakes   my son

וַתֹּאמֶר רָחֵל לָכֵן יִשְׁכַּב עִמָּךְ הַלַּיְלָה תַּחַת דּוּדָאֵי בְּנֵךְ׃
and she said   Rachel   to thus   he lay   with you   the night   under   mandrakes   your sons

15 And she said unto her, Is it a small matter that thou hast taken my husband? and

wouldest thou take away my son's mandrakes also? And Rachel said, Therefore he shall lie with thee to night for thy son's mandrakes.

וַיָּבֹא יַעֲקֹב מִן־הַשָּׂדֶה בָּעֶרֶב
in evening   the field – from   Jacob   and he came

וַתֵּצֵא לֵאָה לִקְרָאתוֹ
to meet him   Leah   and she went out

וַתֹּאמֶר אֵלַי תָּבוֹא כִּי שָׂכֹר שְׂכַרְתִּיךָ בְּדוּדָאֵי בְּנִי
my son   in mandrakes   I hired you   hirer   like   you come   unto him   and she said

וַיִּשְׁכַּב עִמָּהּ בַּלַּיְלָה הוּא:
it   in night   with her   and he layed

16 And Jacob came out of the field in the evening, and Leah went out to meet him, and said, Thou must come in unto me; for surely I have hired thee with my son's mandrakes. And he lay with her that night.

וַיִּשְׁמַע אֱלֹהִים אֶל־לֵאָה וַתַּהַר
and she conceived   Leah – unto   Elohim   and he heard

וַתֵּלֶד לְיַעֲקֹב בֵּן חֲמִישִׁי:
fifth   son   to Jacob   and beget

17 And God hearkened unto Leah, and she conceived, and bare Jacob the fifth son.

וַתֹּאמֶר לֵאָה נָתַן אֱלֹהִים שְׂכָרִי אֲשֶׁר־נָתַתִּי שִׁפְחָתִי לְאִישִׁי
to my man   my maid   I gave – which   my hire   Elohim   given   Leah   and she said

וַתִּקְרָא שְׁמוֹ יִשָּׂשכָר:
Issachar   his name   and she called

18 And Leah said, God hath given me my hire, because I have given my maiden to my husband: and she called his name Issachar.

וַתַּהַר עוֹד לֵאָה וַתֵּלֶד בֵּן־שִׁשִּׁי לְיַעֲקֹב:
to Jacob   sixth – son   and she beget   Leah   again   and she conceived

19 And Leah conceived again, and bare Jacob the sixth son.

וַתֹּאמֶר לֵאָה זְבָדַנִי אֱלֹהִים אֹתִי זֵבֶד טוֹב הַפַּעַם
the twice   good   dowry   to me   Elohim   he dowryed me   Leah   and she said

יִזְבְּלֵנִי אִישִׁי כִּי־יָלַדְתִּי לוֹ שִׁשָּׁה בָנִים
sons   six   to him   I begot – like   my man   he will prefer me

וַתִּקְרָא אֶת־שְׁמוֹ זְבֻלוּן:
Zebulun   his name – that   and she called

20 And Leah said, God hath endued me with a good dowry; now will my husband dwell with me, because I have born him six sons: and she called his name Zebulun.

וְאַחַר יָלְדָה בַת וַתִּקְרָא אֶת־שְׁמָהּ דִּינָה:
Dinah   her name – that   and she called   daughter   she begot   and after

21 And afterwards she bare a daughter, and called her name Dinah.

אֱלֹהִים אֶת־רָחֵל וַיִּשְׁמַע אֵלֶיהָ אֱלֹהִים וַיִּזְכֹּר
Elohim   unto her   and he listened   Rachel – that   Elohim   and he remembered

וַיִּפְתַּח אֶת־רַחְמָהּ:
her womb – that   and he opened

22 And God remembered Rachel, and God hearkened to her, and opened her womb.

וַתַּהַר וַתֵּלֶד בֵּן וַתֹּאמֶר אָסַף אֱלֹהִים אֶת־חֶרְפָּתִי:
my reproach – that   Elohim   gathered   and she said   son   and she begot   and she conceived

23 And she conceived, and bare a son; and said, God hath taken away my reproach:

וַתִּקְרָא אֶת־שְׁמוֹ יוֹסֵף לֵאמֹר יֹסֵף יְהוָה לִי בֵּן אַחֵר:
another   son   to me   ihvh   he added   to say   Joseph   his name - that   and she called

24 And she called his name Joseph; and said, The LORD shall add to me another son.

וַיְהִי כַּאֲשֶׁר יָלְדָה רָחֵל אֶת־יוֹסֵף
Joseph – that   Rachel   she begot   when   and it was

וַיֹּאמֶר יַעֲקֹב אֶל־לָבָן שַׁלְּחֵנִי
send me away   Laban – unto   Jacob   and he said

וְאֵלְכָה אֶל־מְקוֹמִי וּלְאַרְצִי:
and to my land   my place – unto   and I go

25 And it came to pass, when Rachel had born Joseph, that Jacob said unto Laban, Send me away, that I may go unto mine own place, and to my country.

תְּנָה אֶת־נָשַׁי
my women – that   you give

וְאֶת־יְלָדַי אֲשֶׁר עָבַדְתִּי אֹתְךָ בָּהֵן וְאֵלֵכָה
and I go   in them   to you   I served   which   my born ones – and that

כִּי אַתָּה יָדַעְתָּ אֶת־עֲבֹדָתִי אֲשֶׁר עֲבַדְתִּיךָ:
I served you   which   my service – that   you know   you   like

26 Give *me* my wives and my children, for whom I have served thee, and let me go: for thou knowest my service which I have done thee.

וַיֹּאמֶר אֵלָיו לָבָן אִם־נָא מָצָאתִי חֵן בְּעֵינֶיךָ נִחַשְׁתִּי
enchant me   in your eyes   grace   I found   please – with   Laban   unto him   and he said

וַיְבָרֲכֵנִי יְהוָה בִּגְלָלֶךָ:
in your sake   ihvh   and he blessed me

27 And Laban said unto him, I pray thee, if I have found favour in thine eyes, tarry: for I have learned by experience that the LORD hath blessed me for thy sake.

[חמישי]

וַיֹּאמַר נָקְבָה שְׂכָרְךָ עָלַי וְאֶתֵּנָה:
I will give it   upon me   your wages   appoint   and he said

28 And he said, Appoint me thy wages, and I will give it.

וַיֹּאמַר אֵלָיו אַתָּה יָדַעְתָּ אֵת אֲשֶׁר עֲבַדְתִּיךָ
I served you   which   that   you know   you   unto him   and he said

וְאֵת אֲשֶׁר־הָיָה מִקְנְךָ אִתִּי:
with me   your cattle   it was – which   and that

29 And he said unto him, Thou knowest how I have served thee, and how thy cattle was with me.

כִּי מְעַט אֲשֶׁר־הָיָה לְךָ לְפָנַי
before me   to you   it was – which   little   like

וַיִּפְרֹץ לָרֹב וַיְבָרֶךְ יְהוָה אֹתְךָ לְרַגְלִי
to my feet   to you   ihvh   and he blessed   to much   and it fruitful

וְעַתָּה מָתַי אֶעֱשֶׂה גַם־אָנֹכִי לְבֵיתִי:
to my house   I am – also   I will do   when   and now

30 For it was little which thou hadst before I came, and it is now increased unto a multitude; and the LORD hath blessed thee since my coming: and now when shall I provide for mine own house also?

וַיֹּאמַר מָה אֶתֶּן־לָךְ
to you – I give   what   and he said

וַיֹּאמֶר יַעֲקֹב לֹא־תִתֶּן־לִי מְאוּמָה
from speck   to me – give – not   Jacob   and he said

אִם־תַּעֲשֶׂה־לִּי הַדָּבָר הַזֶּה אָשׁוּבָה אֶרְעֶה צֹאנְךָ אֶשְׁמֹר:
I heed   your sheep   I will shepherd   I will return   the this   the matter   to me – you do – with

31 And he said, What shall I give thee? And Jacob said, Thou shalt not give me any thing: if thou wilt do this thing for me, I will again feed and keep thy flock.

אֶעֱבֹר בְּכָל־צֹאנְךָ הַיּוֹם הָסֵר מִשָּׁם כָּל־שֶׂה נָקֹד וְטָלוּא
and spotted   speckled   lamb - all   from there   removing   the day   your sheep – in all   I will pass

וְכָל־שֶׂה־חוּם בַּכְּשָׂבִים
in sheep   brown - lamb - and all

וְטָלוּא וְנָקֹד בָּעִזִּים וְהָיָה שְׂכָרִי:
my hire   and it will be   in goats   and speckled   and spotted

32 I will pass through all thy flock to day, removing from thence all the speckled and spotted cattle, and all the brown cattle among the sheep, and the spotted and speckled among the goats: and of such shall be my hire.

וְעָנְתָה־בִּי צִדְקָתִי בְּיוֹם מָחָר
tomorrow   in day   my righteousness   in me – and answer

כִּי־תָבוֹא עַל־שְׂכָרִי לְפָנֶיךָ כֹּל
all   before you   my hire - upon   you come – like

אֲשֶׁר־אֵינֶנּוּ נָקֹד וְטָלוּא בָּעִזִּים

in goats   and spotted   speckled   isn't – which

וְחוּם   בַּכְּשָׂבִים גָּנוּב הוּא אִתִּי׃

with me   he   stolen   in sheep ones   and brown

33 So shall my righteousness answer for me in time to come, when it shall come for my hire before thy face: every one that is not speckled and spotted among the goats, and brown among the sheep, that shall be counted stolen with me.

וַיֹּאמֶר לָבָן הֵן לוּ יְהִי כִדְבָרֶךָ׃

like your speaking   it will be   to you   grace   Laban   and he said

34 And Laban said, Behold, I would it might be according to thy word.

וַיָּסַר   בַּיּוֹם   הַהוּא אֶת־הַתְּיָשִׁים הָעֲקֻדִּים וְהַטְּלֻאִים

and the spotted   the ringed   the male goats - that   the it   in day   and he removed

וְאֵת   כָּל־הָעִזִּים הַנְּקֻדּוֹת

the ringed   the goats - all   and that

וְהַטְּלֻאֹת כֹּל אֲשֶׁר־לָבָן בּוֹ

in his   Laban – which   all   and the spotted

וְכָל־חוּם בַּכְּשָׂבִים וַיִּתֵּן בְּיַד־בָּנָיו׃

his sons – in hand   and he gave   in mature sheep   brown– and all

35 And he removed that day the he goats that were ring straked and spotted, and all the she goats that were speckled and spotted, and every one that had some white in it, and all the brown among the sheep, and gave them into the hand of his sons.

וַיָּשֶׂם דֶּרֶךְ שְׁלֹשֶׁת יָמִים בֵּינוֹ וּבֵין יַעֲקֹב

Jacob   and between   between him   days   three   way   and he set

וְיַעֲקֹב רֹעֶה אֶת־צֹאן לָבָן הַנּוֹתָרֹת׃

the remainder   Laban   sheep – that   shepherd   and Jacob

36 And he set three days' journey betwixt himself and Jacob: and Jacob fed the rest of Laban's flocks.

וַיִּקַּח־לוֹ יַעֲקֹב מַקַּל לִבְנֶה לַח וְלוּז וְעַרְמוֹן

and plane   and hazel   smooth   white popular   stick   Jacob   to him – the took

וַיְפַצֵּל בָּהֵן פְּצָלוֹת לְבָנוֹת מַחְשֹׂף

baring   white ones   peelings   in them   and he appealing

הַלָּבָן אֲשֶׁר עַל־הַמַּקְלוֹת׃

the sticks - upon   which   the white

37 And Jacob took him rods of green poplar, and of the hazel and chestnut tree; and pilled white strakes in them, and made the white appear which was in the rods.

וַיַּצֵּג אֶת־הַמַּקְלוֹת אֲשֶׁר פִּצֵּל בָּרְהָטִים בְּשִׁקֲתוֹת הַמָּיִם

the water   in drinking basins   in troughs   peeled   which   the sticks – that   and he set up

אֲשֶׁר תָּבֹאןָ הַצֹּאן לִשְׁתּוֹת לְנֹכַח הַצֹּאן
the sheep   to ahead   to drink   the sheep   came them   which

וַיֵּחַמְנָה בְּבֹאָן לִשְׁתּוֹת:
to drink   in females coming   and he conceive

38 And he set the rods which he had pilled before the flocks in the gutters in the
watering troughs when the flocks came to drink, that they should conceive when they
came to drink.

וַיֶּחֱמוּ הַצֹּאן אֶל־הַמַּקְלוֹת
the sticks – unto   the sheep   and they conceived

וַתֵּלַדְןָ הַצֹּאן עֲקֻדִּים נְקֻדִּים וּטְלֻאִים:
spotted ones   speckled ones   ringed ones   the sheep   and they (females) went

39 And the flocks conceived before the rods, and brought forth cattle ringstraked,
speckled, and spotted.

וְהַכְּשָׂבִים הִפְרִיד יַעֲקֹב
Jacob   caused to separated   and the lamb ones

וַיִּתֵּן פְּנֵי הַצֹּאן אֶל־עָקֹד
ringed - upon   the sheep   faces   and he gave

וְכָל־חוּם בְּצֹאן לָבָן וַיָּשֶׁת לוֹ עֲדָרִים לְבַדּוֹ
alone   flocks   to him   and he put   Laban   in sheep   brown – and all

וְלֹא שָׁתָם עַל־צֹאן לָבָן:
Laban   sheep – upon   put them   and not

40 And Jacob did separate the lambs, and set the faces of the flocks toward the
ringstraked, and all the brown in the flock of Laban; and he put his own flocks by
themselves, and put them not unto Laban's cattle.

וְהָיָה בְּכָל־יַחֵם הַצֹּאן הַמְקֻשָּׁרוֹת
the sinewy ones   the sheep   he conceived - in all   and it was

וְשָׂם יַעֲקֹב אֶת־הַמַּקְלוֹת לְעֵינֵי הַצֹּאן בָּרְהָטִים
in gutters   the sheep   to eyes   the sticks - that   Jacob   and put

לְיַחֲמֵנָּה בַּמַּקְלוֹת:
in sticks   to conceive

41 And it came to pass, whensoever the stronger cattle did conceive, that Jacob laid the
rods before the eyes of the cattle in the gutters, that they might conceive among the
rods.

וּבְהַעֲטִיף הַצֹּאן לֹא יָשִׂים
he put them   not   the sheep   and in the feeble

וְהָיָה הָעֲטֻפִים לְלָבָן וְהַקְּשֻׁרִים לְיַעֲקֹב:
to Jacob   and the hardened ones   to Laban   the feeble ones   and it was

42 But when the cattle were feeble, he put them not in: so the feebler were Laban's, and

the stronger Jacob's.

וַיִּפְרֹץ   הָאִישׁ מְאֹד מְאֹד וַיְהִי־לוֹ צֹאן רַבּוֹת
much ones   sheep   to him – and it was   greatly   greatly   the man   and he bared fruit

וּשְׁפָחוֹת וַעֲבָדִים וּגְמַלִּים וַחֲמֹרִים:
and asses   and camels   and servant ones   and maids

43 And the man increased exceedingly, and had much cattle, and maidservants, and menservants, and camels, and asses.

CHAPTER 31

ספר בראשית פרק לא

וַיִּשְׁמַע אֶת־דִּבְרֵי בְנֵי־לָבָן לֵאמֹר
to say   Laban - sons   speaking – that   and he heard

לָקַח יַעֲקֹב אֵת כָּל־אֲשֶׁר לְאָבִינוּ
to our father   which – all   that   Jacob   take

וּמֵאֲשֶׁר לְאָבִינוּ עָשָׂה אֵת כָּל־הַכָּבֹד הַזֶּה:
the this   the glory – all   that   did   to our fathers   and from which

1 And he heard the words of Laban's sons, saying, Jacob hath taken away all that was our father's; and of that which was our father's hath he gotten all this glory.

וַיַּרְא יַעֲקֹב אֶת־פְּנֵי לָבָן
Laban   face – that   Jacob   and he saw

וְהִנֵּה אֵינֶנּוּ עִמּוֹ כִּתְמוֹל שִׁלְשׁוֹם:
three ones (days)   like yesterday   with him   isn't   and here

2 And Jacob beheld the countenance of Laban, and, behold, it was not toward him as before.

וַיֹּאמֶר יְהֹוָה אֶל־יַעֲקֹב
Jacob – unto   ihvh   and he said

שׁוּב אֶל־אֶרֶץ אֲבוֹתֶיךָ וּלְמוֹלַדְתֶּךָ
and to your kindred   your fathers   land – unto   return

וְאֶהְיֶה עִמָּךְ:
with you   and I will be

3 And the LORD said unto Jacob, Return unto the land of thy fathers, and to thy kindred; and I will be with thee.

וַיִּשְׁלַח יַעֲקֹב וַיִּקְרָא לְרָחֵל וּלְלֵאָה הַשָּׂדֶה אֶל־צֹאנוֹ:
his sheep – unto   the field   and to Leah   to Rachel   and he called   Jacob   and he sent

4 And Jacob sent and called Rachel and Leah to the field unto his flock,

וַיֹּאמֶר לָהֶן רֹאֶה אָנֹכִי אֶת־פְּנֵי אֲבִיכֶן
your father   face – that   I am   shepherd   to them   and he said

כִּי־אֵינֶנּוּ אֵלַי כִּתְמֹל שִׁלְשֹׁם

three ones (days) like yesterday these isn't us – like

וֵאלֹהֵי אָבִי הָיָה עִמָּדִי:

with me was my father and Elohim

5 And said unto them, I see your father's countenance, that it is not toward me as
before; but the God of my father hath been with me.

וְאַתֵּנָה יְדַעְתֶּן כִּי בְּכָל־כֹּחִי עָבַדְתִּי אֶת־אֲבִיכֶן:

your father – that I served my power – in all like you know and towards you

6 And ye know that with all my power I have served your father.

וַאֲבִיכֶן הֵתֶל בִּי וְהֶחֱלִף אֶת־מַשְׂכֻּרְתִּי עֲשֶׂרֶת מֹנִים

times ten my wages – that and the changed in me deceived and your father

וְלֹא־נְתָנוֹ אֱלֹהִים לְהָרַע עִמָּדִי:

with me to the bad Elohim his giving – and not

7 And your father hath deceived me, and changed my wages ten times; but God suffered
him not to hurt me.

אִם־כֹּה יֹאמַר נְקֻדִּים יִהְיֶה שְׂכָרֶךָ

your wages it will be speckled ones he said thus - if

וְיָלְדוּ כָל־הַצֹּאן נְקֻדִּים

speckled ones the sheep – all and they begot

וְאִם־כֹּה יֹאמַר עֲקֻדִּים יִהְיֶה שְׂכָרֶךָ

your wages it will be rings ones he said thus – and if

וְיָלְדוּ כָל־הַצֹּאן עֲקֻדִּים:

rings ones the sheep – all and they begot

8 If he said thus, The speckled shall be thy wages; then all the cattle bare speckled: and
if he said thus, The ringstraked shall be thy hire; then bare all the cattle ringstraked.

וַיַּצֵּל אֱלֹהִים אֶת־מִקְנֵה אֲבִיכֶם וַיִּתֶּן־לִי:

to me – he gave your father cattle – that Elohim and he took away

9 Thus God hath taken away the cattle of your father, and given them to me.

וַיְהִי בְּעֵת יַחֵם הַצֹּאן וָאֶשָּׂא עֵינַי וָאֵרֶא בַּחֲלוֹם

in dream and appeared eyes and he lifted the sheep conceived in time and it was

וְהִנֵּה הָעַתֻּדִים הָעֹלִים עַל־הַצֹּאן עֲקֻדִּים נְקֻדִּים וּבְרֻדִּים:

spotted ones speckled ones ringstraked ones the sheep - upon the leaping ones the rams and here

10 And it came to pass at the time that the cattle conceived, that I lifted up mine
eyes, and saw in a dream, and, behold, the rams which leaped upon the cattle were
ringstraked, speckled, and grisled.

וַיֹּאמֶר אֵלַי מַלְאַךְ הָאֱלֹהִים בַּחֲלוֹם יַעֲקֹב

Jacob in dream the Elohim angel unto him and he said

וַיֹּאמֶר   הִנֵּנִי:
here am I   and he said

11 And the angel of God spake unto me in a dream, saying, Jacob: And I said, Here am I.

וַיֹּאמֶר שָׂא־נָא עֵינֶיךָ
your eyes   now – lift   and he said

וּרְאֵה כָּל־הָעַתֻּדִים הָעֹלִים עַל־הַצֹּאן
the sheep - upon   the leaping ones   ringed ones - all   and see

עֲקֻדִּים נְקֻדִּים וּבְרֻדִּים
and spotted ones   speckled ones   the striped ones

כִּי רָאִיתִי אֵת כָּל־אֲשֶׁר לָבָן עֹשֶׂה לָּךְ:
to you   did   Laban   which – all   that   I saw   like

12 And he said, Lift up now thine eyes, and see, all the rams which leap upon the cattle are ringstraked, speckled, and grisled: for I have seen all that Laban doeth unto thee.

אָנֹכִי הָאֵל בֵּית־אֵל אֲשֶׁר מָשַׁחְתָּ שָּׁם מַצֵּבָה
pillar   there   you anointed   which   El – house   the El   I am

אֲשֶׁר נָדַרְתָּ לִּי שָׁם נֶדֶר
vow   there   to me   you vowed   which

עַתָּה קוּם צֵא מִן־הָאָרֶץ הַזֹּאת
the this   the land – from   go out   rise   now

וְשׁוּב אֶל־אֶרֶץ מוֹלַדְתֶּךָ:
your kindred   land - unto   and return

13 I am the God of Beth-el, where thou anointedst the pillar, and where thou vowedst a vow unto me: now arise, get thee out from this land, and return unto the land of thy kindred.

וַתַּעַן רָחֵל וְלֵאָה
and Leah   Rachel   and they answered

וַתֹּאמַרְנָה לוֹ הַעוֹד לָנוּ חֵלֶק וְנַחֲלָה בְּבֵית אָבִינוּ:
our father   in house   and inheritance   portion   to us   the still   to him   and she said

14 And Rachel and Leah answered and said unto him, Is there yet any portion or inheritance for us in our father's house?

הֲלוֹא נָכְרִיּוֹת נֶחְשַׁבְנוּ לוֹ
to him   we are possessions   strangers   the not

כִּי מְכָרָנוּ וַיֹּאכַל גַּם־אָכוֹל אֶת־כַּסְפֵּנוּ:
our silver – that   ate – also   and he ate   hired us out   like

15 Are we not counted of him strangers? for he hath sold us, and hath quite devoured also our money.

כִּי כָל־הָעֹשֶׁר אֲשֶׁר הִצִּיל אֱלֹהִים מֵאָבִינוּ לָנוּ הוּא וּלְבָנֵינוּ

and to ours sons   it   to us   from our father   Elohim   cause to take   which   the riches – all   like

וְעַתָּה כֹּל אֲשֶׁר אָמַר אֱלֹהִים אֵלֶיךָ עֲשֵׂה:

do   unto you   Elohim   said   which   all   and now

16 For all the riches which God hath taken from our father, that is ours, and our children's: now then, whatsoever God hath said unto thee, do.

[ששי]

וַיָּקָם יַעֲקֹב וַיִּשָּׂא אֶת־בָּנָיו וְאֶת־נָשָׁיו עַל־הַגְּמַלִּים:

the camels – upon   his women – and that   his sons – that   and he put   Jacob   and he rose

17 Then Jacob rose up, and set his sons and his wives upon camels;

וַיִּנְהַג אֶת־כָּל־מִקְנֵהוּ וְאֶת־כָּל־רְכֻשׁוֹ אֲשֶׁר רָכָשׁ

he possessed   which   his possessions – all – and that   his cattle – all – that   and he carried away

מִקְנֵה קִנְיָנוֹ אֲשֶׁר רָכַשׁ בְּפַדַּן אֲרָם

Aram   in Padan   possessed   which   his purchased   cattle

לָבוֹא אֶל־יִצְחָק אָבִיו אַרְצָה כְּנָעַן:

Canaan   land   his father   Isaac – unto   to come

18 And he carried away all his cattle, and all his goods which he had gotten, the cattle of his getting, which he had gotten in Padan-aram, for to go to Isaac his father in the land of Canaan.

וְלָבָן הָלַךְ לִגְזֹז אֶת־צֹאנוֹ

his sheep – that   to shear   went   and Laban

וַתִּגְנֹב רָחֵל אֶת־הַתְּרָפִים אֲשֶׁר לְאָבִיהָ:

to her father   which   the deity graven images – that   Rachel   and she stole

19 And Laban went to shear his sheep: and Rachel had stolen the images that were her father's.

וַיִּגְנֹב יַעֲקֹב אֶת־לֵב לָבָן הָאֲרַמִּי

the Syrian   Laban   heart – that   Jacob   and he stole

עַל־בְּלִי הִגִּיד לוֹ כִּי בֹרֵחַ הוּא:

he   fled   like   to him   caused to tell   nothing – upon

20 And Jacob stole away unawares to Laban the Syrian, in that he told him not that he fled.

וַיִּבְרַח הוּא וְכָל־אֲשֶׁר־לוֹ וַיָּקָם וַיַּעֲבֹר אֶת־הַנָּהָר

the river – that   and he passed   and he arose   to him – which – and all   he   and he fled

וַיָּשֶׂם אֶת־פָּנָיו הַר הַגִּלְעָד:

the Gilead   mountain   his face – that   and he set

21 So he fled with all that he had; and he rose up, and passed over the river, and set his face toward the mount Gilead.

וַיֻּגַּד לְלָבָן בַּיּוֹם הַשְּׁלִישִׁי כִּי בָרַח יַעֲקֹב׃

Jacob　fled　like　the third　in day　to Laban　and it told

22 And it was told Laban on the third day that Jacob was fled.

וַיִּקַּח אֶת־אֶחָיו עִמּוֹ

with him　his brother – that　and he took

וַיִּרְדֹּף אַחֲרָיו דֶּרֶךְ שִׁבְעַת יָמִים

days　seven　way　after him　and he pursued

וַיַּדְבֵּק אֹתוֹ בְּהַר הַגִּלְעָד׃

the Gilead　in mountain　to him　and he clingged

23 And he took his brethren with him, and pursued after him seven days' journey; and they overtook him in the mount Gilead.

וַיָּבֹא אֱלֹהִים אֶל־לָבָן הָאֲרַמִּי בַּחֲלֹם הַלָּיְלָה

the night　in dream　the Syrian　Laban – unto　Elohim　and he came

וַיֹּאמֶר לוֹ הִשָּׁמֶר לְךָ

to you　cause to heed　to him　and he said

פֶּן־תְּדַבֵּר עִם־יַעֲקֹב מִטּוֹב עַד־רָע׃

bad – till　from good　Jacob – with　you speak - lest

24 And God came to Laban the Syrian in a dream by night, and said unto him, Take heed that thou speak not to Jacob either good or bad.

וַיַּשֵּׂג לָבָן אֶת־יַעֲקֹב

Jacob – that　Laban　and he overtook

וְיַעֲקֹב תָּקַע אֶת־אָהֳלוֹ בָּהָר

in mountain　his tent – that　pitched　and Jacob

וְלָבָן תָּקַע אֶת־אֶחָיו בְּהַר הַגִּלְעָד׃

the Gilead　in mountain　his brother – that　pitched　and Laban

25 Then Laban overtook Jacob. Now Jacob had pitched his tent in the mount: and Laban with his brethren pitched in the mount of Gilead.

וַיֹּאמֶר לָבָן לְיַעֲקֹב מֶה עָשִׂיתָ

you did　what　to Jacob　Laban　and he said

וַתִּגְנֹב אֶת־לְבָבִי

my heart – that　and you stole

וַתְּנַהֵג אֶת־בְּנֹתַי כִּשְׁבֻיוֹת חָרֶב׃

sword　captives　my sons – that　and you carried away

26 And Laban said to Jacob, What hast thou done, that thou hast stolen away unawares to me, and carried away my daughters, as captives taken with the sword?

לָמָּה נַחְבֵּאתָ לִבְרֹחַ וַתִּגְנֹב אֹתִי וְלֹא־הִגַּדְתָּ לִי

to me　you told - and not　to me　and you stole　to run away　you hid　why

וָאֲשַׁלֵּחֲךָ   בְּשִׂמְחָה   וּבְשִׁרִים   בְּתֹף   וּבְכִנּוֹר:

and harp	in tabret	and in songs	in happiness	and I send you away

27 Wherefore didst thou flee away secretly, and steal away from me; and didst not tell me, that I might have sent thee away with mirth, and with songs, with tabret, and with harp?

וְלֹא נְטַשְׁתַּנִי לְנַשֵּׁק לְבָנַי

to my sons	to kiss	you allowed me	and not

וְלִבְנֹתָי   עַתָּה   הִסְכַּלְתָּ   עֲשׂוֹ:

his doing	it caused foolishness	now	and to my daughters

28 And hast not suffered me to kiss my sons and my daughters? thou hast now done foolishly in so doing.

יֶשׁ־לְאֵל   יָדִי   לַעֲשׂוֹת   עִמָּכֶם   רָע

bad	with you	to doings	my hand	to El - there is

אֱלֹהֵי   אֲבִיכֶם   אֶמֶשׁ   אָמַר   אֵלַי   לֵאמֹר

to say	unto me	said	yester-night	your father	Elohim

הִשָּׁמֶר   לְךָ   מִדַּבֵּר   עִם־יַעֲקֹב   מִטּוֹב   עַד־רָע:

bad – till	from good	Jacob – with	from speaking	to you	cause to heed

29 It is in the power of my hand to do you hurt: but the God of your father spake unto me yesternight, saying, Take thou heed that thou speak not to Jacob either good or bad.

וְעַתָּה   הָלֹךְ   הָלַכְתָּ

you go	go	and now

כִּי־נִכְסֹף   נִכְסַפְתָּה   לְבֵית   אָבִיךָ

your father	to house	longest for	longs for - like

לָמָּה   גָנַבְתָּ   אֶת־אֱלֹהָי:

my elohim – that	you stole	why

30 And now, though thou wouldest needs be gone, because thou sore longedst after thy father's house, yet wherefore hast thou stolen my gods?

וַיַּעַן   יַעֲקֹב   וַיֹּאמֶר   לְלָבָן

to Laban	and he said	Jacob	and he answered

כִּי   יָרֵאתִי   כִּי   אָמַרְתִּי   פֶּן־תִּגְזֹל   אֶת־בְּנוֹתֶיךָ   מֵעִמִּי:

from with me	your daughters – that	forcefully take - lest	I said	like	I afraid	like

31 And Jacob answered and said to Laban, Because I was afraid: for I said, Peradventure thou wouldest take by force thy daughters from me.

עִם   אֲשֶׁר   תִּמְצָא   אֶת־אֱלֹהֶיךָ   לֹא   יִחְיֶה   נֶגֶד   אַחֵינוּ

our brothers	among	he live	not	your elohim – that	you find	which	with

הַכֶּר־לְךָ   מָה   עִמָּדִי   וְקַח־לָךְ

to you – and take	with me	what	to you - discern

וְלֹא־יָדַע יַעֲקֹב כִּי רָחֵל גְּנָבָתַם׃

stole them	Rachel	like	Jacob	knew – and not

32 With whomsoever thou findest thy gods, let him not live: before our brethren discern thou what is thine with me, and take it to thee. For Jacob knew not that Rachel had stolen them.

וַיָּבֹא לָבָן בְּאֹהֶל־יַעֲקֹב

Jacob – in tent	Laban	and he came

וּבְאֹהֶל לֵאָה וּבְאֹהֶל שְׁתֵּי הָאֲמָהֹת

the maids	two	and in tent	Lea	and in tent

וְלֹא מָצָא וַיֵּצֵא מֵאֹהֶל לֵאָה

Leah	from tent	and he went out	he found	and not

וַיָּבֹא בְּאֹהֶל רָחֵל׃

Rachel	in tent	and he came

33 And Laban went into Jacob's tent, and into Leah's tent, and into the two maidservants' tents; but he found them not. Then went he out of Leah's tent, and entered into Rachel's tent.

וְרָחֵל לָקְחָה אֶת־הַתְּרָפִים

the deity graven images - that	took	and Rachel

וַתְּשִׂמֵם בְּכַר הַגָּמָל וַתֵּשֶׁב עֲלֵיהֶם

upon them	and she sat	the camel	in saddle	and she put them

וַיְמַשֵּׁשׁ לָבָן אֶת־כָּל־הָאֹהֶל וְלֹא מָצָא׃

he found	and not	the tent – all - that	Laban	and he searched

34 Now Rachel had taken the images, and put them in the camel's furniture, and sat upon them. And Laban searched all the tent, but found them not.

וַתֹּאמֶר אֶל־אָבִיהָ אַל־יִחַר בְּעֵינֵי אֲדֹנִי

my master	in my eyes	it anger – don't	her father – unto	and she said

כִּי לוֹא אוּכַל לָקוּם מִפָּנֶיךָ כִּי־דֶרֶךְ נָשִׁים לִי

to me	women	way – like	from before you	to rise	I can	to it	like

וַיְחַפֵּשׂ וְלֹא מָצָא אֶת־הַתְּרָפִים׃

images - that	found	and not	and he searched

35 And she said to her father, Let it not displease my lord that I cannot rise up before thee; for the custom of women is upon me. And he searched, but found not the images.

וַיִּחַר לְיַעֲקֹב וַיָּרֶב בְּלָבָן

in Laban	and he quarreled	to Jacob	and he angerd

וַיַּעַן יַעֲקֹב וַיֹּאמֶר לְלָבָן

to Laban	and he said	Jacob	and he answered

מַה־פִּשְׁעִי מַה חַטָּאתִי כִּי דָלַקְתָּ אַחֲרָי׃

after me | you pursued | like | my sin | what | my trespass - what

36 And Jacob was wroth, and chode with Laban: and Jacob answered and said to Laban, What is my trespass? what is my sin, that thou hast so hotly pursued after me?

כִּי־מִשַּׁשְׁתָּ אֶת־כָּל־כֵּלַי מַה־מָּצָאתָ מִכֹּל

from all | you found – what | items - all – that | you searched - like

כְּלֵי־בֵיתֶךָ שִׂים כֹּה נֶגֶד אַחַי וְאַחֶיךָ

and your brothers | my brothers | amongst | here | put | your house - items

וְיוֹכִיחוּ בֵּין שְׁנֵינוּ׃

two of us | between | and they judge you

37 Whereas thou hast searched all my stuff, what hast thou found of all thy household stuff? set it here before my brethren and thy brethren, that they may judge betwixt us both.

זֶה עֶשְׂרִים שָׁנָה אָנֹכִי עִמָּךְ

with you | I am | years | twenty | this

רְחֵלֶיךָ וְעִזֶּיךָ לֹא שִׁכֵּלוּ

aborted | not | and your female goats | your ewes

וְאֵילֵי צֹאנְךָ לֹא אָכָלְתִּי׃

I ate | not | your sheep | and rams

38 This twenty years have I been with thee; thy ewes and thy she goats have not cast their young, and the rams of thy flock have I not eaten.

טְרֵפָה לֹא־הֵבֵאתִי אֵלֶיךָ אָנֹכִי אֲחַטֶּנָּה מִיָּדִי תְּבַקְשֶׁנָּה

you required it | from my hand | bearer loss | I am | unto you | the I brought – not | torn

גְּנֻבְתִי יוֹם וּגְנֻבְתִי לָיְלָה׃

night | and my stolen | day | my stolen

39 That which was torn of beasts I brought not unto thee; I bare the loss of it; of my hand didst thou require it, whether stolen by day, or stolen by night.

הָיִיתִי בַיּוֹם אֲכָלַנִי חֹרֶב וְקֶרַח בַּלָּיְלָה

in night | and frost | drought | consumed me | in day | I was

וַתִּדַּד שְׁנָתִי מֵעֵינָי׃

from my eyes | my sleep | and departed

40 Thus I was; in the day the drought consumed me, and the frost by night; and my sleep departed from mine eyes.

זֶה־לִּי עֶשְׂרִים שָׁנָה בְּבֵיתֶךָ

in your house | year | twenty | to me - this

עֲבַדְתִּיךָ אַרְבַּע־עֶשְׂרֵה שָׁנָה בִּשְׁתֵּי בְנֹתֶיךָ

your daughters | in two | year | --- fourteen --- | I served you

וְשֵׁשׁ שָׁנִים בְּצֹאנֶךָ וַתַּחֲלֵף אֶת־מַשְׂכֻּרְתִּי עֲשֶׂרֶת מֹנִים:

      times   ten   my wages – that   and changed   in your sheep   years   and six

41 Thus have I been twenty years in thy house; I served thee fourteen years for thy two daughters, and six years for thy cattle: and thou hast changed my wages ten times.

לוּלֵי אֱלֹהֵי אָבִי אֱלֹהֵי אַבְרָהָם וּפַחַד יִצְחָק הָיָה לִי

   to me   it was   Isaac   and fear   Abraham   Elohim   my father   Elohim   perhaps

כִּי עַתָּה רֵיקָם שִׁלַּחְתָּנִי אֶת־עָנְיִי

      my affliction – that   you sent me   empty   now   like

וְאֶת־יְגִיעַ כַּפַּי רָאָה אֱלֹהִים וַיּוֹכַח אָמֶשׁ:

   yester - night   and he rebuked   Elohim   saw   my palms   he touched – and that

42 Except the God of my father, the God of Abraham, and the fear of Isaac, had been with me, surely thou hadst sent me away now empty. God hath seen mine affliction and the labour of my hands, and rebuked thee yesternight.

[שביעי]

וַיַּעַן לָבָן וַיֹּאמֶר אֶל־יַעֲקֹב

      Jacob – unto   and he said   Laban   and he answered

הַבָּנוֹת בְּנֹתַי וְהַבָּנִים בָּנַי

      my sons   and the sons   my daughters   the daughters

וְהַצֹּאן צֹאנִי וְכֹל אֲשֶׁר־אַתָּה רֹאֶה לִי הוּא

     it   to me   see   you – which   and all   my sheep   and the sheep

וְלִבְנֹתַי מָה־אֶעֱשֶׂה לָאֵלֶּה הַיּוֹם אוֹ לִבְנֵיהֶן אֲשֶׁר יָלָדוּ:

  they begot   which   to their sons   or   the day   to these   I do – what   and to my daughters

43 And Laban answered and said unto Jacob, These daughters are my daughters, and these children are my children, and these cattle are my cattle, and all that thou seest is mine: and what can I do this day unto these my daughters, or unto their children which they have born?

וְעַתָּה לְכָה נִכְרְתָה בְרִית אֲנִי וָאָתָּה

   and you   I   covenant   we cut   come   and now

וְהָיָה לְעֵד בֵּינִי וּבֵינֶךָ:

   and between you   between me   to witness   and it be

44 Now therefore come thou, let us make a covenant, I and thou; and let it be for a witness between me and thee.

וַיִּקַּח יַעֲקֹב אָבֶן וַיְרִימֶהָ מַצֵּבָה:

   pillar   and he set it upright   stone   Jacob   and he took

45 And Jacob took a stone, and set it up for a pillar.

וַיֹּאמֶר יַעֲקֹב לְאֶחָיו לִקְטוּ אֲבָנִים

   stones   you gather   to his brothers   Jacob   and he said

וַיִּקְחוּ אֲבָנִים וַיַּעֲשׂוּ־גָל וַיֹּאכְלוּ שָׁם עַל־הַגָּל:

the heap – upon there and they ate heap – and they made stones and they took

46 And Jacob said unto his brethren, Gather stones; and they took stones, and made an heap: and they did eat there upon the heap.

וַיִּקְרָא־לוֹ לָבָן יְגַר שָׂהֲדוּתָא

sahadutha Jegar Laban to it – and he called

וְיַעֲקֹב קָרָא לוֹ גַּלְעֵד:

Galeed to it called and Jacob

47 And Laban called it Jegar-sahadutha: but Jacob called it Galeed.

וַיֹּאמֶר לָבָן הַגַּל הַזֶּה עֵד בֵּינִי וּבֵינְךָ הַיּוֹם

the day and between you between me witness the this the heap Laban and he said

עַל־כֵּן קָרָא־שְׁמוֹ גַּלְעֵד:

Galeed its name – called thus – upon

48 And Laban said, This heap is a witness between me and thee this day. Therefore was the name of it called Galeed;

וְהַמִּצְפָּה אֲשֶׁר אָמַר יִצֶף יְהֹוָה בֵּינִי וּבֵינֶךָ

and between you between me ihvh watch over said which and the Mizpah

כִּי נִסָּתֵר אִישׁ מֵרֵעֵהוּ:

from his neighbor man absent like

49 And Mizpah; for he said, The LORD watch between me and thee, when we are absent one from another.

אִם־תְּעַנֶּה אֶת־בְּנֹתַי

my daughters – that you afflict - if

וְאִם־תִּקַּח נָשִׁים עַל־בְּנֹתַי אֵין אִישׁ עִמָּנוּ

with us man isn't my daughters – upon women you take – and if

רְאֵה אֱלֹהִים עֵד בֵּינִי וּבֵינֶךָ:

and between you between me witness Elohim see

50 If thou shalt afflict my daughters, or if thou shalt take other wives beside my daughters, no man is with us; see, God is witness betwixt me and thee.

וַיֹּאמֶר לָבָן לְיַעֲקֹב הִנֵּה הַגַּל הַזֶּה

the this the heap here to Jacob Laban and he said

וְהִנֵּה הַמַּצֵּבָה אֲשֶׁר יָרִיתִי בֵּינִי וּבֵינֶךָ:

and between you between me he sees which the pillar and here

51 And Laban said to Jacob, Behold this heap, and behold this pillar, which I have cast betwixt me and thee;

עֵד הַגַּל הַזֶּה

the this the heap witness

וְעֵדָה הַמַּצֵּבָה אִם־אָנִי לֹא־אֶעֱבֹר אֵלֶיךָ אֶת־הַגַּל הַזֶּה

the this   the heap – that   unto you   pass – not   I – with   the pillar   and witness

וְאִם־אַתָּה לֹא־תַעֲבֹר אֵלַי אֶת־הַגַּל הַזֶּה

the this   the heap – that   unto me   pass over – not   you – and with

וְאֶת־הַמַּצֵּבָה הַזֹּאת לְרָעָה:

to bad   the this   the pillar – and that

52 This heap be witness, and this pillar be witness, that I will not pass over this heap to thee, and that thou shalt not pass over this heap and this pillar unto me, for harm.

אֱלֹהֵי אַבְרָהָם וֵאלֹהֵי נָחוֹר יִשְׁפְּטוּ בֵינֵינוּ אֱלֹהֵי אֲבִיהֶם

their father   Elohim   between us   they judge   Nahor   and Elohim   Abraham   Elohim

וַיִּשָּׁבַע יַעֲקֹב בְּפַחַד אָבִיו יִצְחָק:

Isaac   his father   in awe   Jacob   and he swore

53 The God of Abraham, and the God of Nahor, the God of their father, judge betwixt us. And Jacob sware by the fear of his father Isaac.

וַיִּזְבַּח יַעֲקֹב זֶבַח בָּהָר

in mountain   sacrifice   Jacob   and he offered

וַיִּקְרָא לְאֶחָיו לֶאֱכָל־לָחֶם וַיֹּאכְלוּ לֶחֶם וַיָּלִינוּ בָּהָר:

in mountain   and they spent night   bread   and they ate   bread – to eat   to his brothers   and he called

54 Then Jacob offered sacrifice upon the mount, and called his brethren to eat bread: and they did eat bread, and tarried all night in the mount.

CHAPTER 32 (TORAH)

ספר בראשית פרק לב

[מפטיר]

וַיַּשְׁכֵּם לָבָן בַּבֹּקֶר וַיְנַשֵּׁק לְבָנָיו וְלִבְנוֹתָיו

and to his daughters   to his sons   and he kissed   in morning   Laban   and he arose early

וַיְבָרֶךְ אֶתְהֶם וַיֵּלֶךְ וַיָּשָׁב לָבָן לִמְקֹמוֹ:

to his place   Laban   and he returned   and he went   to them   and he blessed

55 And early in the morning Laban rose up, and kissed his sons and his daughters, and blessed them: and Laban departed, and returned unto his place.

CHAPTER 32 (KING JAMES)

וְיַעֲקֹב הָלַךְ לְדַרְכּוֹ וַיִּפְגְּעוּ־בוֹ מַלְאֲכֵי אֱלֹהִים:

Elohim   angels   in it – and they touched   to his way   went   and Jacob

1 And Jacob went on his way, and the angels of God met him.

וַיֹּאמֶר יַעֲקֹב כַּאֲשֶׁר רָאָם מַחֲנֵה אֱלֹהִים זֶה

this   Elohim   tent   saw them   when   Jacob   and he said

וַיִּקְרָא שֵׁם־הַמָּקוֹם הַהוּא מַחֲנָיִם:

Mahanaim	the it	the place – name	and he called

2 And when Jacob saw them, he said, This is God's host: and he called the name of that place Mahanaim.

פ פ פ

8 VAYISHLACH

CHAPTER 32 CONT

וַיִּשְׁלַח יַעֲקֹב מַלְאָכִים לְפָנָיו אֶל־עֵשָׂו אָחִיו

his brother	Esau – El	before him	messengers	Jacob	and he sent

אַרְצָה שֵׂעִיר שְׂדֵה אֱדוֹם:

Edom	field	Seir	towards land

3 And Jacob sent messengers before him to Esau his brother unto the land of Seir, the country of Edom.

וַיְצַו אֹתָם לֵאמֹר כֹּה תֹאמְרוּן לַאדֹנִי לְעֵשָׂו

to Esau	to my lord	you say to him	thus	to say	to them	and he commanded

כֹּה אָמַר עַבְדְּךָ יַעֲקֹב עִם־לָבָן גַּרְתִּי וָאֵחַר עַד־עָתָּה:

now – till	and I delayed	I sojourned	Laban – with	Jacob	your servant	say	thus

4 And he commanded them, saying, Thus shall ye speak unto my lord Esau; Thy servant Jacob saith thus, I have sojourned with Laban, and stayed there until now:

וַיְהִי־לִי שׁוֹר וַחֲמוֹר צֹאן וְעֶבֶד וְשִׁפְחָה

and maids	and men servants	sheep	and asses	oxen	to me and it was

וָאֶשְׁלְחָה לְהַגִּיד לַאדֹנִי לִמְצֹא־חֵן בְּעֵינֶיךָ:

in your eyes	grace – to find	to my lord	to the telling	and I sent

5 And I have oxen, and asses, flocks, and menservants, and women servants: and I have sent to tell my lord, that I may find grace in thy sight.

וַיָּשֻׁבוּ הַמַּלְאָכִים אֶל־יַעֲקֹב לֵאמֹר

to say	Jacob – unto	the messenger	and they returned

בָּאנוּ אֶל־אָחִיךָ אֶל־עֵשָׂו

Esau – unto	your brother – unto	we came

וְגַם הֹלֵךְ לִקְרָאתְךָ וְאַרְבַּע־מֵאוֹת אִישׁ עִמּוֹ:

with him	man	hundred - and four	to meet you	he goes	and also

6 And the messengers returned to Jacob, saying, We came to thy brother Esau, and also he cometh to meet thee, and four hundred men with him.

וַיִּירָא יַעֲקֹב מְאֹד וַיֵּצֶר לוֹ

to him	and it distressed	greatly	Jacob	and he was afraid

וַיַּחַץ אֶת־הָעָם אֲשֶׁר־אִתּוֹ

with him – which	the people – that	and he halved

וְאֶת־הַצֹּאן וְאֶת־הַבָּקָר וְהַגְּמַלִּים לִשְׁנֵי מַחֲנוֹת:

camps	to two	and the camels	the cattle - and that	the sheep – and that

7 Then Jacob was greatly afraid and distressed: and he divided the people that was with

him, and the flocks, and herds, and the camels, into two bands;

וַיֹּאמֶר אִם־יָבוֹא עֵשָׂו אֶל־הַמַּחֲנֶה הָאַחַת וְהִכָּהוּ
and he said   he come – with   Esau   the camp – unto   the one   and slaughter it

וְהָיָה הַמַּחֲנֶה הַנִּשְׁאָר לִפְלֵיטָה:
and it will be   the camp   the remainder   to escape

8 And said, If Esau come to the one company, and smite it, then the other company
which is left shall escape.

וַיֹּאמֶר יַעֲקֹב אֱלֹהֵי אָבִי אַבְרָהָם
and he said   Jacob   Elohim   my father   Abraham

וֵאלֹהֵי אָבִי יִצְחָק יְהֹוָה הָאֹמֵר אֵלַי שׁוּב לְאַרְצְךָ וּלְמוֹלַדְתְּךָ
and Elohim   my father   Isaac   ihvh   the sayer   unto me   return   to your land   and to your kindred

וְאֵיטִיבָה עִמָּךְ:
and I do good   with you

9 And Jacob said, O God of my father Abraham, and God of my father Isaac, the
LORD which saidst unto me, Return unto thy country, and to thy kindred, and I will
deal well with thee:

קָטֹנְתִּי מִכֹּל הַחֲסָדִים
I am small   from all   the merciful ones

וּמִכָּל־הָאֱמֶת אֲשֶׁר עָשִׂיתָ אֶת־עַבְדֶּךָ
the truth – and from all   which   you did   your servant – that

כִּי בְמַקְלִי עָבַרְתִּי אֶת־הַיַּרְדֵּן הַזֶּה
like   in my staff   I passed   the Jordan – that   the this

וְעַתָּה הָיִיתִי לִשְׁנֵי מַחֲנוֹת:
and now   I am   to two   camps

10 I am not worthy of the least of all the mercies, and of all the truth, which thou hast
shewed unto thy servant; for with my staff I passed over this Jordan; and now I am
become two bands.

הַצִּילֵנִי נָא מִיַּד אָחִי מִיַּד עֵשָׂו
rescue me   now   from hand   my brother   from hand   Esau

כִּי־יָרֵא אָנֹכִי אֹתוֹ פֶּן־יָבוֹא
I fear - like   I am   to him   he will come - lest

וְהִכַּנִי אֵם עַל־בָּנִים:
and smite me   mother   sons – upon

11 Deliver me, I pray thee, from the hand of my brother, from the hand of Esau: for I
fear him, lest he will come and smite me, and the mother with the children.

וְאַתָּה אָמַרְתָּ הֵיטֵב אֵיטִיב עִמָּךְ
and you   you said   the good   I do good   with you

וְשַׂמְתִּי אֶת־זַרְעֲךָ כְּחוֹל הַיָּם אֲשֶׁר לֹא־יִסָּפֵר מֵרֹב׃

from many | it number – not | which | the sea | like sand | your seed – that | and I put

12 And thou saidst, I will surely do thee good, and make thy seed as the sand of the sea, which cannot be numbered for multitude.

[שני]

וַיָּלֶן שָׁם בַּלַּיְלָה הַהוּא

the it | in night | there | and he spend night

וַיִּקַּח מִן־הַבָּא בְיָדוֹ מִנְחָה לְעֵשָׂו אָחִיו׃

his brother | to Esau | offering | in his hand | the come – from | and he took

13 And he lodged there that same night; and took of that which came to his hand a present for Esau his brother;

עִזִּים מָאתַיִם וּתְיָשִׁים עֶשְׂרִים רְחֵלִים מָאתַיִם

200 | ewes | 20 | and he goats | 200 | she goats

וְאֵילִים עֶשְׂרִים׃

20 | and rams

14 Two hundred she goats, and twenty he goats, two hundred ewes, and twenty rams,

גְּמַלִּים מֵינִיקוֹת וּבְנֵיהֶם שְׁלֹשִׁים פָּרוֹת אַרְבָּעִים

40 | kine | 30 | and their sons | milch | camels

וּפָרִים עֲשָׂרָה אֲתֹנֹת עֶשְׂרִים וַעְיָרִם עֲשָׂרָה׃

10 | and foals | 20 | she asses | 10 | and bulls

15 Thirty milch camels with their colts, forty kine, and ten bulls, twenty she asses, and ten foals.

וַיִּתֵּן בְּיַד־עֲבָדָיו עֵדֶר עֵדֶר לְבַדּוֹ

alone | drove | drove | his servants – in hand | and he gave

וַיֹּאמֶר אֶל־עֲבָדָיו עִבְרוּ לְפָנַי

before | you pass | his servants – unto | and he said

וְרֶוַח תָּשִׂימוּ בֵּין עֵדֶר וּבֵין עֵדֶר׃

drove | and between | drove | between | you put it | and interval

16 And he delivered them into the hand of his servants, every drove by themselves; and said unto his servants, Pass over before me, and put a space betwixt drove and drove.

וַיְצַו אֶת־הָרִאשׁוֹן לֵאמֹר כִּי יִפְגָּשְׁךָ עֵשָׂו אָחִי

my brother | Esau | he meets you | like | to say | the first – that | and he commanded

וּשְׁאֵלְךָ לֵאמֹר לְמִי־אַתָּה וְאָנָה תֵלֵךְ

you go | and where | you – to who | to say | and asks you

וּלְמִי אֵלֶּה לְפָנֶיךָ׃

before you | these | and to who

17 And he commanded the foremost, saying, When Esau my brother meeteth thee,

and asketh thee, saying, Whose art thou? and whither goest thou? and whose are these
before thee?

וְאָמַרְתָּ לְעַבְדְּךָ לְיַעֲקֹב מִנְחָה הִוא שְׁלוּחָה לַאדֹנִי לְעֵשָׂו

| to Esau | to my master | a sent present | it | offering | to Jacob | to your servant | and you say |

וְהִנֵּה גַם־הוּא אַחֲרֵינוּ:

| after us | it – also | and here |

18 Then thou shalt say, They be thy servant Jacob's; it is a present sent unto my lord
Esau: and, behold, also he is behind us.

וַיְצַו גַּם אֶת־הַשֵּׁנִי גַּם אֶת־הַשְּׁלִישִׁי

| the third – that | also | the second – that | also | and he commanded |

גַּם אֶת־כָּל־הַהֹלְכִים אַחֲרֵי הָעֲדָרִים לֵאמֹר כַּדָּבָר הַזֶּה

| the this | like speak | to say | the droves | after | the walking ones – all – that | also |

תְּדַבְּרוּן אֶל־עֵשָׂו בְּמֹצַאֲכֶם אֹתוֹ:

| to him | in you finding | Esau - unto | you will speak |

19 And so commanded he the second, and the third, and all that followed the droves,
saying, On this manner shall ye speak unto Esau, when ye find him.

וַאֲמַרְתֶּם גַּם הִנֵּה עַבְדְּךָ יַעֲקֹב אַחֲרֵינוּ

| after us | Jacob | your servant | here | also | and you say |

כִּי־אָמַר אֲכַפְּרָה פָנָיו בַּמִּנְחָה הַהֹלֶכֶת לְפָנָי

| before me | the goings | in offering | his face | I will appease | he said - like |

וְאַחֲרֵי־כֵן אֶרְאֶה פָנָיו אוּלַי יִשָּׂא פָנָי:

| face | he will lift | perhaps | his face | I will see | thus – and after |

20 And say ye moreover, Behold, thy servant Jacob is behind us. For he said, I will
appease him with the present that goeth before me, and afterward I will see his face;
peradventure he will accept of me.

וַתַּעֲבֹר הַמִּנְחָה עַל־פָּנָיו

| his face – upon | the offering | and it passed |

וְהוּא לָן בַּלַּיְלָה־הַהוּא בַּמַּחֲנֶה:

| in camp | the it – in night | spent night | and he |

21 So went the present over before him: and himself lodged that night in the company.

וַיָּקָם בַּלַּיְלָה הוּא וַיִּקַּח אֶת־שְׁתֵּי נָשָׁיו

| wives | two – that | and he took | it | in night | and he arose |

וְאֶת־שְׁתֵּי שִׁפְחֹתָיו וְאֶת־אַחַד עָשָׂר יְלָדָיו

| his children | ----11------ - and that | his maids | two – and that |

וַיַּעֲבֹר אֵת מַעֲבַר יַבֹּק:

| Jabbok | crossing | that | and he passed |

22 And he rose up that night, and took his two wives, and his two women servants, and

his eleven sons, and passed over the ford Jabbok.

וַיִּקָּחֵם   וַיַּעֲבִרֵם   אֶת־הַנָּחַל   וַיַּעֲבֵר   אֶת־אֲשֶׁר־לֽוֹ׃
and he took them   and he passes over   the river – that   and he passed   to him – which – that

23 And he took them, and sent them over the brook, and sent over that he had.

וַיִּוָּתֵר   יַעֲקֹב   לְבַדּוֹ
and he tarried   Jacob   alone

וַיֵּאָבֵק   אִישׁ   עִמּוֹ   עַד   עֲלוֹת   הַשָּֽׁחַר׃
and he wrestled   man   with him   till   rose up   the morning sun

24 And Jacob was left alone; and there wrestled a man with him until the breaking of the day.

וַיַּרְא   כִּי   לֹא   יָכֹל   לוֹ   וַיִּגַּע   בְּכַף־יְרֵכוֹ
and he saw   like   not   he able   to him   and he touched   his thigh - in palm

וַתֵּקַע   כַּף־יֶרֶךְ   יַעֲקֹב   בְּהֵאָבְקוֹ   עִמּֽוֹ׃
and it broke   thigh - palm   Jacob   in the his wrestling   with him

25 And when he saw that he prevailed not against him, he touched the hollow of his thigh; and the hollow of Jacob's thigh was out of joint, as he wrestled with him.

וַיֹּאמֶר   שַׁלְּחֵנִי   כִּי   עָלָה   הַשָּׁחַר
and he said   send me   like   rises   morning sun

וַיֹּאמֶר   לֹא   אֲשַׁלֵּחֲךָ   כִּי   אִם־בֵּרַכְתָּֽנִי׃
and he said   not   I will send you   like   you bless me – if

26 And he said, Let me go, for the day breaketh. And he said, I will not let thee go, except thou bless me.

וַיֹּאמֶר   אֵלָיו   מַה־שְּׁמֶךָ   וַיֹּאמֶר   יַעֲקֹֽב׃
and he said   unto him   your name – what   and he said   Jacob

27 And he said unto him, What is thy name? And he said, Jacob.

וַיֹּאמֶר   לֹא   יַעֲקֹב   יֵאָמֵר   עוֹד   שִׁמְךָ
and he said   not   Jacob   it will be said   again   your name

כִּי   אִם־יִשְׂרָאֵל   כִּי־שָׂרִיתָ   עִם־אֱלֹהִים   וְעִם־אֲנָשִׁים   וַתּוּכָֽל׃
like   Israel – with   you prince – like   Elohim – with   men – and with   and you prevailed

28 And he said, Thy name shall be called no more Jacob, but Israel: for as a prince hast thou power with God and with men, and hast prevailed.

וַיִּשְׁאַל   יַעֲקֹב   וַיֹּאמֶר   הַגִּידָה־נָּא   שְׁמֶךָ
and he asked   Jacob   and he said   now – the you tell   your name

וַיֹּאמֶר   לָמָּה   זֶּה   תִּשְׁאַל   לִשְׁמִי   וַיְבָרֶךְ   אֹתוֹ   שָֽׁם׃
and he said   why   this   you ask   to my name   and he blessed   to him   there

29 And Jacob asked him, and said, Tell me, I pray thee, thy name. And he said, Wherefore is it that thou dost ask after my name? And he blessed him there.

[שלישי]

וַיִּקְרָא יַעֲקֹב שֵׁם הַמָּקוֹם פְּנִיאֵל
Peniel   the place   name   Jacob   and he called

כִּי־רָאִיתִי אֱלֹהִים פָּנִים אֶל־פָּנִים וַתִּנָּצֵל נַפְשִׁי׃
my soul   and it preserved   faces – unto   faces   Elohim   I saw – like

30 And Jacob called the name of the place Peniel: for I have seen God face to face, and my life is preserved.

וַיִּזְרַח־לוֹ הַשֶּׁמֶשׁ כַּאֲשֶׁר עָבַר אֶת־פְּנוּאֵל
Penuel – that   passed   when   the sun   to him – and it sunrise

וְהוּא צֹלֵעַ עַל־יְרֵכוֹ׃
his thigh – upon   halted   and he

31 And as he passed over Penuel the sun rose upon him, and he halted upon his thigh.

עַל־כֵּן לֹא־יֹאכְלוּ בְנֵי־יִשְׂרָאֵל אֶת־גִּיד הַנָּשֶׁה
the shank   sinew - that   Israel – sons   they eat – not   thus - upon

אֲשֶׁר עַל־כַּף הַיָּרֵךְ עַד הַיּוֹם הַזֶּה
the this   the day   till   the thigh   palm – upon   which

כִּי נָגַע בְּכַף־יֶרֶךְ יַעֲקֹב בְּגִיד הַנָּשֶׁה׃
the shank   in sinew   Jacob   thigh – in palm   touched   like

32 Therefore the children of Israel eat not of the sinew which shrank, which is upon the hollow of the thigh, unto this day: because he touched the hollow of Jacob's thigh in the sinew that shrank.

Chapter 33

ספר בראשית פרק לג

וַיִּשָּׂא יַעֲקֹב עֵינָיו וַיַּרְא וְהִנֵּה עֵשָׂו בָּא
comes   Esau   and here   and he saw   his eye   Jacob   and he lifted

וְעִמּוֹ אַרְבַּע מֵאוֹת אִישׁ
man   hundred   four   and with him

וַיַּחַץ אֶת־הַיְלָדִים עַל־לֵאָה וְעַל־רָחֵל
Rachel – and upon   Leah – upon   the children – that   and he proportioned

וְעַל שְׁתֵּי הַשְּׁפָחוֹת׃
the maids   two   and upon

1 And Jacob lifted up his eyes, and looked, and, behold, Esau came, and with him four hundred men. And he divided the children unto Leah, and unto Rachel, and unto the two handmaids.

וַיָּשֶׂם אֶת־הַשְּׁפָחוֹת וְאֶת־יַלְדֵיהֶן רִאשֹׁנָה
towards first   their children – and that   the maids – that   and he put

וְאֶת־לֵאָה וִילָדֶיהָ אַחֲרֹנִים
after ones   and her children   Leah – and that

וְאֶת־רָחֵל וְאֶת־יוֹסֵף אַחֲרֹנִים:
after ones   Joseph – and that   Rachel – and that

2 And he put the handmaids and their children foremost, and Leah and her children after, and Rachel and Joseph hindermost.

וְהוּא עָבַר לִפְנֵיהֶם
before them   passed   and he

וַיִּשְׁתַּחוּ אַרְצָה שֶׁבַע פְּעָמִים עַד־גִּשְׁתּוֹ עַד־אָחִיו:
his brother - till   drew near - till   times   seven   towards ground   and he bowed

3 And he passed over before them, and bowed himself to the ground seven times, until he came near to his brother.

וַיָּרָץ עֵשָׂו לִקְרָאתוֹ וַיְחַבְּקֵהוּ
and he embraced him   to his meeting   Esau   and he ran

וַיִּפֹּל עַל־צַוָּארָו וַיִּשָּׁקֵהוּ וַיִּבְכּוּ:
and they wept   and he kissed him   his neck – upon   and he fell

4 And Esau ran to meet him, and embraced him, and fell on his neck, and kissed him: and they wept.

וַיִּשָּׂא אֶת־עֵינָיו וַיַּרְא אֶת־הַנָּשִׁים וְאֶת־הַיְלָדִים
the children – and that   the women – that   and he saw   his eyes – that   and he lifted

וַיֹּאמֶר מִי־אֵלֶּה לָּךְ
to you   these – who   and he said

וַיֹּאמַר הַיְלָדִים אֲשֶׁר־חָנַן אֱלֹהִים אֶת־עַבְדֶּךָ:
your servant – that   Elohim   graced – which   the children   and he said

5 And he lifted up his eyes, and saw the women and the children; and said, Who are those with thee? And he said, The children which God hath graciously given thy servant.

[רביעי]

וַתִּגַּשְׁןָ הַשְּׁפָחוֹת הֵנָּה וְיַלְדֵיהֶן וַתִּשְׁתַּחֲוֶיןָ:
and they bowed themselves   and their children   there   the handmaidens   and they came near

6 Then the handmaidens came near, they and their children, and they bowed themselves.

וַתִּגַּשׁ גַּם־לֵאָה וִילָדֶיהָ וַיִּשְׁתַּחֲווּ
and they bowed   and her children   Leah – also   and she came near

וְאַחַר נִגַּשׁ יוֹסֵף וְרָחֵל וַיִּשְׁתַּחֲווּ:
and they bowed   and Rachel   Joseph   came near   and after

7 And Leah also with her children came near, and bowed themselves: and after came Joseph near and Rachel, and they bowed themselves.

וַיֹּאמֶר מִי לְךָ כָּל־הַמַּחֲנֶה הַזֶּה אֲשֶׁר פָּגָשְׁתִּי
I met   which   the this   the camp – all   to you   who   and he said

וַיֹּאמֶר לִמְצֹא־חֵן בְּעֵינֵי אֲדֹנִי׃
my lord   in eyes   grace – to find   and he said

8 And he said, What meanest thou by all this drove which I met? And he said, These are
to find grace in the sight of my lord.

וַיֹּאמֶר עֵשָׂו יֶשׁ־לִי רָב אָחִי יְהִי לְךָ אֲשֶׁר־לָךְ׃
to you – which   to you   it be   my brother   much   to me – there is   Esau   and he said

9 And Esau said, I have enough, my brother; keep that thou hast unto thyself.

וַיֹּאמֶר יַעֲקֹב אַל־נָא אִם־נָא מָצָאתִי חֵן בְּעֵינֶיךָ
In your eyes   grace   my finding   please – if   please – unto   Jacob   and he said

וְלָקַחְתָּ מִנְחָתִי מִיָּדִי כִּי עַל־כֵּן רָאִיתִי פָנֶיךָ
your face   I saw   thus – upon   like   from my hand   my offering   and you take

כִּרְאֹת פְּנֵי אֱלֹהִים וַתִּרְצֵנִי׃
and you were pleased me   Elohim   face   like I see

10 And Jacob said, Nay, I pray thee, if now I have found grace in thy sight, then receive
my present at my hand: for therefore I have seen thy face, as though I had seen the face
of God, and thou wast pleased with me.

קַח־נָא אֶת־בִּרְכָתִי אֲשֶׁר הֻבָאת לָךְ כִּי־חַנַּנִי אֱלֹהִים
Elohim   granted me – like   to you   brought   which   my blessing – that   please - take

וְכִי יֶשׁ־לִי־כֹל
all – to me – there is   and like

וַיִּפְצַר־בּוֹ וַיִּקָּח׃
and he took   in him – he urged

11 Take, I pray thee, my blessing that is brought to thee; because God hath dealt
graciously with me, and because I have enough. And he urged him, and he took it.

וַיֹּאמֶר נִסְעָה וְנֵלֵכָה וְאֵלְכָה לְנֶגְדֶּךָ׃
to before you   and I go   and we go   we journey   and he said

12 And he said, Let us take our journey, and let us go, and I will go before thee.

וַיֹּאמֶר אֵלָיו אֲדֹנִי יֹדֵעַ כִּי־הַיְלָדִים רַכִּים
tender ones   the children – like   knows   my lord   unto him   and he said

וְהַצֹּאן וְהַבָּקָר עָלוֹת עָלָי
upon me   calves   and cattle   and the sheep

וּדְפָקוּם יוֹם אֶחָד וָמֵתוּ כָּל־הַצֹּאן׃
the sheep – all   and they die   one   day   and over driving

13 And he said unto him, My lord knoweth that the children are tender, and the flocks
and herds with young are with me: and if men should overdrive them one day, all the
flock will die.

יַעֲבָר־נָא אֲדֹנִי לִפְנֵי עַבְדּוֹ
his servant   before   my lord   please – he pass

וַאֲנִי אֶתְנַהֲלָה לְאִטִּי לְרֶגֶל הַמְּלָאכָה אֲשֶׁר־לְפָנַי
before me – which   the work   to moment   to softly   that will lead   and I

וּלְרֶגֶל הַיְלָדִים עַד אֲשֶׁר־אָבֹא אֶל־אֲדֹנִי שֵׂעִירָה׃
towards Seir   my lord – unto   I come – which   till   the children   and to moment

14 Let my lord, I pray thee, pass over before his servant: and I will lead on softly, according as the cattle that goeth before me and the children be able to endure, until I come unto my lord unto Seir.

וַיֹּאמֶר עֵשָׂו אַצִּיגָה־נָּא עִמְּךָ מִן־הָעָם אֲשֶׁר אִתִּי
with me   which   the people – from   with you   please – leave behind   Esau   and he said

וַיֹּאמֶר לָמָּה זֶּה אֶמְצָא־חֵן בְּעֵינֵי אֲדֹנִי׃
my lord   in eyes   grace – I find   this   why   and he said

15 And Esau said, Let me now leave with thee some of the folk that are with me. And he said, What needeth it? let me find grace in the sight of my lord.

וַיָּשָׁב בַּיּוֹם הַהוּא עֵשָׂו לְדַרְכּוֹ שֵׂעִירָה׃
towards Seir   to his way   Esau   the it   in day   and he returned

16 So Esau returned that day on his way unto Seir.

וְיַעֲקֹב נָסַע סֻכֹּתָה וַיִּבֶן לוֹ בָּיִת
house   to him   and he built   towards Succoth   journeyed   and Jacob

וּלְמִקְנֵהוּ עָשָׂה סֻכֹּת עַל־כֵּן קָרָא שֵׁם־הַמָּקוֹם סֻכּוֹת׃
Succoth   the place – name   called   thus – upon   Succoth   did   and to his cattle

17 And Jacob journeyed to Succoth, and built him an house, and made booths for his cattle: therefore the name of the place is called Succoth.

ס

וַיָּבֹא יַעֲקֹב שָׁלֵם עִיר שְׁכֶם אֲשֶׁר בְּאֶרֶץ כְּנַעַן
Canaan   in earth   which   Shechem   city   Shalem   Jacob   and he came

בְּבֹאוֹ מִפַּדַּן אֲרָם וַיִּחַן אֶת־פְּנֵי הָעִיר׃
the city   face – that   and he pitched   aram   from Padan   in his coming

18 And Jacob came to Shalem, a city of Shechem, which is in the land of Canaan, when he came from Padan-aram; and pitched his tent before the city.

וַיִּקֶן אֶת־חֶלְקַת הַשָּׂדֶה אֲשֶׁר נָטָה־שָׁם אָהֳלוֹ
his tent   there – spread   which   the field   portion – that   and he bought

מִיַּד בְּנֵי־חֲמוֹר אֲבִי שְׁכֶם בְּמֵאָה קְשִׂיטָה׃
Casita   in hundred   Shechem   father   Hamor – son   from hand

19 And he bought a parcel of a field, where he had spread his tent, at the hand of the children of Hamor, Shechem's father, for an hundred pieces of money.

וַיַּצֶּב־שָׁם מִזְבֵּחַ וַיִּקְרָא־לוֹ אֵל אֱלֹהֵי יִשְׂרָאֵל׃

Israel Elohai El to him – and he called altar there – and he erected

20 And he erected there an altar, and called it El-elohe-Israel.

ס

Chapter 34

ספר בראשית פרק לד

[חמישי]

וַתֵּצֵא דִינָה בַּת־לֵאָה

Leah – daughter Dina and came out

אֲשֶׁר יָלְדָה לְיַעֲקֹב לִרְאוֹת בִּבְנוֹת הָאָרֶץ׃

the earth in daughters to see to Jacob begot which

1 And Dinah the daughter of Leah, which she bare unto Jacob, went out to see the daughters of the land.

וַיַּרְא אֹתָהּ שְׁכֶם בֶּן־חֲמוֹר הַחִוִּי נְשִׂיא הָאָרֶץ

the land prince the Hivite Hamor – son Shechem to her and he saw

וַיִּקַּח אֹתָהּ וַיִּשְׁכַּב אֹתָהּ וַיְעַנֶּהָ׃

and he defiled her to her and he laid to her and he took her

2 And when Shechem the son of Hamor the Hivite, prince of the country, saw her, he took her, and lay with her, and defiled her.

וַתִּדְבַּק נַפְשׁוֹ בְּדִינָה בַּת־יַעֲקֹב

Jacob – daughter in Dina his soul and it clung

וַיֶּאֱהַב אֶת־הַנַּעֲרָ וַיְדַבֵּר עַל־לֵב הַנַּעֲרָ׃

the girl heart – upon and he spoke the girl – that and he loved

3 And his soul clave unto Dinah the daughter of Jacob, and he loved the damsel, and spake kindly unto the damsel.

וַיֹּאמֶר שְׁכֶם אֶל־חֲמוֹר אָבִיו לֵאמֹר

to say his father Hamor – unto Shechem and he said

קַח־לִי אֶת־הַיַּלְדָּה הַזֹּאת לְאִשָּׁה׃

to wife the this the girl – that to me – take

4 And Shechem spake unto his father Hamor, saying, Get me this damsel to wife.

וְיַעֲקֹב שָׁמַע כִּי טִמֵּא אֶת־דִּינָה בִתּוֹ

his daughter Dina – that defiled like heard and Jacob

וּבָנָיו הָיוּ אֶת־מִקְנֵהוּ בַּשָּׂדֶה וְהֶחֱרִשׁ יַעֲקֹב עַד־בֹּאָם׃

their coming – till Jacob and the held silence in field his cattle – that they were and his sons

5 And Jacob heard that he had defiled Dinah his daughter: now his sons were with his cattle in the field: and Jacob held his peace until they were come.

וַיֵּצֵא   חֲמוֹר אֲבִי־שְׁכֶם אֶל־יַעֲקֹב לְדַבֵּר אִתּֽוֹ׃

with him	to speak	Jacob – unto	Shecem – his father	Hamor	and he went out

6 And Hamor the father of Shechem went out unto Jacob to commune with him.

וּבְנֵי יַעֲקֹב בָּאוּ   מִן־הַשָּׂדֶה כְּשָׁמְעָם

like they heard	the field – from	they came	Jacob	and sons

וַיִּֽתְעַצְּבוּ הָֽאֲנָשִׁים וַיִּחַר   לָהֶם מְאֹד

greatly	to them	and it infuriated	the men	and they grieved

כִּי נְבָלָה עָשָׂה בְיִשְׂרָאֵל לִשְׁכַּב אֶת־בַּת־יַעֲקֹב

Jacob – daughter – that	to lay	in Israel	did	folly	like

וְכֵן לֹא יֵעָשֶֽׂה׃

it done	not	and thus

7 And the sons of Jacob came out of the field when they heard it: and the men were grieved, and they were very wroth, because he had wrought folly in Israel in lying with Jacob's daughter; which thing ought not to be done.

וַיְדַבֵּר חֲמוֹר אִתָּם לֵאמֹר

to say	with them	Hamor	and he spoke

שְׁכֶם בְּנִי חָשְׁקָה נַפְשׁוֹ בְּבִתְּכֶם

in your daughter	his soul	longeth	my son	Shechem

תְּנוּ נָא אֹתָהּ לוֹ לְאִשָּֽׁה׃

to wife	to him	to her	please	give you

8 And Hamor communed with them, saying, The soul of my son Shechem longeth for your daughter: I pray you give her him to wife.

וְהִֽתְחַתְּנוּ   אֹתָנוּ בְּנֹתֵיכֶם תִּתְּנוּ־לָנוּ

to us – you give	your daughters	to us	and you cause to marry

וְאֶת־בְּנֹתֵינוּ תִּקְחוּ לָכֶֽם׃

to you	you take	our daughters – and that

9 And make ye marriages with us, and give your daughters unto us, and take our daughters unto you.

וְאִתָּנוּ תֵּשֵׁבוּ וְהָאָרֶץ תִּהְיֶה לִפְנֵיכֶם

before you	it will be	and the earth	you will dwell it	and with us

שְׁבוּ וּסְחָרוּהָ וְהֵֽאָחֲזוּ בָּֽהּ׃

in it	and you the take possession	and trade in it	you dwell

10 And ye shall dwell with us: and the land shall be before you; dwell and trade ye therein, and get you possessions therein.

וַיֹּאמֶר שְׁכֶם אֶל־אָבִיהָ

her father – unto	Shechem	and he said

וְאֶל־אַחֶיהָ אֶמְצָא־חֵן בְּעֵינֵיכֶם
in your eyes   grace – I find   her brothers – and unto

וַאֲשֶׁר תֹּאמְרוּ אֵלַי אֶתֵּן:
I will give   unto me   you say it   and which

11 And Shechem said unto her father and unto her brethren, Let me find grace in your
eyes, and what ye shall say unto me I will give.

הַרְבּוּ עָלַי מְאֹד מֹהַר וּמַתָּן
and gift   dowry   greatly   upon me   the much it

וְאֶתְּנָה כַּאֲשֶׁר תֹּאמְרוּ אֵלָי
unto me   you say it   when   and I will give

וּתְנוּ־לִי אֶת־הַנַּעֲרָ לְאִשָּׁה:
to wife   the girl – that   to me – and you give

12 Ask me never so much dowry and gift, and I will give according as ye shall say unto
me: but give me the damsel to wife.

וַיַּעֲנוּ בְנֵי־יַעֲקֹב אֶת־שְׁכֶם
Shechem - that   Jacob - sons   and they answered

וְאֶת־חֲמוֹר אָבִיו בְּמִרְמָה
in deceit   his father   Hamor – and that

וַיְדַבֵּרוּ אֲשֶׁר טִמֵּא אֵת דִּינָה אֲחֹתָם:
their sister   Dinah   that   defiled   which   and they spoke

13 And the sons of Jacob answered Shechem and Hamor his father deceitfully, and said,
because he had defiled Dinah their sister:

וַיֹּאמְרוּ אֲלֵיהֶם לֹא נוּכַל לַעֲשׂוֹת הַדָּבָר הַזֶּה
the this   the matter   to doings   we able   not   unto them   and they said

לָתֵת אֶת־אֲחֹתֵנוּ לְאִישׁ אֲשֶׁר־לוֹ עָרְלָה
foreskin   to him – which   to wife   our sisters – that   to give

כִּי־חֶרְפָּה הוּא לָנוּ:
to us   it   reproach - like

14 And they said unto them, We cannot do this thing, to give our sister to one that is
uncircumcised; for that were a reproach unto us:

אַךְ־בְּזֹאת נֵאוֹת לָכֶם אִם תִּהְיוּ כָמֹנוּ
like be us   they will be   with   to them   consent   in this - only

לְהִמֹּל לָכֶם כָּל־זָכָר:
male – all   to you   to circumcise

15 But in this will we consent unto you: If ye will be as we be, that every male of you be
circumcised;

וְנָתַ֤נּוּ אֶת־בְּנֹתֵ֙ינוּ֙ לָכֶ֔ם וְאֶת־בְּנֹתֵיכֶ֖ם נִקַּֽח־לָ֑נוּ

to us – we take   your daughters - and that   to you   our daughters – that   and we will give you

וְיָשַׁ֣בְנוּ אִתְּכֶ֔ם וְהָיִ֖ינוּ לְעַ֥ם אֶחָֽד׃

one   to people   and we will be   with you   and we will dwell

16 Then will we give our daughters unto you, and we will take your daughters to us, and we will dwell with you, and we will become one people.

וְאִם־לֹ֧א תִשְׁמְע֛וּ אֵלֵ֖ינוּ לְהִמּ֑וֹל

to circumcise   unto us   you hear   not – and if

וְלָקַ֥חְנוּ אֶת־בִּתֵּ֖נוּ וְהָלָֽכְנוּ׃

and we go   our daughter – that   and we take

17 But if ye will not hearken unto us, to be circumcised; then will we take our daughter, and we will be gone.

וַיִּֽיטְב֥וּ דִבְרֵיהֶ֖ם בְּעֵינֵ֣י חֲמ֑וֹר

Hamor   in eyes   their speaking   and they pleased

וּבְעֵינֵ֖י שְׁכֶ֥ם בֶּן־חֲמֽוֹר׃

Hamor – son   Shechem   and in eyes

18 And their words pleased Hamor, and Shechem Hamor's son.

וְלֹֽא־אֵחַ֤ר הַנַּ֙עַר֙ לַעֲשׂ֣וֹת הַדָּבָ֔ר כִּ֥י חָפֵ֖ץ בְּבַת־יַעֲקֹ֑ב

Jacob – in daughter   delight   like   the matter   to doings   the young man   deferred – and not

וְה֣וּא נִכְבָּ֔ד מִכֹּ֖ל בֵּ֥ית אָבִֽיו׃

his father   house   from all   most honored   and he

19 And the young man deferred not to do the thing, because he had delight in Jacob's daughter: and he was more honourable than all the house of his father.

וַיָּבֹ֥א חֲמ֛וֹר וּשְׁכֶ֥ם בְּנ֖וֹ אֶל־שַׁ֣עַר עִירָ֑ם

their city   gate – unto   his son   and Shechem   Hamor   and he came

וַיְדַבְּר֛וּ אֶל־אַנְשֵׁ֥י עִירָ֖ם לֵאמֹֽר׃

to say   their city   men – unto   they spoke

20 And Hamor and Shechem his son came unto the gate of their city, and communed with the men of their city, saying,

הָאֲנָשִׁ֨ים הָאֵ֜לֶּה שְׁלֵמִ֧ים הֵ֣ם אִתָּ֗נוּ

with us   them   peaceful ones   the these   the men

וְיֵשְׁב֤וּ בָאָ֙רֶץ֙ וְיִסְחֲר֣וּ אֹתָ֔הּ

to it   and they will trade   in land   and they will dwell

וְהָאָ֙רֶץ֙ הִנֵּ֣ה רַֽחֲבַת־יָדַ֔יִם לִפְנֵיהֶ֑ם

before them   hands – wide   here   and the land

אֶת־בְּנֹתָ֞ם נִֽקַּח־לָ֣נוּ לְנָשִׁ֗ים

to wives   to us – we take   their daughters – that

וְאֶת־בְּנֹתֵינוּ נִתֵּן לָהֶם:

<small>to them　we give　our daughters – and that</small>

21 These men are peaceable with us; therefore let them dwell in the land, and trade therein; for the land, behold, it is large enough for them; let us take their daughters to us for wives, and let us give them our daughters.

אַךְ־בְּזֹאת יֵאֹתוּ לָנוּ הָאֲנָשִׁים לָשֶׁבֶת אִתָּנוּ

<small>with us　to dwell　the men　to us　they consent　in this - only</small>

לִהְיוֹת לְעַם אֶחָד בְּהִמּוֹל לָנוּ כָּל־זָכָר כַּאֲשֶׁר הֵם נִמֹּלִים:

<small>we circumcised ones　them　when　male - all　to us　in circumcised　one　to people　to be</small>

22 Only herein will the men consent unto us for to dwell with us, to be one people, if every male among us be circumcised, as they are circumcised.

מִקְנֵהֶם וְקִנְיָנָם וְכָל־בְּהֶמְתָּם הֲלוֹא לָנוּ הֵם

<small>them　to us　the not　their beasts – and all　and their possessions　their cattle</small>

אַךְ נֵאוֹתָה לָהֶם וְיֵשְׁבוּ אִתָּנוּ:

<small>with us　and they will dwell　to them　we consent　only</small>

23 Shall not their cattle and their substance and every beast of theirs be ours? only let us consent unto them, and they will dwell with us.

וַיִּשְׁמְעוּ אֶל־חֲמוֹר וְאֶל־שְׁכֶם בְּנוֹ כָּל־יֹצְאֵי שַׁעַר עִירוֹ

<small>his city　gate　come out – all　his son　Shechem – and unto　Hamor – unto　and they heard</small>

וַיִּמֹּלוּ כָּל־זָכָר כָּל־יֹצְאֵי שַׁעַר עִירוֹ:

<small>his city　gate　coming out ones – all　male – all　and they circumcised</small>

24 And unto Hamor and unto Shechem his son hearkened all that went out of the gate of his city; and every male was circumcised, all that went out of the gate of his city.

וַיְהִי בַיּוֹם הַשְּׁלִישִׁי בִּהְיוֹתָם כֹּאֲבִים

<small>pain ones　in them being　the third　in day　and it was</small>

וַיִּקְחוּ שְׁנֵי־בְנֵי־יַעֲקֹב שִׁמְעוֹן וְלֵוִי אֲחֵי דִינָה

<small>Dinah　brothers　and Levi　Simon　Jacob – sons – two　and they took</small>

אִישׁ חַרְבּוֹ וַיָּבֹאוּ עַל־הָעִיר בֶּטַח

<small>securely　the city – upon　and they came　his sword　each man</small>

וַיַּהַרְגוּ כָּל־זָכָר:

<small>males – all　and they slew</small>

25 And it came to pass on the third day, when they were sore, that two of the sons of Jacob, Simeon and Levi, Dinah's brethren, took each man his sword, and came upon the city boldly, and slew all the males.

וְאֶת־חֲמוֹר וְאֶת־שְׁכֶם בְּנוֹ הָרְגוּ לְפִי־חָרֶב

<small>sword – to edge　and they slew　his son　Shechem – and that　Hamor – and that</small>

וַיִּקְחוּ אֶת־דִּינָה מִבֵּית שְׁכֶם וַיֵּצֵאוּ:

<small>and they went out　Shechem　from house　Dinah – that　and they took</small>

26 And they slew Hamor and Shechem his son with the edge of the sword, and took Dinah out of Shechem's house, and went out.

בְּנֵי יַעֲקֹב בָּאוּ עַל־הַחֲלָלִים

sons	Jacob	they came	upon - the slain

וַיָּבֹזּוּ הָעִיר אֲשֶׁר טִמְּאוּ אֲחוֹתָם׃

and they spoiled it	the city	which	defiled	their sister

27 The sons of Jacob came upon the slain, and spoiled the city, because they had defiled their sister.

אֶת־צֹאנָם וְאֶת־בְּקָרָם וְאֶת־חֲמֹרֵיהֶם

that - their sheep	and that - their cattle	and that - their asses

וְאֵת אֲשֶׁר־בָּעִיר וְאֶת־אֲשֶׁר בַּשָּׂדֶה לָקָחוּ׃

and that	which - in city	and that - which	in field	they took

28 They took their sheep, and their oxen, and their asses, and that which was in the city, and that which was in the field,

וְאֶת־כָּל־חֵילָם וְאֶת־כָּל־טַפָּם וְאֶת־נְשֵׁיהֶם שָׁבוּ

and that - all - their force	and that - all - little ones	and that - their women	they returned

וַיָּבֹזּוּ וְאֵת כָּל־אֲשֶׁר בַּבָּיִת׃

and they spoiled it	and that	all - which	in house

29 And all their wealth, and all their little ones, and their wives took they captive, and spoiled even all that was in the house.

וַיֹּאמֶר יַעֲקֹב אֶל־שִׁמְעוֹן וְאֶל־לֵוִי

and he said	Jacob	unto - Simon	and unto - Levi

עֲכַרְתֶּם אֹתִי לְהַבְאִישֵׁנִי בְּיֹשֵׁב הָאָרֶץ בַּכְּנַעֲנִי וּבַפְּרִזִּי

you troubled	me	to the stink me	in dwelling	the land	in Canaanites	in Perizzites

וַאֲנִי מְתֵי מִסְפָּר וְנֶאֶסְפוּ עָלַי

and I	few	number	and they gather	upon me

וְהִכּוּנִי וְנִשְׁמַדְתִּי אֲנִי וּבֵיתִי׃

and cause to slay me	and destroy me	I	and my house

30 And Jacob said to Simeon and Levi, Ye have troubled me to make me to stink among the inhabitants of the land, among the Canaanites and the Perizzites: and I being few in number, they shall gather themselves together against me, and slay me; and I shall be destroyed, I and my house.

פ

וַיֹּאמְרוּ הַכְזוֹנָה יַעֲשֶׂה אֶת־אֲחוֹתֵנוּ׃

and they said	the like harlot	he does	that - our sister

31 And they said, Should he deal with our sister as with an harlot?

CHAPTER 35

ספר בראשית פרק לה

וַיֹּאמֶר אֱלֹהִים אֶל־יַעֲקֹב קוּם עֲלֵה בֵית־אֵל וְשֶׁב־שָׁם

there – and dwell   El – house   ascend   rise   Jacob – unto   Elohim   and he said

וַעֲשֵׂה־שָׁם מִזְבֵּחַ לָאֵל הַנִּרְאֶה אֵלֶיךָ בְּבָרְחֲךָ מִפְּנֵי עֵשָׂו אָחִיךָ׃

your brother   Esau   from face   in your fleeing   unto you   the appeared   to El   altar   there – and do

1 And God said unto Jacob, Arise, go up to Beth-el, and dwell there: and make there an altar unto God, that appeared unto thee when thou fleddest from the face of Esau thy brother.

וַיֹּאמֶר יַעֲקֹב אֶל־בֵּיתוֹ וְאֶל כָּל־אֲשֶׁר עִמּוֹ

with him   which – all   and unto   his house – unto   Jacob   and he said

הָסִרוּ אֶת־אֱלֹהֵי הַנֵּכָר אֲשֶׁר בְּתֹכְכֶם

among you   which   the foreign   gods – that   remove it

וְהִטַּהֲרוּ וְהַחֲלִיפוּ שִׂמְלֹתֵיכֶם׃

your garments   and the you change   and cause to clean you

2 Then Jacob said unto his household, and to all that were with him, Put away the strange gods that are among you, and be clean, and change your garments:

וְנָקוּמָה וְנַעֲלֶה בֵּית־אֵל

El – house   and we ascend   and we rise

וְאֶעֱשֶׂה־שָּׁם מִזְבֵּחַ לָאֵל הָעֹנֶה אֹתִי בְּיוֹם צָרָתִי

my distress   in day   to me   the answerer   to El   altar   there – and I will make

וַיְהִי עִמָּדִי בַּדֶּרֶךְ אֲשֶׁר הָלָכְתִּי׃

I went   which   in way   with me   and it be

3 And let us arise, and go up to Beth-el; and I will make there an altar unto God, who answered me in the day of my distress, and was with me in the way which I went.

וַיִּתְּנוּ אֶל־יַעֲקֹב אֵת כָּל־אֱלֹהֵי הַנֵּכָר אֲשֶׁר בְּיָדָם

in their hands   which   the foreign   gods – all   that   Jacob – unto   and they gave

וְאֶת־הַנְּזָמִים אֲשֶׁר בְּאָזְנֵיהֶם

in their ears   which   earrings - and that

וַיִּטְמֹן אֹתָם יַעֲקֹב תַּחַת הָאֵלָה אֲשֶׁר עִם־שְׁכֶם׃

Shechem – with   which   oak   under   Jacob   them   and he hid

4 And they gave unto Jacob all the strange gods which were in their hand, and all their earrings which were in their ears; and Jacob hid them under the oak which was by Shechem.

וַיִּסָּעוּ

and they journeyed

וַיְהִי חִתַּת אֱלֹהִים עַל־הֶעָרִים אֲשֶׁר סְבִיבֹתֵיהֶם

around them / which / the cities – upon / Elohim / terror / and there was

וְלֹא רָדְפוּ אַחֲרֵי בְּנֵי יַעֲקֹב׃

Jacob / sons / after / they pursue / and not

5 And they journeyed: and the terror of God was upon the cities that were round about them, and they did not pursue after the sons of Jacob.

וַיָּבֹא יַעֲקֹב לוּזָה אֲשֶׁר בְּאֶרֶץ כְּנַעַן הִוא בֵּית־אֵל

El – house / it / Canaan / in land / which / towards Luz / Jacob / and he came

הוּא וְכָל־הָעָם אֲשֶׁר־עִמּוֹ׃

with him – which / the people – and all / he

6 So Jacob came to Luz, which is in the land of Canaan, that is, Beth-el, he and all the people that were with him.

וַיִּבֶן שָׁם מִזְבֵּחַ

altar / there / and he built

וַיִּקְרָא לַמָּקוֹם אֵל בֵּית־אֵל

El – Beth / El / to place / and he called

כִּי שָׁם נִגְלוּ אֵלָיו הָאֱלֹהִים בְּבָרְחוֹ מִפְּנֵי אָחִיו׃

his brother / from face / in his fleeing / the Elohim / unto him / it touched / there / like

7 And he built there an altar, and called the place El-beth-el: because there God appeared unto him, when he fled from the face of his brother.

וַתָּמָת דְּבֹרָה מֵינֶקֶת רִבְקָה

Rebekah / nurse / Deborah / and she died

וַתִּקָּבֵר מִתַּחַת לְבֵית־אֵל תַּחַת הָאַלּוֹן

the oak / under / El – to house / beneath / and she buried

וַיִּקְרָא שְׁמוֹ אַלּוֹן בָּכוּת׃

Bachuth – Allon / its name / and he called

8 But Deborah Rebekah's nurse died, and she was buried beneath Beth-el under an oak: and the name of it was called Allon-bachuth.

פ

וַיֵּרָא אֱלֹהִים אֶל־יַעֲקֹב עוֹד בְּבֹאוֹ מִפַּדַּן אֲרָם

Aram / from Padan / in his coming / again / Jacob – unto / Elohim / and he appeared

וַיְבָרֶךְ אֹתוֹ׃

to him / and he blessed

9 And God appeared unto Jacob again, when he came out of Padan-aram, and blessed him.

וַיֹּאמֶר־לוֹ אֱלֹהִים שִׁמְךָ יַעֲקֹב לֹא־יִקָּרֵא שִׁמְךָ עוֹד יַעֲקֹב

Jacob / again / your name / he calls – not / Jacob / your name / Elohim / to him – and he said

כִּי אִם־יִשְׂרָאֵל יִהְיֶה שְׁמֶךָ
your name   it will be   Israel – with   like

וַיִּקְרָא אֶת־שְׁמוֹ יִשְׂרָאֵל:
Israel   his name – that   and he called

10 And God said unto him, Thy name is Jacob: thy name shall not be called any more
Jacob, but Israel shall be thy name: and he called his name Israel.

וַיֹּאמֶר לוֹ אֱלֹהִים אֲנִי אֵל שַׁדַּי
Shadai   El   I   Elohim   to him   and he said

פְּרֵה וּרְבֵה גּוֹי וּקְהַל גּוֹיִם יִהְיֶה מִמֶּךָּ
from you   it will be   nations   and [a] league   nation   multiply   you be fruitful

וּמְלָכִים מֵחֲלָצֶיךָ יֵצֵאוּ:
they will come out   from your loins   and kings

11 And God said unto him, I am God Almighty: be fruitful and multiply; a nation and a
company of nations shall be of thee, and kings shall come out of thy loins;

[שׁשׁי]

וְאֶת־הָאָרֶץ אֲשֶׁר נָתַתִּי לְאַבְרָהָם וּלְיִצְחָק
and to Issac   to Abraham   I gave   which   the land – and that

לְךָ אֶתְּנֶנָּה וּלְזַרְעֲךָ אַחֲרֶיךָ אֶתֵּן אֶת־הָאָרֶץ:
the land – that   I will give   after you   and to your seed   I will give it   to you

12 And the land which I gave Abraham and Isaac, to thee I will give it, and to thy seed
after thee will I give the land.

וַיַּעַל מֵעָלָיו אֱלֹהִים בַּמָּקוֹם אֲשֶׁר־דִּבֶּר אִתּוֹ:
with him   spoke – which   in place   Elohim   from upon him   and he ascended

13 And God went up from him in the place where he talked with him.

וַיַּצֵּב יַעֲקֹב מַצֵּבָה בַּמָּקוֹם
in place   pillar   Jacob   and he set up

אֲשֶׁר־דִּבֶּר אִתּוֹ מַצֶּבֶת אָבֶן
stone   pillar   with him   spoke – which

וַיַּסֵּךְ עָלֶיהָ נֶסֶךְ וַיִּצֹק עָלֶיהָ שָׁמֶן:
oil   upon it   and he poured   drink offering   upon it   he poured

14 And Jacob set up a pillar in the place where he talked with him, even a pillar of
stone: and he poured a drink offering thereon, and he poured oil thereon.

וַיִּקְרָא יַעֲקֹב אֶת־שֵׁם הַמָּקוֹם
the place   name – that   Jacob   and he called

אֲשֶׁר דִּבֶּר אִתּוֹ שָׁם אֱלֹהִים בֵּית־אֵל:
El – house   Elohim   there   to him   spoke   which

15 And Jacob called the name of the place where God spake with him, Beth-el.

וַיִּסְעוּ֙   מִבֵּ֣ית   אֵ֔ל
and they journeyed   from Beth   El

וַֽיְהִי־ע֥וֹד   כִּבְרַת־הָאָ֖רֶץ   לָב֣וֹא   אֶפְרָ֑תָה
again – and it was   the land – like distance   to come   towards Ephrath

וַתֵּ֥לֶד   רָחֵ֖ל   וַתְּקַ֥שׁ   בְּלִדְתָּֽהּ׃
and she bare   Rachel   and she hard   in her birthing

16 And they journeyed from Beth-el; and there was but a little way to come to Ephrath: and Rachel travailed, and she had hard labour.

וַיְהִ֥י   בְהַקְשֹׁתָ֖הּ   בְּלִדְתָּ֑הּ   וַתֹּ֨אמֶר   לָ֤הּ   הַֽמְיַלֶּ֨דֶת֙
and it was   in the hardness   in her birthing   and she said   to her   the midwife

אַל־תִּ֣ירְאִ֔י   כִּֽי־גַם־זֶ֥ה   לָ֖ךְ   בֵּֽן׃
don't – you fear   like – also – this   to you   son

17 And it came to pass, when she was in hard labour, that the midwife said unto her, Fear not; thou shalt have this son also.

וַיְהִ֞י   בְּצֵ֤את   נַפְשָׁהּ֙   כִּ֣י   מֵ֔תָה
and it was   in going out   her soul   like   she died

וַתִּקְרָ֥א   שְׁמ֖וֹ   בֶּן־אוֹנִ֑י   וְאָבִ֖יו   קָֽרָא־ל֥וֹ   בִנְיָמִֽין׃
and she called   his name   Ben – oni   and his father   called – to him   Benjamin

18 And it came to pass, as her soul was in departing, (for she died) that she called his name Ben-oni: but his father called him Benjamin.

וַתָּ֣מָת   רָחֵ֔ל   וַתִּקָּבֵר֙   בְּדֶ֣רֶךְ   אֶפְרָ֔תָה   הִ֖וא   בֵּ֥ית   לָֽחֶם׃
and she died   Rachel   and she was buried   in way   towards Ephrath   it   Beth   lehem

19 And Rachel died, and was buried in the way to Ephrath, which is Beth-lehem.

וַיַּצֵּ֧ב   יַעֲקֹ֛ב   מַצֵּבָ֖ה   עַל־קְבֻרָתָ֑הּ
and he set up   Jacob   pillar   upon – her grave

הִ֛וא   מַצֶּ֥בֶת   קְבֻרַת־רָחֵ֖ל   עַד־הַיּֽוֹם׃
it   pillar   grave – Rachel   till – the day

20 And Jacob set a pillar upon her grave: that is the pillar of Rachel's grave unto this day.

וַיִּסַּ֖ע   יִשְׂרָאֵ֑ל   וַיֵּ֣ט   אָֽהֳלֹ֔ה   מֵהָ֖לְאָה   לְמִגְדַּל־עֵֽדֶר׃
and he traveled   Israel   and he pitched   tent   from beyond   Edar – to tower

21 And Israel journeyed, and spread his tent beyond the tower of Edar.

וַיְהִ֗י   בִּשְׁכֹּ֤ן   יִשְׂרָאֵל֙   בָּאָ֣רֶץ   הַהִ֔וא
and it was   in dwelling   Israel   in land   the it

וַיֵּ֣לֶךְ   רְאוּבֵ֗ן   וַיִּשְׁכַּב֙   אֶת־בִּלְהָה֙   פִּילֶ֣גֶשׁ   אָבִ֔יו   וַיִּשְׁמַ֖ע   יִשְׂרָאֵ֑ל
and he went   Ruben   and he lay   that – Bilhah   concubine   his father   and he heard   Israel

וַיִּהְיוּ בְנֵי־יַעֲקֹב שְׁנֵים עָשָׂר׃

- twelve -   Jacob – son   and they were

22 And it came to pass, when Israel dwelt in that land, that Reuben went and lay with
Bilhah his father's concubine: and Israel heard it. Now the sons of Jacob were twelve:

פ

בְּנֵי לֵאָה בְּכוֹר יַעֲקֹב רְאוּבֵן

Reuben   Jacob   first born   Leah   sons

וְשִׁמְעוֹן וְלֵוִי וִיהוּדָה וְיִשָּׂשכָר וּזְבֻלוּן׃

and Zebulun   and Issachar   and Judah   and Levi   and Simeon

23 The sons of Leah; Reuben, Jacob's firstborn, and Simeon, and Levi, and Judah, and
Issachar, and Zebulun:

בְּנֵי רָחֵל יוֹסֵף וּבִנְיָמִן׃

and Benjamin   Joseph   Rachel   sons

24 The sons of Rachel; Joseph, and Benjamin:

וּבְנֵי בִלְהָה שִׁפְחַת רָחֵל דָּן וְנַפְתָּלִי׃

and Naphtali   Dan   Rachel   maid   Bilhah   and sons

25 And the sons of Bilhah, Rachel's handmaid; Dan, and Naphtali:

וּבְנֵי זִלְפָּה שִׁפְחַת לֵאָה גָּד וְאָשֵׁר

and Asher   Gad   Leah   maid   Zilpah   and sons

אֵלֶּה בְּנֵי יַעֲקֹב אֲשֶׁר יֻלַּד־לוֹ בְּפַדַּן אֲרָם׃

Aram   in Padan   to him – begot   which   Jacob   sons   these

26 And the sons of Zilpah, Leah's handmaid; Gad, and Asher: these are the sons of
Jacob, which were born to him in Padan-aram.

וַיָּבֹא יַעֲקֹב אֶל־יִצְחָק אָבִיו מַמְרֵא קִרְיַת הָאַרְבַּע

the Arbah   city   Mamre   his father   Isaac – unto   Jacob   and he came

הִוא חֶבְרוֹן אֲשֶׁר־גָּר־שָׁם אַבְרָהָם וְיִצְחָק׃

and Isaac   Abraham   there – lived – which   Hebron   it

27 And Jacob came unto Isaac his father unto Mamre, unto the city of Arbah, which is
Hebron, where Abraham and Isaac sojourned.

וַיִּהְיוּ יְמֵי יִצְחָק מְאַת שָׁנָה וּשְׁמֹנִים שָׁנָה׃

years   and sixty   year   hundred   Isaac   days   and they were

28 And the days of Isaac were an hundred and fourscore years.

וַיִּגְוַע יִצְחָק וַיָּמָת וַיֵּאָסֶף אֶל־עַמָּיו

his people – unto   and he gathered   and he died   Isaac   and he expired

זָקֵן וּשְׂבַע יָמִים וַיִּקְבְּרוּ אֹתוֹ עֵשָׂו וְיַעֲקֹב בָּנָיו׃

his sons   and Jacob   Esau   to him   and they buried   days   and full   old

29 And Isaac gave up the ghost, and died, and was gathered unto his people, being old
and full of days: and his sons Esau and Jacob buried him.

CHAPTER 36

ספר בראשית פרק לו

וְאֵ֣לֶּה תֹּלְד֥וֹת עֵשָׂ֖ו ה֥וּא אֱדֽוֹם׃

and these	begettings	Esau	he	Edom

1 Now these are the generations of Esau, who is Edom.

עֵשָׂ֞ו לָקַ֧ח אֶת־נָשָׁ֛יו מִבְּנ֖וֹת כְּנָ֑עַן

Esau	took	women – that	from daughters	Canaan

אֶת־עָדָ֗ה בַּת־אֵילוֹן֙ הַֽחִתִּ֔י

Adah – that	Elon – daughter	the Hittite

וְאֶת־אׇהֳלִ֣יבָמָ֔ה בַּת־עֲנָ֖ה בַּת־צִבְע֥וֹן הַֽחִוִּֽי׃

Aholibamah – that	Anah – daughter	Zibeon – daughter	the Hivite

2 Esau took his wives of the daughters of Canaan; Adah the daughter of Elon the
Hittite, and Aholibamah the daughter of Anah the daughter of Zibeon the Hivite;

וְאֶת־בָּ֣שְׂמַ֔ת בַּת־יִשְׁמָעֵ֖אל אֲח֥וֹת נְבָיֽוֹת׃

Bashemath – that	Ishmael – daughter	sister	Nebajoth

3 And Bashemath Ishmael's daughter, sister of Nebajoth.

וַתֵּ֧לֶד עָדָ֛ה לְעֵשָׂ֖ו אֶת־אֱלִיפָ֑ז וּבָ֣שְׂמַ֔ת יָֽלְדָ֖ה אֶת־רְעוּאֵֽל׃

and she begot	Adah	to Esau	Eliphaz – that	and Bashemath	begot	Reuel – that

4 And Adah bare to Esau Eliphaz; and Bashemath bare Reuel;

וְאׇהֳלִֽיבָמָה֙ יָֽלְדָ֔ה אֶת־יְעִ֥ישׁ [יְעוּשׁ] וְאֶת־יַעְלָ֖ם וְאֶת־קֹֽרַח

and Aholibamah	begot	Jeush – that	Jaalam – and that	Korah – and that

אֵ֖לֶּה בְּנֵ֣י עֵשָׂ֑ו אֲשֶׁ֥ר יֻלְּדוּ־ל֖וֹ בְּאֶ֥רֶץ כְּנָֽעַן׃

these	sons	Esau	which	to him – they begot	in earth	Canaan

5 And Aholibamah bare Jeush, and Jaalam, and Korah: these are the sons of Esau,
which were born unto him in the land of Canaan.

וַיִּקַּ֣ח עֵשָׂ֡ו אֶת־נָשָׁיו֩ וְאֶת־בָּנָ֨יו וְאֶת־בְּנֹתָ֜יו

and he took	Esau	his women – that	his sons – and that	his daughters – and that

וְאֶת־כׇּל־נַפְשׁ֣וֹת בֵּית֗וֹ וְאֶת־מִקְנֵ֙הוּ֙

his souls – all – and that	his house	his cattle – and that

וְאֶת־כׇּל־בְּהֶמְתּ֔וֹ וְאֵת֙ כׇּל־קִנְיָנ֔וֹ אֲשֶׁ֥ר רָכַ֖שׁ בְּאֶ֣רֶץ כְּנָ֑עַן

his beasts – all – and that	and that	his possessions – all	which	possessed	in land	Canaan

וַיֵּ֣לֶךְ אֶל־אֶ֔רֶץ מִפְּנֵ֖י יַעֲקֹ֥ב אָחִֽיו׃

and he went	land – unto	from face	Jacob	his brother

6 And Esau took his wives, and his sons, and his daughters, and all the persons of his
house, and his cattle, and all his beasts, and all his substance, which he had got in the
land of Canaan; and went into the country from the face of his brother Jacob.

כִּי־הָיָה רְכוּשָׁם רָב מִשֶּׁבֶת יַחְדָּו
together   from dwelling   much   riches   it was - like

וְלֹא יָכְלָה אֶרֶץ מְגוּרֵיהֶם לָשֵׂאת אֹתָם מִפְּנֵי מִקְנֵיהֶם:
their cattle   from face   to them   to set   as strangers them   land   it able   and not

7 For their riches were more than that they might dwell together; and the land wherein
they were strangers could not bear them because of their cattle.

וַיֵּשֶׁב עֵשָׂו בְּהַר שֵׂעִיר עֵשָׂו הוּא אֱדוֹם:
Edom   he   Esau   Seir   in mountain   Esau   and he dwelt

8 Thus dwelt Esau in mount Seir: Esau is Edom.

וְאֵלֶּה תֹּלְדוֹת עֵשָׂו אֲבִי אֱדוֹם בְּהַר שֵׂעִיר:
Seir   in mount   Edom   father   Esau   generations   and these

9 And these are the generations of Esau the father of the Edomites in mount Seir:

אֵלֶּה שְׁמוֹת בְּנֵי־עֵשָׂו אֱלִיפַז בֶּן־עָדָה אֵשֶׁת עֵשָׂו
Esau   wife   Adah – son   Eliphaz   Esau – sons   names   these

רְעוּאֵל בֶּן־בָּשְׂמַת אֵשֶׁת עֵשָׂו:
Esau   wife   Bashemath - son   Reuel

10 These are the names of Esau's sons; Eliphaz the son of Adah the wife of Esau,
Reuel the son of Bashemath the wife of Esau.

וַיִּהְיוּ בְּנֵי אֱלִיפָז תֵּימָן אוֹמָר צְפוֹ וְגַעְתָּם וּקְנַז:
and Kenaz   and Gatam   Zepho   Omar   Teman   Eliphaz   sons   and they were

11 And the sons of Eliphaz were Teman, Omar, Zepho, and Gatam, and Kenaz.

וְתִמְנַע הָיְתָה פִילֶגֶשׁ לֶאֱלִיפַז בֶּן־עֵשָׂו
Esau – son   to Eliphaz   concubine   she was   and Timna

וַתֵּלֶד לֶאֱלִיפַז אֶת־עֲמָלֵק
Amalek – that   to Eliphaz   and she begot

אֵלֶּה בְּנֵי עָדָה אֵשֶׁת עֵשָׂו:
Esau   wife   Adah   sons   these

12 And Timna was concubine to Eliphaz Esau's son; and she bare to Eliphaz Amalek:
these were the sons of Adah Esau's wife.

וְאֵלֶּה בְּנֵי רְעוּאֵל נַחַת וָזֶרַח שַׁמָּה וּמִזָּה
and Mizzah   Shammah   and Zerah   Nahath   Reuel   sons   and these

אֵלֶּה הָיוּ בְּנֵי בָשְׂמַת אֵשֶׁת עֵשָׂו:
Esau   wife   Bashemath   sons   they were   these

13 And these are the sons of Reuel; Nahath, and Zerah, Shammah, and Mizzah: these
were the sons of Bashemath Esau's wife.

וְאֵלֶּה הָיוּ בְּנֵי אָהֳלִיבָמָה
Aholibamah   sons   they were   and these

בַת־עֲנָה   בַּת־צִבְעוֹן   אֵשֶׁת   עֵשָׂו
Anah – daughter   Zibeon – daughter   wife   Esau

וַתֵּלֶד   לְעֵשָׂו   אֶת־יעיש   [יְעוּשׁ]   וְאֶת־יַעְלָם   וְאֶת־קֹרַח:
and she begot   to Esau   Jeush – that   Jaalam – and that   Korah – and that

14 And these were the sons of Aholibamah, the daughter of Anah the daughter of
Zibeon, Esau's wife: and she bare to Esau Jeush, and Jaalam, and Korah.

אֵלֶּה   אַלּוּפֵי   בְנֵי־עֵשָׂו   בְּנֵי   אֱלִיפַז   בְּכוֹר   עֵשָׂו
these   dukes   Esau – sons   sons   Eliphaz   first born   Esau

אַלּוּף   תֵּימָן   אַלּוּף   אוֹמָר   אַלּוּף   צְפוֹ   אַלּוּף   קְנַז:
duke   Teman   duke   Omar   duke   Zepho   duke   Kenaz

15 These were dukes of the sons of Esau: the sons of Eliphaz the firstborn son of
Esau; duke Teman, duke Omar, duke Zepho, duke Kenaz,

אַלּוּף־קֹרַח   אַלּוּף   גַּעְתָּם   אַלּוּף   עֲמָלֵק
Korah - duke   duke   Gatam   duke   Amalek

אֵלֶּה   אַלּוּפֵי   אֱלִיפַז
these   dukes   Eliphaz

בְּאֶרֶץ   אֱדוֹם   אֵלֶּה   בְּנֵי   עָדָה:
in land   Edom   these   sons   Adah

16 Duke Korah, duke Gatam, and duke Amalek: these are the dukes that came of
Eliphaz in the land of Edom; these were the sons of Adah.

וְאֵלֶּה   בְּנֵי   רְעוּאֵל   בֶּן־עֵשָׂו
and these   sons   Ruel   Esau – son

אַלּוּף   נַחַת   אַלּוּף   זֶרַח   אַלּוּף   שַׁמָּה   אַלּוּף   מִזָּה
duke   Nahath   duke   Zerah   duke   Shammah   duke   Mizzah

אֵלֶּה   אַלּוּפֵי   רְעוּאֵל
these   dukes   Reuel

בְּאֶרֶץ   אֱדוֹם   אֵלֶּה   בְּנֵי   בָשְׂמַת   אֵשֶׁת   עֵשָׂו:
in land   Edom   these   sons   Bashemath   wife   Esau

17 And these are the sons of Reuel Esau's son; duke Nahath, duke Zerah, duke
Shammah, duke Mizzah: these are the dukes that came of Reuel in the land of Edom;
these are the sons of Bashemath Esau's wife.

וְאֵלֶּה   בְּנֵי   אָהֳלִיבָמָה   אֵשֶׁת   עֵשָׂו
and these   sons   Aholibamah   wife   Esau

אַלּוּף   יְעוּשׁ   אַלּוּף   יַעְלָם   אַלּוּף   קֹרַח
duke   Jeush   duke   Jaalam   duke   Korah

אֵלֶּה   אַלּוּפֵי   אָהֳלִיבָמָה   בַּת־עֲנָה   אֵשֶׁת   עֵשָׂו:
these   dukes   Aholibamah   Anah – daughter   wife   Esau

18 And these are the sons of Aholibamah Esau's wife; duke Jeush, duke Jaalam, duke Korah: these were the dukes that came of Aholibamah the daughter of Anah, Esau's wife.

אֵלֶּה בְנֵי־עֵשָׂו וְאֵלֶּה אַלּוּפֵיהֶם הוּא אֱדוֹם:

| Edom | he | their dukes | and these | Esau – sons | these |

19 These are the sons of Esau, who is Edom, and these are their dukes.

ס

[שביעי]

אֵלֶּה בְנֵי־שֵׂעִיר הַחֹרִי יֹשְׁבֵי הָאָרֶץ

| the land | he inhabited | the Horite | Seir – sons | these |

לוֹטָן וְשׁוֹבָל וְצִבְעוֹן וַעֲנָה:

| and Anah | and Zibeon | and Shobal | Lotan |

20 These are the sons of Seir the Horite, who inhabited the land; Lotan, and Shobal, and Zibeon, and Anah,

וְדִשׁוֹן וְאֵצֶר וְדִישָׁן

| and Dishan | and Ezer | and Dishon |

אֵלֶּה אַלּוּפֵי הַחֹרִי בְּנֵי שֵׂעִיר בְּאֶרֶץ אֱדוֹם:

| Edom | in land | Seir | sons | the Horites | dukes | these |

21 And Dishon, and Ezer, and Dishan: these are the dukes of the Horites, the children of Seir in the land of Edom.

וַיִּהְיוּ בְנֵי־לוֹטָן

| Lotan – sons | and they were |

חֹרִי וְהֵימָם וַאֲחוֹת לוֹטָן תִּמְנָע:

| Timna | Lotan | and sister | and Hemam | Hori |

22 And the children of Lotan were Hori and Hemam; and Lotan's sister was Timna.

וְאֵלֶּה בְּנֵי שׁוֹבָל עַלְוָן וּמָנַחַת וְעֵיבָל שְׁפוֹ וְאוֹנָם:

| and Onam | Shepho | and Ebal | and Manahath | Alvan | Shobal | sons | and these |

23 And the children of Shobal were these; Alvan, and Manahath, and Ebal, Shepho, and Onam.

וְאֵלֶּה בְנֵי־צִבְעוֹן וְאַיָּה וַעֲנָה

| and Anah | and Ajah | Zibeon – sons | and these |

הוּא עֲנָה אֲשֶׁר מָצָא אֶת־הַיֵּמִם בַּמִּדְבָּר

| in wilderness | the mules – that | found | which | Anah | he |

בִּרְעֹתוֹ אֶת־הַחֲמֹרִים לְצִבְעוֹן אָבִיו:

| his father | to Zibeon | the asses – that | in his shepherding |

24 And these are the children of Zibeon; both Ajah, and Anah: this was that Anah that found the mules in the wilderness, as he fed the asses of Zibeon his father.

וְאֵ֣לֶּה בְנֵֽי־עֲנָ֔ה דִּשֹׁ֖ן וְאׇהֳלִיבָמָ֥ה בַת־עֲנָֽה:

Anah - daughter   and Aholibamah   Dishon   Anah – sons   and these

25 And the children of Anah were these; Dishon, and Aholibamah the daughter of Anah.

וְאֵ֛לֶּה בְּנֵ֥י דִישָׁ֖ן חֶמְדָּ֣ן וְאֶשְׁבָּ֑ן וְיִתְרָ֖ן וּכְרָֽן:

and Cheran   and Ithran   and Esh-ban   Hemdan   Dishon   sons   and these

26 And these are the children of Dishon; Hemdan, and Esh-ban, and Ithran, and Cheran.

אֵ֖לֶּה בְּנֵי־אֵ֑צֶר בִּלְהָ֥ן וְזַעֲוָ֖ן וַעֲקָֽן:

and Akan   and Zaavan   Bilhan   Ezer – sons   these

27 The children of Ezer are these; Bilhan, and Zaavan, and Akan.

אֵ֥לֶּה בְנֵֽי־דִישָׁ֖ן ע֥וּץ וַאֲרָֽן:

and Aran   Uz   Dishan – sons   these

28 The children of Dishan are these; Uz, and Aran.

אֵ֖לֶּה אַלּוּפֵ֣י הַחֹרִ֑י

the Horites   dukes   these

אַלּ֤וּף לוֹטָן֙ אַלּ֣וּף שׁוֹבָ֔ל אַלּ֥וּף צִבְע֖וֹן אַלּ֥וּף עֲנָֽה:

Anah   duke   Zibeon   duke   Shobal   duke   Lotan   duke

29 These are the dukes that came of the Horites; duke Lotan, duke Shobal, duke Zibeon, duke Anah,

אַלּ֥וּף דִּשֹׁ֛ן אַלּ֥וּף אֵ֖צֶר אַלּ֥וּף דִּישָֽׁן

Dishan   duke   Ezer   duke   Dishon   duke

אֵ֣לֶּה אַלּוּפֵ֧י הַחֹרִ֛י לְאַלֻּפֵיהֶ֖ם בְּאֶ֥רֶץ שֵׂעִֽיר:

Seir   in land   to their dukes   the Hori   dukes   these

30 Duke Dishon, duke Ezer, duke Dishan: these are the dukes that came of Hori, among their dukes in the land of Seir.

פ

וְאֵ֣לֶּה הַמְּלָכִ֗ים אֲשֶׁ֤ר מָלְכוּ֙ בְּאֶ֣רֶץ אֱד֔וֹם

Edom   in land   reigned   which   the kings   and these

לִפְנֵ֥י מְלׇךְ־מֶ֖לֶךְ לִבְנֵ֥י יִשְׂרָאֵֽל:

Israel   to sons   king – reigned   before

31 And these are the kings that reigned in the land of Edom, before there reigned any king over the children of Israel.

וַיִּמְלֹ֣ךְ בֶּאֱד֔וֹם בֶּ֖לַע בֶּן־בְּע֑וֹר וְשֵׁ֥ם עִיר֖וֹ דִּנְהָֽבָה:

Dinhabah   his city   and name   Beor – son   Bela   in Edom   and he reigned

32 And Bela the son of Beor reigned in Edom: and the name of his city was Dinhabah.

וַיָּ֖מׇת בָּ֑לַע וַיִּמְלֹ֣ךְ תַּחְתָּ֔יו יוֹבָ֥ב בֶּן־זֶ֖רַח מִבׇּצְרָֽה:

from Bozrah   Zerah – son   Jobab   in his stead   and he reigned   Bela   and he died

33 And Bela died, and Jobab the son of Zerah of Bozrah reigned in his stead.

וַיָּ֣מָת יוֹבָ֑ב וַיִּמְלֹ֣ךְ תַּחְתָּ֗יו חֻשָׁ֛ם מֵאֶ֥רֶץ הַתֵּימָנִֽי׃

the Temani　from land　Husham　in his stead　and he reigned　Jobab　and he died

34 And Jobab died, and Husham of the land of Temani reigned in his stead.

וַיָּ֖מָת חֻשָׁ֑ם וַיִּמְלֹ֣ךְ תַּחְתָּ֗יו הֲדַ֡ד

Hadad　in his stead　and he reigned　Husham　and he died

בֶּן־בְּדַ֞ד הַמַּכֶּ֤ה אֶת־מִדְיָן֙ בִּשְׂדֵ֣ה מוֹאָ֔ב

Moab　in field　Midian – that　the smoter　Bedad - son

וְשֵׁ֥ם עִיר֖וֹ עֲוִֽית׃

Avith　his city　and name

35 And Husham died, and Hadad the son of Bedad, who smote Midian in the field of Moab, reigned in his stead: and the name of his city was Avith.

וַיָּ֖מָת הֲדָ֑ד וַיִּמְלֹ֣ךְ תַּחְתָּ֗יו שַׂמְלָ֖ה מִמַּשְׂרֵקָֽה׃

from Masrekah　Samlah　in his stead　and he reigned　Hadad　and he died

36 And Hadad died, and Samlah of Masrekah reigned in his stead.

וַיָּ֖מָת שַׂמְלָ֑ה וַיִּמְלֹ֣ךְ תַּחְתָּ֗יו שָׁא֖וּל מֵרְחֹב֥וֹת הַנָּהָֽר׃

the river　from Rehoboth　Saul　in his stead　and he reigned　Samlah　and he died

37 And Samlah died, and Saul of Rehoboth by the river reigned in his stead.

וַיָּ֖מָת שָׁא֑וּל וַיִּמְלֹ֣ךְ תַּחְתָּ֗יו בַּ֥עַל חָנָ֖ן בֶּן־עַכְבּֽוֹר׃

Achbor – son　hanan　Baal　in his stead　and he reigned　Saul　and he died

38 And Saul died, and Baal-hanan the son of Achbor reigned in his stead.

וַיָּ֗מָת בַּ֤עַל חָנָן֙ בֶּן־עַכְבּ֔וֹר

Achbor – son　hanan　Baal　and died

וַיִּמְלֹ֤ךְ תַּחְתָּיו֙ הֲדַ֔ר וְשֵׁ֥ם עִיר֖וֹ פָּ֑עוּ

Pau　his city　and name　Hadar　his stead　and he reigned

וְשֵׁ֨ם אִשְׁתּ֤וֹ מְהֵֽיטַבְאֵל֙ בַּת־מַטְרֵ֔ד בַּ֖ת מֵ֥י זָהָֽב׃

Mezahab　daughter　Matred - daughter　Mehetabel　his wife　and name

39 And Baal-hanan the son of Achbor died, and Hadar reigned in his stead: and the name of his city was Pau; and his wife's name was Mehetabel, the daughter of Matred, the daughter of Mezahab.

[מפטיר]

וְאֵ֗לֶּה שְׁמ֛וֹת אַלּוּפֵ֥י עֵשָׂ֖ו

Esau　dukes　names　and these

לְמִשְׁפְּחֹתָ֖ם לִמְקֹמֹתָ֑ם בִּשְׁמֹתָ֑ם

in their names　to their places　to their families

אַלּ֥וּף תִּמְנָ֛ע אַלּ֥וּף עַלְוָ֖ה אַלּ֥וּף יְתֵֽת׃

Jetheth　duke　Alvah　duke　Timnah　duke

40 And these are the names of the dukes that came of Esau, according to their families, after their places, by their names; duke Timnah, duke Alvah, duke Jetheth,

אַלּוּף אָהֳלִיבָמָה אַלּוּף אֵלָה אַלּוּף פִּינֹן׃

Pinon   duke   Elah   duke   Aholibamah   duke

41 Duke Aholibamah, duke Elah, duke Pinon,

אַלּוּף קְנַז אַלּוּף תֵּימָן אַלּוּף מִבְצָר׃

Mibzar   duke   Teman   duke   Kenaz   duke

42 Duke Kenaz, duke Teman, duke Mibzar,

אַלּוּף מַגְדִּיאֵל אַלּוּף עִירָם

Iram   duke   Magdiel   duke

אֵלֶּה אַלּוּפֵי אֱדוֹם לְמֹשְׁבֹתָם בְּאֶרֶץ אֲחֻזָּתָם

their possession   in land   to their habitations   Edom   dukes   these

הוּא עֵשָׂו אֲבִי אֱדוֹם׃

Edom   father   Esau   he

43 Duke Magdiel, duke Iram: these be the dukes of Edom, according to their habitations in the land of their possession: he is Esau the father of the Edomites.

פ פ פ

9 Vayeishev

[פרשת וישב]

Chapter 37

ספר בראשית פרק לז

וַיֵּשֶׁב יַעֲקֹב בְּאֶרֶץ מְגוּרֵי אָבִיו

his father · a stranger · in land · Jacob · and he dwelt

בְּאֶרֶץ כְּנָעַן:

Canaan · in land

1 And Jacob dwelt in the land wherein his father was a stranger, in the land of Canaan.

אֵלֶּה תֹּלְדוֹת יַעֲקֹב

Jacob · begettings · these

יוֹסֵף בֶּן־שְׁבַע־עֶשְׂרֵה שָׁנָה הָיָה רֹעֶה אֶת־אֶחָיו בַּצֹּאן

in sheep · his brothers – that · shepherd · was · years · -17 - age · Joseph

וְהוּא נַעַר אֶת־בְּנֵי בִלְהָה

Bilhah · sons – that · child · and he

וְאֶת־בְּנֵי זִלְפָּה נְשֵׁי אָבִיו

his father · women · Zilpah · sons – and that

וַיָּבֵא יוֹסֵף אֶת־דִּבָּתָם רָעָה אֶל־אֲבִיהֶם:

their fathers – unto · evil · their speakings – that · Joseph · and he brought

2 These are the generations of Jacob. Joseph, being seventeen years old, was feeding the flock with his brethren; and the lad was with the sons of Bilhah, and with the sons of Zilpah, his father's wives: and Joseph brought unto his father their evil report.

וְיִשְׂרָאֵל אָהַב אֶת־יוֹסֵף מִכָּל־בָּנָיו כִּי־בֶן־זְקֻנִים הוּא לוֹ

to him · he · old ones – age – like · his sons – from all · Joseph – that · loved · and Israel

וְעָשָׂה לוֹ כְּתֹנֶת פַּסִּים:

many colors · coat · to him · and he made

3 Now Israel loved Joseph more than all his children, because he was the son of his old age: and he made him a coat of many colours.

וַיִּרְאוּ אֶחָיו כִּי־אֹתוֹ אָהַב אֲבִיהֶם מִכָּל־אֶחָיו

his brothers – from all · their father · loved · to him like · his brothers · and they saw

וַיִּשְׂנְאוּ אֹתוֹ וְלֹא יָכְלוּ דַּבְּרוֹ לְשָׁלֹם:

to peace · his speak · they able · and not · to him · and they hated

4 And when his brethren saw that their father loved him more than all his brethren, they hated him, and could not speak peaceably unto him.

וַיַּחֲלֹם יוֹסֵף חֲלוֹם וַיַּגֵּד לְאֶחָיו
to his brothers   and he told   dream   Joseph   and he dreamed

וַיּוֹסִפוּ עוֹד שְׂנֹא אֹתוֹ׃
to him   hated   again   and they storied

5 And Joseph dreamed a dream, and he told it his brethren: and they hated him yet the more.

וַיֹּאמֶר אֲלֵיהֶם שִׁמְעוּ־נָא הַחֲלוֹם הַזֶּה אֲשֶׁר חָלָמְתִּי׃
I dreamed   which   the this   the dream   please – you hear   unto them   and he said

6 And he said unto them, Hear, I pray you, this dream which I have dreamed:

וְהִנֵּה אֲנַחְנוּ מְאַלְּמִים אֲלֻמִּים בְּתוֹךְ הַשָּׂדֶה
the field   midst   sheaves   binding ones   we   and here

וְהִנֵּה קָמָה אֲלֻמָּתִי וְגַם־נִצָּבָה
stood up - and also   my sheaf   rose up   and here

וְהִנֵּה תְסֻבֶּינָה אֲלֻמֹּתֵיכֶם
your sheaves   it stood around   and here

וַתִּשְׁתַּחֲוֶיןָ לַאֲלֻמָּתִי׃
to my sheaf   and you bowed them

7 For, behold, we were binding sheaves in the field, and, lo, my sheaf arose, and also stood upright; and, behold, your sheaves stood round about, and made obeisance to my sheaf.

וַיֹּאמְרוּ לוֹ אֶחָיו
his brothers   to him   and they said

הֲמָלֹךְ תִּמְלֹךְ עָלֵינוּ אִם־מָשׁוֹל תִּמְשֹׁל בָּנוּ
in us   you rule   ruler – with   upon us   you reign   the reign

וַיּוֹסִפוּ עוֹד שְׂנֹא אֹתוֹ עַל־חֲלֹמֹתָיו וְעַל־דְּבָרָיו׃
his speaking – and upon   his dreams – upon   to him   hatred   again   and they storied

8 And his brethren said to him, Shalt thou indeed reign over us? or shalt thou indeed have dominion over us? And they hated him yet the more for his dreams, and for his words.

וַיַּחֲלֹם עוֹד חֲלוֹם אַחֵר וַיְסַפֵּר אֹתוֹ לְאֶחָיו
to his brothers   to it   and he storied   another   dream   again   and he dreamed

וַיֹּאמֶר הִנֵּה חָלַמְתִּי חֲלוֹם עוֹד וְהִנֵּה הַשֶּׁמֶשׁ וְהַיָּרֵחַ
and moon   the sun   and here   again   dream   I dreamed   here   and he said

וְאַחַד עָשָׂר כּוֹכָבִים מִשְׁתַּחֲוִים לִי׃
to me   bowing ones   stars   and eleven -

9 And he dreamed yet another dream, and told it his brethren, and said, Behold, I have dreamed a dream more; and, behold, the sun and the moon and the eleven stars made obeisance to me.

וַיְסַפֵּר אֶל־אָבִיו וְאֶל־אֶחָיו וַיִּגְעַר־בּוֹ אָבִיו
his father　in him - rebuked　his brothers – and unto　his father – and unto　and he storied

וַיֹּאמֶר לוֹ מָה הַחֲלוֹם הַזֶּה אֲשֶׁר חָלָמְתָּ
you dreamed　which　the this　the dream　what　to him　and he said

הֲבוֹא נָבוֹא אֲנִי וְאִמְּךָ וְאַחֶיךָ לְהִשְׁתַּחֲוֺת לְךָ אָרְצָה׃
towards earth　to you　to cause bowing　and your brothers　and your mother　I　we come　the come

10 And he told it to his father, and to his brethren: and his father rebuked him, and said
unto him, What is this dream that thou hast dreamed? Shall I and thy mother and thy
brethren indeed come to bow down ourselves to thee to the earth?

וַיְקַנְאוּ־בוֹ אֶחָיו וְאָבִיו שָׁמַר אֶת־הַדָּבָר׃
the speaking – that　heeded　and his father　his brothers　in him – and they envied

11 And his brethren envied him; but his father observed the saying.

[שני]

וַיֵּלְכוּ אֶחָיו לִרְעוֹת אֶת־צֹאן אֲבִיהֶם בִּשְׁכֶם׃
in Shechem　their fathers　sheep – that　to shepherd　his brothers　and they went

12 And his brethren went to feed their father's flock in Shechem.

וַיֹּאמֶר יִשְׂרָאֵל אֶל־יוֹסֵף הֲלוֹא אַחֶיךָ רֹעִים בִּשְׁכֶם
in Shechem　shepherd ones　your brothers　the to it　Joseph – unto　Israel　and he said

לְכָה וְאֶשְׁלָחֲךָ אֲלֵיהֶם וַיֹּאמֶר לוֹ הִנֵּנִי׃
here am I　to him　and he said　unto them　and I will send you　to thus

13 And Israel said unto Joseph, Do not thy brethren feed the flock in Shechem? come,
and I will send thee unto them. And he said to him, Here am I.

וַיֹּאמֶר לוֹ לֶךְ־נָא רְאֵה אֶת־שְׁלוֹם אַחֶיךָ
your brothers　peace – that　see　please – go　to him　and he said

וְאֶת־שְׁלוֹם הַצֹּאן וַהֲשִׁבֵנִי דָּבָר
speak　and the return me　the sheep　peace – and that

וַיִּשְׁלָחֵהוּ מֵעֵמֶק חֶבְרוֹן וַיָּבֹא שְׁכֶמָה׃
towards Shechem　and he came　Hebron　from vale　and he send him

14 And he said to him, Go, I pray thee, see whether it be well with thy brethren, and
well with the flocks; and bring me word again. So he sent him out of the vale of
Hebron, and he came to Shechem.

וַיִּמְצָאֵהוּ אִישׁ וְהִנֵּה תֹעֶה בַּשָּׂדֶה
in field　wandering　and here　man　and he found him

וַיִּשְׁאָלֵהוּ הָאִישׁ לֵאמֹר מַה־תְּבַקֵּשׁ׃
you seek – what　to say　the man　and he asked him

15 And a certain man found him, and, behold, he was wandering in the field: and the
man asked him, saying, What seekest thou?

וַיֹּאמֶר אֶת־אַחַי אָנֹכִי מְבַקֵּשׁ

and he said brothers – that I am seeking

הַגִּידָה־נָּא לִי אֵיפֹה הֵם רֹעִים:

the you tell please – to me where them shepherding

16 And he said, I seek my brethren: tell me, I pray thee, where they feed their flocks.

וַיֹּאמֶר הָאִישׁ נָסְעוּ מִזֶּה

and he said the man they traveled from this

כִּי שָׁמַעְתִּי אֹמְרִים נֵלְכָה דֹּתָיְנָה

like I heard sayings we go towards to Dothan

וַיֵּלֶךְ יוֹסֵף אַחַר אֶחָיו וַיִּמְצָאֵם בְּדֹתָן:

and he went Joseph after his brothers and he found them in Dothan

17 And the man said, They are departed hence; for I heard them say, Let us go to Dothan. And Joseph went after his brethren, and found them in Dothan.

וַיִּרְאוּ אֹתוֹ מֵרָחֹק וּבְטֶרֶם יִקְרַב אֲלֵיהֶם

and they saw to him from far and in before he neared unto them

וַיִּתְנַכְּלוּ אֹתוֹ לַהֲמִיתוֹ:

and they conspired to him to the his kill

18 And when they saw him afar off, even before he came near unto them, they conspired against him to slay him.

וַיֹּאמְרוּ אִישׁ אֶל־אָחִיו

and they said man his brothers – unto

הִנֵּה בַּעַל הַחֲלֹמוֹת הַלָּזֶה בָּא:

here master the dreams the to this come

19 And they said one to another, Behold, this dreamer cometh.

וְעַתָּה לְכוּ וְנַהַרְגֵהוּ

and now you go and we slay him

וְנַשְׁלִכֵהוּ בְּאַחַד הַבֹּרוֹת וְאָמַרְנוּ חַיָּה רָעָה אֲכָלָתְהוּ

and we throw him in one the pit and we say animal evil ate him

וְנִרְאֶה מַה־יִּהְיוּ חֲלֹמֹתָיו:

and we see what – they will be his dreams

20 Come now therefore, and let us slay him, and cast him into some pit, and we will say, Some evil beast hath devoured him: and we shall see what will become of his dreams.

וַיִּשְׁמַע רְאוּבֵן וַיַּצִּלֵהוּ מִיָּדָם

and he heard Rueben and he delivered him from their hands

וַיֹּאמֶר לֹא נַכֶּנּוּ נָפֶשׁ:

and he said not we murder soul

21 And Reuben heard it, and he delivered him out of their hands; and said, Let us not kill him.

וַיֹּאמֶר אֲלֵהֶם רְאוּבֵן אַל־תִּשְׁפְּכוּ־דָם

blood – you shed - don't   Rueben   unto them   and he said

הַשְׁלִיכוּ אֹתוֹ אֶל־הַבּוֹר הַזֶּה אֲשֶׁר בַּמִּדְבָּר

in wilderness   which   the this   the pit – unto   to him   the you cast

וְיָד   אַל־תִּשְׁלְחוּ־בוֹ

in him - you strike it– don't   and hand

לְמַעַן הַצִּיל אֹתוֹ מִיָּדָם לַהֲשִׁיבוֹ אֶל־אָבִיו:

his father – unto   to his the return   from their hands   to him   the rescue   to end

22 And Reuben said unto them, Shed no blood, but cast him into this pit that is in the wilderness, and lay no hand upon him; that he might rid him out of their hands, to deliver him to his father again.

[שלישי]

וַיְהִי כַּאֲשֶׁר־בָּא יוֹסֵף אֶל־אֶחָיו

his brothers – unto   Joseph   came – when   and it was

וַיַּפְשִׁיטוּ אֶת־יוֹסֵף אֶת־כֻּתָּנְתּוֹ

his coat - that   Joseph – that   and they stripped

אֶת־כְּתֹנֶת הַפַּסִּים אֲשֶׁר עָלָיו:

upon him   which   the colors   coat - that

23 And it came to pass, when Joseph was come unto his brethren, that they stripped Joseph out of his coat, his coat of many colours that was on him;

וַיִּקָּחֻהוּ וַיַּשְׁלִכוּ אֹתוֹ הַבֹּרָה

toward the pit   to him   and they cast him   and they took him

וְהַבּוֹר רֵק אֵין בּוֹ מָיִם:

water   in it   isn't   empty   and the pit

24 And they took him, and cast him into a pit: and the pit was empty, there was no water in it.

וַיֵּשְׁבוּ לֶאֱכָל־לֶחֶם וַיִּשְׂאוּ עֵינֵיהֶם וַיִּרְאוּ

and they saw   their eyes   and they lifted   bread – to eat   and they sat

וְהִנֵּה אֹרְחַת יִשְׁמְעֵאלִים בָּאָה מִגִּלְעָד

from Gilead   coming   Ishmeelites   company   and here

וּגְמַלֵּיהֶם נֹשְׂאִים נְכֹאת וּצְרִי וָלֹט

and myrrh   and balm   spicery   bearing ones   and their camels

הוֹלְכִים לְהוֹרִיד מִצְרָיְמָה:

towards Egypt   to descend   going ones

25 And they sat down to eat bread: and they lifted up their eyes and looked, and,

behold, a company of Ishmeelites came from Gilead with their camels bearing spicery and balm and myrrh, going to carry it down to Egypt.

וַיֹּאמֶר יְהוּדָה אֶל־אֶחָיו מַה־בֶּצַע

and he said	Judah	his brothers – unto	gain - what

כִּי נַהֲרֹג אֶת־אָחִינוּ וְכִסִּינוּ אֶת־דָּמוֹ:

like	we kill	our brothers – that	and we cover	his blood – that

26 And Judah said unto his brethren, What profit is it if we slay our brother, and conceal his blood?

לְכוּ וְנִמְכְּרֶנּוּ לַיִּשְׁמְעֵאלִים

lets go	and we sell	to Ishmeelites

וְיָדֵנוּ אַל־תְּהִי־בוֹ כִּי־אָחִינוּ בְשָׂרֵנוּ הוּא

and our hand	in it – you be – don't	our brother – like	our flesh	he

וַיִּשְׁמְעוּ אֶחָיו:

and they heard	his brothers

27 Come, and let us sell him to the Ishmeelites, and let not our hand be upon him; for he is our brother and our flesh. And his brethren were content.

וַיַּעַבְרוּ אֲנָשִׁים מִדְיָנִים סֹחֲרִים

and they passed	men	Midianites	merchants

וַיִּמְשְׁכוּ וַיַּעֲלוּ אֶת־יוֹסֵף מִן־הַבּוֹר

and they drew out	and they ascended	Joseph – that	the pit – from

וַיִּמְכְּרוּ אֶת־יוֹסֵף לַיִּשְׁמְעֵאלִים בְּעֶשְׂרִים כָּסֶף

and they sold	Joseph – that	to Ishmeelites	in twenty	silver

וַיָּבִיאוּ אֶת־יוֹסֵף מִצְרָיְמָה:

and they brought	Joseph – that	towards Egypt

28 Then there passed by Midianites merchantmen; and they drew and lifted up Joseph out of the pit, and sold Joseph to the Ishmeelites for twenty pieces of silver: and they brought Joseph into Egypt.

וַיָּשָׁב רְאוּבֵן אֶל־הַבּוֹר וְהִנֵּה אֵין־יוֹסֵף בַּבּוֹר

and he returned	Rueben	the pit – unto	and here	Joseph – isn't	in pit

וַיִּקְרַע אֶת־בְּגָדָיו:

and he tore	his clothes – that

29 And Reuben returned unto the pit; and, behold, Joseph was not in the pit; and he rent his clothes.

וַיָּשָׁב אֶל־אֶחָיו וַיֹּאמַר הַיֶּלֶד אֵינֶנּוּ

and he returned	his brothers – unto	and he said	the child	isn't with us

וַאֲנִי אָנָה אֲנִי־בָא:

and I	where	come – I

30 And he returned unto his brethren, and said, The child is not; and I, whither shall I go?

וַיִּקְחוּ אֶת־כְּתֹנֶת יוֹסֵף וַיִּשְׁחֲטוּ שְׂעִיר עִזִּים
and they took — coat – that — Joseph — and they slaughtered — kid — goat

וַיִּטְבְּלוּ אֶת־הַכֻּתֹּנֶת בַּדָּם:
and they dipped — the coat – that — in blood

31 And they took Joseph's coat, and killed a kid of the goats, and dipped the coat in the blood;

וַיְשַׁלְּחוּ אֶת־כְּתֹנֶת הַפַּסִּים וַיָּבִיאוּ אֶל־אֲבִיהֶם
and they sent — coat – that — the colors — and they came — unto – their father

וַיֹּאמְרוּ זֹאת מָצָאנוּ הַכֶּר־נָא הַכְּתֹנֶת בִּנְךָ הִוא אִם־לֹא:
and he said — this — we found — please – recognized — the coat — your son — it — if – not

32 And they sent the coat of many colours, and they brought it to their father; and said, This have we found: know now whether it be thy son's coat or no.

וַיַּכִּירָהּ וַיֹּאמֶר כְּתֹנֶת בְּנִי
and he recognized — and he said — coat — my son

חַיָּה רָעָה אֲכָלָתְהוּ טָרֹף טֹרַף יוֹסֵף:
animal — bad — ate him — tore — tearer — Joseph

33 And he knew it, and said, It is my son's coat; an evil beast hath devoured him; Joseph is without doubt rent in pieces.

וַיִּקְרַע יַעֲקֹב שִׂמְלֹתָיו וַיָּשֶׂם שַׂק בְּמָתְנָיו
and he ripped — Jacob — his dress — and he put — sackcloth — in his loins

וַיִּתְאַבֵּל עַל־בְּנוֹ יָמִים רַבִּים:
and he mourned — upon – his son — days — many

34 And Jacob rent his clothes, and put sackcloth upon his loins, and mourned for his son many days.

וַיָּקֻמוּ כָל־בָּנָיו וְכָל־בְּנֹתָיו לְנַחֲמוֹ וַיְמָאֵן לְהִתְנַחֵם
and they got up — all – his sons — and all – his daughters — his comfort — and he refused — to cause comfort

וַיֹּאמֶר כִּי־אֵרֵד אֶל־בְּנִי אָבֵל שְׁאֹלָה
and he said — like – I will descend — unto – my son — mourning — grave

וַיֵּבְךְּ אֹתוֹ אָבִיו:
and he wept — to him — his father

35 And all his sons and all his daughters rose up to comfort him; but he refused to be comforted; and he said, For I will go down into the grave unto my son mourning. Thus his father wept for him.

וְהַמְּדָנִים מָכְרוּ אֹתוֹ אֶל־מִצְרָיִם
and the Midianites — they sold — to him — unto – Egypt

לְפוֹטִיפַר סְרִיס פַּרְעֹה שַׂר הַטַּבָּחִים׃

the guard　captain　Pharaoh　officer　to Potiphar

36 And the Midianites sold him into Egypt unto Potiphar, an officer of Pharaoh's, and captain of the guard.

פ

Chapter 38

ספר בראשית פרק לח

[רביעי]

וַיְהִי בָּעֵת הַהִוא וַיֵּרֶד יְהוּדָה מֵאֵת אֶחָיו

his brothers　from that　Judah　and he descended　the it　in time　and it was

וַיֵּט עַד־אִישׁ עֲדֻלָּמִי וּשְׁמוֹ חִירָה׃

Hirah　and his name　Adullamite　man – till　and he turned

1 And it came to pass at that time, that Judah went down from his brethren, and turned in to a certain Adullamite, whose name was Hirah.

וַיַּרְא־שָׁם יְהוּדָה בַּת־אִישׁ כְּנַעֲנִי

Canaanite　man – daughter　Judah　there – and he saw

וּשְׁמוֹ שׁוּעַ וַיִּקָּחֶהָ וַיָּבֹא אֵלֶיהָ׃

unto her　the came　and he took her　Shuah　and his name

2 And Judah saw there a daughter of a certain Canaanite, whose name was Shuah; and he took her, and went in unto her.

וַתַּהַר וַתֵּלֶד בֵּן וַיִּקְרָא אֶת־שְׁמוֹ עֵר׃

Er　his name – that　and he called　son　and she bore　and she conceived

3 And she conceived, and bare a son; and he called his name Er.

וַתַּהַר עוֹד וַתֵּלֶד בֵּן וַתִּקְרָא אֶת־שְׁמוֹ אוֹנָן׃

Onan　his name – that　and she called　son　and she begot　again　and she conceived

4 And she conceived again, and bare a son; and she called his name Onan.

וַתֹּסֶף עוֹד וַתֵּלֶד בֵּן

son　and she begot　again　and she continued

וַתִּקְרָא אֶת־שְׁמוֹ שֵׁלָה

Shelah　his name – that　she called

וְהָיָה בִכְזִיב בְּלִדְתָּהּ אֹתוֹ׃

to him　in her begetting　in Chezib　and it was

5 And she yet again conceived, and bare a son; and called his name Shelah: and he was at Chezib, when she bare him.

וַיִּקַּח יְהוּדָה אִשָּׁה לְעֵר בְּכוֹרוֹ וּשְׁמָהּ תָּמָר׃

Tamar　and her name　his firstborn　to Er　wife　Judah　and he took

6 And Judah took a wife for Er his firstborn, whose name was Tamar.

וַיְהִי עֵר בְּכוֹר יְהוּדָה רַע בְּעֵינֵי יְהֹוָה וַיְמִתֵהוּ יְהֹוָה:

ihvh   and he slew him   ihvh   in eyes   bad   Judah   first born   Er   and it was

7 And Er, Judah's firstborn, was wicked in the sight of the LORD; and the LORD slew him.

וַיֹּאמֶר יְהוּדָה לְאוֹנָן בֹּא אֶל־אֵשֶׁת אָחִיךָ

your brother   wife – unto   come   to Onan   Judah   and he said

וְיַבֵּם אֹתָהּ וְהָקֵם זֶרַע לְאָחִיךָ:

to his brother   seed   and the rise up   to her   and he came

8 And Judah said unto Onan, Go in unto thy brother's wife, and marry her, and raise up seed to thy brother.

וַיֵּדַע אוֹנָן כִּי לֹּא לוֹ יִהְיֶה הַזָּרַע

the seed   it be   to him   not   like   Onan   and he knew

וְהָיָה אִם־בָּא אֶל־אֵשֶׁת אָחִיו

his brother   wife – unto   come – with   and it was

וְשִׁחֵת אַרְצָה לְבִלְתִּי נְתָן־זֶרַע לְאָחִיו:

to his brother   seed – give   to without   towards ground   and spilled

9 And Onan knew that the seed should not be his; and it came to pass, when he went in unto his brother's wife, that he spilled it on the ground, lest that he should give seed to his brother.

וַיֵּרַע בְּעֵינֵי יְהֹוָה אֲשֶׁר עָשָׂה וַיָּמֶת גַּם־אֹתוֹ:

to him – also   and he slew   did   which   ihvh   in eyes   and he bad

10 And the thing which he did displeased the LORD: wherefore he slew him also.

וַיֹּאמֶר יְהוּדָה לְתָמָר כַּלָּתוֹ שְׁבִי אַלְמָנָה בֵית־אָבִיךְ

your father – house   widow   you dwell   his daughter in law   to Tamar   Judah   and he said

עַד־יִגְדַּל שֵׁלָה בְנִי כִּי אָמַר פֶּן־יָמוּת גַּם־הוּא כְּאֶחָיו

like his brothers   he – also   he die – lest   said   like   my son   Shelah   he grew – till

וַתֵּלֶךְ תָּמָר וַתֵּשֶׁב בֵּית אָבִיהָ:

her father   house   and she dwelt   Tamar   and she went

11 Then said Judah to Tamar his daughter in law, Remain a widow at thy father's house, till Shelah my son be grown: for he said, Lest peradventure he die also, as his brethren did. And Tamar went and dwelt in her father's house.

וַיִּרְבּוּ הַיָּמִים וַתָּמָת בַּת־שׁוּעַ אֵשֶׁת־יְהוּדָה

Judah – wife   Shuah - daughter   and she died   the days   and they multiplied

וַיִּנָּחֶם יְהוּדָה וַיַּעַל עַל־גֹּזְזֵי צֹאנוֹ

his sheep   sheep shearers - upon   and he ascended   Judah   and he comforted

הוּא וְחִירָה רֵעֵהוּ הָעֲדֻלָּמִי תִּמְנָתָה:

towards Timnath   the Adullamite   his neighbor   and Hirah   he

12 And in process of time the daughter of Shuah Judah's wife died; and Judah was

comforted, and went up unto his sheep shearers to Timnath, he and his friend Hirah the Adullamite.

וַיֻּגַּד לְתָמָר לֵאמֹר
and he told   to Tamar   to say

הִנֵּה חָמִיךְ עֹלֶה תִמְנָתָה לָגֹז צֹאנוֹ:
here   your father in law   ascends   toward Timnath   to shear   his sheep

13 And it was told Tamar, saying, Behold thy father in law goeth up to Timnath to shear his sheep.

וַתָּסַר בִּגְדֵי אַלְמְנוּתָהּ מֵעָלֶיהָ
and she removed   clothes   widow   from upon her

וַתְּכַס בַּצָּעִיף וַתִּתְעַלָּף
and she covered   in veil   and she wrapped

וַתֵּשֶׁב בְּפֶתַח עֵינַיִם אֲשֶׁר עַל־דֶּרֶךְ תִּמְנָתָה
and she sat   in opening   eyes   which   way – upon   towards Timnath

כִּי רָאֲתָה כִּי־גָדַל שֵׁלָה וְהִוא לֹא־נִתְּנָה לוֹ לְאִשָּׁה:
like   she saw   big – like   Shelah   and she   given – not   to him   to wife

14 And she put her widow's garments off from her, and covered her with a veil, and wrapped herself, and sat in an open place, which is by the way to Timnath; for she saw that Shelah was grown, and she was not given unto him to wife.

וַיִּרְאֶהָ יְהוּדָה וַיַּחְשְׁבֶהָ לְזוֹנָה כִּי כִסְּתָה פָּנֶיהָ:
and he saw her   Judah   and he thought her   to harlot   like   covered   her face

15 When Judah saw her, he thought her to be an harlot; because she had covered her face.

וַיֵּט אֵלֶיהָ אֶל־הַדֶּרֶךְ
and he turned   unto her   the way – unto

וַיֹּאמֶר הָבָה נָּא אָבוֹא אֵלַיִךְ
and he said   the towards   now   I come   unto you

כִּי לֹא יָדַע כִּי כַלָּתוֹ הִוא
like   not   he knew   like   his daughter in law   she

וַתֹּאמֶר מַה־תִּתֶּן־לִי כִּי תָבוֹא אֵלָי:
and she said   like to me - you give – what   like   you come   unto me

16 And he turned unto her by the way, and said, Go to, I pray thee, let me come in unto thee; (for he knew not that she was his daughter in law.) And she said, What wilt thou give me, that thou mayest come in unto me?

וַיֹּאמֶר אָנֹכִי אֲשַׁלַּח גְּדִי־עִזִּים מִן־הַצֹּאן
and he said   I am   I will send   goats - kid   the sheep – from

וַתֹּאמֶר אִם־תִּתֵּן עֵרָבוֹן עַד שָׁלְחֶךָ:

your sending   till   pledge   you will give – if   and she said

17 And he said, I will send thee a kid from the flock. And she said, Wilt thou give me a pledge, till thou send it?

וַיֹּאמֶר מָה הָעֵרָבוֹן אֲשֶׁר אֶתֶּן־לָךְ

to you – I give   which   the pledge   what   and he said

וַתֹּאמֶר חֹתָמְךָ וּפְתִילֶךָ וּמַטְּךָ אֲשֶׁר בְּיָדֶךָ

in your hand   which   and your staff   and your bracelets   your signet   and she said

וַיִּתֶּן־לָהּ וַיָּבֹא אֵלֶיהָ וַתַּהַר לוֹ:

to him   and she conceived   unto her   and he came   to her – and gave

18 And he said, What pledge shall I give thee? And she said, Thy signet, and thy bracelets, and thy staff that is in thine hand. And he gave it her, and came in unto her, and she conceived by him.

וַתָּקָם וַתֵּלֶךְ וַתָּסַר צְעִיפָהּ מֵעָלֶיהָ

from upon her   veil   and she removed   and she went   and she arose

וַתִּלְבַּשׁ בִּגְדֵי אַלְמְנוּתָהּ:

her widowhood   clothes   and she dressed

19 And she arose, and went away, and laid by her veil from her, and put on the garments of her widowhood.

וַיִּשְׁלַח יְהוּדָה

Judah   and he sent

אֶת־גְּדִי הָעִזִּים בְּיַד רֵעֵהוּ הָעֲדֻלָּמִי

the Adullamite   his neighbor   in hand   the goats   kid – that

לָקַחַת הָעֵרָבוֹן מִיַּד הָאִשָּׁה וְלֹא מְצָאָהּ:

he found her   and not   the woman   from hand   the pledge   to take

20 And Judah sent the kid by the hand of his friend the Adullamite, to receive his pledge from the woman's hand: but he found her not.

וַיִּשְׁאַל אֶת־אַנְשֵׁי מְקֹמָהּ לֵאמֹר

to say   towards place   men – that   and he asked

אַיֵּה הַקְּדֵשָׁה הִוא בָעֵינַיִם עַל־הַדָּרֶךְ

the way – upon   in eyes   she   the holy woman   where

וַיֹּאמְרוּ לֹא־הָיְתָה בָזֶה קְדֵשָׁה:

holy woman   in this   has been – not   and they said

21 Then he asked the men of that place, saying, Where is the harlot, that was openly by the way side? And they said, There was no harlot in this place.

וַיָּשָׁב אֶל־יְהוּדָה וַיֹּאמֶר לֹא מְצָאתִיהָ

I found her   not   and he said   Judah – unto   and he returned

וְגַם אַנְשֵׁי הַמָּקוֹם אָמְרוּ לֹא־הָיְתָה בָזֶה קְדֵשָׁה:
holy woman   in this   there was – not   they said   the place   men   and also

22 And he returned to Judah, and said, I cannot find her; and also the men of the place said, that there was no harlot in this place.

וַיֹּאמֶר יְהוּדָה תִּקַּח־לָהּ פֶּן נִהְיֶה לָבוּז
to shame   we be   lest   to her – you take   Judah   and he said

הִנֵּה שָׁלַחְתִּי הַגְּדִי הַזֶּה וְאַתָּה לֹא מְצָאתָהּ:
found her   not   and you   the this   the kid   I sent   here

23 And Judah said, Let her take it to her, lest we be shamed: behold, I sent this kid, and thou hast not found her.

וַיְהִי כְּמִשְׁלֹשׁ חֳדָשִׁים
months   like from three   and it was

וַיֻּגַּד לִיהוּדָה לֵאמֹר זָנְתָה תָּמָר כַּלָּתֶךָ
your daughter in law   Tamar   harlot   to say   to Judah   and he was told

וְגַם הִנֵּה הָרָה לִזְנוּנִים
to whoredom ones   pregnant   here   and also

וַיֹּאמֶר יְהוּדָה הוֹצִיאוּהָ וְתִשָּׂרֵף:
and she be burned   bring her out   Judah   and he said

24 And it came to pass about three months after, that it was told Judah, saying, Tamar thy daughter in law hath played the harlot; and also, behold, she is with child by whoredom. And Judah said, Bring her forth, and let her be burnt.

הִוא מוּצֵאת וְהִיא שָׁלְחָה אֶל־חָמִיהָ לֵאמֹר
to say   father in law - unto   sent   and she   brought forth   she

לְאִישׁ אֲשֶׁר־אֵלֶּה לּוֹ אָנֹכִי הָרָה
pregnant   I am   to him   these – which   to man

וַתֹּאמֶר הַכֶּר־נָא לְמִי הַחֹתֶמֶת וְהַפְּתִילִים וְהַמַּטֶּה הָאֵלֶּה:
the these   and the staff   and the bracelets   the signet   to who   now - discern   and she said

25 When she was brought forth, she sent to her father in law, saying, By the man, whose these are, am I with child: and she said, Discern, I pray thee, whose arethese, the signet, and bracelets, and staff.

וַיַּכֵּר יְהוּדָה וַיֹּאמֶר צָדְקָה מִמֶּנִּי
from myself   she righteous   and he said   Judah   and he acknowledged

כִּי־עַל־כֵּן לֹא־נְתַתִּיהָ לְשֵׁלָה בְנִי
my son   to Shelah   I gave her – not   thus – upon – like

וְלֹא־יָסַף עוֹד לְדַעְתָּהּ:
to know her   again   he added - and not

26 And Judah acknowledged them, and said, She hath been more righteous than I; because that I gave her not to Shelah my son. And he knew her again no more.

וַיְהִי בְּעֵת לִדְתָּהּ וְהִנֵּה תְאוֹמִים בְּבִטְנָהּ:

in her stomach   twins   and here   to birthing   in time   and it was

27 And it came to pass in the time of her travail, that, behold, twins were in her womb.

וַיְהִי בְלִדְתָּהּ וַיִּתֶּן־יָד וַתִּקַּח הַמְיַלֶּדֶת

the midwife   and she took   hand – and he gave   in her birthing   and it was

וַתִּקְשֹׁר עַל־יָדוֹ שָׁנִי לֵאמֹר זֶה יָצָא רִאשֹׁנָה:

first   came out   this   to say   ribbon   his hand – upon   and she bound

28 And it came to pass, when she travailed, that the one put out his hand: and the midwife took and bound upon his hand a scarlet thread, saying, This came out first.

וַיְהִי כְּמֵשִׁיב יָדוֹ וְהִנֵּה יָצָא אָחִיו

his brother   came out   and here   his hand   like drew back   and it was

וַתֹּאמֶר מַה־פָּרַצְתָּ עָלֶיךָ פָּרֶץ וַיִּקְרָא שְׁמוֹ פָּרֶץ:

Pharez   his name   and he called   breach   upon you   opened you - what   and she said

29 And it came to pass, as he drew back his hand, that, behold, his brother came out: and she said, How hast thou broken forth? this breach be upon thee: therefore his name was called Pharez.

וְאַחַר יָצָא אָחִיו אֲשֶׁר עַל־יָדוֹ הַשָּׁנִי

the ribbon   his hand – upon   which   his brother   came out   and after

וַיִּקְרָא שְׁמוֹ זָרַח:

Zarah   his name   and he called

30 And afterward came out his brother, that had the scarlet thread upon his hand: and his name was called Zarah.

ס

CHAPTER 39

ספר בראשית פרק לט

[חמישי]

וְיוֹסֵף הוּרַד מִצְרָיְמָה

towards Egypt   brought down   and Joseph

וַיִּקְנֵהוּ פּוֹטִיפַר סְרִיס פַּרְעֹה שַׂר הַטַּבָּחִים אִישׁ מִצְרִי

Egyptian   man   the guard   captain   Pharoah   officer   Potiphar   and he bought him

מִיַּד הַיִּשְׁמְעֵאלִים אֲשֶׁר הוֹרִדֻהוּ שָׁמָּה:

towards there   brought down him   which   the Ishmeelites   from hand

1 And Joseph was brought down to Egypt; and Potiphar, an officer of Pharaoh, captain of the guard, an Egyptian, bought him of the hands of the Ishmeelites, which had brought him down thither.

וַיְהִי מַצְלִיחַ אִישׁ וַיְהִי אֶת־יוֹסֵף יְהוָה וַיְהִי
and he was   prosperous   man   and he was   Joseph – that   ihvh   and he was

הַמִּצְרִי׃ אֲדֹנָיו בְּבֵית
the Egyptian   his master   in house   and he was

2 And the LORD was with Joseph, and he was a prosperous man; and he was in the
house of his master the Egyptian.

אִתּוֹ יְהוָה כִּי אֲדֹנָיו וַיַּרְא
to him   ihvh   like   his master   and he saw

בְּיָדוֹ׃ מַצְלִיחַ יְהוָה עֹשֶׂה וְכֹל אֲשֶׁר־הוּא
in his hand   prospered   ihvh   did   he – which   and all

3 And his master saw that the LORD was with him, and that the LORD made all that
he did to prosper in his hand.

אֹתוֹ וַיְשָׁרֶת בְּעֵינָיו חֵן יוֹסֵף וַיִּמְצָא
to him   and served   in his eyes   grace   Joseph   and he found

בְּיָדוֹ׃ נָתַן וְכָל־יֶשׁ־לוֹ עַל־בֵּיתוֹ וַיַּפְקִדֵהוּ
in his hand   gave   to him – there – and all   his house – upon   and he made overseer him

4 And Joseph found grace in his sight, and he served him: and he made him overseer
over his house, and all that he had he put into his hand.

בְּבֵיתוֹ אֹתוֹ הִפְקִיד מֵאָז וַיְהִי
in his house   to him   made overseer   from passing   and it was

יֶשׁ־לוֹ כָּל־אֲשֶׁר וְעַל
to him – there is   which – all   and upon

יוֹסֵף בִּגְלַל הַמִּצְרִי אֶת־בֵּית יְהוָה וַיְבָרֶךְ
Joseph   in sake   the Egyptian   house – that   ihvh   and he blessed

וּבַשָּׂדֶה׃ בַּבַּיִת יֶשׁ־לוֹ בְּכָל־אֲשֶׁר יְהוָה בִּרְכַּת וַיְהִי
and in field   in house   to him – there is   which – in all   ihvh   blessing   and it was

5 And it came to pass from the time that he had made him overseer in his house, and
over all that he had, that the LORD blessed the Egyptian's house for Joseph's sake; and
the blessing of the LORD was upon all that he had in the house, and in the field.

כָּל־אֲשֶׁר־לוֹ בְּיַד־יוֹסֵף וַיַּעֲזֹב
Joseph – in hand   to him – which – all   and he entrusted

אֹכֵל אֲשֶׁר־הוּא הַלֶּחֶם כִּי אִם־ מְאוּמָה אִתּוֹ וְלֹא־יָדַע
eat   he – which   the bread – with   like   speck   with him   he knew – and not

מַרְאֶה׃ וִיפֵה יְפֵה־תֹאַר יוֹסֵף וַיְהִי
appearance   and beautiful   countenance - beautiful   Joseph   and it was

6 And he left all that he had in Joseph's hand; and he knew not ought he had, save the
bread which he did eat. And Joseph was a goodly person, and well favoured.

[ששי]

וַיְהִי אַחַר הַדְּבָרִים הָאֵלֶּה
the these   the speakings   after   and it was

וַתִּשָּׂא אֵשֶׁת־אֲדֹנָיו אֶת־עֵינֶיהָ אֶל־יוֹסֵף
Joseph – unto   her eyes – that   his master - wife   and she lifted

וַתֹּאמֶר שִׁכְבָה עִמִּי:
with me   lay   and she said

7 And it came to pass after these things, that his master's wife cast her eyes upon Joseph; and she said, Lie with me.

וַיְמָאֵן וַיֹּאמֶר אֶל־אֵשֶׁת אֲדֹנָיו
his master   wife – unto   and he said   and he refused

הֵן אֲדֹנִי לֹא־יָדַע אִתִּי מַה־בַּבָּיִת
in house – what   to me   know – not   my master   thus

וְכֹל אֲשֶׁר־יֶשׁ־לוֹ נָתַן בְּיָדִי:
in my hand   gave   to him – there is – which   and all

8 But he refused, and said unto his master's wife, Behold, my master wotteth not what is with me in the house, and he hath committed all that he hath to my hand;

אֵינֶנּוּ גָדוֹל בַּבַּיִת הַזֶּה מִמֶּנִּי
from me   the this   in house   greater   isn't

וְלֹא־חָשַׂךְ מִמֶּנִּי מְאוּמָה
from speck   from myself   kept back - and not

כִּי אִם־אוֹתָךְ בַּאֲשֶׁר אַתְּ־אִשְׁתּוֹ
his wife – that   in which   to you – with   like

וְאֵיךְ אֶעֱשֶׂה הָרָעָה הַגְּדֹלָה הַזֹּאת
the this   the big one   the bad   I do   and how

וְחָטָאתִי לֵאלֹהִים:
to Elohim   and my sin

9 There is none greater in this house than I; neither hath he kept back any thing from me but thee, because thou art his wife: how then can I do this great wickedness, and sin against God?

וַיְהִי כְּדַבְּרָהּ אֶל־יוֹסֵף יוֹם יוֹם
day   day   Joseph – unto   like she spoke   and it was

וְלֹא־שָׁמַע אֵלֶיהָ לִשְׁכַּב אֶצְלָהּ לִהְיוֹת עִמָּהּ:
with her   to be   beside her   to lay   unto her   hear – and not

10 And it came to pass, as she spake to Joseph day by day, that he hearkened not unto her, to lie by her, or to be with her.

וַיְהִי   כְּהַיּוֹם הַזֶּה
the this   like the day   and it was

וַיָּבֹא   הַבַּיְתָה לַעֲשׂוֹת מְלַאכְתּוֹ
his kingdom   to doings   the house   and he came

וְאֵין אִישׁ מֵאַנְשֵׁי הַבַּיִת שָׁם בַּבָּיִת:
in house   there   the house   from men   man   and isn't

11 And it came to pass about this time, that Joseph went into the house to do his
business; and there was none of the men of the house there within.

וַתִּתְפְּשֵׂהוּ   בְּבִגְדוֹ לֵאמֹר שִׁכְבָה עִמִּי
with me   lie   to say   in his garment   and she grasped him

וַיַּעֲזֹב   בִּגְדוֹ בְּיָדָהּ וַיָּנָס וַיֵּצֵא   הַחוּצָה:
the outside   and he went out   and he fled   in her hand   in his garment   and he left behind

12 And she caught him by his garment, saying, Lie with me: and he left his garment in
her hand, and fled, and got him out.

וַיְהִי כִּרְאוֹתָהּ כִּי־עָזַב בִּגְדוֹ בְּיָדָהּ וַיָּנָס הַחוּצָה:
the outside   and he fled   in her hand   his garment   left behind - like   like she saw   and it was

13 And it came to pass, when she saw that he had left his garment in her hand, and was
fled forth,

וַתִּקְרָא לְאַנְשֵׁי בֵיתָהּ וַתֹּאמֶר לָהֶם לֵאמֹר
to say   to them   and she said   her house   to men   and she called

רְאוּ הֵבִיא לָנוּ אִישׁ עִבְרִי לְצַחֶק בָּנוּ
in us   to laugh   Hebrew   man   to us   the bring   you saw

בָּא אֵלַי לִשְׁכַּב עִמִּי וָאֶקְרָא בְּקוֹל גָּדוֹל:
big   in voice   and I called   with me   to lie   unto me   come

14 That she called unto the men of her house, and spake unto them, saying, See, he
hath brought in an Hebrew unto us to mock us; he came in unto me to lie with me, and
I cried with a loud voice:

וַיְהִי כְשָׁמְעוֹ כִּי־הֲרִימֹתִי קוֹלִי
my voice   the I raised high - like   like his hearing   and it was

וָאֶקְרָא וַיַּעֲזֹב בִּגְדוֹ אֶצְלִי
beside me   his garment   and he left behind   and I called

וַיָּנָס וַיֵּצֵא הַחוּצָה:
the outside   and he went out   and he fled

15 And it came to pass, when he heard that I lifted up my voice and cried, that he left
his garment with me, and fled, and got him out.

וַתַּנַּח בִּגְדוֹ אֶצְלָהּ עַד־בּוֹא אֲדֹנָיו אֶל־בֵּיתוֹ:
his house – unto   his master   he came – till   beside her   his garment   and she leaving

16 And she laid up his garment by her, until his lord came home.

וַתְּדַבֵּר אֵלָיו כַּדְּבָרִים הָאֵלֶּה לֵאמֹר
to say   the these   like speakings   unto him   and she spoke

בָּא אֵלַי הָעֶבֶד הָעִבְרִי
the Hebrew   the servant   unto me   come

אֲשֶׁר־הֵבֵאתָ לָּנוּ לְצַחֶק בִּי:
in me   to laugh   to us   you brought – which

17 And she spake unto him according to these words, saying, The Hebrew servant,
which thou hast brought unto us, came in unto me to mock me:

וַיְהִי כַּהֲרִימִי קוֹלִי וָאֶקְרָא
and I called   my voice   like I raised high   and it was

וַיַּעֲזֹב בִּגְדוֹ אֶצְלִי וַיָּנָס הַחוּצָה:
the outside   and he fled   beside me   his garment   and he left behind

18 And it came to pass, as I lifted up my voice and cried, that he left his garment with
me, and fled out.

וַיְהִי כִשְׁמֹעַ אֲדֹנָיו אֶת־דִּבְרֵי אִשְׁתּוֹ
his wife   speakings – that   his master   like heard   and it was

אֲשֶׁר דִּבְּרָה אֵלָיו לֵאמֹר
to say   unto him   she spoke   which

כַּדְּבָרִים הָאֵלֶּה עָשָׂה לִי עַבְדֶּךָ
your servant   to me   did   the these   like speakings

וַיִּחַר אַפּוֹ:
his anger   and he kindled

19 And it came to pass, when his master heard the words of his wife, which she spake
unto him, saying, After this manner did thy servant to me; that his wrath was kindled.

וַיִּקַּח אֲדֹנֵי יוֹסֵף אֹתוֹ וַיִּתְּנֵהוּ אֶל־בֵּית הַסֹּהַר
the bound   house – unto   and he gave him   to him   Joseph   master   and he took

מְקוֹם אֲשֶׁר־אֲסוּרֵי [אֲסִירֵי] הַמֶּלֶךְ אֲסוּרִים
bound ones   the king   bindings – which   place

וַיְהִי־שָׁם בְּבֵית הַסֹּהַר:
the bound   in house   there – and he was

20 And Joseph's master took him, and put him into the prison, a place where the king's
prisoners were bound: and he was there in the prison.

וַיְהִי יְהוָֹה אֶת־יוֹסֵף וַיֵּט אֵלָיו חָסֶד
kindness   unto him   and he turned   Joseph – that   ihvh   and he was

וַיִּתֵּן חִנּוֹ בְּעֵינֵי שַׂר בֵּית־הַסֹּהַר:
the bound – house   officer   in eyes   his favor   and he gave

21 But the LORD was with Joseph, and shewed him mercy, and gave him favour in the sight of the keeper of the prison.

וַיִּתֵּן שַׂר בֵּית־הַסֹּהַר בְּיַד־יוֹסֵף
Joseph – in hand   the bound – house   officer   and he gave

אֵת כָּל־הָאֲסִירִם אֲשֶׁר בְּבֵית הַסֹּהַר
the bound   in house   which   the bound ones – all   that

וְאֵת כָּל־אֲשֶׁר עֹשִׂים שָׁם הוּא הָיָה עֹשֶׂה:
doer   was   he   there   doings   which – all   and that

22 And the keeper of the prison committed to Joseph's hand all the prisoners that were in the prison; and whatsoever they did there, he was the doer of it.

אֵין שַׂר בֵּית־הַסֹּהַר רֹאֶה אֶת־כָּל־מְאוּמָה בְּיָדוֹ
in his hand   speck - all – that   seer   the bound – house   officer   isn't

בַּאֲשֶׁר יְהוָה אִתּוֹ
with him   ihvh   in which

וַאֲשֶׁר־הוּא עֹשֶׂה יְהוָה מַצְלִיחַ:
prosper   ihvh   doer   he – and which

23 The keeper of the prison looked not to any thing that was under his hand; because the LORD was with him, and that which he did, the LORD made it to prosper.

פ

CHAPTER 40

ספר בראשית פרק מ

[שביעי]

וַיְהִי אַחַר הַדְּבָרִים הָאֵלֶּה חָטְאוּ מַשְׁקֵה מֶלֶךְ־מִצְרַיִם
Egypt – king   butler   sinned him   the these   the speakings   after   and it was

וְהָאֹפֶה לַאֲדֹנֵיהֶם לְמֶלֶךְ מִצְרָיִם:
Egypt   to king   to their master   and the baker

1 And it came to pass after these things, that the butler of the king of Egypt and his baker had offended their lord the king of Egypt.

וַיִּקְצֹף פַּרְעֹה עַל שְׁנֵי סָרִיסָיו
his officers   two   upon   Pharaoh   and he wroth

עַל שַׂר הַמַּשְׁקִים וְעַל שַׂר הָאוֹפִים:
the baking ones   officer   and upon   the butlers   officer   upon

2 And Pharaoh was wroth against two of his officers, against the chief of the butlers, and against the chief of the bakers.

וַיִּתֵּן אֹתָם בְּמִשְׁמַר בֵּית שַׂר הַטַּבָּחִים אֶל־בֵּית הַסֹּהַר
the bound   house – unto   the guard ones   officer   house   in ward   to them   and he gave

מְקוֹם אֲשֶׁר יוֹסֵף אָסוּר שָׁם:
there　bound　Joseph　which　place

3 And he put them in ward in the house of the captain of the guard, into the prison, the place where Joseph was bound.

וַיִּפְקֹד　שַׂר　הַטַּבָּחִים אֶת־יוֹסֵף אִתָּם
with him　Joseph – that　the guard ones　officer　and he charged

וַיְשָׁרֶת　אֹתָם　וַיִּהְיוּ　יָמִים בְּמִשְׁמָר:
in ward　days　and they were　to them　and he ministered

4 And the captain of the guard charged Joseph with them, and he served them: and they continued a season in ward.

וַיַּחַלְמוּ　חֲלוֹם שְׁנֵיהֶם אִישׁ חֲלֹמוֹ בְּלַיְלָה אֶחָד
one　in night　his dream　man　two of them　dream　and they dreamed

אִישׁ כְּפִתְרוֹן　חֲלֹמוֹ הַמַּשְׁקֶה וְהָאֹפֶה
and the baker　the butler　his dream　like interpretation　man

אֲשֶׁר לְמֶלֶךְ מִצְרַיִם אֲשֶׁר אֲסוּרִים בְּבֵית הַסֹּהַר:
the bound　in house　bound ones　which　Egypt　to king　which

5 And they dreamed a dream both of them, each man his dream in one night, each man according to the interpretation of his dream, the butler and the baker of the king of Egypt, which were bound in the prison.

וַיָּבֹא　אֲלֵיהֶם יוֹסֵף בַּבֹּקֶר
in morning　Joseph　unto them　and he came

וַיַּרְא　אֹתָם וְהִנָּם זֹעֲפִים:
turbulent ones　and behold　to them　and he looked

6 And Joseph came in unto them in the morning, and looked upon them, and, behold, they were sad.

וַיִּשְׁאַל אֶת־סְרִיסֵי פַרְעֹה
Pharaoh　officers – that　and he asked

אֲשֶׁר אִתּוֹ בְמִשְׁמַר בֵּית אֲדֹנָיו לֵאמֹר
to say　his master　house　in ward　with him　which

מַדּוּעַ פְּנֵיכֶם רָעִים הַיּוֹם:
the day　bad ones　your faces　why

7 And he asked Pharaoh's officers that were with him in the ward of his lord's house, saying, Wherefore look ye so sadly to day?

וַיֹּאמְרוּ אֵלָיו חֲלוֹם חָלַמְנוּ וּפֹתֵר אֵין אֹתוֹ
to it　isn't　and interpreter　we dreamed　dream　unto him　and they said

וַיֹּאמֶר אֲלֵהֶם יוֹסֵף
Joseph　unto them　and he said

הֲלוֹא לֵאלֹהִים פִּתְרֹנִים סַפְּרוּ־נָא לִי׃

the not   to Elohim   interpretations   story – you please   to me

8 And they said unto him, We have dreamed a dream, and there is no interpreter of it.
And Joseph said unto them, Do not interpretations belong to God? tell me them, I pray
you.

וַיְסַפֵּר שַׂר־הַמַּשְׁקִים אֶת־חֲלֹמוֹ לְיוֹסֵף

and he storied   the butler ones - officer   that his dream   to Joseph

וַיֹּאמֶר לוֹ בַּחֲלוֹמִי וְהִנֵּה־גֶפֶן לְפָנָי׃

and he said   to him   in my dream   and here – vine   before me

9 And the chief butler told his dream to Joseph, and said to him, In my dream, behold,
a vine was before me;

וּבַגֶּפֶן שְׁלֹשָׁה שָׂרִיגִם

and in vine   three   branches

וְהִוא כְפֹרַחַת עָלְתָה נִצָּה הִבְשִׁילוּ אַשְׁכְּלֹתֶיהָ עֲנָבִים׃

and it   budded   rising   brought forth   blossoming it   it's clusters   grapes

10 And in the vine were three branches: and it was as though it budded, and her
blossoms shot forth; and the clusters thereof brought forth ripe grapes:

וְכוֹס פַּרְעֹה בְּיָדִי וָאֶקַּח אֶת־הָעֲנָבִים

and glass   Pharaoh   in my hand   and I took   that – the grapes

וָאֶשְׂחַט אֹתָם אֶל־כוֹס פַּרְעֹה

and I pressed   to them   unto – glass   Pharaoh

וָאֶתֵּן אֶת־הַכּוֹס עַל־כַּף פַּרְעֹה׃

and I gave   that – the glass   upon – palm   Pharaoh

11 And Pharaoh's cup was in my hand: and I took the grapes, and pressed them into
Pharaoh's cup, and I gave the cup into Pharaoh's hand.

וַיֹּאמֶר לוֹ יוֹסֵף זֶה פִּתְרֹנוֹ

and he said   to him   Joseph   this   its interpretation

שְׁלֹשֶׁת הַשָּׂרִגִים שְׁלֹשֶׁת יָמִים הֵם׃

three   the branches   three   days   them

12 And Joseph said unto him, This is the interpretation of it: The three branches are
three days:

בְּעוֹד שְׁלֹשֶׁת יָמִים יִשָּׂא פַרְעֹה אֶת־רֹאשֶׁךָ

in another   three   days   he will lift   Pharaoh   that – your head

וַהֲשִׁיבְךָ עַל־כַּנֶּךָ וְנָתַתָּ כוֹס־פַּרְעֹה בְּיָדוֹ

and the return you   upon – your place   and you give   glass – Pharaoh   in his hand

כַּמִּשְׁפָּט הָרִאשׁוֹן אֲשֶׁר הָיִיתָ מַשְׁקֵהוּ׃

like judgment   the first   which   you were   his butler

13 Yet within three days shall Pharaoh lift up thine head, and restore thee unto thy place: and thou shalt deliver Pharaoh's cup into his hand, after the former manner when thou wast his butler.

כִּי אִם־זְכַרְתַּנִי אִתְּךָ כַּאֲשֶׁר יִיטַב לָךְ
to you   it will be good   when   with you   remember me – if   like

וְעָשִׂיתָ־נָּא עִמָּדִי חָסֶד וְהִזְכַּרְתַּנִי אֶל־פַּרְעֹה
Pharaoh – unto   and cause to remember me   mercy   with me   now – and you do

וְהוֹצֵאתַנִי מִן־הַבַּיִת הַזֶּה:
the this   the house – from   and bring me out

14 But think on me when it shall be well with thee, and shew kindness, I pray thee, unto me, and make mention of me unto Pharaoh, and bring me out of this house:

כִּי־גֻנֹּב גֻּנַּבְתִּי מֵאֶרֶץ הָעִבְרִים
the Hebrews   from earth   I was stolen   stole - like

וְגַם־פֹּה לֹא־עָשִׂיתִי מְאוּמָה
from speck   I did – not   here – and also

כִּי־שָׂמוּ אֹתִי בַּבּוֹר:
in pit   to me   they put me – like

15 For indeed I was stolen away out of the land of the Hebrews: and here also have I done nothing that they should put me into the dungeon.

וַיַּרְא שַׂר־הָאֹפִים כִּי טוֹב פָּתָר
interpretation   good   like   the baking ones – officer   and he saw

וַיֹּאמֶר אֶל־יוֹסֵף אַף־אֲנִי בַּחֲלוֹמִי
in my dream   I – then   Joseph – unto   and he said

וְהִנֵּה שְׁלֹשָׁה סַלֵּי חֹרִי עַל־רֹאשִׁי:
my head – upon   wicker   baskets   three   and here

16 When the chief baker saw that the interpretation was good, he said unto Joseph, I also was in my dream, and, behold, I had three white baskets on my head:

וּבַסַּל הָעֶלְיוֹן מִכֹּל מַאֲכַל פַּרְעֹה מַעֲשֵׂה אֹפֶה
baker   works   Pharoah   food   from all   the highest   and in basket

וְהָעוֹף אֹכֵל אֹתָם מִן־הַסַּל מֵעַל רֹאשִׁי:
my head   from upon   the basket - from   to them   ate   and the bird

17 And in the uppermost basket there was of all manner of bakemeats for Pharaoh; and the birds did eat them out of the basket upon my head.

וַיַּעַן יוֹסֵף וַיֹּאמֶר זֶה פִּתְרֹנוֹ
its interpretation   this   and he said   Joseph   and he answered

שְׁלֹשֶׁת הַסַּלִּים שְׁלֹשֶׁת יָמִים הֵם:
them   days   three   baskets   three

18 And Joseph answered and said, This is the interpretation thereof: The three baskets are three days:

בְּעוֹד שְׁלֹשֶׁת יָמִים יִשָּׂא פַרְעֹה אֶת־רֹאשְׁךָ מֵעָלֶיךָ
from upon you   your head – that   Pharaoh   he will lift   days   three   in another

וְתָלָה אוֹתְךָ עַל־עֵץ
tree – upon   to you   and hang

וְאָכַל הָעוֹף אֶת־בְּשָׂרְךָ מֵעָלֶיךָ:
from upon you   your flesh – that   the bird   and eat

19 Yet within three days shall Pharaoh lift up thy head from off thee, and shall hang thee on a tree; and the birds shall eat thy flesh from off thee.

[מפטיר]

וַיְהִי בַּיּוֹם הַשְּׁלִישִׁי יוֹם הֻלֶּדֶת אֶת־פַּרְעֹה
Pharaoh – that   birthday   day   the third   in day   and it was

וַיַּעַשׂ מִשְׁתֶּה לְכָל־עֲבָדָיו
his servants – to all   feast   and he did

וַיִּשָּׂא אֶת־רֹאשׁ שַׂר הַמַּשְׁקִים
the butler ones   officer   head – that   and he lifted

וְאֶת־רֹאשׁ שַׂר הָאֹפִים בְּתוֹךְ עֲבָדָיו:
his servants   midst   the baking ones   officer   head – and that

20 And it came to pass the third day, which was Pharaoh's birthday, that he made a feast unto all his servants: and he lifted up the head of the chief butler and of the chief baker among his servants.

וַיָּשֶׁב אֶת־שַׂר הַמַּשְׁקִים עַל־מַשְׁקֵהוּ
his butlership - upon   the butler ones   officer – that   and he returned

וַיִּתֵּן הַכּוֹס עַל־כַּף פַּרְעֹה:
Pharaoh   palm – upon   the cup   and he gave

21 And he restored the chief butler unto his butlership again; and he gave the cup into Pharaoh's hand:

וְאֵת שַׂר הָאֹפִים תָּלָה
hanged   the baking ones   officer   and that

כַּאֲשֶׁר פָּתַר לָהֶם יוֹסֵף:
Joseph   to them   interpretation   when

22 But he hanged the chief baker: as Joseph had interpreted to them.

וְלֹא־זָכַר שַׂר־הַמַּשְׁקִים אֶת־יוֹסֵף וַיִּשְׁכָּחֵהוּ:
and he forgot him   Joseph – that   the butler ones - officer   he remembered – and not

23 Yet did not the chief butler remember Joseph, but forgot him.

פ פ פ

10 Mikeitz

[פרשת מקץ]

Chapter 41

ספר בראשית פרק מא

וַיְהִי מִקֵּץ שְׁנָתַיִם יָמִים
days　two years　from end　and it was

וּפַרְעֹה חֹלֵם וְהִנֵּה עֹמֵד עַל־הַיְאֹר:
the river - upon　stood　and here　dreamer　and Pharaoh

40: 1 And it came to pass at the end of two full years, that Pharaoh dreamed: and, behold, he stood by the river.

וְהִנֵּה מִן־הַיְאֹר עֹלֹת שֶׁבַע פָּרוֹת יְפוֹת מַרְאֶה
appearance　beautiful ones　cows　seven　ascender　the river– from　and here

וּבְרִיאֹת בָּשָׂר וַתִּרְעֶינָה בָּאָחוּ:
in meadow　and she grazed　flesh　and in seeing

2 And, behold, there came up out of the river seven well favoured kine and fat fleshed; and they fed in a meadow.

וְהִנֵּה שֶׁבַע פָּרוֹת אֲחֵרוֹת עֹלוֹת אַחֲרֵיהֶן מִן־הַיְאֹר
the river – from　after them　ascenders　after ones　cows　seven　and here

רָעוֹת מַרְאֶה וְדַקּוֹת בָּשָׂר
flesh　and thin ones　appearance　bad ones

וַתַּעֲמֹדְנָה אֵצֶל הַפָּרוֹת עַל־שְׂפַת הַיְאֹר:
the river　shore – upon　the cows　side　and she stood

3 And, behold, seven other kine came up after them out of the river, ill favoured and lean fleshed; and stood by the other kine upon the brink of the river.

וַתֹּאכַלְנָה הַפָּרוֹת רָעוֹת הַמַּרְאֶה וְדַקֹּת הַבָּשָׂר
the flesh　and thin ones　the appearance　bad ones　the cows　and she ate up

אֵת שֶׁבַע הַפָּרוֹת יְפֹת הַמַּרְאֶה וְהַבְּרִיאֹת
and the quality　the appearance　beautiful ones　the cows　seven　that

וַיִּיקַץ פַּרְעֹה:
Pharaoh　and he awoke

4 And the ill favoured and lean fleshed kine did eat up the seven well favoured and fat kine. So Pharaoh awoke.

וַיִּישָׁן וַיַּחֲלֹם שֵׁנִית
second　and he dreamed　and he slept

וְהִנֵּה שֶׁבַע שִׁבֳּלִים עֹלוֹת בְּקָנֶה אֶחָד בְּרִיאוֹת וְטֹבוֹת:
and good ones quality one stalk ascending ears corn seven and here

5 And he slept and dreamed the second time: and, behold, seven ears of corn came up upon one stalk, rank and good.

וְהִנֵּה שֶׁבַע שִׁבֳּלִים דַּקּוֹת וּשְׁדוּפֹת קָדִים צֹמְחוֹת אַחֲרֵיהֶן:
after them sprouted ones east wind and wind blasted thin ones ears corn seven and here

6 And, behold, seven thin ears and blasted with the east wind sprung up after them.

וַתִּבְלַעְנָה הַשִּׁבֳּלִים הַדַּקּוֹת
the thin ones the ears corn and it devoured

אֵת שֶׁבַע הַשִּׁבֳּלִים הַבְּרִיאוֹת וְהַמְּלֵאוֹת
and the full ones the quality ones the ears corn seven that

וַיִּיקַץ פַּרְעֹה וְהִנֵּה חֲלוֹם:
dream and here Pharaoh and he awoke

7 And the seven thin ears devoured the seven rank and full ears. And Pharaoh awoke, and, behold, it was a dream.

וַיְהִי בַבֹּקֶר וַתִּפָּעֶם רוּחוֹ
his spirit and it troubled in morning and it was

וַיִּשְׁלַח וַיִּקְרָא אֶת־כָּל־חַרְטֻמֵּי מִצְרַיִם וְאֶת־כָּל־חֲכָמֶיהָ
wise men- all - and that Egyptian magicians - all - that and he called and he sent

וַיְסַפֵּר פַּרְעֹה לָהֶם אֶת־חֲלֹמוֹ
his dream - that to them Pharaoh and he storied

וְאֵין־פּוֹתֵר אוֹתָם לְפַרְעֹה:
to Pharaoh to them interpretation - and it isn't

8 And it came to pass in the morning that his spirit was troubled; and he sent and called for all the magicians of Egypt, and all the wise men thereof: and Pharaoh told them his dream; but there was none that could interpret them unto Pharaoh.

וַיְדַבֵּר שַׂר הַמַּשְׁקִים אֶת־פַּרְעֹה
Pharaoh - that the butler ones officer and he spoke

לֵאמֹר אֶת־חֲטָאַי אֲנִי מַזְכִּיר הַיּוֹם:
the day remember I my sins - that to say

9 Then spake the chief butler unto Pharaoh, saying, I do remember my faults this day:

פַּרְעֹה קָצַף עַל־עֲבָדָיו
his servant - upon wroth Pharaoh

וַיִּתֵּן אֹתִי בְּמִשְׁמַר בֵּית שַׂר הַטַּבָּחִים אֹתִי
to me the guards officer house in ward to me and he gave

וְאֵת שַׂר הָאֹפִים:
the bakers officer and that

10 Pharaoh was wroth with his servants, and put me in ward in the captain of the guard's house, both me and the chief baker:

וַנַּחַלְמָה חֲלוֹם בְּלַיְלָה אֶחָד
and we dreamed   dream   in night   one

אֲנִי וָהוּא אִישׁ כְּפִתְרוֹן חֲלֹמוֹ חָלָמְנוּ:
I   and he   man   like interpretation   his dream   we dreamed

11 And we dreamed a dream in one night, I and he; we dreamed each man according to the interpretation of his dream.

וְשָׁם אִתָּנוּ נַעַר עִבְרִי עֶבֶד לְשַׂר הַטַּבָּחִים
and there   to us   young man   Hebrew   servant   to officer   the guards

וַנְּסַפֶּר־לוֹ וַיִּפְתָּר־לָנוּ אֶת־חֲלֹמֹתֵינוּ אִישׁ כַּחֲלֹמוֹ פָּתָר:
and we storied - to him   to us - and he interpreted   that - our dreams   each man   like his dream   interpreted

12 And there was there with us a young man, an Hebrew, servant to the captain of the guard; and we told him, and he interpreted to us our dreams; to each man according to his dream he did interpret.

וַיְהִי כַּאֲשֶׁר פָּתַר־לָנוּ
and it was   when   interpreted - to us

כֵּן הָיָה אֹתִי הֵשִׁיב עַל־כַּנִּי וְאֹתוֹ תָלָה:
thus   it was   to me   the return   upon office -   and to him   hanged

13 And it came to pass, as he interpreted to us, so it was; me he restored unto mine office, and him he hanged.

וַיִּשְׁלַח פַּרְעֹה וַיִּקְרָא אֶת־יוֹסֵף
and he sent   Pharaoh   and he called   Joseph - that

וַיְרִיצֻהוּ מִן־הַבּוֹר וַיְגַלַּח וַיְחַלֵּף שִׂמְלֹתָיו
and they hurriedly brought   from - the dungeon   and he shaved   and he changed   his clothes

וַיָּבֹא אֶל־פַּרְעֹה:
and he came   Pharaoh - unto

14 Then Pharaoh sent and called Joseph, and they brought him hastily out of the dungeon: and he shaved himself, and changed his raiment, and came in unto Pharaoh.

[שני]

וַיֹּאמֶר פַּרְעֹה אֶל־יוֹסֵף חֲלוֹם חָלָמְתִּי
and he said   Pharaoh   Joseph – unto   dream   I dreamed

וּפֹתֵר אֵין אֹתוֹ
and interpretation   isn't   to it

וַאֲנִי שָׁמַעְתִּי עָלֶיךָ לֵאמֹר תִּשְׁמַע חֲלוֹם לִפְתֹּר אֹתוֹ:
and I   my hearing   upon you   to say   you heard   dream   to interpret   to it

15 And Pharaoh said unto Joseph, I have dreamed a dream, and there is none that

can interpret it: and I have heard say of thee, that thou canst understand a dream to interpret it.

בִּלְעָדָי	לֵאמֹר	אֶת־פַּרְעֹה	יוֹסֵף	וַיַּעַן
not to me	to say	Pharaoh – that	Joseph	and he answered.

פַּרְעֹה׃	אֶת־שְׁלוֹם	יַעֲנֶה	אֱלֹהִים
Pharaoh	peace -- that	he will answer	Elohim

16 And Joseph answered Pharaoh, saying, It is not in me: God shall give Pharaoh an answer of peace.

אֶל־יוֹסֵף	פַּרְעֹה	וַיְדַבֵּר
Joseph – unto	Paraoh	and he spoke

הַיְאֹר׃	עַל־שְׂפַת	עֹמֵד	הִנְנִי	בַּחֲלֹמִי
the river	beach – upon	stood	here I	in my dream

17 And Pharaoh said unto Joseph, In my dream, behold, I stood upon the bank of the river:

בָּשָׂר	בְּרִיאוֹת	פָּרוֹת	שֶׁבַע	עֹלֹת	וְהִנֵּה מִן־הַיְאֹר
flesh	quality	cows	seven	ascends	the river -- from and here

בָּאָחוּ׃	וַתִּרְעֶינָה	תֹּאַר	וִיפֹת
in meadow	and she grazed	countenance	and beautiful

18 And, behold, there came up out of the river seven kine, fat fleshed and well favoured; and they fed in a meadow:

אַחֲרֵיהֶן	עֹלוֹת	אֲחֵרוֹת	פָּרוֹת	שֶׁבַע	וְהִנֵּה
after them	ascended	after one's	cows	seven	and here

בָּשָׂר	וְרַקּוֹת	מְאֹד	תֹּאַר	וְרָעוֹת דַּלּוֹת
flesh	and thin ones	very	countenance	and bad ones thin ones

לָרֹעַ׃	מִצְרַיִם	בְּכָל־אֶרֶץ	כָהֵנָּה	לֹא־רָאִיתִי
to badness	Egypt	land - in all	like here	I saw - not

19 And, behold, seven other kine came up after them, poor and very ill favoured and lean fleshed, such as I never saw in all the land of Egypt for badness:

וְהָרָעוֹת	הָרַקּוֹת	הַפָּרוֹת	וַתֹּאכַלְנָה
and the bad ones	the thin ones	the calves	and it ate up

הַבְּרִיאֹת׃	הָרִאשֹׁנוֹת	הַפָּרוֹת	שֶׁבַע	אֵת
the quality ones	the first ones	the cows	seven	that

20 And the lean and the ill favoured kine did eat up the first seven fat kine:

אֶל־קִרְבֶּנָה	כִּי־בָאוּ	וְלֹא נוֹדַע	אֶל־קִרְבֶּנָה	וַתָּבֹאנָה
inwards - unto	they came – like	it known and not	inwards - unto	and it came

וָאִיקָץ׃	בַּתְּחִלָּה	כַּאֲשֶׁר	רַע	וּמַרְאֵיהֶן
and I awoke	in start	when	bad	and they appeared

21 And when they had eaten them up, it could not be known that they had eaten them; but they were still ill favoured, as at the beginning. So I awoke.

וָאֵרֶא בַּחֲלֹמִי
and I saw — in my dream

וְהִנֵּה שֶׁבַע שִׁבֳּלִים עֹלֹת בְּקָנֶה אֶחָד מְלֵאֹת וְטֹבוֹת:
and here — seven — ears corn — ascending — in stalk — one — full ones — and good ones

22 And I saw in my dream, and, behold, seven ears came up in one stalk, full and good:

וְהִנֵּה שֶׁבַע שִׁבֳּלִים צְנֻמוֹת דַּקוֹת
and here — seven — ears corn — withered ones — thin ones

שְׁדֻפוֹת קָדִים צֹמְחוֹת אַחֲרֵיהֶם:
that blasted ones — east wind — sprung up ones — after them

23 And, behold, seven ears, withered, thin, and blasted with the east wind, sprung up after them:

וַתִּבְלַעְןָ הַשִּׁבֳּלִים הַדַּקֹת אֵת שֶׁבַע הַשִּׁבֳּלִים הַטֹּבוֹת
and it devoured — the ears corn — the thin ones — that — seven — the ears corn — the good ones

וָאֹמַר אֶל־הַחַרְטֻמִּים וְאֵין מַגִּיד לִי:
and I said — the magicians – unto — and isn't — telling — to me

24 And the thin ears devoured the seven good ears: and I told this unto the magicians; but there was none that could declare it to me.

וַיֹּאמֶר יוֹסֵף אֶל־פַּרְעֹה חֲלוֹם פַּרְעֹה אֶחָד הוּא
and he said — Joseph — Pharaoh -- unto — dream — Pharaoh — one — it

אֵת אֲשֶׁר הָאֱלֹהִים עֹשֶׂה הִגִּיד לְפַרְעֹה:
that — which — the Elohim — does — tells — to Pharaoh

25 And Joseph said unto Pharaoh, The dream of Pharaoh is one: God hath shewed Pharaoh what he is about to do.

שֶׁבַע פָּרֹת הַטֹּבֹת שֶׁבַע שָׁנִים הֵנָּה
seven — cows — the good ones — seven — years — here

וְשֶׁבַע הַשִּׁבֳּלִים הַטֹּבֹת שֶׁבַע שָׁנִים הֵנָּה
and seven. — the ears corn — the good ones — seven — years — here

חֲלוֹם אֶחָד הוּא:
dream — one — it

26 The seven good kine are seven years; and the seven good ears are seven years: the dream is one.

וְשֶׁבַע הַפָּרוֹת הָרַקּוֹת וְהָרָעֹת הָעֹלֹת אַחֲרֵיהֶן
and seven — the cows — the thin ones — and bad ones — the ascended ones — and after them

שֶׁבַע שָׁנִים הֵנָּה
seven — years — here

וְשֶׁבַע הַשִׁבֳּלִים הָרֵקוֹת שְׁדֻפוֹת הַקָּדִים

and seven | the ears corn | the thin ones | blasted ones | the east wind

יִהְיוּ שֶׁבַע שְׁנֵי רָעָב:

they are | seven | years | famine

27 And the seven thin and ill favoured kine that came up after them are seven years; and the seven empty ears blasted with the east wind shall be seven years of famine.

הוּא הַדָּבָר אֲשֶׁר דִּבַּרְתִּי אֶל־פַּרְעֹה

it | the matter | which | I spoke | Pharaoh – unto

אֲשֶׁר הָאֱלֹהִים עֹשֶׂה הֶרְאָה אֶת־פַּרְעֹה:

which | the Elohim | does | the see | Pharaoh – that

28 This is the thing which I have spoken unto Pharaoh: What God is about to do he sheweth unto Pharaoh.

הִנֵּה שֶׁבַע שָׁנִים

here | seven | years

בָּאוֹת שָׂבָע גָּדוֹל בְּכָל־אֶרֶץ מִצְרָיִם:

coming ones | full | big | earth -- in all | Egypt

29 Behold, there come seven years of great plenty throughout all the land of Egypt:

וְקָמוּ שֶׁבַע שְׁנֵי רָעָב אַחֲרֵיהֶן

and it will arise | seven | years | famine | after them

וְנִשְׁכַּח כָּל־הַשָּׂבָע בְּאֶרֶץ מִצְרָיִם

and will be forgotten | the full - all | in earth | Egypt

וְכִלָּה הָרָעָב אֶת־הָאָרֶץ:

and will consume | the famine | the earth – that

30 And there shall arise after them seven years of famine; and all the plenty shall be forgotten in the land of Egypt; and the famine shall consume the land;

וְלֹא־יִוָּדַע הַשָּׂבָע בָּאֶרֶץ מִפְּנֵי הָרָעָב הַהוּא אַחֲרֵי־כֵן

will known -- and not | the full | in earth | from before | the hunger | the it | thus -- after

כִּי־כָבֵד הוּא מְאֹד:

heavy – like | it | greatly

31 And the plenty shall not be known in the land by reason of that famine following; for it shall be very grievous.

וְעַל הִשָּׁנוֹת הַחֲלוֹם אֶל־פַּרְעֹה פַּעֲמָיִם

and upon | doubled | the dream | Pharaoh – unto | twice

כִּי־נָכוֹן הַדָּבָר מֵעִם הָאֱלֹהִים

right -- like | the matter | from with | the Elohim

וּמְמַהֵר הָאֱלֹהִים לַעֲשֹׂתוֹ:

and from tomorrow | the Elohim | to his doing

32 And for that the dream was doubled unto Pharaoh twice; it is because the thing is established by God, and God will shortly bring it to pass.

וְעַתָּה יֵרֶא פַרְעֹה אִישׁ נָבוֹן וְחָכָם

and wise   correct   man   Pharaoh   he will see   and now

וִישִׁיתֵהוּ עַל־אֶרֶץ מִצְרָיִם:

Egyptian   earth – upon   and he set him

33 Now therefore let Pharaoh look out a man discreet and wise, and set him over the land of Egypt.

יַעֲשֶׂה פַרְעֹה וְיַפְקֵד פְּקִדִים עַל־הָאָרֶץ

the earth -- upon   officers   and he appointed   Pharaoh   he did

וְחִמֵּשׁ אֶת־אֶרֶץ מִצְרַיִם בְּשֶׁבַע שְׁנֵי הַשָּׂבָע:

the fullness   years   in seven   Egyptian   Earth – that   and fifth part

34 Let Pharaoh do this, and let him appoint officers over the land, and take up the fifth part of the land of Egypt in the seven plenteous years.

וְיִקְבְּצוּ אֶת־כָּל־אֹכֶל הַשָּׁנִים הַטֹּבוֹת הַבָּאֹת הָאֵלֶּה

the these   the coming ones   the good ones   the years   food -- all -- that   and they gathered

וְיִצְבְּרוּ־בָר תַּחַת יַד־פַּרְעֹה אֹכֶל בֶּעָרִים וְשָׁמָרוּ:

and they heeded   in cities   food   Pharaoh –hand   under   corn - and they laid up

35 And let them gather all the food of those good years that come, and lay up corn under the hand of Pharaoh, and let them keep food in the cities.

וְהָיָה הָאֹכֶל לְפִקָּדוֹן לָאָרֶץ לְשֶׁבַע שְׁנֵי הָרָעָב

the hunger   years   to full   to earth   to store   the food   and there was

אֲשֶׁר תִּהְיֶיןָ בְּאֶרֶץ מִצְרָיִם וְלֹא־תִכָּרֵת הָאָרֶץ בָּרָעָב:

in hunger   the land   it perish -- and to not   Egyptians   in land   it well be   which

36 And that food shall be for store to the land against the seven years of famine, which shall be in the land of Egypt; that the land perish not through the famine.

וַיִּיטַב הַדָּבָר בְּעֵינֵי פַרְעֹה

Pharaoh   in eyes   the matter   and it was good

וּבְעֵינֵי כָּל־עֲבָדָיו:

his servants – all   and in eyes

37 And the thing was good in the eyes of Pharaoh, and in the eyes of all his servants.

וַיֹּאמֶר פַּרְעֹה אֶל־עֲבָדָיו

his servants -- unto   Pharaoh   and he said

הֲנִמְצָא כָזֶה אִישׁ אֲשֶׁר רוּחַ אֱלֹהִים בּוֹ:

in him   Elohim   spirit   which   man   like this   the we find

38 And Pharaoh said unto his servants, Can we find such a one as this is, a man in whom the Spirit of God is?

[שְׁלִישִׁי]

וַיֹּאמֶר פַּרְעֹה אֶל־יוֹסֵף אַחֲרֵי הוֹדִיעַ אֱלֹהִים אוֹתְךָ

to you   Elohim   made known   after   Joseph – unto   Pharaoh   and he said

אֶת־כָּל־זֹאת אֵין־נָבוֹן וְחָכָם כָּמוֹךָ:

like you   and wise   correct - isn't   this -- all -- that

39 And Pharaoh said unto Joseph, For as much as God hath shewed thee all this, there is none so discreet and wise as thou art:

אַתָּה תִּהְיֶה עַל־בֵּיתִי

my house -- upon   you will be   you

וְעַל־פִּיךָ   יִשַּׁק כָּל־עַמִּי רַק הַכִּסֵּא אֶגְדַּל מִמֶּךָּ:

from you   I greater   the throne   only   my people - all   will rule   your mouth -- and upon

40 Thou shalt be over my house, and according unto thy word shall all my people be ruled: only in the throne will I be greater than thou.

וַיֹּאמֶר פַּרְעֹה אֶל־יוֹסֵף

Joseph – unto   Pharaoh   and he said

רְאֵה נָתַתִּי אֹתְךָ עַל כָּל־אֶרֶץ מִצְרָיִם:

Egypt   land -- all   upon   to you   I give   see

41 And Pharaoh said unto Joseph, See, I have set thee over all the land of Egypt.

וַיָּסַר   פַּרְעֹה אֶת־טַבַּעְתּוֹ מֵעַל   יָדוֹ

his hand   from upon   his ring -- that   Pharaoh   and he removed

וַיִּתֵּן אֹתָהּ עַל־יַד יוֹסֵף

Joseph   hand – upon   to it   and he gave

וַיַּלְבֵּשׁ אֹתוֹ בִּגְדֵי־שֵׁשׁ

silk – clothes   to him   and he dressed

וַיָּשֶׂם רְבִד הַזָּהָב עַל־צַוָּארוֹ:

his neck – upon   the gold   chain   and he put

42 And Pharaoh took off his ring from his hand, and put it upon Joseph's hand, and arrayed him in vestures of fine linen, and put a gold chain about his neck;

וַיַּרְכֵּב אֹתוֹ בְּמִרְכֶּבֶת הַמִּשְׁנֶה אֲשֶׁר־לוֹ

to him - which   the second most   in chariot   to him   and he rode

וַיִּקְרְאוּ לְפָנָיו אַבְרֵךְ

bow knee   before him   and they called

וְנָתוֹן אֹתוֹ עַל כָּל־אֶרֶץ מִצְרָיִם:

Egypt   land -- all   upon   to him   and he gave

43 And he made him to ride in the second chariot which he had; and they cried before him, Bow the knee: and he made him ruler over all the land of Egypt.

וַיֹּ֧אמֶר פַּרְעֹ֛ה אֶל־יוֹסֵ֖ף אֲנִ֣י פַרְעֹ֑ה

Pharaoh   I   Joseph – unto   Pharaoh   and he said

וּבִלְעָדֶ֗יךָ לֹֽא־יָרִ֨ים אִ֧ישׁ אֶת־יָד֛וֹ וְאֶת־רַגְל֖וֹ

his foot -- and that   his hand – that   man   lift high – not   and without you

בְּכָל־אֶ֥רֶץ מִצְרָֽיִם:

Egypt   land - in all

44 And Pharaoh said unto Joseph, I am Pharaoh, and without thee shall no man lift up
his hand or foot in all the land of Egypt.

וַיִּקְרָ֨א פַרְעֹ֤ה שֵׁם־יוֹסֵף֙ צָֽפְנַ֣ת פַּעְנֵ֔חַ

paaneah   Zaph-nath   Joseph -- name   Pharaoh   and he called

וַיִּתֶּן־ל֣וֹ אֶת־אָֽסְנַ֗ת בַּת־פּ֥וֹטִי פֶ֛רַע כֹּהֵ֥ן אֹ֖ן לְאִשָּׁ֑ה

to wife   On   priest   pherah   Poti – daughter   Asenath – that   to him - and he gave

וַיֵּצֵ֥א יוֹסֵ֖ף עַל־אֶ֥רֶץ מִצְרָֽיִם:

Egypt   land -- upon   Joseph   and he went out

45 And Pharaoh called Joseph's name Zaph-nath-paaneah; and he gave him to wife
Asenath the daughter of Poti-pherah priest of On. And Joseph went out over all the
land of Egypt.

וְיוֹסֵף֙ בֶּן־שְׁלֹשִׁ֣ים שָׁנָ֔ה בְּעָמְד֕וֹ לִפְנֵ֖י פַּרְעֹ֣ה מֶֽלֶךְ־מִצְרָ֑יִם

Egypt -- king   Pharaoh   before   in his standing   year   thirty – age   and Joseph

וַיֵּצֵ֤א יוֹסֵף֙ מִלִּפְנֵ֣י פַרְעֹ֔ה וַֽיַּעֲבֹ֖ר בְּכָל־אֶ֥רֶץ מִצְרָֽיִם:

Egypt   land -- in all   and he passed   Pharaoh   from before   Joseph   and he went out

46 And Joseph was thirty years old when he stood before Pharaoh king of Egypt. And
Joseph went out from the presence of Pharaoh, and went throughout all the land of
Egypt.

וַתַּ֣עַשׂ הָאָ֔רֶץ בְּשֶׁ֖בַע שְׁנֵ֣י הַשָּׂבָ֑ע לִקְמָצִֽים:

to handfuls   the full   years   in seven   the land   and he did

47 And in the seven plenteous years the earth brought forth by handfuls.

וַיִּקְבֹּ֞ץ אֶת־כָּל־אֹ֣כֶל ׀ שֶׁ֣בַע שָׁנִ֗ים אֲשֶׁ֤ר הָיוּ֙ בְּאֶ֣רֶץ מִצְרַ֔יִם

Egypt   in land   they were   which   years   seven   food -- all -- that   and he gathered

וַיִּתֶּן־אֹ֖כֶל בֶּֽעָרִ֑ים אֹ֧כֶל שְׂדֵֽה־הָעִ֛יר אֲשֶׁ֥ר סְבִֽיבֹתֶ֖יהָ

around it   which   the city – field   food   in cities   food -- and he gave

נָתַ֥ן בְּתוֹכָֽהּ:

in amongst it   he gave

48 And he gathered up all the food of the seven years, which were in the land of Egypt,
and laid up the food in the cities: the food of the field, which was round about every
city, laid he up in the same.

וַיִּצְבֹּ֨ר יוֹסֵ֥ף בָּ֛ר כְּח֥וֹל הַיָּ֖ם הַרְבֵּ֣ה מְאֹ֑ד

very   the much   the sea   like sand   corn   Joseph   and he heaping

עַד כִּי־חָדַל לִסְפֹּר כִּי־אֵין מִסְפָּר׃
number isn't -- like to number left off - like till

49 And Joseph gathered corn as the sand of the sea, very much, until he left numbering;
for it was without number.

וּלְיוֹסֵף יֻלַּד שְׁנֵי בָנִים בְּטֶרֶם תָּבוֹא שְׁנַת הָרָעָב
the hunger year it came in before sons two begot and to Joseph

אֲשֶׁר יָלְדָה־לּוֹ אָסְנַת בַּת־פּוֹטִי פֶרַע כֹּהֵן אוֹן׃
On priest pherah Poti – daughter Asenath to him – she begot which

50 And unto Joseph were born two sons before the years of famine came, which
Asenath the daughter of Poti-pherah priest of On bare unto him.

וַיִּקְרָא יוֹסֵף אֶת־שֵׁם הַבְּכוֹר מְנַשֶּׁה
Manasseh the firstborn name -- that Joseph and he called

כִּי־נַשַּׁנִי אֱלֹהִים אֶת־כָּל־עֲמָלִי
my labor - all - that Elohim made me forget -- like

וְאֵת כָּל־בֵּית אָבִי׃
my father house - all and that

51 And Joseph called the name of the firstborn Manasseh: For God, said he, hath made
me forget all my toil, and all my father's house.

וְאֵת שֵׁם הַשֵּׁנִי קָרָא אֶפְרָיִם
Ephraim he called the second name and that

כִּי־הִפְרַנִי אֱלֹהִים בְּאֶרֶץ עָנְיִי׃
my affliction in land Elohim caused me to be fruitful -- like

52 And the name of the second called he Ephraim: For God hath caused me to be
fruitful in the land of my affliction.

[רביעי]

וַתִּכְלֶינָה שֶׁבַע שְׁנֵי הַשָּׂבָע
the full years seven and it finishing

אֲשֶׁר הָיָה בְּאֶרֶץ מִצְרָיִם׃
Egypt in land it was which

53 And the seven years of plenteousness, that was in the land of Egypt, were ended.

וַתְּחִלֶּינָה שֶׁבַע שְׁנֵי הָרָעָב לָבוֹא כַּאֲשֶׁר אָמַר יוֹסֵף
Joseph said when to come the famine years seven and it towards start

וַיְהִי רָעָב בְּכָל־הָאֲרָצוֹת
the lands – in all famine and it was

וּבְכָל־אֶרֶץ מִצְרַיִם הָיָה לָחֶם׃
bread it was Egypt earth – and in all

54 And the seven years of dearth began to come, according as Joseph had said: and the

dearth was in all lands; but in all the land of Egypt there was bread.

וַתִּרְעַב כָּל־אֶרֶץ מִצְרַיִם

Egypt   land – all   and it famine

וַיִּצְעַק הָעָם אֶל־פַּרְעֹה לַלָּחֶם
to bread   Pharaoh – unto   the people   and it cried

וַיֹּאמֶר פַּרְעֹה לְכָל־מִצְרַיִם לְכוּ אֶל־יוֹסֵף
Joseph – unto   you go   Egyptians – to all   Pharaoh   and he said

אֲשֶׁר־יֹאמַר לָכֶם תַּעֲשׂוּ׃
you do it   to you   he says – which

55 And when all the land of Egypt was famished, the people cried to Pharaoh for bread: and Pharaoh said unto all the Egyptians, Go unto Joseph; what he saith to you, do.

וְהָרָעָב הָיָה עַל כָּל־פְּנֵי הָאָרֶץ
the earth   face – all   upon   was   and the famine

וַיִּפְתַּח יוֹסֵף אֶת־כָּל־אֲשֶׁר בָּהֶם
in them   which – all – that   Joseph   and he opened

וַיִּשְׁבֹּר לְמִצְרַיִם וַיֶּחֱזַק הָרָעָב בְּאֶרֶץ מִצְרָיִם׃
Egypt   in land   the famine   and it was strong   to Egyptians   and he sold

56 And the famine was over all the face of the earth: And Joseph opened all the storehouses, and sold unto the Egyptians; and the famine waxed sore in the land of Egypt.

וְכָל־הָאָרֶץ בָּאוּ מִצְרַיְמָה לִשְׁבֹּר אֶל־יוֹסֵף
Joseph – unto   to buy   towards Egypt   they came   the earth – and all

כִּי־חָזַק הָרָעָב בְּכָל־הָאָרֶץ׃
the earth – in all   the famine   strong – like

57 And all countries came into Egypt to Joseph for to buy corn; because that the famine was so sore in all lands.

CHAPTER 42

ספר בראשית פרק מב

וַיַּרְא יַעֲקֹב כִּי יֶשׁ־שֶׁבֶר בְּמִצְרָיִם
In Egypt   corn – there is   like   Jacob   and he saw

וַיֹּאמֶר יַעֲקֹב לְבָנָיו לָמָּה תִּתְרָאוּ׃
you look it   why   to his sons   Jacob   and he said

48:1 Now when Jacob saw that there was corn in Egypt, Jacob said unto his sons, Why do ye look one upon another?

וַיֹּאמֶר הִנֵּה שָׁמַעְתִּי כִּי יֶשׁ־שֶׁבֶר בְּמִצְרָיִם רְדוּ־שָׁמָּה
towards there – you descend   in Egypt   corn – there is   like   I heard   here   and he said

וְשִׁבְרוּ־לָנוּ מִשָּׁם וְנִחְיֶה וְלֹא נָמוּת:

we die   and not   and we live   from there   to us – and you return

2 And he said, Behold, I have heard that there is corn in Egypt: get you down thither,
and buy for us from thence; that we may live, and not die.

וַיֵּרְדוּ   אֲחֵי־יוֹסֵף עֲשָׂרָה לִשְׁבֹּר בָּר מִמִּצְרָיִם:

from Egypt   corn   to buy   ten   Joseph – brothers   and they descended

3 And Joseph's ten brethren went down to buy corn in Egypt.

וְאֶת־בִּנְיָמִין אֲחִי יוֹסֵף לֹא־שָׁלַח יַעֲקֹב אֶת־אֶחָיו

his brother - that   Jacob   send – not   Joseph   brother   Benjamin – and that

כִּי אָמַר פֶּן־יִקְרָאֶנּוּ אָסוֹן:

mischief   they meet – lest   said   like

4 But Benjamin, Joseph's brother, Jacob sent not with his brethren; for he said, Lest
peradventure mischief befall him.

וַיָּבֹאוּ   בְּנֵי יִשְׂרָאֵל לִשְׁבֹּר בְּתוֹךְ הַבָּאִים

the coming ones   among   to buy   Israel   sons   and they came

כִּי־הָיָה הָרָעָב בְּאֶרֶץ כְּנָעַן:

Canaan   in land   the famine   there was – like

5 And the sons of Israel came to buy corn among those that came: for the famine was
in the land of Canaan.

וְיוֹסֵף הוּא הַשַּׁלִּיט עַל־הָאָרֶץ

the land – upon   the governor   he   and Joseph

הוּא הַמַּשְׁבִּיר לְכָל־עַם הָאָרֶץ

the earth   people – to all   the merchant   he

וַיָּבֹאוּ אֲחֵי יוֹסֵף וַיִּשְׁתַּחֲווּ־לוֹ אַפַּיִם אָרְצָה:

towards land   faces   to him – and they bowed   Joseph   brothers   and they came

6 And Joseph was the governor over the land, and he it was that sold to all the people
of the land: and Joseph's brethren came, and bowed down themselves before him with
their faces to the earth.

וַיַּרְא יוֹסֵף אֶת־אֶחָיו

his brothers – that   Joseph   and he saw

וַיַּכִּרֵם   וַיִּתְנַכֵּר   אֲלֵיהֶם

unto them   and he strangered   and he recognized them

וַיְדַבֵּר אִתָּם קָשׁוֹת וַיֹּאמֶר אֲלֵהֶם מֵאַיִן בָּאתֶם

come you   from where   unto them   and he said   hard   with them   and he spoke

וַיֹּאמְרוּ מֵאֶרֶץ כְּנַעַן לִשְׁבָּר־אֹכֶל:

food – to buy   Canaan   from land   and they said

7 And Joseph saw his brethren, and he knew them, but made himself strange unto
them, and spake roughly unto them; and he said unto them, Whence come ye? And they

said, From the land of Canaan to buy food.

וַיַּכֵּ֥ר יוֹסֵ֖ף אֶת־אֶחָ֑יו וְהֵ֖ם לֹ֥א הִכִּרֻֽהוּ׃

recognized him   not   and them   his brothers – that   Joseph   and he recognized

8 And Joseph knew his brethren, but they knew not him.

וַיִּזְכֹּ֣ר יוֹסֵ֔ף אֵ֚ת הַחֲלֹמ֔וֹת אֲשֶׁ֥ר חָלַ֖ם לָהֶ֑ם

to them   dreamed   which   the dreams   that   Joseph   and he remembered

וַיֹּ֣אמֶר אֲלֵהֶ֗ם

unto them   and he said

מְרַגְּלִ֣ים אַתֶּ֔ם לִרְא֛וֹת אֶת־עֶרְוַ֥ת הָאָ֖רֶץ בָּאתֶֽם׃

you come   the earth   nakedness – that   to see   you   spies

9 And Joseph remembered the dreams which he dreamed of them, and said unto them,
Ye are spies; to see the nakedness of the land ye are come.

וַיֹּאמְר֥וּ אֵלָ֖יו לֹ֣א אֲדֹנִ֑י

my lord   not   unto him   and they said

וַעֲבָדֶ֥יךָ בָּ֖אוּ לִשְׁבָּר־אֹֽכֶל׃

food - to buy   they came   and your servants

10 And they said unto him, Nay, my lord, but to buy food are thy servants come.

כֻּלָּ֕נוּ בְּנֵ֥י אִישׁ־אֶחָ֖ד

one – man   sons   all us

נָ֑חְנוּ כֵּנִ֣ים אֲנַ֔חְנוּ

we   truthful men   we

לֹא־הָי֥וּ עֲבָדֶ֖יךָ מְרַגְּלִֽים׃

spies   your servants   they were – not

11 We are all one man's sons; we are true men, thy servants are no spies.

וַיֹּ֖אמֶר אֲלֵהֶ֑ם לֹ֕א כִּֽי־עֶרְוַ֥ת הָאָ֖רֶץ בָּאתֶ֥ם לִרְאֽוֹת׃

to see   you came   the earth   nakedness – like   not   unto them   and he said

12 And he said unto them, Nay, but to see the nakedness of the land ye are come.

וַיֹּאמְר֗וּ שְׁנֵ֣ים עָשָׂ֩ר עֲבָדֶ֨יךָ אַחִ֥ים

brothers   your servants   - twelve -   and they said

אֲנַ֛חְנוּ בְּנֵ֥י אִישׁ־אֶחָ֖ד בְּאֶ֣רֶץ כְּנָ֑עַן

Canaan   in land   one – man   sons   we

וְהִנֵּ֨ה הַקָּטֹ֤ן אֶת־אָבִ֙ינוּ֙ הַיּ֔וֹם וְהָאֶחָ֖ד אֵינֶֽנּוּ׃

is not with us   and the one   the day   our father – that   the small   and here

13 And they said, Thy servants are twelve brethren, the sons of one man in the land of
Canaan; and, behold, the youngest is this day with our father, and one is not.

וַיֹּ֥אמֶר אֲלֵהֶ֖ם יוֹסֵ֑ף

Joseph   unto them   and he said

הוּא אֲשֶׁר דִּבַּרְתִּי אֲלֵכֶם לֵאמֹר מְרַגְּלִים אַתֶּם׃

you   spies   to say   unto you   I spoke   which   it

14 And Joseph said unto them, That is it that I spake unto you, saying, Ye are spies:

בְּזֹאת תִּבָּחֵנוּ חֵי פַרְעֹה אִם־תֵּצְאוּ מִזֶּה

from this   you go out – which   Pharaoh   life   you prove it   in this

כִּי אִם־בְּבוֹא אֲחִיכֶם הַקָּטֹן הֵנָּה׃

here   the little   your brother   in come – with   like

15 Hereby ye shall be proved: By the life of Pharaoh ye shall not go forth hence, except your youngest brother come hither.

שִׁלְחוּ מִכֶּם אֶחָד

one   from you   you send

וְיִקַּח אֶת־אֲחִיכֶם וְאַתֶּם הֵאָסְרוּ

the bound it   and you   your brothers – that   and he take

וְיִבָּחֲנוּ דִּבְרֵיכֶם הַאֱמֶת אִתְּכֶם

with you   the truth   your speakings   and they prove

וְאִם־לֹא חֵי פַרְעֹה כִּי מְרַגְּלִים אַתֶּם׃

you   spies   like   Pharaoh   life   not – and if

16 Send one of you, and let him fetch your brother, and ye shall be kept in prison, that your words may be proved, whether there be any truth in you: or else by the life of Pharaoh surely ye are spies.

וַיֶּאֱסֹף אֹתָם אֶל־מִשְׁמָר שְׁלֹשֶׁת יָמִים׃

days   three   ward – unto   to them   and he added

17 And he put them all together into ward three days.

וַיֹּאמֶר אֲלֵהֶם יוֹסֵף בַּיּוֹם הַשְּׁלִישִׁי

the third   in day   Joseph   unto them   and he said

זֹאת עֲשׂוּ וִחְיוּ אֶת־הָאֱלֹהִים אֲנִי יָרֵא׃

fear   I   the Elohim – that   and you live   you do   this

18 And Joseph said unto them the third day, This do, and live; for I fear God:

[חמישי]

אִם־כֵּנִים אַתֶּם אֲחִיכֶם אֶחָד יֵאָסֵר בְּבֵית מִשְׁמַרְכֶם

from your prison   in house   he bound   one   your brother   you   true men - if

וְאַתֶּם לְכוּ הָבִיאוּ שֶׁבֶר רַעֲבוֹן בָּתֵּיכֶם׃

your house   famine   corn   the bring you   you go   and you

19 If ye be true men, let one of your brethren be bound in the house of your prison: go ye, carry corn for the famine of your houses:

וְאֶת־אֲחִיכֶם הַקָּטֹן תָּבִיאוּ אֵלַי

unto me   you bring him   the small   your brother – that

וְיֵאָמְנ֤וּ   דִבְרֵיכֶ֖ם   וְלֹ֣א תָמ֑וּתוּ
you will die it   and not   your speaking   and it we will verify

וַיַּעֲשׂוּ־כֵֽן׃
thus – and they did

20 But bring your youngest brother unto me; so shall your words be verified, and ye shall not die. And they did so.

וַיֹּאמְר֞וּ אִ֣ישׁ אֶל־אָחִ֗יו
his brother – unto   man   and they said

אֲבָל֮ אֲשֵׁמִ֣ים אֲנַ֣חְנוּ עַל־אָחִ֒ינוּ֒
our brother – upon   we   guilty ones   but

אֲשֶׁ֨ר רָאִ֜ינוּ צָרַ֥ת נַפְשׁ֛וֹ בְּהִתְחַֽנְנ֥וֹ אֵלֵ֖ינוּ
unto us   in his supplication   his soul   distress   we saw   which

וְלֹ֣א שָׁמָ֑עְנוּ עַל־כֵּן֙ בָּ֣אָה אֵלֵ֔ינוּ הַצָּרָ֖ה הַזֹּֽאת׃
the this   the trouble   unto us   come   thus – upon   we heard   and not

21 And they said one to another, We are verily guilty concerning our brother, in that we saw the anguish of his soul, when he besought us, and we would not hear; therefore is this distress come upon us.

וַיַּ֩עַן֩ רְאוּבֵ֨ן אֹתָ֜ם לֵאמֹ֗ר הֲלוֹא֩ אָמַ֨רְתִּי אֲלֵיכֶ֧ם
unto you   I said   the not   to say   to them   Reuben   and answered

לֵאמֹ֛ר אַל־תֶּחֶטְא֥וּ בַיֶּ֖לֶד
in child   you sin it - don't   to say

וְלֹ֣א שְׁמַעְתֶּ֑ם וְגַם־דָּמ֖וֹ הִנֵּ֥ה נִדְרָֽשׁ׃
required   here   his blood – and also   you heard   and not

22 And Reuben answered them, saying, Spake I not unto you, saying, Do not sin against the child; and ye would not hear? therefore, behold, also his blood is required.

וְהֵם֙ לֹ֣א יָֽדְע֔וּ כִּ֥י שֹׁמֵ֖עַ יוֹסֵ֑ף כִּ֥י הַמֵּלִ֖יץ בֵּינֹתָֽם׃
isn't between them   the interpreter   like   Joseph   hearer   like   they knew   not   and them

23 And they knew not that Joseph understood them; for he spake unto them by an interpreter.

וַיִּסֹּ֥ב מֵֽעֲלֵיהֶ֖ם וַיֵּֽבְךְּ
and he wept   from upon them   and he turned

וַיָּ֤שָׁב אֲלֵהֶם֙ וַיְדַבֵּ֣ר אֲלֵהֶ֔ם
unto them   and he spoke   unto them   and he returned

וַיִּקַּ֤ח מֵֽאִתָּם֙ אֶת־שִׁמְע֔וֹן וַיֶּֽאֱסֹ֥ר אֹת֖וֹ לְעֵינֵיהֶֽם׃
to their eyes   to him   and he bound   Simeon – that   from with them   and he took

24 And he turned himself about from them, and wept; and returned to them again, and communed with them, and took from them Simeon, and bound him before their eyes.

וַיְצַו יוֹסֵף וַיְמַלְאוּ אֶת־כְּלֵיהֶם בָּר
and he commanded   Joseph   and they filled   pots - that   corn

וּלְהָשִׁיב כַּסְפֵּיהֶם אִישׁ אֶל־שַׂקּוֹ
and to the return   their money   man   his sack – unto

וְלָתֵת לָהֶם צֵדָה לַדָּרֶךְ וַיַּעַשׂ לָהֶם כֵּן׃
and to give   to them   provision   to way   and he did   to them   thus

25 Then Joseph commanded to fill their sacks with corn, and to restore every man's
money into his sack, and to give them provision for the way: and thus did he unto them.

וַיִּשְׂאוּ אֶת־שִׁבְרָם עַל־חֲמֹרֵיהֶם וַיֵּלְכוּ מִשָּׁם׃
and they lifted   bag saddles - that   their donkeys – upon   and they went   from there

26 And they laded their asses with the corn, and departed thence.

וַיִּפְתַּח הָאֶחָד אֶת־שַׂקּוֹ לָתֵת מִסְפּוֹא לַחֲמֹרוֹ בַּמָּלוֹן
and he opened   the one   his sack – that   to give   provender   to his donkey   in inn

וַיַּרְא אֶת־כַּסְפּוֹ וְהִנֵּה־הוּא בְּפִי אַמְתַּחְתּוֹ׃
and he saw   his money – that   it – here   in mouth   his sack opening

27 And as one of them opened his sack to give his ass provender in the inn, he espied
his money; for, behold, it was in his sack's mouth.

וַיֹּאמֶר אֶל־אֶחָיו הוּשַׁב כַּסְפִּי וְגַם הִנֵּה בְאַמְתַּחְתִּי
and he said   his brother – unto   restored   my money   and also   here   my sack opening

וַיֵּצֵא לִבָּם וַיֶּחֶרְדוּ אִישׁ אֶל־אָחִיו לֵאמֹר
and it came out   their hearts   and they afraid   man   his brother – unto   to say

מַה־זֹּאת עָשָׂה אֱלֹהִים לָנוּ׃
this – what   did   Elohim   to us

28 And he said unto his brethren, My money is restored; and, lo, it is even in my sack:
and their heart failed them, and they were afraid, saying one to another, What is this that
God hath done unto us?

וַיָּבֹאוּ אֶל־יַעֲקֹב אֲבִיהֶם אַרְצָה כְּנָעַן
and they came   Jacob – unto   their father   land   Canaan

וַיַּגִּידוּ לוֹ אֵת כָּל־הַקֹּרֹת אֹתָם לֵאמֹר׃
and they told   to him   that   the happenings - all   to them   to say

29 And they came unto Jacob their father unto the land of Canaan, and told him all that
befell unto them; saying,

דִּבֶּר הָאִישׁ אֲדֹנֵי הָאָרֶץ אִתָּנוּ קָשׁוֹת
spoke   the man   master   the land   with us   hard ones

וַיִּתֵּן אֹתָנוּ כִּמְרַגְּלִים אֶת־הָאָרֶץ׃
to us and he gave   like spies   the land – that

30 The man, who is the lord of the land, spake roughly to us, and took us for spies of
the country.

וַנֹּאמֶר אֵלָיו כֵּנִים אֲנַחְנוּ לֹא הָיִינוּ מְרַגְּלִים׃

spies   we were   not   we   true men   unto him   and we said

31 And we said unto him, We are true men; we are no spies:

שְׁנֵים־עָשָׂר אֲנַחְנוּ אַחִים בְּנֵי אָבִינוּ

our father   son   brothers   we   - twelve -

הָאֶחָד אֵינֶנּוּ וְהַקָּטֹן הַיּוֹם אֶת־אָבִינוּ בְּאֶרֶץ כְּנָעַן׃

Canaan   in land   our father – that   the day   and the small   isn't to us   the one

32 We be twelve brethren, sons of our father; one is not, and the youngest is this day with our father in the land of Canaan.

וַיֹּאמֶר אֵלֵינוּ הָאִישׁ אֲדֹנֵי הָאָרֶץ

the land   master   the man   unto us   and he said

בְּזֹאת אֵדַע כִּי כֵנִים אַתֶּם אֲחֵיכֶם

your brothers   you   true men   like   I know   in this

הָאֶחָד הַנִּיחוּ אִתִּי

with me   leave you   the one

וְאֶת־רַעֲבוֹן בָּתֵּיכֶם קְחוּ וָלֵכוּ׃

and you go   you take   your house   famine food - and that

33 And the man, the lord of the country, said unto us, Hereby shall I know that ye are true men; leave one of your brethren here with me, and take food for the famine of your households, and be gone:

וְהָבִיאוּ אֶת־אֲחִיכֶם הַקָּטֹן אֵלַי

unto me   the small   your brother – that   and the bring you

וְאֵדְעָה כִּי לֹא מְרַגְּלִים אַתֶּם כִּי כֵנִים אַתֶּם

you are   true men   like   you   spies   not   like   and I know

אֶת־אֲחִיכֶם אֶתֵּן לָכֶם

to you   I will give   your brother – that

וְאֶת־הָאָרֶץ תִּסְחָרוּ׃

you will be merchants   the land – and that

34 And bring your youngest brother unto me: then shall I know that ye are no spies, but that ye are true men: so will I deliver you your brother, and ye shall traffick in the land.

וַיְהִי הֵם מְרִיקִים שַׂקֵּיהֶם וְהִנֵּה־אִישׁ צְרוֹר־כַּסְפּוֹ בְּשַׂקּוֹ

in his sack   money - bundle   man – and here   their sacks   empty ones   them   and it was

וַיִּרְאוּ אֶת־צְרֹרוֹת כַּסְפֵּיהֶם הֵמָּה

they were   money   bundles - that   and they saw

וַאֲבִיהֶם וַיִּירָאוּ׃

and they afraid   and their father

35 And it came to pass as they emptied their sacks, that, behold, every man's bundle of

money was in his sack: and when both they and their father saw the bundles of money, they were afraid.

וַיֹּאמֶר אֲלֵהֶם יַעֲקֹב אֲבִיהֶם אֹתִי שִׁכַּלְתֶּם

you bereaved   to me   their father   Jacob   unto them   and he said

יוֹסֵף אֵינֶנּוּ וְשִׁמְעוֹן אֵינֶנּוּ וְאֶת־בִּנְיָמִן תִּקָּחוּ

you will take him   Benjamin – and that   not with us   and Simeon   not of us   Joseph

עָלַי הָיוּ כֻלָּנָה׃

towards all   it was   upon me

36 And Jacob their father said unto them, Me have ye bereaved of my children: Joseph is not, and Simeon is not, and ye will take Benjamin away: all these things are against me.

וַיֹּאמֶר רְאוּבֵן אֶל־אָבִיו לֵאמֹר

to say   his father – unto   Reuben   and he said

אֶת־שְׁנֵי בָנַי תָּמִית אִם־לֹא אֲבִיאֶנּוּ אֵלֶיךָ

unto you   I bring you   not – if   you kill   my sons   two – that

תְּנָה אֹתוֹ עַל־יָדִי

my hand – upon   to him   you give

וַאֲנִי אֲשִׁיבֶנּוּ אֵלֶיךָ׃

unto you   I return him   and I

37 And Reuben spake unto his father, saying, Slay my two sons, if I bring him not to thee: deliver him into my hand, and I will bring him to thee again.

וַיֹּאמֶר לֹא־יֵרֵד בְּנִי עִמָּכֶם כִּי־אָחִיו מֵת

dead   his brother – like   with you   my son   he will descend – not   and he said

וְהוּא לְבַדּוֹ נִשְׁאָר

remains   alone   and he

וּקְרָאָהוּ אָסוֹן בַּדֶּרֶךְ אֲשֶׁר תֵּלְכוּ־בָהּ

in it – you go   which   in way   mischief   and comes near him

וְהוֹרַדְתֶּם אֶת־שֵׂיבָתִי בְּיָגוֹן שְׁאוֹלָה׃

towards grave   in sorrow   my gray hair – that   and bringer down

38 And he said, My son shall not go down with you; for his brother is dead, and he is left alone: if mischief befall him by the way in the which ye go, then shall ye bring down my gray hairs with sorrow to the grave.

CHAPTER 43

ספר בראשית פרק מג

וְהָרָעָב כָּבֵד בָּאָרֶץ׃

in land   already   and the famine

1 And the famine was sore in the land.

וַיְהִי כַּאֲשֶׁר כִּלּוּ לֶאֱכֹל אֶת־הַשֶּׁבֶר אֲשֶׁר הֵבִיאוּ מִמִּצְרָיִם
<small>from Egypt   they brought   which   the corn – that   to eat   they finished   when   and it was</small>

וַיֹּאמֶר אֲלֵיהֶם אֲבִיהֶם שֻׁבוּ שִׁבְרוּ־לָנוּ מְעַט־אֹכֶל:
<small>food – little   to us – you buy   you return   their father   unto them   and he said</small>

2 And it came to pass, when they had eaten up the corn which they had brought out of Egypt, their father said unto them, Go again, buy us a little food.

וַיֹּאמֶר אֵלָיו יְהוּדָה לֵאמֹר
<small>to say   Judah   unto him   and he said</small>

הָעֵד הֵעִד בָּנוּ הָאִישׁ לֵאמֹר
<small>to say   the man   in us   the testimony   the testify</small>

לֹא־תִרְאוּ פָנַי בִּלְתִּי אֲחִיכֶם אִתְּכֶם:
<small>with you   your brother   without   my face   you see it – not</small>

3 And Judah spake unto him, saying, The man did solemnly protest unto us, saying, Ye shall not see my face, except your brother be with you.

אִם־יֶשְׁךָ מְשַׁלֵּחַ אֶת־אָחִינוּ אִתָּנוּ
<small>with us   our brother – that   send   it is your - if</small>

נֵרְדָה וְנִשְׁבְּרָה לְךָ אֹכֶל:
<small>food   to you   and we buy   we descend</small>

4 If thou wilt send our brother with us, we will go down and buy thee food:

וְאִם־אֵינְךָ מְשַׁלֵּחַ לֹא נֵרֵד
<small>we will descend   not   send   isn't you - if</small>

כִּי־הָאִישׁ אָמַר אֵלֵינוּ
<small>unto us   said   the man – like</small>

לֹא־תִרְאוּ פָנַי בִּלְתִּי אֲחִיכֶם אִתְּכֶם:
<small>with you   your brother   without   my face   you will see – not</small>

5 But if thou wilt not send him, we will not go down: for the man said unto us, Ye shall not see my face, except your brother be with you.

וַיֹּאמֶר יִשְׂרָאֵל לָמָה הֲרֵעֹתֶם לִי
<small>to me   the bad you   why   Israel   and he said</small>

לְהַגִּיד לָאִישׁ הַעוֹד לָכֶם אָח:
<small>brother   to you   the again   to man   to the tell</small>

6 And Israel said, Wherefore dealt ye so ill with me, as to tell the man whether ye had yet a brother?

וַיֹּאמְרוּ שָׁאוֹל שָׁאַל־הָאִישׁ לָנוּ
<small>to us   the man – heb asked   ask   and they said</small>

וּלְמוֹלַדְתֵּנוּ לֵאמֹר הַעוֹד אֲבִיכֶם חַי הֲיֵשׁ לָכֶם אָח
<small>brother   to you   the there is   life   your father   the again   to say   and to our kindred</small>

וַנַּגֶּד־לוֹ   עַל־פִּי הַדְּבָרִים הָאֵלֶּה
the these   the words   face – upon   to him – and we told

הֲיָדוֹעַ נֵדַע   כִּי יֹאמַר הוֹרִדוּ אֶת־אֲחִיכֶם:
your brother – that   bring down him   he said   like   we know   the knower

7 And they said, The man asked us straitly of our state, and of our kindred, saying, Is your father yet alive? have ye another brother? and we told him according to the tenor of these words: could we certainly know that he would say, Bring your brother down?

וַיֹּאמֶר יְהוּדָה אֶל־יִשְׂרָאֵל אָבִיו
his father   Israel – unto   Judah   and he said

שִׁלְחָה הַנַּעַר אִתִּי וְנָקוּמָה וְנֵלֵכָה וְנִחְיֶה
and we live   and we go   and we rise   with me   the boy   send

וְלֹא נָמוּת גַּם־אֲנַחְנוּ גַם־אַתָּה גַּם־טַפֵּנוּ:
our little ones - also   you – also   we – also   we die   and not

8 And Judah said unto Israel his father, Send the lad with me, and we will arise and go; that we may live, and not die, both we, and thou, and also our little ones.

אָנֹכִי אֶעֶרְבֶנּוּ מִיָּדִי   תְּבַקְשֶׁנּוּ
you will seek him   from my hand   will surety it   I am

אִם־לֹא הֲבִיאֹתִיו אֵלֶיךָ וְהִצַּגְתִּיו לְפָנֶיךָ
to your face   and to set him   unto you   the bring him   not – if

וְחָטָאתִי לְךָ כָּל־הַיָּמִים:
the days – all   to you   and my sin

9 I will be surety for him; of my hand shalt thou require him: if I bring him not unto thee, and set him before thee, then let me bear the blame for ever:

כִּי לוּלֵא הִתְמַהְמָהְנוּ כִּי־עַתָּה שַׁבְנוּ זֶה פַעֲמָיִם:
second time   this   we return   now – like   you cause to us linger   except   like

10 For except we had lingered, surely now we had returned this second time.

וַיֹּאמֶר אֲלֵהֶם יִשְׂרָאֵל אֲבִיהֶם
their father   Israel   unto them   and he said

אִם־כֵּן אֵפוֹא זֹאת
this   where   thus – if

עֲשׂוּ קְחוּ מִזִּמְרַת הָאָרֶץ בִּכְלֵיכֶם
in your vessels   the earth   from fruit trees   you take   you make

וְהוֹרִידוּ לָאִישׁ מִנְחָה מְעַט צֳרִי
balm   little   offering   to man   and you bring down

וּמְעַט דְּבַשׁ נְכֹאת וָלֹט בָּטְנִים וּשְׁקֵדִים:
and almonds   nuts   and myrrh   spices   honey   and little

11 And their father Israel said unto them, If it must be so now, do this; take of the best

fruits in the land in your vessels, and carry down the man a present, a little balm, and a little honey, spices, and myrrh, nuts, and almonds:

וְכֶ֧סֶף מִשְׁנֶ֛ה קְח֥וּ בְיֶדְכֶ֖ם
and silver   twice   you take   in your hand

וְאֶת־הַכֶּ֨סֶף הַמּוּשָׁ֜ב בְּפִ֣י אַמְתְּחֹֽתֵיכֶ֗ם
the silver – and that   the returned   in mouth   your bags

תָּשִׁ֧יבוּ בְיֶדְכֶ֛ם אוּלַ֥י מִשְׁגֶּ֖ה הֽוּא׃
you return it   in your hand   perhaps   mistake   it

12 And take double money in your hand; and the money that was brought again in the mouth of your sacks, carry it again in your hand; peradventure it was an oversight:

וְאֶת־אֲחִיכֶ֖ם קָ֑חוּ וְק֥וּמוּ שׁ֖וּבוּ אֶל־הָאִֽישׁ׃
your brother – and that   you take   and you get up   you return   the man – unto

13 Take also your brother, and arise, go again unto the man:

וְאֵ֣ל שַׁדַּ֗י יִתֵּ֨ן לָכֶ֤ם רַחֲמִים֙ לִפְנֵ֣י הָאִ֔ישׁ
and El   Shadai   he gives   to you   mercies   before   the man

וְשִׁלַּ֥ח לָכֶ֛ם אֶת־אֲחִיכֶ֥ם אַחֵ֖ר וְאֶת־בִּנְיָמִ֑ין
and he will send   to you   your brother – that   other   Benjamin – and that

וַאֲנִ֕י כַּאֲשֶׁ֥ר שָׁכֹ֖לְתִּי שָׁכָֽלְתִּי׃
and I   when   I bereaver   I bereaved

14 And God Almighty give you mercy before the man, that he may send away your other brother, and Benjamin. If I be bereaved of my children, I am bereaved.

וַיִּקְח֤וּ הָֽאֲנָשִׁים֙ אֶת־הַמִּנְחָ֣ה הַזֹּ֔את
and they took   the men   the offering – that   the this

וּמִשְׁנֶה־כֶּ֛סֶף לָקְח֥וּ בְיָדָ֖ם וְאֶת־בִּנְיָמִ֑ן
silver - and twice   to take it   in their hand   Benjamin – and that

וַיָּקֻ֨מוּ֙ וַיֵּרְד֣וּ מִצְרַ֔יִם
and they rose up   and they descended   Egypt

וַיַּעַמְד֖וּ לִפְנֵ֥י יוֹסֵֽף׃
and they stood   before   Joseph

15 And the men took that present, and they took double money in their hand, and Benjamin; and rose up, and went down to Egypt, and stood before Joseph.

[ששי]

וַיַּ֨רְא יוֹסֵ֣ף אִתָּם֮ אֶת־בִּנְיָמִין֒
and he saw   Joseph   with them   Benjamin – that

וַיֹּ֨אמֶר֙ לַֽאֲשֶׁ֣ר עַל־בֵּית֔וֹ הָבֵ֥א אֶת־הָאֲנָשִׁ֖ים הַבָּֽיְתָה
and he said   to which   his house – upon   the bring   the men – that   the house

וּטְבֹחַ טֶבַח וְהָכֵן כִּי אִתִּי יֹאכְלוּ הָאֲנָשִׁים בַּצָּהֳרָיִם׃

in noon the men they will eat with me like and prepare you slaughter and slay

16 And when Joseph saw Benjamin with them, he said to the ruler of his house, Bring these men home, and slay, and make ready; for these men shall dine with me at noon.

וַיַּעַשׂ הָאִישׁ כַּאֲשֶׁר אָמַר יוֹסֵף

Joseph said when the man and he did

וַיָּבֵא הָאִישׁ אֶת־הָאֲנָשִׁים בֵּיתָה יוֹסֵף׃

Joseph towards house the men – that the man and he brought

17 And the man did as Joseph bade; and the man brought the men into Joseph's house.

וַיִּירְאוּ הָאֲנָשִׁים כִּי הוּבְאוּ בֵּית יוֹסֵף

Joseph house they brought like the men and they afraid

וַיֹּאמְרוּ עַל־דְּבַר הַכֶּסֶף הַשָּׁב בְּאַמְתְּחֹתֵינוּ

in our sacks the returned the money matter – upon and they said

בַּתְּחִלָּה אֲנַחְנוּ מוּבָאִים לְהִתְגֹּלֵל עָלֵינוּ

upon us to cause to roll brought in ones we in start

וּלְהִתְנַפֵּל עָלֵינוּ וְלָקַחַת אֹתָנוּ לַעֲבָדִים וְאֶת־חֲמֹרֵינוּ׃

our asses – and that to slaves to us and to take upon us and to cause to fall

18 And the men were afraid, because they were brought into Joseph's house; and they said, Because of the money that was returned in our sacks at the first time are we brought in; that he may seek occasion against us, and fall upon us, and take us for bondmen, and our asses.

וַיִּגְּשׁוּ אֶל־הָאִישׁ אֲשֶׁר עַל־בֵּית יוֹסֵף

Joseph house – upon which the man – unto and they touched

וַיְדַבְּרוּ אֵלָיו פֶּתַח הַבָּיִת׃

the house opening unto him and they spoke

19 And they came near to the steward of Joseph's house, and they communed with him at the door of the house,

וַיֹּאמְרוּ בִּי אֲדֹנִי יָרֹד יָרַדְנוּ בַּתְּחִלָּה לִשְׁבָּר־אֹכֶל׃

food – to buy in start we descended descend master in me and they said

20 And said, O sir, we came indeed down at the first time to buy food:

וַיְהִי כִּי־בָאנוּ אֶל־הַמָּלוֹן

the inn – unto we came – like and it was

וַנִּפְתְּחָה אֶת־אַמְתְּחֹתֵינוּ

our sacks – that and we opened

וְהִנֵּה כֶסֶף־אִישׁ בְּפִי אַמְתַּחְתּוֹ

his sack in mouth man – money and here

כַּסְפֵּנוּ בְּמִשְׁקָלוֹ   וַנָּשֶׁב אֹתוֹ בְּיָדֵנוּ:

in our hands   to it   and we return   in its full weight   our money

21 And it came to pass, when we came to the inn, that we opened our sacks, and, behold, every man's money was in the mouth of his sack, our money in full weight: and we have brought it again in our hand.

וְכֶסֶף אַחֵר הוֹרַדְנוּ   בְּיָדֵנוּ לִשְׁבָּר־אֹכֶל

food – to buy   in our hands   we brought down   other   and money

לֹא יָדַעְנוּ מִי־שָׂם כַּסְפֵּנוּ בְּאַמְתְּחֹתֵינוּ:

in our sacks   our money   put – who   we knew   not

22 And other money have we brought down in our hands to buy food: we cannot tell who put our money in our sacks.

וַיֹּאמֶר שָׁלוֹם לָכֶם אַל־תִּירָאוּ

your fear – don't   to you   peace   and he said

אֱלֹהֵיכֶם וֵאלֹהֵי אֲבִיכֶם נָתַן לָכֶם מַטְמוֹן בְּאַמְתְּחֹתֵיכֶם

in your sacks   buried treasure   to you   gave   your fathers   and Elohim   your Elohim

כַּסְפְּכֶם בָּא אֵלָי

unto me   come   your money

וַיּוֹצֵא   אֲלֵהֶם אֶת־שִׁמְעוֹן:

Simeon – that   unto them   and he brought out

23 And he said, Peace be to you, fear not: your God, and the God of your father, hath given you treasure in your sacks: I had your money. And he brought Simeon out unto them.

וַיָּבֵא   הָאִישׁ אֶת־הָאֲנָשִׁים בֵּיתָה יוֹסֵף

Joseph   house   the men – that   the man   and he brought

וַיִּתֶּן־מַיִם   וַיִּרְחֲצוּ רַגְלֵיהֶם וַיִּתֵּן מִסְפּוֹא לַחֲמֹרֵיהֶם:

to their asses   provender   and he gave   their feet   and they washed   water – and he gave

24 And the man brought the men into Joseph's house, and gave them water, and they washed their feet; and he gave their asses provender.

וַיָּכִינוּ   אֶת־הַמִּנְחָה עַד־בּוֹא יוֹסֵף בַּצָּהֳרָיִם

in noon   Joseph   came – till   the offering – that   and they made ready

כִּי שָׁמְעוּ כִּי־שָׁם יֹאכְלוּ לָחֶם:

bread   they will eat   there – like   they heard   like

25 And they made ready the present against Joseph came at noon: for they heard that they should eat bread there.

וַיָּבֹא   יוֹסֵף הַבַּיְתָה

the house   Joseph   and he came

וַיָּבִיאוּ   לוֹ   אֶת־הַמִּנְחָה אֲשֶׁר־בְּיָדָם הַבַּיְתָה

the house   in their hands – which   the offering – that   to him   and they brought

וַיִּשְׁתַּחֲווּ־לוֹ　אָֽרְצָה:
towards ground　to him – and they bowed

26 And when Joseph came home, they brought him the present which was in their hand into the house, and bowed themselves to him to the earth.

וַיִּשְׁאַל　לָהֶם　לְשָׁלוֹם
to peace　to them　and he asked

וַיֹּאמֶר　הֲשָׁלוֹם　אֲבִיכֶם　הַזָּקֵן　אֲשֶׁר　אֲמַרְתֶּם　הַעוֹדֶנּוּ　חָֽי:
life　the still he　you spoke　which　the old one　your father　the peace　and he said

27 And he asked them of their welfare, and said, Is your father well, the old man of whom ye spake? Is he yet alive?

וַיֹּאמְרוּ　שָׁלוֹם　לְעַבְדְּךָ　לְאָבִינוּ　עוֹדֶנּוּ　חָי
life　still he　to our father　to your servant　peace　and they said

וַיִּקְּדוּ　וַיִּשְׁתַּחוּ　[וַיִּשְׁתַּחֲווּ]　:
and they bowed　and they bowed heads

28 And they answered, Thy servant our father is in good health, he is yet alive. And they bowed down their heads, and made obeisance.

וַיִּשָּׂא　עֵינָיו
his eye　and he lifted

וַיַּרְא　אֶת־בִּנְיָמִין　אָחִיו　בֶן־אִמּוֹ
his mother son　his brother　Benjamin – that　and he saw

וַיֹּאמֶר　הֲזֶה　אֲחִיכֶם　הַקָּטֹן　אֲשֶׁר　אֲמַרְתֶּם　אֵלָי
unto me　your said　which　the small　your brother　the this　and he said

וַיֹּאמַר　אֱלֹהִים　יָחְנְךָ　בְּנִֽי:
my son　he graces you　Elohim　and he said

29 And he lifted up his eyes, and saw his brother Benjamin, his mother's son, and said, Is this your younger brother, of whom ye spake unto me? And he said, God be gracious unto thee, my son.

[שביעי]

וַיְמַהֵר　יוֹסֵף　כִּי־נִכְמְרוּ　רַחֲמָיו　אֶל־אָחִיו
his brothers – unto　his bowels　he yearned - like　Joseph　and he quickly

וַיְבַקֵּשׁ　לִבְכּוֹת　וַיָּבֹא　הַחַדְרָה　וַיֵּבְךְּ　שָֽׁמָּה:
there　and he wept　the personal room　and he came　to weep　and he seeking

30 And Joseph made haste; for his bowels did yearn upon his brother: and he sought where to weep; and he entered into his chamber, and wept there.

וַיִּרְחַץ　פָּנָיו　וַיֵּצֵא　וַיִּתְאַפַּק　וַיֹּאמֶר　שִׂימוּ　לָֽחֶם:
bread　you set　and he said　and he refrained　and he went out　his face　and he washed

31 And he washed his face, and went out, and refrained himself, and said, Set on bread.

וַיָּשִׂימוּ לוֹ לְבַדּוֹ וְלָהֶם לְבַדָּם
alone them and to them   alone to him and they set

וְלַמִּצְרִים הָאֹכְלִים אִתּוֹ לְבַדָּם
alone them with him the eating ones and to Egyptians

כִּי לֹא יוּכְלוּן הַמִּצְרִים לֶאֱכֹל אֶת־הָעִבְרִים לֶחֶם
bread the Israelites - that to eat the Egyptians they will eat not like

כִּי־תוֹעֵבָה הוּא לְמִצְרָיִם:
to Egyptians it abomination – like

32 And they set on for him by himself, and for them by themselves, and for the
Egyptians, which did eat with him, by themselves: because the Egyptians might not eat
bread with the Hebrews; for that is an abomination unto the Egyptians.

וַיֵּשְׁבוּ לְפָנָיו הַבְּכֹר כִּבְכֹרָתוֹ
like his birth right the first born to his face and they sat

וְהַצָּעִיר כִּצְעִרָתוֹ
like his youngness and the youngest

וַיִּתְמְהוּ הָאֲנָשִׁים אִישׁ אֶל־רֵעֵהוּ:
neighbor – unto man the men and they marveled

33 And they sat before him, the firstborn according to his birthright, and the youngest
according to his youth: and the men marveled one at another.

וַיִּשָּׂא מַשְׂאֹת מֵאֵת פָּנָיו אֲלֵהֶם
unto them before him from that helpings and he lifted

וַתֵּרֶב מַשְׂאַת בִּנְיָמִן
Benjamin helpings and it much

מִמַּשְׂאֹת כֻּלָּם חָמֵשׁ יָדוֹת וַיִּשְׁתּוּ וַיִּשְׁכְּרוּ עִמּוֹ:
with him and they merry and they drank handfuls five all them from helpings

34 And he took and sent messes unto them from before him: but Benjamin's mess was
five times so much as any of theirs. And they drank, and were merry with him.

CHAPTER 44

ספר בראשית פרק מד

וַיְצַו אֶת־אֲשֶׁר עַל־בֵּיתוֹ לֵאמֹר
to say his house – upon which – that and he commanded

מַלֵּא אֶת־אַמְתְּחֹת הָאֲנָשִׁים אֹכֶל כַּאֲשֶׁר יוּכְלוּן שְׂאֵת
carry they able when food the men sacks – that fill

וְשִׂים כֶּסֶף־אִישׁ בְּפִי אַמְתַּחְתּוֹ:
his sack in mouth man – money and put

1 And he commanded the steward of his house, saying, Fill the men's sacks with food, as much as they can carry, and put every man's money in his sack's mouth.

וְאֶת־גְּבִיעִי גְּבִיעַ הַכֶּסֶף

the silver   cup   and my cup – and that

תָּשִׂים בְּפִי אַמְתַּחַת הַקָּטֹן וְאֶת כֶּסֶף שִׁבְרוֹ

his corn   money   and that   the small   sack   in mouth   you put

וַיַּעַשׂ כִּדְבַר יוֹסֵף אֲשֶׁר דִּבֵּר:

spoke   which   Joseph   like spoke   and he did

2 And put my cup, the silver cup, in the sack's mouth of the youngest, and his corn money. And he did according to the word that Joseph had spoken.

הַבֹּקֶר אוֹר וְהָאֲנָשִׁים שֻׁלְּחוּ הֵמָּה וַחֲמֹרֵיהֶם:

and their asses   to them   he sent away   and the men   light   the morning

3 As soon as the morning was light, the men were sent away, they and their asses.

הֵם יָצְאוּ אֶת־הָעִיר לֹא הִרְחִיקוּ

it was far   not   the city – that   they went out   them

וְיוֹסֵף אָמַר לַאֲשֶׁר עַל־בֵּיתוֹ

his house – upon   to which   said   and Joseph

קוּם רְדֹף אַחֲרֵי הָאֲנָשִׁים וְהִשַּׂגְתָּם

and overtake   the men   after   pursue   rise

וְאָמַרְתָּ אֲלֵהֶם לָמָּה שִׁלַּמְתֶּם רָעָה תַּחַת טוֹבָה:

good   instead of   bad   you repay   why   unto them   and you say

4 And when they were gone out of the city, and not yet far off, Joseph said unto his steward, Up, follow after the men; and when thou dost overtake them, say unto them, Wherefore have ye rewarded evil for good?

הֲלוֹא זֶה אֲשֶׁר יִשְׁתֶּה אֲדֹנִי בּוֹ

in it   my master   he drinks   which   this   the not it

וְהוּא נַחֵשׁ יְנַחֵשׁ בּוֹ הֲרֵעֹתֶם אֲשֶׁר עֲשִׂיתֶם:

you did   which   the bad you   in it   he deceives   deceive   in it

5 Is not this it in which my lord drinketh, and whereby indeed he divineth? ye have done evil in so doing.

וַיַּשִּׂגֵם וַיְדַבֵּר אֲלֵהֶם אֶת־הַדְּבָרִים הָאֵלֶּה:

the these   the speaking – that   unto them   and he said   and he overtook

6 And he overtook them, and he spake unto them these same words.

וַיֹּאמְרוּ אֵלָיו לָמָּה יְדַבֵּר אֲדֹנִי כַּדְּבָרִים הָאֵלֶּה

the these   like speakings   my master   he speaks   why   unto him   and they said

חָלִילָה לַעֲבָדֶיךָ מֵעֲשׂוֹת כַּדָּבָר הַזֶּה:

the this   like matter   from doings   to your servants   God forbid

7 And they said unto him, Wherefore saith my lord these words? God forbid that thy servants should do according to this thing:

הֵן כֶּסֶף אֲשֶׁר מָצָאנוּ בְּפִי אַמְתְּחֹתֵינוּ

our sacks · in mouth · we found · which · money · thus

הֱשִׁיבֹנוּ אֵלֶיךָ מֵאֶרֶץ כְּנָעַן

Cannan · from land · unto you · the returned us

וְאֵיךְ נִגְנֹב מִבֵּית אֲדֹנֶיךָ כֶּסֶף אוֹ זָהָב:

gold · or · silver · your master · from house · we steal · and how

8 Behold, the money, which we found in our sacks' mouths, we brought again unto thee out of the land of Canaan: how then should we steal out of thy lord's house silver or gold?

אֲשֶׁר יִמָּצֵא אִתּוֹ מֵעֲבָדֶיךָ וָמֵת

and die · from your servants · with him · he finds · which

וְגַם־אֲנַחְנוּ נִהְיֶה לַאדֹנִי לַעֲבָדִים:

to servants · to master · we will be · we – and also

9 With whomsoever of thy servants it be found, both let him die, and we also will be my lord's bondmen.

וַיֹּאמֶר גַּם־עַתָּה כְדִבְרֵיכֶם

like you spoke · now – also · and he said

כֶּן־הוּא אֲשֶׁר יִמָּצֵא אִתּוֹ יִהְיֶה־לִּי עָבֶד

servant · to me – it be · with him · he finds · which · it – thus

וְאַתֶּם תִּהְיוּ נְקִיִּם:

blameless ones · you will be · and you all

10 And he said, Now also let it be according unto your words: he with whom it is found shall be my servant; and ye shall be blameless.

וַיְמַהֲרוּ וַיּוֹרִדוּ אִישׁ אֶת־אַמְתַּחְתּוֹ אָרְצָה

towards ground · his sack – that · man · and they descended · and they speedily

וַיִּפְתְּחוּ אִישׁ אַמְתַּחְתּוֹ:

his sack · man · and he opened

11 Then they speedily took down every man his sack to the ground, and opened every man his sack.

וַיְחַפֵּשׂ בַּגָּדוֹל הֵחֵל וּבַקָּטֹן כִּלָּה

finished · and in smallest · started · in biggest · and he searched

וַיִּמָּצֵא הַגָּבִיעַ בְּאַמְתַּחַת בִּנְיָמִן:

Benjamin · in sack · the cup · and he found

12 And he searched, and began at the eldest, and left at the youngest: and the cup was found in Benjamin's sack.

וַיִּקְרְעוּ שִׂמְלֹתָם
their dresses   and they tore

וַיַּעֲמֹס אִישׁ עַל־חֲמֹרוֹ וַיָּשֻׁבוּ הָעִירָה:
the towards city and they returned his ass – upon man and he laded

13 Then they rent their clothes, and laded every man his ass, and returned to the city.

[מפטיר]

וַיָּבֹא יְהוּדָה וְאֶחָיו בֵּיתָה יוֹסֵף
Joseph   home   and his brothers   Judah   and he came

וְהוּא עוֹדֶנּוּ שָׁם וַיִּפְּלוּ לְפָנָיו אָרְצָה:
towards ground before him and they fell him there still he and he

14 And Judah and his brethren came to Joseph's house; for he was yet there: and they fell before him on the ground.

וַיֹּאמֶר לָהֶם יוֹסֵף מָה־הַמַּעֲשֶׂה הַזֶּה אֲשֶׁר עֲשִׂיתֶם
you did   which   the this   the act – what   Joseph   to them   and he said

הֲלוֹא יְדַעְתֶּם כִּי־נַחֵשׁ יְנַחֵשׁ אִישׁ אֲשֶׁר כָּמֹנִי:
like me   which   man   he deceive   deceit – like   you know   the not

15 And Joseph said unto them, What deed is this that ye have done? wot ye not that such a man as I can certainly divine?

וַיֹּאמֶר יְהוּדָה
Judah   and he said

מַה־נֹּאמַר לַאדֹנִי מַה־נְּדַבֵּר וּמַה־נִּצְטַדָּק
we will justify – and what we speak – what to master we say – what

הָאֱלֹהִים מָצָא אֶת־עֲוֹן עֲבָדֶיךָ הִנֶּנּוּ עֲבָדִים לַאדֹנִי
to master serving ones here us your servants inequity – that found the Elohim

גַּם־אֲנַחְנוּ גַּם אֲשֶׁר־נִמְצָא הַגָּבִיעַ בְּיָדוֹ:
in his hand the cup we found – which also we – also

16 And Judah said, What shall we say unto my lord? what shall we speak? or how shall we clear ourselves? God hath found out the iniquity of thy servants: behold, we are my lord's servants, both we, and he also with whom the cup is found.

וַיֹּאמֶר חָלִילָה לִּי מֵעֲשׂוֹת זֹאת
this   from doing   to me   God forbid   and he said

הָאִישׁ אֲשֶׁר נִמְצָא הַגָּבִיעַ בְּיָדוֹ הוּא יִהְיֶה־לִּי עָבֶד
servant to me – will be he in his hand the cup found which the man

וְאַתֶּם עֲלוּ לְשָׁלוֹם אֶל־אֲבִיכֶם:
your father – unto to peace you go up and you

17 And he said, God forbid that I should do so: but the man in whose hand the cup is found, he shall be my servant; and as for you, get you up in peace unto your father.

ם ם ם

11 VAIGASH

CHAPTER 44 CONT

וַיִּגַּ֨שׁ אֵלָ֜יו יְהוּדָ֗ה
and he touched unto him Judah

וַיֹּאמֶר֮ בִּ֣י אֲדֹנִי֒ יְדַבֶּר־נָ֤א עַבְדְּךָ֙ דָבָ֜ר בְּאָזְנֵ֣י אֲדֹנִ֗י
and he said in me my master now – he speak your servant speak in my ear my master

וְאַל־יִ֥חַר אַפְּךָ֖ בְּעַבְדֶּ֑ךָ כִּ֥י כָמ֖וֹךָ כְּפַרְעֹֽה׃
anger – and don't your anger in your servant like like you like Pharaoh

18 Then Judah came near unto him, and said, Oh my lord, let thy servant, I pray thee, speak a word in my lord's ears, and let not thine anger burn against thy servant: for thou art even as Pharaoh.

אֲדֹנִ֣י שָׁאַ֔ל אֶת־עֲבָדָ֖יו לֵאמֹ֑ר
my master ask his servants – that to say

הֲיֵשׁ־לָכֶ֥ם אָ֖ב אוֹ־אָֽח׃
the there is to you father brother – or

19 My lord asked his servants, saying, Have ye a father, or a brother?

וַנֹּ֙אמֶר֙ אֶל־אֲדֹנִ֔י יֶשׁ־לָ֙נוּ֙ אָ֣ב זָקֵ֔ן
and we said my master – unto to us – there is father old

וְיֶ֥לֶד זְקֻנִ֖ים קָטָ֑ן וְאָחִ֣יו מֵ֔ת
and child old ones small and his brother dead

וַיִּוָּתֵ֨ר ה֤וּא לְבַדּוֹ֙ לְאִמּ֔וֹ וְאָבִ֖יו אֲהֵבֽוֹ׃
and he remainder he alone to his mother and his father his love

20 And we said unto my lord, We have a father, an old man, and a child of his old age, a little one; and his brother is dead, and he alone is left of his mother, and his father loveth him.

וַתֹּ֙אמֶר֙ אֶל־עֲבָדֶ֔יךָ הוֹרִדֻ֖הוּ אֵלָ֑י
and you said your servant – unto bring down him unto me

וְאָשִׂ֥ימָה עֵינִ֖י עָלָֽיו׃
and will I set my eye upon him

21 And thou saidst unto thy servants, Bring him down unto me, that I may set mine eyes upon him.

וַנֹּ֙אמֶר֙ אֶל־אֲדֹנִ֔י לֹא־יוּכַ֥ל הַנַּ֖עַר לַעֲזֹ֣ב אֶת־אָבִ֑יו
and we said my master – unto able – not the young boy to leave his father – that

וְעָזַב אֶת־אָבִיו וָמֵת׃
and die · his father – that · and leave

22 And we said unto my lord, The lad cannot leave his father: for if he should leave his father, his father would die.

וַתֹּאמֶר אֶל־עֲבָדֶיךָ
your servant – unto · and you said

אִם־לֹא יֵרֵד אֲחִיכֶם הַקָּטֹן אִתְּכֶם
with you · the small · your brother · he come down · not – with

לֹא תֹסִפוּן לִרְאוֹת פָּנָי׃
my face · to see · you again · not

23 And thou saidst unto thy servants, Except your youngest brother come down with you, ye shall see my face no more.

וַיְהִי כִּי עָלִינוּ אֶל־עַבְדְּךָ אָבִי
my father · your servant – unto · upon us · like · and it was

וַנַּגֶּד־לוֹ אֵת דִּבְרֵי אֲדֹנִי׃
my master · speakings · that · to him – and we told

24 And it came to pass when we came up unto thy servant my father, we told him the words of my lord.

וַיֹּאמֶר אָבִינוּ שֻׁבוּ שִׁבְרוּ־לָנוּ מְעַט־אֹכֶל׃
food – little · us – you buy · you return · our father · and he said

25 And our father said, Go again, and buy us a little food.

וַנֹּאמֶר לֹא נוּכַל לָרֶדֶת אִם־יֵשׁ אָחִינוּ הַקָּטֹן אִתָּנוּ
with us · the small · our brother · without – with · to go down · we can · not · and we said

וְיָרַדְנוּ כִּי־לֹא נוּכַל לִרְאוֹת פְּנֵי הָאִישׁ
the man · face · to see · we able · not - like · and we went down

וְאָחִינוּ הַקָּטֹן אֵינֶנּוּ אִתָּנוּ׃
with us · isn't · the small · and our brother

26 And we said, We cannot go down: if our youngest brother be with us, then will we go down: for we may not see the man's face, except our youngest brother be with us.

וַיֹּאמֶר עַבְדְּךָ אָבִי אֵלֵינוּ
unto us · father · your servant · and he said

אַתֶּם יְדַעְתֶּם כִּי שְׁנַיִם יָלְדָה־לִּי אִשְׁתִּי׃
my wife · to me – born · two · like · you know · you

27 And thy servant my father said unto us, Ye know that my wife bare me two sons:

וַיֵּצֵא הָאֶחָד מֵאִתִּי
from with me · the one · and he went out

וַיֹּ֕אמֶר אַ֛ךְ טָרֹ֥ף טֹרָ֖ף וְלֹ֥א רְאִיתִ֖יו עַד־הֵֽנָּה׃

here – till   his seeing   and not   torn   tear   surely   and said

28 And the one went out from me, and I said, Surely he is torn in pieces; and I saw him not since:

וּלְקַחְתֶּ֧ם גַּם־אֶת־זֶ֛ה מֵעִ֥ם פָּנַ֖י וְקָרָ֥הוּ אָס֑וֹן

mischief   and meet him   face   from with   this – that – also   and to take you

וְהֽוֹרַדְתֶּ֧ם אֶת־שֵׂיבָתִ֛י בְּרָעָ֖ה שְׁאֹֽלָה׃

towards grave   in evil   my gray hair – that   and you bring down

29 And if ye take this also from me, and mischief befall him, ye shall bring down my gray hairs with sorrow to the grave.

וְעַתָּ֗ה כְּבֹאִי֙ אֶל־עַבְדְּךָ֣ אָבִ֔י

my father   your servant – unto   like I come   and now

וְהַנַּ֖עַר אֵינֶ֣נּוּ אִתָּ֑נוּ

with us   is not   and the young man

וְנַפְשׁ֖וֹ קְשׁוּרָ֥ה בְנַפְשֽׁוֹ׃

in his soul   bound up   and his soul

30 Now therefore when I come to thy servant my father, and the lad be not with us; seeing that his life is bound up in the lad's life;

[שני]

וְהָיָ֗ה כִּרְאוֹת֛וֹ כִּי־אֵ֥ין הַנַּ֖עַר וָמֵ֑ת

and death   the boy   isn't – like   like his seeing   and it was

וְהוֹרִ֨ידוּ עֲבָדֶ֜יךָ אֶת־שֵׂיבַ֨ת עַבְדְּךָ֥ אָבִ֛ינוּ בְּיָג֖וֹן שְׁאֹֽלָה׃

towards grave   in affliction   our father   your servant   gray hair – that   your servant   and you bring down

31 It shall come to pass, when he seeth that the lad is not with us, that he will die: and thy servants shall bring down the gray hairs of thy servant our father with sorrow to the grave.

כִּ֤י עַבְדְּךָ֙ עָרַ֣ב אֶת־הַנַּ֔עַר מֵעִ֥ם אָבִ֖י לֵאמֹ֑ר

to say   my father   from with   the young man – that   surety   your servant   like

אִם־לֹ֤א אֲבִיאֶ֨נּוּ֙ אֵלֶ֔יךָ

unto you   I bring you   not – with

וְחָטָ֥אתִי לְאָבִ֖י כָּל־הַיָּמִֽים׃

the days – all   to my father   and my sin

32 For thy servant became surety for the lad unto my father, saying, If I bring him not unto thee, then I shall bear the blame to my father for ever.

וְעַתָּ֗ה יֵֽשֶׁב־נָ֤א עַבְדְּךָ֙ תַּ֣חַת הַנַּ֔עַר עֶ֖בֶד לַֽאדֹנִ֑י

to my master   serve   the boy   instead   your servant   please – he dwells   and now

וְהַנַּעַר יַעַל עִם־אֶחָיו:
his brothers – with he ascends and the boy

33 Now therefore, I pray thee, let thy servant abide instead of the lad a bondman to my lord; and let the lad go up with his brethren.

כִּי־אֵיךְ אֶעֱלֶה אֶל־אָבִי
my father – unto I go up how – like

וְהַנַּעַר אֵינֶנּוּ אִתִּי
with me isn't and the boy

פֶּן אֶרְאֶה בָרָע אֲשֶׁר יִמְצָא אֶת־אָבִי:
my father – that he finds which in bad I will see then

34 For how shall I go up to my father, and the lad be not with me? lest peradventure I see the evil that shall come on my father.

CHAPTER 45

ספר בראשית פרק מה
וְלֹא־יָכֹל יוֹסֵף לְהִתְאַפֵּק לְכֹל הַנִּצָּבִים עָלָיו
upon him the standing ones to all to refrain Joseph he able – and not

וַיִּקְרָא הוֹצִיאוּ כָל־אִישׁ מֵעָלָי
from upon me man – all go out you and he called

וְלֹא־עָמַד אִישׁ אִתּוֹ בְּהִתְוַדַּע יוֹסֵף אֶל־אֶחָיו:
his brothers – unto Joseph in make known with him man stood – and not

1 Then Joseph could not refrain himself before all them that stood by him; and he cried, Cause every man to go out from me. And there stood no man with him, while Joseph made himself known unto his brethren.

וַיִּתֵּן אֶת־קֹלוֹ בִּבְכִי
in crying his voice – that and he gave

וַיִּשְׁמְעוּ מִצְרַיִם וַיִּשְׁמַע בֵּית פַּרְעֹה:
Pharaoh house and he heard Egyptians and they heard

2 And he wept aloud: and the Egyptians and the house of Pharaoh heard.

וַיֹּאמֶר יוֹסֵף אֶל־אֶחָיו
his brothers – unto Joseph and he said

אֲנִי יוֹסֵף הַעוֹד אָבִי חָי
life my father the still Joseph I

וְלֹא־יָכְלוּ אֶחָיו לַעֲנוֹת אֹתוֹ כִּי נִבְהֲלוּ מִפָּנָיו:
from his presence they troubled like to him to answer his brothers they able – and not

3 And Joseph said unto his brethren, I am Joseph; doth my father yet live? And his brethren could not answer him; for they were troubled at his presence.

וַיֹּאמֶר יוֹסֵף אֶל־אֶחָיו גְּשׁוּ־נָא אֵלַי
<small>unto me　please – you touch　his brothers – unto　Joseph　and he said</small>

וַיִּגָּשׁוּ　וַיֹּאמֶר אֲנִי יוֹסֵף אֲחִיכֶם
<small>your brother　Joseph　I　and he said　and they touched</small>

אֲשֶׁר־מְכַרְתֶּם אֹתִי מִצְרָיְמָה:
<small>towards Egypt　to me　you sold – which</small>

4 And Joseph said unto his brethren, Come near to me, I pray you. And they came near. And he said, I am Joseph your brother, whom ye sold into Egypt.

וְעַתָּה אַל־תֵּעָצְבוּ וְאַל־יִחַר בְּעֵינֵיכֶם
<small>in your eyes　angry – and don't　you grieve – don't　and now</small>

כִּי־מְכַרְתֶּם אֹתִי הֵנָּה כִּי לְמִחְיָה שְׁלָחַנִי אֱלֹהִים לִפְנֵיכֶם:
<small>before you　Elohim　sent me　to preserve life　like　here　to me　you sold – like</small>

5 Now therefore be not grieved, nor angry with yourselves, that ye sold me hither: for God did send me before you to preserve life.

כִּי־זֶה שְׁנָתַיִם הָרָעָב בְּקֶרֶב הָאָרֶץ
<small>the land　in close　the famine　two years　this – like</small>

וְעוֹד חָמֵשׁ שָׁנִים אֲשֶׁר אֵין־חָרִישׁ וְקָצִיר:
<small>and harvest　plowing - isn't　which　years　five　and still</small>

6 For these two years hath the famine been in the land: and yet there are five years, in the which there shall neither be earing nor harvest.

וַיִּשְׁלָחֵנִי אֱלֹהִים לִפְנֵיכֶם לָשׂוּם לָכֶם שְׁאֵרִית בָּאָרֶץ
<small>in earth　remanet　to you　to preserve　before you　Elohim　and he sent me</small>

וּלְהַחֲיוֹת לָכֶם לִפְלֵיטָה גְדֹלָה:
<small>big　to deliver me　to you　and to the life</small>

7 And God sent me before you to preserve you a posterity in the earth, and to save your lives by a great deliverance.

[שלישי]

וְעַתָּה לֹא־אַתֶּם שְׁלַחְתֶּם אֹתִי הֵנָּה כִּי הָאֱלֹהִים
<small>the Elohim　like　here　to me　you sent　that you – not　and now</small>

וַיְשִׂימֵנִי לְאָב לְפַרְעֹה
<small>to Pharaoh　to father　and he placed me</small>

וּלְאָדוֹן לְכָל־בֵּיתוֹ וּמֹשֵׁל בְּכָל־אֶרֶץ מִצְרָיִם:
<small>Egyptian　land – in all　and ruler　his house – to all　and to master</small>

8 So now it was not you that sent me hither, but God: and he hath made me a father to Pharaoh, and lord of all his house, and a ruler throughout all the land of Egypt.

מַהֲרוּ וַעֲלוּ אֶל־אָבִי וַאֲמַרְתֶּם אֵלָיו
<small>unto him　and you tell　my father – unto　and you ascend　you haste</small>

כֹּה אָמַר בִּנְךָ יוֹסֵף שָׂמַנִי אֱלֹהִים לְאָדוֹן לְכָל־מִצְרָיִם
Egypt – to all   to master   Elohim   put me   Joseph   your son   say   thus

רְדָה אֵלַי אַל־תַּעֲמֹד:
you stand – don't   unto me   come down

9 Haste ye, and go up to my father, and say unto him, Thus saith thy son Joseph, God hath made me lord of all Egypt: come down unto me, tarry not:

וְיָשַׁבְתָּ בְאֶרֶץ־גֹּשֶׁן וְהָיִיתָ קָרוֹב אֵלַי
unto me   near   and it will be   Goshen – in land   and he will dwell

אַתָּה וּבָנֶיךָ וּבְנֵי בָנֶיךָ
your sons   and sons   and your sons   you

וְצֹאנְךָ וּבְקָרְךָ וְכָל־אֲשֶׁר־לָךְ:
to you – which – and all   and your herds   and your flocks

10 And thou shalt dwell in the land of Goshen, and thou shalt be near unto me, thou, and thy children, and thy children's children, and thy flocks, and thy herds, and all that thou hast:

וְכִלְכַּלְתִּי אֹתְךָ שָׁם
there   to you   and I will nourish

כִּי־עוֹד חָמֵשׁ שָׁנִים רָעָב פֶּן־תִּוָּרֵשׁ
you will be destitute – lest   famine   years   five   still – like

אַתָּה וּבֵיתְךָ וְכָל־אֲשֶׁר־לָךְ:
to you – which – and all   and your house   you

11 And there will I nourish thee; for yet there are five years of famine; lest thou, and thy household, and all that thou hast, come to poverty.

וְהִנֵּה עֵינֵיכֶם רֹאוֹת וְעֵינֵי אָחִי בִנְיָמִין
Benjamin   my brother   and my eyes   see   your eyes   and here

כִּי־פִי הַמְדַבֵּר אֲלֵיכֶם:
unto you   the speaks   my mouth – like

12 And, behold, your eyes see, and the eyes of my brother Benjamin, that it is my mouth that speaketh unto you.

וְהִגַּדְתֶּם לְאָבִי אֶת־כָּל־כְּבוֹדִי בְּמִצְרַיִם
in Egyptians   my honor – all – that   to my father   and you will tell

וְאֵת כָּל־אֲשֶׁר רְאִיתֶם
you seen   which – all   and that

וּמִהַרְתֶּם וְהוֹרַדְתֶּם אֶת־אָבִי הֵנָּה:
here   my father – that   and you will bring down   and you will haste

13 And ye shall tell my father of all my glory in Egypt, and of all that ye have seen; and ye shall haste and bring down my father hither.

וַיִּפֹּל עַל־צַוְּארֵי בִנְיָמִן־אָחִיו וַיֵּבְךְּ

and he wept   his brother - Benjamin   neck – upon   and he fell

וּבִנְיָמִן בָּכָה עַל־צַוָּארָיו:

his neck – upon   wept   and Benjamin

14 And he fell upon his brother Benjamin's neck, and wept; and Benjamin wept upon
his neck.

וַיְנַשֵּׁק לְכָל־אֶחָיו וַיֵּבְךְּ עֲלֵהֶם

upon them   and he wept   his brothers – to all   and he kissed

וְאַחֲרֵי כֵן דִּבְּרוּ אֶחָיו אִתּוֹ:

with him   his brothers   they spoke   thus   and after

15 Moreover he kissed all his brethren, and wept upon them: and after that his brethren
talked with him.

וְהַקֹּל נִשְׁמַע בֵּית פַּרְעֹה לֵאמֹר בָּאוּ אֲחֵי יוֹסֵף

Joseph   brothers   they came   to say   Pharaoh   house   heard   and the voice

וַיִּיטַב בְּעֵינֵי פַרְעֹה וּבְעֵינֵי עֲבָדָיו:

his servant   in eyes   Pharaoh   in eyes   and it pleased

16 And the fame thereof was heard in Pharaoh's house, saying, Joseph's brethren are
come: and it pleased Pharaoh well, and his servants.

וַיֹּאמֶר פַּרְעֹה אֶל־יוֹסֵף אֱמֹר אֶל־אַחֶיךָ זֹאת עֲשׂוּ

you do   this   your brothers – unto   say   Joseph – unto   Pharaoh   and he said

טַעֲנוּ אֶת־בְּעִירְכֶם

your brutes – that   you load up

וּלְכוּ־בֹאוּ אַרְצָה כְּנָעַן:

Canaan   land   you come – and you go

17 And Pharaoh said unto Joseph, Say unto thy brethren, This do ye; lade your beasts,
and go, get you unto the land of Canaan;

וּקְחוּ אֶת־אֲבִיכֶם וְאֶת־בָּתֵּיכֶם וּבֹאוּ אֵלָי

unto me   and you come   your house – and that   your father – that   and you take

וְאֶתְּנָה לָכֶם אֶת־טוּב אֶרֶץ מִצְרַיִם

Egypt   land   good – that   to you   and I give

וְאִכְלוּ אֶת־חֵלֶב הָאָרֶץ:

the land   fat – that   and will you eat

18 And take your father and your households, and come unto me: and I will give you
the good of the land of Egypt, and ye shall eat the fat of the land.

וְאַתָּה צֻוֵּיתָה זֹאת עֲשׂוּ

you do   this   are commanded   and you

קְחוּ־לָכֶם מֵאֶרֶץ מִצְרַיִם עֲגָלוֹת לְטַפְּכֶם

to your little ones   wagons   Egyptians   from land   to you – you take

וְלִנְשֵׁיכֶם וּנְשָׂאתֶם אֶת־אֲבִיכֶם וּבָאתֶם׃

and you come   your father – that   and you carry   and to your women

19 Now thou art commanded, this do ye; take you wagons out of the land of Egypt for your little ones, and for your wives, and bring your father, and come.

וְעֵינְכֶם אַל־תָּחֹס עַל־כְּלֵיכֶם

your stuff – upon   regard - don't   and your eyes

כִּי־טוּב כָּל־אֶרֶץ מִצְרַיִם לָכֶם הוּא׃

it   to you   Egypt   land – all   good – like

20 Also regard not your stuff; for the good of all the land of Egypt is yours.

וַיַּעֲשׂוּ־כֵן בְּנֵי יִשְׂרָאֵל

Israel   sons   thus – and they did

וַיִּתֵּן לָהֶם יוֹסֵף עֲגָלוֹת עַל־פִּי פַרְעֹה

Pharaoh   mouth – upon   wagons   Joseph   to them   and he gave

וַיִּתֵּן לָהֶם צֵדָה לַדָּרֶךְ׃

to way   provisions   to them   and he gave

21 And the children of Israel did so: and Joseph gave them wagons, according to the commandment of Pharaoh, and gave them provision for the way.

לְכֻלָּם נָתַן לָאִישׁ חֲלִפוֹת שְׂמָלֹת

dresses   changes of   to man   gave   to all them

וּלְבִנְיָמִן נָתַן שְׁלֹשׁ מֵאוֹת כֶּסֶף

silver   hundred   three   gave   and to Benjamin

וְחָמֵשׁ חֲלִפֹת שְׂמָלֹת׃

dresses   changes   and five

22 To all of them he gave each man changes of raiment; but to Benjamin he gave three hundred pieces of silver, and five changes of raiment.

וּלְאָבִיו שָׁלַח כְּזֹאת עֲשָׂרָה חֲמֹרִים נֹשְׂאִים מִטּוּב מִצְרָיִם

Egypt   from good   carrying   asses   ten   like this   sent   and to his father

וְעֶשֶׂר אֲתֹנֹת נֹשְׂאֹת בָּר וָלֶחֶם וּמָזוֹן לְאָבִיו לַדָּרֶךְ׃

to way   to his father   and sustenance   and bread   corn   carrying   she asses   and ten

23 And to his father he sent after this manner; ten asses laden with the good things of Egypt, and ten she asses laden with corn and bread and meat for his father by the way.

וַיְשַׁלַּח אֶת־אֶחָיו וַיֵּלֵכוּ

and they went   his brother – that   and he sent

וַיֹּאמֶר אֲלֵהֶם אַל־תִּרְגְּזוּ בַּדָּרֶךְ׃

in the way   you off course - don't   unto them   and he said

24 So he sent his brethren away, and they departed: and he said unto them, See that ye fall not out by the way.

וַיַּעֲלוּ   מִמִּצְרָיִם
from Egypt   and they went up

וַיָּבֹאוּ   אֶרֶץ   כְּנַעַן   אֶל־יַעֲקֹב   אֲבִיהֶם׃
their father   Jacob - unto   Canaan   land   and they came

25 And they went up out of Egypt, and came into the land of Canaan unto Jacob their father,

וַיַּגִּדוּ   לוֹ   לֵאמֹר   עוֹד   יוֹסֵף   חַי
life   Joseph   still   to say   to him   and he told

וְכִי־הוּא   מֹשֵׁל   בְּכָל־אֶרֶץ   מִצְרָיִם
Egypt   land – in all   ruler   he – and like

וַיָּפָג   לִבּוֹ   כִּי   לֹא־הֶאֱמִין   לָהֶם׃
to them   the believe - not   like   his heart   and fainted

26 And told him, saying, Joseph is yet alive, and he is governor over all the land of Egypt. And Jacob's heart fainted, for he believed them not.

וַיְדַבְּרוּ   אֵלָיו   אֵת   כָּל־דִּבְרֵי   יוֹסֵף   אֲשֶׁר   דִּבֶּר   אֲלֵהֶם
unto them   spoke   which   Joseph   speaking – all   that   unto him   and they spoke

וַיַּרְא   אֶת־הָעֲגָלוֹת   אֲשֶׁר־שָׁלַח   יוֹסֵף   לָשֵׂאת   אֹתוֹ
to him   to carry   Joseph   sent – which   the wagons – that   and he saw

וַתְּחִי   רוּחַ   יַעֲקֹב   אֲבִיהֶם׃
their father   Jacob   spirit   and it life

27 And they told him all the words of Joseph, which he had said unto them: and when he saw the wagons which Joseph had sent to carry him, the spirit of Jacob their father revived:

[רביעי]

וַיֹּאמֶר   יִשְׂרָאֵל   רַב
much   Israel   and he said

עוֹד־יוֹסֵף   בְּנִי   חָי
life   my son   Joseph – still

אֵלְכָה   וְאֶרְאֶנּוּ   בְּטֶרֶם   אָמוּת׃
I die   in before   and I will see him   I will go

28 And Israel said, It is enough; Joseph my son is yet alive: I will go and see him before I die.

CHAPTER 46

ספר בראשית פרק מו

וַיִּסַּע יִשְׂרָאֵל וְכָל־אֲשֶׁר־לוֹ וַיָּבֹא בְּאֵרָה שָּׁבַע

Sheba   Beer   and he came   to him – which – and all   Israel   and he traveled

וַיִּזְבַּח זְבָחִים לֵאלֹהֵי אָבִיו יִצְחָק:

Isaac   his father   to Elohim   offerings   and he offered

1 And Israel took his journey with all that he had, and came to Beer-sheba, and offered sacrifices unto the God of his father Isaac.

וַיֹּאמֶר אֱלֹהִים לְיִשְׂרָאֵל בְּמַרְאֹת הַלַּיְלָה

the night   in visions   to Israel   Elohim   and he said

וַיֹּאמֶר יַעֲקֹב יַעֲקֹב וַיֹּאמֶר הִנֵּנִי:

here am I   and he said   Jacob   Jacob   and he said

2 And God spake unto Israel in the visions of the night, and said, Jacob, Jacob. And he said, Here am I.

וַיֹּאמֶר אָנֹכִי הָאֵל אֱלֹהֵי אָבִיךָ

your father   Elohim   the El   I am   and he said

אַל־תִּירָא מֵרְדָה מִצְרַיְמָה

towards Egypt   from going down   you fear – don't

כִּי־לְגוֹי גָּדוֹל אֲשִׂימְךָ שָׁם:

there   I make you   great   to nations – like

3 And he said, I am God, the God of thy father: fear not to go down into Egypt; for I will there make of thee a great nation:

אָנֹכִי אֵרֵד עִמְּךָ מִצְרַיְמָה

towards Egypt   with you   will go down   I am

וְאָנֹכִי אַעַלְךָ גַם־עָלֹה

go up – also   I will bring up you   and I am

וְיוֹסֵף יָשִׁית יָדוֹ עַל־עֵינֶיךָ:

your eyes – upon   his hand   he will put   and Joseph

4 I will go down with thee into Egypt; and I will also surely bring thee up again: and Joseph shall put his hand upon thine eyes.

וַיָּקָם יַעֲקֹב מִבְּאֵר שָׁבַע

Sheba   from Beer   Jacob   and he rose up

וַיִּשְׂאוּ בְנֵי־יִשְׂרָאֵל אֶת־יַעֲקֹב אֲבִיהֶם

their father   Jacob – that   Israel – sons   and they carried

וְאֶת־טַפָּם וְאֶת־נְשֵׁיהֶם בָּעֲגָלוֹת

in wagons   their women – and that   little ones – and that

אֲשֶׁר־שָׁלַח פַּרְעֹה לָשֵׂאת אֹתֽוֹ׃

to him   to carry   Pharaoh   sent – which

5 And Jacob rose up from Beer-sheba: and the sons of Israel carried Jacob their father, and their little ones, and their wives, in the wagons which Pharaoh had sent to carry him.

וַיִּקְחוּ אֶת־מִקְנֵיהֶם

their cattle – that   and they took

וְאֶת־רְכוּשָׁם אֲשֶׁר רָכְשׁוּ בְּאֶרֶץ כְּנַעַן

Canaan   in land   they possessed   which   their possessions – and that

וַיָּבֹאוּ מִצְרַיְמָה יַעֲקֹב וְכָל־זַרְעוֹ אִתּֽוֹ׃

with him   his seed – and all   Jacob   towards Egypt   and they came

6 And they took their cattle, and their goods, which they had gotten in the land of Canaan, and came into Egypt, Jacob, and all his seed with him:

בָּנָיו וּבְנֵי בָנָיו אִתּוֹ

with him   his sons   and sons   his son

בְּנֹתָיו וּבְנוֹת בָּנָיו

his sons   and daughters   his daughter

וְכָל־זַרְעוֹ הֵבִיא אִתּוֹ מִצְרָיְמָה׃

towards Egypt   with him   the bring   his seed – and all

7 His sons, and his sons' sons with him, his daughters, and his sons' daughters, and all his seed brought he with him into Egypt.

ס

[חמישי]

וְאֵלֶּה שְׁמוֹת בְּנֵי־יִשְׂרָאֵל הַבָּאִים מִצְרַיְמָה

towards Egypt   the coming ones   Israel – your sons   names   and these

יַעֲקֹב וּבָנָיו בְּכֹר יַעֲקֹב רְאוּבֵן׃

Rueben   Jacob   first born   and his son   Jacob

8 And these are the names of the children of Israel, which came into Egypt, Jacob and his sons: Reuben, Jacob's firstborn.

וּבְנֵי רְאוּבֵן חֲנוֹךְ וּפַלּוּא וְחֶצְרֹן וְכַרְמִי׃

and Carmi   and Hezron   and Phallu   Hanoch   Reuben   and sons

9 And the sons of Reuben; Hanoch, and Phallu, and Hezron, and Carmi.

וּבְנֵי שִׁמְעוֹן יְמוּאֵל וְיָמִין וְאֹהַד וְיָכִין

and Jachin   and Ohad   and Jamin   Jemuel   Simeon   and sons

וְצֹחַר וְשָׁאוּל בֶּן־הַכְּנַעֲנִית׃

Canaanitish woman – son   and Shaul   and Zohar

10 And the sons of Simeon; Jemuel, and Jamin, and Ohad, and Jachin, and Zohar, and
Shaul the son of a Canaanitish woman.

וּבְנֵי לֵוִי גֵּרְשׁוֹן קְהָת וּמְרָרִי:

and Merari   Kohath   Gershon   Levi   and sons

11 And the sons of Levi; Gershon, Kohath, and Merari.

וּבְנֵי יְהוּדָה עֵר וְאוֹנָן וְשֵׁלָה וָפֶרֶץ וָזָרַח

and Zarah   and Pharez   and Shelah   and Onan   Er   Judah   and sons

וַיָּמָת עֵר וְאוֹנָן בְּאֶרֶץ כְּנַעַן

Canaan   in land   and Onan   Er   and he died

וַיִּהְיוּ בְנֵי־פֶרֶץ חֶצְרוֹן וְחָמוּל:

and Hamul   Hezron   Pharez – sons   and they were

12 And the sons of Judah; Er, and Onan, and Shelah, and Pharez, and Zarah: but
Er and Onan died in the land of Canaan. And the sons of Pharez were Hezron and
Hamul.

וּבְנֵי יִשָּׂשכָר תּוֹלָע וּפֻוָּה וְיוֹב וְשִׁמְרֹן:

and Shimron   and Job   and Phuvah   Tola   Issachar   and sons

13 And the sons of Issachar; Tola, and Phuvah, and Job, and Shimron.

וּבְנֵי זְבוּלֻן סֶרֶד וְאֵלוֹן וְיַחְלְאֵל:

and Jahleel   and Elon   Sered   Zebulun   and sons

14 And the sons of Zebulun; Sered, and Elon, and Jahleel.

אֵלֶּה בְּנֵי לֵאָה אֲשֶׁר יָלְדָה לְיַעֲקֹב בְּפַדַּן אֲרָם

aram   in Padan   to Jacob   she bore   which   Lea   sons   these

וְאֵת דִּינָה בִתּוֹ

his daughter   Dinah   and that

כָּל־נֶפֶשׁ בָּנָיו וּבְנוֹתָיו שְׁלֹשִׁים וְשָׁלֹשׁ:

and three   thirty   his daughters   and his sons   soul - all

15 These be the sons of Leah, which she bare unto Jacob in Padan-aram, with his
daughter Dinah: all the souls of his sons and his daughters were thirty and three.

וּבְנֵי גָד צִפְיוֹן וְחַגִּי שׁוּנִי וְאֶצְבֹּן

and Ezbon   Shuni   and Haggi   Ziphion   Gad   sons and

עֵרִי וַאֲרוֹדִי וְאַרְאֵלִי:

and Areli   and Arodi   Eri

16 And the sons of Gad; Ziphion, and Haggi, Shuni, and Ezbon, Eri, and Arodi, and
Areli.

וּבְנֵי אָשֵׁר יִמְנָה וְיִשְׁוָה וְיִשְׁוִי וּבְרִיעָה וְשֶׂרַח אֲחֹתָם

their sister   and Serah   and Beriah   and Isui   and Ishuah   Jimnah   Asher   and sons

וּבְנֵי בְרִיעָה חֶבֶר וּמַלְכִּיאֵל:
and Malchiel   Heber   Beriah   and sons

17 And the sons of Asher; Jimnah, and Ishuah, and Isui, and Beriah, and Serah their sister: and the sons of Beriah; Heber, and Malchiel.

אֵלֶּה בְּנֵי זִלְפָּה אֲשֶׁר־נָתַן לָבָן לְלֵאָה בִתּוֹ
his daughter   to Leah   Laban   gave – which   Zipah   sons   these

וַתֵּלֶד אֶת־אֵלֶּה לְיַעֲקֹב שֵׁשׁ עֶשְׂרֵה נָפֶשׁ:
soul   -- six teen --   to Jacob   these - that   and she bare

18 These are the sons of Zilpah, whom Laban gave to Leah his daughter, and these she bare unto Jacob, even sixteen souls.

בְּנֵי רָחֵל אֵשֶׁת יַעֲקֹב יוֹסֵף וּבִנְיָמִן:
and Benjamin   Joseph   Jacob   wife   Rachel   sons

19 The sons of Rachel Jacob's wife; Joseph, and Benjamin.

וַיִּוָּלֵד לְיוֹסֵף בְּאֶרֶץ מִצְרַיִם
Egypt   in land   to Joseph   and he born

אֲשֶׁר יָלְדָה־לּוֹ אָסְנַת בַּת־פּוֹטִי פֶרַע כֹּהֵן אֹן
On   priest   pherah   Poti - daughter   Asenath   to him - he born   which

אֶת־מְנַשֶּׁה וְאֶת־אֶפְרָיִם:
Ephraim - and that   Manasseh - that

20 And unto Joseph in the land of Egypt were born Manasseh and Ephraim, which Asenath the daughter of Poti-pherah priest of On bare unto him.

וּבְנֵי בִנְיָמִן בֶּלַע וָבֶכֶר וְאַשְׁבֵּל
and Ashbel   and Becher   Belah   Benjamin   and sons

גֵּרָא וְנַעֲמָן אֵחִי וָרֹאשׁ
and Rosh   Ehi   and Naaman   Gera

מֻפִּים וְחֻפִּים וָאָרְדְּ:
and Ard   and Huppim   Muppim

21 And the sons of Benjamin were Belah, and Becher, and Ashbel, Gera, and Naaman, Ehi, and Rosh, Muppim, and Huppim, and Ard.

אֵלֶּה בְּנֵי רָחֵל אֲשֶׁר יֻלַּד לְיַעֲקֹב
to Jacob   born   which   Rachel   sons   these

כָּל־נֶפֶשׁ אַרְבָּעָה עָשָׂר:
-- fourteen --   soul - all

22 These are the sons of Rachel, which were born to Jacob: all the souls were fourteen.

וּבְנֵי־דָן חֻשִׁים:
Hushim   Dan - and sons

23 And the sons of Dan; Hushim.

וּבְנֵי נַפְתָּלִי יַחְצְאֵל וְגוּנִי וְיֵצֶר וְשִׁלֵּם:

and Shillem   and Jezer   and Guni   Jahzeel   Naphtali   and sons

24 And the sons of Naphtali; Jahzeel, and Guni, and Jezer, and Shillem.

אֵלֶּה בְּנֵי בִלְהָה אֲשֶׁר־נָתַן לָבָן לְרָחֵל בִּתּוֹ

his daughter   to Rachel   Laban   gave - which   Bilhah   sons   these

וַתֵּלֶד אֶת־אֵלֶּה לְיַעֲקֹב כָּל־נֶפֶשׁ שִׁבְעָה:

seven   soul - all   to Jacob   these - that   and she bare

25 These are the sons of Bilhah, which Laban gave unto Rachel his daughter, and she bare these unto Jacob: all the souls were seven.

כָּל־הַנֶּפֶשׁ הַבָּאָה לְיַעֲקֹב מִצְרַיְמָה יֹצְאֵי יְרֵכוֹ

his loins   came out   towards Egypt   to Jacob   the came   the soul - all

מִלְּבַד נְשֵׁי בְנֵי־יַעֲקֹב כָּל־נֶפֶשׁ שִׁשִּׁים וָשֵׁשׁ:

and three   thirty   soul - all   Jacob - sons   wives   besides

26 All the souls that came with Jacob into Egypt, which came out of his loins, besides Jacob's sons' wives, all the souls were threescore and six;

וּבְנֵי יוֹסֵף אֲשֶׁר־יֻלַּד־לוֹ בְמִצְרַיִם נֶפֶשׁ שְׁנָיִם

two   soul   in Egypt   to him – bore - which   Joseph   and sons

כָּל־הַנֶּפֶשׁ לְבֵית־יַעֲקֹב הַבָּאָה מִצְרַיְמָה שִׁבְעִים:

seventy   towards Egypt   the came   Jacob - to house   the soul - all

27 And the sons of Joseph, which were born him in Egypt, were two souls: all the souls of the house of Jacob, which came into Egypt, were threescore and ten.

ס

[שׁשׁי]

וְאֶת־יְהוּדָה שָׁלַח לְפָנָיו אֶל־יוֹסֵף

Joseph - unto   before him   sent   Judah - and that

לְהוֹרֹת לְפָנָיו גֹּשְׁנָה וַיָּבֹאוּ אַרְצָה גֹּשֶׁן:

Goshen   land   and they came   towards Goshen   before him   to direct

28 And he sent Judah before him unto Joseph, to direct his face unto Goshen; and they came into the land of Goshen.

וַיֶּאְסֹר יוֹסֵף מֶרְכַּבְתּוֹ

his chariot   Joseph   and he made ready

וַיַּעַל לִקְרַאת־יִשְׂרָאֵל אָבִיו גֹּשְׁנָה וַיֵּרָא אֵלָיו

unto him   and he saw   towards Goshen   his father   Israel - to meet   and he went up

וַיִּפֹּל עַל־צַוָּארָיו וַיֵּבְךְּ עַל־צַוָּארָיו עוֹד:

still   his neck - upon   and he wept   his neck - upon   and he fell

29 And Joseph made ready his chariot, and went up to meet Israel his father, to Goshen, and presented himself unto him; and he fell on his neck, and wept on his neck a good

while.

וַיֹּאמֶר יִשְׂרָאֵל אֶל־יוֹסֵף אָמוּתָה הַפָּעַם
the once | I will die | Joseph - unto | Israel | and he said

אַחֲרֵי רְאוֹתִי אֶת־פָּנֶיךָ כִּי עוֹדְךָ חָי:
live | still you | like | your face – that | I have seen | after

30 And Israel said unto Joseph, Now let me die, since I have seen thy face, because thou art yet alive.

וַיֹּאמֶר יוֹסֵף אֶל־אֶחָיו וְאֶל־בֵּית אָבִיו אֶעֱלֶה
I will ascend | his father | house - and unto | his brothers – unto | Joseph | and he said

וְאַגִּידָה לְפַרְעֹה וְאֹמְרָה אֵלָיו
unto him | and I say | to Pharaoh | and I will tell

אַחַי וּבֵית־אָבִי אֲשֶׁר בְּאֶרֶץ־כְּנַעַן בָּאוּ אֵלָי:
unto me | they came | Canaan - in land | which | my father - and house | my brothers

31 And Joseph said unto his brethren, and unto his father's house, I will go up, and shew Pharaoh, and say unto him, My brethren, and my father's house, which were in the land of Canaan, are come unto me;

וְהָאֲנָשִׁים רֹעֵי צֹאן כִּי־אַנְשֵׁי מִקְנֶה הָיוּ
they were | cattle | men - like | sheep | shepherds | and the men

וְצֹאנָם וּבְקָרָם וְכָל־אֲשֶׁר לָהֶם הֵבִיאוּ:
they brought | to them | which - and all | and their herds | and their flocks

32 And the men are shepherds, for their trade hath been to feed cattle; and they have brought their flocks, and their herds, and all that they have.

וְהָיָה כִּי־יִקְרָא לָכֶם פַּרְעֹה וְאָמַר מַה־מַּעֲשֵׂיכֶם:
your occupation - what | and say | Pharaoh | to you | he will call - like | and it was

33 And it shall come to pass, when Pharaoh shall call you, and shall say, What is your occupation?

וַאֲמַרְתֶּם אַנְשֵׁי מִקְנֶה הָיוּ עֲבָדֶיךָ מִנְּעוּרֵינוּ
from our youth | your servants | they were | cattle | men | and you will say

וְעַד־עַתָּה גַּם־אֲנַחְנוּ גַּם־אֲבֹתֵינוּ בַּעֲבוּר
in past | our fathers - also | we - also | now - and till

תֵּשְׁבוּ בְּאֶרֶץ גֹּשֶׁן כִּי־תוֹעֲבַת מִצְרַיִם כָּל־רֹעֵה צֹאן:
sheep | shepherd - all | Egyptians | abomination - like | Goshen | in land | you dwell

34 That ye shall say, Thy servants' trade hath been about cattle from our youth even until now, both we, and also our fathers: that ye may dwell in the land of Goshen; for every shepherd is an abomination unto the Egyptians.

CHAPTER 47

ספר בראשית פרק מז

וַיָּבֹא יוֹסֵף וַיַּגֵּד לְפַרְעֹה וַיֹּאמֶר
and he said   to Pharaoh   and he told   Joseph   and he came

אָבִי וְאַחַי וְצֹאנָם וּבְקָרָם
and their cattle   and their sheep   and my brothers   my father

וְכָל־אֲשֶׁר לָהֶם בָּאוּ מֵאֶרֶץ כְּנָעַן
Canaan   from land   they came   to them   which - and all

וְהִנָּם בְּאֶרֶץ גֹּשֶׁן:
Goshen   in land   and here them

1 Then Joseph came and told Pharaoh, and said, My father and my brethren, and their flocks, and their herds, and all that they have, are come out of the land of Canaan; and, behold, they are in the land of Goshen.

וּמִקְצֵה אֶחָיו לָקַח חֲמִשָּׁה אֲנָשִׁים
men   five   to take   his brothers   and from half

וַיַּצִּגֵם לִפְנֵי פַרְעֹה:
Pharaoh   before   and he presented

2 And he took some of his brethren, even five men, and presented them unto Pharaoh.

וַיֹּאמֶר פַּרְעֹה אֶל־אֶחָיו מַה־מַּעֲשֵׂיכֶם
your occupations – what   his brothers - unto   Pharaoh   and he said

וַיֹּאמְרוּ אֶל־פַּרְעֹה רֹעֵה צֹאן עֲבָדֶיךָ
your servants   sheep   shepherd   Pharaoh - unto   and they said

גַּם־אֲנַחְנוּ גַּם־אֲבוֹתֵינוּ:
our fathers - also   we - also

3 And Pharaoh said unto his brethren, What is your occupation? And they said unto Pharaoh, Thy servants are shepherds, both we, and also our fathers.

וַיֹּאמְרוּ אֶל־פַּרְעֹה לָגוּר בָּאָרֶץ בָּאנוּ
we came   in land   to sojourn   Pharaoh – unto   and he said

כִּי־אֵין מִרְעֶה לַצֹּאן אֲשֶׁר לַעֲבָדֶיךָ
to your servants   which   to sheep   pasture   isn't - like

כִּי־כָבֵד הָרָעָב בְּאֶרֶץ כְּנָעַן
Canaan   in land   the famine   hard - like

וְעַתָּה יֵשְׁבוּ־נָא עֲבָדֶיךָ בְּאֶרֶץ גֹּשֶׁן:
Goshen   in land   your servants   please - they dwell   and now

4 They said moreover unto Pharaoh, For to sojourn in the land are we come; for thy servants have no pasture for their flocks; for the famine is sore in the land of Canaan: now therefore, we pray thee, let thy servants dwell in the land of Goshen.

וַיֹּאמֶר פַּרְעֹה אֶל־יוֹסֵף לֵאמֹר
to say   Joseph - unto   Pharaoh   and he said

אָבִיךָ וְאַחֶיךָ בָּאוּ אֵלֶיךָ:
unto you   they came   and your brothers   your father

5 And Pharaoh spake unto Joseph, saying, Thy father and thy brethren are come unto thee:

אֶרֶץ מִצְרַיִם לְפָנֶיךָ הִוא בְּמֵיטַב הָאָרֶץ הוֹשֵׁב אֶת־אָבִיךָ
your father - that   dweller   the land   in best   it   before you   Egypt   land

וְאֶת־אַחֶיךָ יֵשְׁבוּ בְּאֶרֶץ גֹּשֶׁן
Goshen   in land   they dwell   your brothers - and that

וְאִם־יָדַעְתָּ וְיֶשׁ־בָּם אַנְשֵׁי־חַיִל
ability - men   in them - and there is   you know - and if

וְשַׂמְתָּם שָׂרֵי מִקְנֶה עַל־אֲשֶׁר־לִי:
to me - which - upon   cattle   rulers   and put them

6 The land of Egypt is before thee; in the best of the land make thy father and brethren to dwell; in the land of Goshen let them dwell: and if thou knowest any men of activity among them, then make them rulers over my cattle.

וַיָּבֵא יוֹסֵף אֶת־יַעֲקֹב אָבִיו וַיַּעֲמִדֵהוּ לִפְנֵי פַרְעֹה
Pharaoh   before   and he stood him   his father   Jacob – that   Joseph   and he brought

וַיְבָרֶךְ יַעֲקֹב אֶת־פַּרְעֹה:
Pharaoh - that   Jacob   and he blessed

7 And Joseph brought in Jacob his father, and set him before Pharaoh: and Jacob blessed Pharaoh.

וַיֹּאמֶר פַּרְעֹה אֶל־יַעֲקֹב כַּמָּה יְמֵי שְׁנֵי חַיֶּיךָ:
your life   years   days   how much   Jacob - unto   Pharaoh   and he said

8 And Pharaoh said unto Jacob, How old art thou?

וַיֹּאמֶר יַעֲקֹב אֶל־פַּרְעֹה יְמֵי שְׁנֵי מְגוּרַי
my pilgrimage   years   days   Pharaoh - unto   Jacob   and he said

שְׁלֹשִׁים וּמְאַת שָׁנָה
year   and hundred   thirty

מְעַט וְרָעִים הָיוּ יְמֵי שְׁנֵי חַיַּי
my life   years   days   they were   and bad ones   few

וְלֹא הִשִּׂיגוּ אֶת־יְמֵי שְׁנֵי חַיֵּי אֲבֹתַי בִּימֵי מְגוּרֵיהֶם:
their pilgrimage   in days   my fathers   life   years   days – that   it attained   and not

9 And Jacob said unto Pharaoh, The days of the years of my pilgrimage are an hundred and thirty years: few and evil have the days of the years of my life been, and have

not attained unto the days of the years of the life of my fathers in the days of their
pilgrimage.

וַיְבָרֶךְ יַעֲקֹב אֶת־פַּרְעֹה וַיֵּצֵא מִלִּפְנֵי פַרְעֹה:

Pharaoh   from before   and he went out   Pharaoh – that   Jacob   and he blessed

10 And Jacob blessed Pharaoh, and went out from before Pharaoh.

[שביעי]

וַיּוֹשֵׁב יוֹסֵף אֶת־אָבִיו וְאֶת־אֶחָיו

brothers – and that   his father – that   Joseph   and he settled

וַיִּתֵּן לָהֶם אֲחֻזָּה בְּאֶרֶץ מִצְרַיִם

Egypt   in land   possession   to them   and he gave

בְּמֵיטַב הָאָרֶץ בְּאֶרֶץ רַעְמְסֵס כַּאֲשֶׁר צִוָּה פַרְעֹה:

Pharaoh   commanded   when   Rameses   in land   the land   in best

11 And Joseph placed his father and his brethren, and gave them a possession in
the land of Egypt, in the best of the land, in the land of Rameses, as Pharaoh had
commanded.

וַיְכַלְכֵּל יוֹסֵף אֶת־אָבִיו

his father – that   Joseph   and he nourished

וְאֶת־אֶחָיו וְאֵת כָּל־בֵּית אָבִיו לֶחֶם לְפִי הַטָּף:

allotted   to mouth   bread   his father   house – all   and that   and his brothers – and that

12 And Joseph nourished his father, and his brethren, and all his father's household,
with bread, according to their families.

וְלֶחֶם אֵין בְּכָל־הָאָרֶץ כִּי־כָבֵד הָרָעָב מְאֹד

very   the famine   heavy – like   the land – in all   isn't   and bread

וַתֵּלַהּ אֶרֶץ מִצְרַיִם וְאֶרֶץ כְּנַעַן מִפְּנֵי הָרָעָב:

the famine   from face   Canaan   and land   Egypt   land   and it frantic

13 And there was no bread in all the land; for the famine was very sore, so that the land
of Egypt and all the land of Canaan fainted by reason of the famine.

וַיְלַקֵּט יוֹסֵף אֶת־כָּל־הַכֶּסֶף הַנִּמְצָא בְּאֶרֶץ־מִצְרַיִם

Egypt – in land   the found   the silver – all – that   Joseph   and he gathered

וּבְאֶרֶץ כְּנַעַן בַּשֶּׁבֶר אֲשֶׁר־הֵם שֹׁבְרִים

purchasing ones   them – which   in food provisions   Canaan   and in land

וַיָּבֵא יוֹסֵף אֶת־הַכֶּסֶף בֵּיתָה פַרְעֹה:

Pharaoh   house   the sliver – that   Joseph   and he brought

14 And Joseph gathered up all the money that was found in the land of Egypt, and in
the land of Canaan, for the corn which they bought: and Joseph brought the money
into Pharaoh's house.

וַיִּתֹּם הַכֶּסֶף מֵאֶרֶץ מִצְרַיִם וּמֵאֶרֶץ כְּנַעַן
Canaan   and from land   Egypt   from land   the silver   and he spent

וַיָּבֹאוּ כָל־מִצְרַיִם אֶל־יוֹסֵף לֵאמֹר הָבָה־לָּנוּ לֶחֶם
bread   to us – the it   to say   Joseph – unto   Egyptians – all   and they came

וְלָמָּה נָמוּת נֶגְדֶּךָ כִּי אָפֵס כָּסֶף:
silver   fails   like   in your presence   we die   and why

15 And when money failed in the land of Egypt, and in the land of Canaan, all the
Egyptians came unto Joseph, and said, Give us bread: for why should we die in thy
presence? for the money faileth.

וַיֹּאמֶר יוֹסֵף הָבוּ מִקְנֵיכֶם
your cattle   grant   Joseph   and he said

וְאֶתְּנָה לָכֶם בְּמִקְנֵיכֶם אִם־אָפֵס כָּסֶף:
silver   fail - if   in your cattle   to you   and I give

16 And Joseph said, Give your cattle; and I will give you for your cattle, if money fail.

וַיָּבִיאוּ אֶת־מִקְנֵיהֶם אֶל־יוֹסֵף
Joseph – unto   their cattle – that   and they brought

וַיִּתֵּן לָהֶם יוֹסֵף לֶחֶם בַּסּוּסִים
in horses   bread   Joseph   to them   and he gave

וּבְמִקְנֵה הַצֹּאן וּבְמִקְנֵה הַבָּקָר וּבַחֲמֹרִים
and in asses   the herds   and in cattle   the sheep   and in cattle

וַיְנַהֲלֵם בַּלֶּחֶם בְּכָל־מִקְנֵהֶם בַּשָּׁנָה הַהִוא:
the it   in year   their cattle – in all   in bread   and he managing them

17 And they brought their cattle unto Joseph: and Joseph gave them bread in exchange
for horses, and for the flocks, and for the cattle of the herds, and for the asses: and he
fed them with bread for all their cattle for that year.

וַתִּתֹּם הַשָּׁנָה הַהִוא
the it   the year   and it spent

וַיָּבֹאוּ אֵלָיו בַּשָּׁנָה הַשֵּׁנִית
the second   in year   unto him   and they came

וַיֹּאמְרוּ לוֹ לֹא־נְכַחֵד מֵאֲדֹנִי
from my master   we will suppress – not   to him   and they said

כִּי אִם־תַּם הַכֶּסֶף וּמִקְנֵה הַבְּהֵמָה אֶל־אֲדֹנִי
my master – unto   the beasts   and cattle   the silver   ended - if   like

לֹא נִשְׁאַר לִפְנֵי אֲדֹנִי בִּלְתִּי אִם־גְּוִיָּתֵנוּ וְאַדְמָתֵנוּ:
and our lands   our bodies – with   nothing   my master   before   we remain   not

18 When that year was ended, they came unto him the second year, and said unto him,
We will not hide it from my lord, how that our money is spent; my lord also hath our

herds of cattle; there is not ought left in the sight of my lord, but our bodies, and our
lands:

לָמָּה נָמוּת לְעֵינֶיךָ גַּם־אֲנַחְנוּ

why | we will die | to your eye | we – also

גַּם־אַדְמָתֵנוּ קְנֵה־אֹתָנוּ וְאֶת־אַדְמָתֵנוּ בַּלָּחֶם

our land – also | to us – buy | our land – and that | in bread

וְנִהְיֶה אֲנַחְנוּ וְאַדְמָתֵנוּ עֲבָדִים לְפַרְעֹה וְתֶן־זֶרַע

we and we will be | and our land | servants | to Pharaoh | seed – and give

וְנִחְיֶה וְלֹא נָמוּת וְהָאֲדָמָה לֹא תֵשָׁם׃

and we live | and not | we die | and the ground | not | desolate

19 Wherefore shall we die before thine eyes, both we and our land? buy us and our land
for bread, and we and our land will be servants unto Pharaoh: and give us seed, that we
may live, and not die, that the land be not desolate.

וַיִּקֶן יוֹסֵף אֶת־כָּל־אַדְמַת מִצְרַיִם לְפַרְעֹה

and he bought | Joseph | land – all – that | Egypt | to Pharaoh

כִּי־מָכְרוּ מִצְרַיִם אִישׁ שָׂדֵהוּ

they sold – like | Egyptians | man | his field

כִּי־חָזַק עֲלֵהֶם הָרָעָב

strong – like | upon them | the famine

וַתְּהִי הָאָרֶץ לְפַרְעֹה׃

and it was | he land | to Pharaoh

20 And Joseph bought all the land of Egypt for Pharaoh; for the Egyptians sold every
man his field, because the famine prevailed over them: so the land became Pharaoh's.

וְאֶת־הָעָם הֶעֱבִיר אֹתוֹ לְעָרִים

the people – and that | the transfer | to him | to cities

מִקְצֵה גְבוּל־מִצְרַיִם וְעַד־קָצֵהוּ׃

from far end | Egypt – border | its very end - and till

21 And as for the people, he removed them to cities from one end of the borders of
Egypt even to the other end thereof.

רַק אַדְמַת הַכֹּהֲנִים לֹא קָנָה

only | land | the priest ones | not | bought

כִּי חֹק לַכֹּהֲנִים מֵאֵת פַּרְעֹה

like | statute | priest ones | from that | Pharaoh

וְאָכְלוּ אֶת־חֻקָּם אֲשֶׁר נָתַן לָהֶם פַּרְעֹה

and they ate | their portion – that | which | gave | to them | Pharaoh

עַל־כֵּן לֹא מָכְרוּ אֶת־אַדְמָתָם׃

thus – upon | not | they sold | their land – that

22 Only the land of the priests bought he not; for the priests had a portion assigned them of Pharaoh, and did eat their portion which Pharaoh gave them: wherefore they sold not their lands.

וַיֹּאמֶר יוֹסֵף אֶל־הָעָם הֵן קָנִיתִי אֶתְכֶם הַיּוֹם

the day   to you   I bought   here   the people – unto   Joseph   and he said

וְאֶת־אַדְמַתְכֶם לְפַרְעֹה

to Pharaoh   your land – and that

הֵא־לָכֶם זֶרַע וּזְרַעְתֶּם אֶת־הָאֲדָמָה:

the ground – that   and you will seed   seed   to you - here

23 Then Joseph said unto the people, Behold, I have bought you this day and your land for Pharaoh: lo, here is seed for you, and ye shall sow the land.

וְהָיָה בַּתְּבוּאֹת

in produce   and it will be

וּנְתַתֶּם חֲמִישִׁית לְפַרְעֹה

to Pharaoh   fifth part   and you give

וְאַרְבַּע הַיָּדֹת יִהְיֶה לָכֶם לְזֶרַע הַשָּׂדֶה

the field   to seed   to you   it will be   the handfuls   and four

וּלְאָכְלְכֶם וְלַאֲשֶׁר בְּבָתֵּיכֶם וְלֶאֱכֹל לְטַפְּכֶם:

to little ones   to food   in your houses   and to which   and to your food

24 And it shall come to pass in the increase, that ye shall give the fifth part unto Pharaoh, and four parts shall be your own, for seed of the field, and for your food, and for them of your households, and for food for your little ones.

[מפטיר]

וַיֹּאמְרוּ הֶחֱיִתָנוּ נִמְצָא־חֵן בְּעֵינֵי אֲדֹנִי

my master   in eyes   grace – we found   the our lives   and they said

וְהָיִינוּ עֲבָדִים לְפַרְעֹה:

to Pharaoh   servants   and we will be

25 And they said, Thou hast saved our lives: let us find grace in the sight of my lord, and we will be Pharaoh's servants.

וַיָּשֶׂם אֹתָהּ יוֹסֵף לְחֹק עַד־הַיּוֹם הַזֶּה

the this   the day – until   to statute   Joseph   to it   and he put

עַל־אַדְמַת מִצְרַיִם לְפַרְעֹה לַחֹמֶשׁ

to fifth part   to Pharaoh   Egypt   ground – upon

רַק אַדְמַת הַכֹּהֲנִים לְבַדָּם

them alone   the priest ones   ground   only

לֹא הָיְתָה לְפַרְעֹה:

to Pharaoh   it was   not

26 And Joseph made it a law over the land of Egypt unto this day, that Pharaoh should have the fifth part; except the land of the priests only, which became not Pharaoh's.

וַיֵּשֶׁב יִשְׂרָאֵל בְּאֶרֶץ מִצְרַיִם בְּאֶרֶץ גֹּשֶׁן

Goshen   in land   Egypt   in land   Israel   and he dwelled

וַיֵּאָחֲזוּ בָהּ וַיִּפְרוּ וַיִּרְבּוּ מְאֹד:

greatly   and they multiplied   and they grew   in it   and they became strong

27 And Israel dwelt in the land of Egypt, in the country of Goshen; and they had possessions therein, and grew, and multiplied exceedingly.

12 VAIKI

CHAPTER 47 CONT

וַיְחִי יַעֲקֹב בְּאֶרֶץ מִצְרַיִם שְׁבַע עֶשְׂרֵה שָׁנָה
year - seventeen - Egypt in land Jacob and he lived

וַיְהִי יְמֵי־יַעֲקֹב שְׁנֵי חַיָּיו
his life years Jacob – days and it was

שֶׁבַע שָׁנִים וְאַרְבָּעִים וּמְאַת שָׁנָה:
year and hundred and forty years seven

28 And Jacob lived in the land of Egypt seventeen years: so the whole age of Jacob was an hundred forty and seven years.

וַיִּקְרְבוּ יְמֵי־יִשְׂרָאֵל לָמוּת
to die Israel – days and they drew near

וַיִּקְרָא לִבְנוֹ לְיוֹסֵף וַיֹּאמֶר לוֹ
to him and he said to Joseph to his son and he called

אִם־נָא מָצָאתִי חֵן בְּעֵינֶיךָ שִׂים־נָא יָדְךָ תַּחַת יְרֵכִי
my thigh under your hand now – put in your sight grace I found now – if

וְעָשִׂיתָ עִמָּדִי חֶסֶד וֶאֱמֶת אַל־נָא תִקְבְּרֵנִי בְּמִצְרָיִם:
in Egypt you bury me now – don't and truth mercy with me and you do

29 And the time drew nigh that Israel must die: and he called his son Joseph, and said unto him, If now I have found grace in thy sight, put, I pray thee, thy hand under my thigh, and deal kindly and truly with me; bury me not, I pray thee, in Egypt:

וְשָׁכַבְתִּי עִם־אֲבֹתַי
my father – with and I will lie

וּנְשָׂאתַנִי מִמִּצְרַיִם וּקְבַרְתַּנִי בִּקְבֻרָתָם
in their burying place and bury me from Egypt and carry me

וַיֹּאמַר אָנֹכִי אֶעֱשֶׂה כִדְבָרֶךָ:
like your speaking I will do I am and he said

30 But I will lie with my fathers, and thou shalt carry me out of Egypt, and bury me in their burying place. And he said, I will do as thou hast said.

וַיֹּאמֶר הִשָּׁבְעָה לִי
to me swear and he said

וַיִּשָּׁבַע לוֹ וַיִּשְׁתַּחוּ יִשְׂרָאֵל עַל־רֹאשׁ הַמִּטָּה:
the bed head – upon Israel and he bowed to him and he swore

31 And he said, Swear unto me. And he sware unto him. And Israel bowed himself upon the bed's head.

CHAPTER 48

ספר בראשית פרק מח

וַיְהִי אַחֲרֵי הַדְּבָרִים הָאֵלֶּה
the these   the speakings   after   and it was

וַיֹּאמֶר לְיוֹסֵף הִנֵּה אָבִיךָ חֹלֶה
sick   your father   here   to Joseph   and he said

וַיִּקַּח אֶת־שְׁנֵי בָנָיו עִמּוֹ אֶת־מְנַשֶּׁה וְאֶת־אֶפְרָיִם:
Ephraim – and that   Manasseh – that   with him   his sons   two – that   and he took

48:1 And it came to pass after these things, that one told Joseph, Behold, thy father is
sick: and he took with him his two sons, Manasseh and Ephraim.

וַיַּגֵּד לְיַעֲקֹב וַיֹּאמֶר הִנֵּה בִּנְךָ יוֹסֵף בָּא אֵלֶיךָ
unto you   come   Joseph   your son   here   and he said   to Jacob   and he told

וַיִּתְחַזֵּק יִשְׂרָאֵל וַיֵּשֶׁב עַל־הַמִּטָּה:
the bed – upon   and he sat   Israel   and he strengthened

2 And one told Jacob, and said, Behold, thy son Joseph cometh unto thee: and Israel
strengthened himself, and sat upon the bed.

וַיֹּאמֶר יַעֲקֹב אֶל־יוֹסֵף
Joseph – unto   Jacob   and he said

אֵל שַׁדַּי נִרְאָה־אֵלַי בְּלוּז בְּאֶרֶץ כְּנָעַן וַיְבָרֶךְ אֹתִי:
to me   and he blessed   Canaan   in land   in Luz   unto me – appeared   Shadai   El

3 And Jacob said unto Joseph, God Almighty appeared unto me at Luz in the land of
Canaan, and blessed me,

וַיֹּאמֶר אֵלַי הִנְנִי מַפְרְךָ וְהִרְבִּיתִךָ
and multiply you   will make you fruitful   here I   unto me   and he said

וּנְתַתִּיךָ לִקְהַל עַמִּים
people   to multitude   and will I give you

וְנָתַתִּי אֶת־הָאָרֶץ הַזֹּאת
the this   the land – that   and I give

לְזַרְעֲךָ אַחֲרֶיךָ אֲחֻזַּת עוֹלָם:
forever   possession   after you   to your seed

4 And said unto me, Behold, I will make thee fruitful, and multiply thee, and I will
make of thee a multitude of people; and will give this land to thy seed after thee for an
everlasting possession.

וְעַתָּה שְׁנֵי־בָנֶיךָ הַנּוֹלָדִים לְךָ בְּאֶרֶץ מִצְרַיִם
Egypt   in land   to you   the born ones   your sons – two   and now

עַד־בֹּאִי אֵלֶיךָ מִצְרַיְמָה לִי־הֶם

them – to me   towards Egypt   unto you   I come – till

אֶפְרַיִם וּמְנַשֶּׁה כִּרְאוּבֵן וְשִׁמְעוֹן יִהְיוּ־לִי:

to me – they will be   and Simeon   like Reuben   and Manasseh   Ephraim

5 And now thy two sons, Ephraim and Manasseh, which were born unto thee in the land of Egypt before I came unto thee into Egypt, are mine; as Reuben and Simeon, they shall be mine.

וּמוֹלַדְתְּךָ אֲשֶׁר־הוֹלַדְתָּ אַחֲרֵיהֶם

after them   you begot – which   and your offspring

לְךָ יִהְיוּ עַל שֵׁם אֲחֵיהֶם יִקָּרְאוּ בְּנַחֲלָתָם:

in their inheritance   they call   their brothers   name   upon   they be   to you

6 And thy issue, which thou begettest after them, shall be thine, and shall be called after the name of their brethren in their inheritance.

וַאֲנִי בְּבֹאִי מִפַּדָּן מֵתָה עָלַי רָחֵל בְּאֶרֶץ כְּנַעַן

Canaan   in land   Rachael   upon me   died   from Pardan   in my coming   and I

בַּדֶּרֶךְ בְּעוֹד כִּבְרַת־אֶרֶץ לָבֹא אֶפְרָתָה

towards Ephrath   to come   land – distance   in still   in way

וָאֶקְבְּרֶהָ שָּׁם בְּדֶרֶךְ אֶפְרָת הִוא בֵּית לָחֶם:

lechem   Beth   it   Ephath   in way   there   and I buried her

7 And as for me, when I came from Padan, Rachel died by me in the land of Canaan in the way, when yet there was but a little way to come unto Ephrath: and I buried her there in the way of Ephrath; the same is Beth-lehem.

וַיַּרְא יִשְׂרָאֵל אֶת־בְּנֵי יוֹסֵף וַיֹּאמֶר מִי־אֵלֶּה:

these – who   and he said   Joseph   son – that   Israel   and he saw

8 And Israel beheld Joseph's sons, and said, Who are these?

וַיֹּאמֶר יוֹסֵף אֶל־אָבִיו בָּנַי הֵם אֲשֶׁר־נָתַן־לִי אֱלֹהִים בָּזֶה

in this   Elohim   to me – gave – which   them   my sons   his father – unto   Joseph   and he said

וַיֹּאמַר קָחֶם־נָא אֵלַי וַאֲבָרֲכֵם:

and I will bless them   unto me   now – take them   and he said

9 And Joseph said unto his father, They are my sons, whom God hath given me in this place. And he said, Bring them, I pray thee, unto me, and I will bless them.

[שני]

וְעֵינֵי יִשְׂרָאֵל כָּבְדוּ מִזֹּקֶן לֹא יוּכַל לִרְאוֹת

to see   he able   not   from age   they heavy   Israel   and eyes

וַיַּגֵּשׁ אֹתָם אֵלָיו וַיִּשַּׁק לָהֶם וַיְחַבֵּק לָהֶם:

to them   and he embraced   to them   and he kissed   unto him   to them   and he touched

10 Now the eyes of Israel were dim for age, so that he could not see. And he brought them near unto him; and he kissed them, and embraced them.

וַיֹּאמֶר יִשְׂרָאֵל אֶל־יוֹסֵף רְאֹה פָנֶיךָ לֹא פִלָּלְתִּי

| I prayed | not | your face | see | Joseph – unto | Israel | and he said |

וְהִנֵּה הֶרְאָה אֹתִי אֱלֹהִים גַּם אֶת־זַרְעֶךָ:

| your seed – that | also | Elohim | to me | the see | and here |

11 And Israel said unto Joseph, I had not thought to see thy face: and, lo, God hath shewed me also thy seed.

וַיּוֹצֵא יוֹסֵף אֹתָם מֵעִם בִּרְכָּיו

| his knees | from with | to them | Joseph | and he brought out |

וַיִּשְׁתַּחוּ לְאַפָּיו אָרְצָה:

| towards ground | to his nose | and he bowed |

12 And Joseph brought them out from between his knees, and he bowed himself with his face to the earth.

וַיִּקַּח יוֹסֵף אֶת־שְׁנֵיהֶם

| two of them – that | Joseph | and he took |

אֶת־אֶפְרַיִם בִּימִינוֹ מִשְּׂמֹאל יִשְׂרָאֵל

| Israel | from left | in his right hand | Ephraim – that |

וְאֶת־מְנַשֶּׁה בִשְׂמֹאלוֹ מִימִין יִשְׂרָאֵל וַיַּגֵּשׁ אֵלָיו:

| unto him | and he touched | Israel | from right | in his left | Manasseh – and that |

13 And Joseph took them both, Ephraim in his right hand toward Israel's left hand, and Manasseh in his left hand toward Israel's right hand, and brought them near unto him.

וַיִּשְׁלַח יִשְׂרָאֵל אֶת־יְמִינוֹ

| his right hand – that | Israel | and he sent |

וַיָּשֶׁת עַל־רֹאשׁ אֶפְרַיִם וְהוּא הַצָּעִיר

| the younger | and he | Ephram | head – upon | and he put |

וְאֶת־שְׂמֹאלוֹ עַל־רֹאשׁ מְנַשֶּׁה שִׂכֵּל אֶת־יָדָיו

| his hand – that | guiding | Manasseh | head – upon | his left – and that |

כִּי מְנַשֶּׁה הַבְּכוֹר:

| the first born | Manasseh | like |

14 And Israel stretched out his right hand, and laid itupon Ephraim's head, who was the younger, and his left hand upon Manasseh's head, guiding his hands wittingly; for Manasseh was the firstborn.

וַיְבָרֶךְ אֶת־יוֹסֵף וַיֹּאמַר

| and he said | Joseph – that | and he blessed |

הָאֱלֹהִים אֲשֶׁר הִתְהַלְּכוּ אֲבֹתַי לְפָנָיו אַבְרָהָם וְיִצְחָק

| and Isaac | Abraham | before him | my father | caused they to walk | which | the Elohim |

הָאֱלֹהִים הָרֹעֶה אֹתִי מֵעוֹדִי עַד־הַיּוֹם הַזֶּה:

| the this | the day – till | from my being | to me | the shepherd | the Elohim |

15 And he blessed Joseph, and said, God, before whom my fathers Abraham and Isaac did walk, the God which fed me all my life long unto this day,

הַמַּלְאָךְ הַגֹּאֵל אֹתִי מִכָּל־רָע יְבָרֵךְ אֶת־הַנְּעָרִים

the young boys – that   he blesses   evil – from all   to me   the redeemer   the angel

וְיִקָּרֵא בָהֶם שְׁמִי וְשֵׁם אֲבֹתַי אַבְרָהָם וְיִצְחָק

and Isaac   Abraham   fathers   and name   my name   in them   and he called

וְיִדְגּוּ לָרֹב בְּקֶרֶב הָאָרֶץ׃

the earth   in among   to many   and they grow

16 The Angel which redeemed me from all evil, bless the lads; and let my name be named on them, and the name of my fathers Abraham and Isaac; and let them grow into a multitude in the midst of the earth.

[שלישי]

וַיַּרְא יוֹסֵף כִּי־יָשִׁית אָבִיו יַד־יְמִינוֹ עַל־רֹאשׁ אֶפְרַיִם

Ephraim   head – upon   his right - hand   his father   he put – like   Joseph   and he saw

וַיֵּרַע בְּעֵינָיו

in his eyes   and it bad

וַיִּתְמֹךְ יַד־אָבִיו לְהָסִיר אֹתָהּ

to it   to remove   his father – hand   and he held up

מֵעַל רֹאשׁ־אֶפְרַיִם עַל־רֹאשׁ מְנַשֶּׁה׃

Manasseh   hand – upon   Ephraim – head   from upon

17 And when Joseph saw that his father laid his right hand upon the head of Ephraim, it displeased him: and he held up his father's hand, to remove it from Ephraim's head unto Manasseh's head.

וַיֹּאמֶר יוֹסֵף אֶל־אָבִיו לֹא־כֵן אָבִי

my father   thus – not   his father – unto   Joseph   and he said

כִּי־זֶה הַבְּכֹר שִׂים יְמִינְךָ עַל־רֹאשׁוֹ׃

his head – upon   your right   put   the first born   this – this

18 And Joseph said unto his father, Not so, my father: for this is the firstborn; put thy right hand upon his head.

וַיְמָאֵן אָבִיו

his father   and he refused

וַיֹּאמֶר יָדַעְתִּי בְנִי יָדַעְתִּי

I know   my son   I know   and he said

גַּם־הוּא יִהְיֶה־לְּעָם וְגַם־הוּא יִגְדָּל

he will be big   he - and also   to people – he will be   he – also

וְאוּלָם אָחִיו הַקָּטֹן יִגְדַּל מִמֶּנּוּ וְזַרְעוֹ יִהְיֶה מְלֹא־הַגּוֹיִם׃

the nation – full   it will be   and his seed   from it   he will be big   the small   his brother   and certainly

19 And his father refused, and said, I know it, my son, I know it: he also shall become a people, and he also shall be great: but truly his younger brother shall be greater than he, and his seed shall become a multitude of nations.

וַיְבָרֲכֵ֞ם בַּיּ֤וֹם הַהוּא֙ לֵאמוֹר֒
and he blessed them and in day   the it   to say

בְּךָ֗ יְבָרֵ֤ךְ יִשְׂרָאֵל֙ לֵאמֹ֔ר יְשִֽׂמְךָ֣ אֱלֹהִ֔ים כְּאֶפְרַ֖יִם וְכִמְנַשֶּׁ֑ה
and like Manasseh like Ephraim Elohim he set you   to say   Israel   he blessed   in it

וַיָּ֥שֶׂם אֶת־אֶפְרַ֖יִם לִפְנֵ֥י מְנַשֶּֽׁה׃
Manasseh   before   Ephraim – that   and he set

20 And he blessed them that day, saying, In thee shall Israel bless, saying, God make thee as Ephraim and as Manasseh: and he set Ephraim before Manasseh.

וַיֹּ֤אמֶר יִשְׂרָאֵל֙ אֶל־יוֹסֵ֔ף הִנֵּ֥ה אָנֹכִ֖י מֵ֑ת
dieing   I am   here   Joseph – unto   Israel   and he said

וְהָיָ֤ה אֱלֹהִים֙ עִמָּכֶ֔ם
with you   Elohim   and it will be

וְהֵשִׁ֣יב אֶתְכֶ֔ם אֶל־אֶ֖רֶץ אֲבֹתֵיכֶֽם׃
your father   land – unto   to you   and the return

21 And Israel said unto Joseph, Behold, I die: but God shall be with you, and bring you again unto the land of your fathers.

וַאֲנִ֞י נָתַ֧תִּי לְךָ֛ שְׁכֶ֥ם אַחַ֖ד עַל־אַחֶ֑יךָ
your brother – upon   one   mountain slope   to you   give   and I

אֲשֶׁ֤ר לָקַ֙חְתִּי֙ מִיַּ֣ד הָאֱמֹרִ֔י בְּחַרְבִּ֖י וּבְקַשְׁתִּֽי׃
and in my bow   in my sword   the Amorite   from hand   I took   which

22 Moreover I have given to thee one portion above thy brethren, which I took out of the hand of the Amorite with my sword and with my bow.

פ

CHAPTER 49

ספר בראשית פרק מט

[רביעי]

וַיִּקְרָ֥א יַעֲקֹ֖ב אֶל־בָּנָ֑יו
his sons – unto   Jacob   and he called

וַיֹּ֕אמֶר הֵאָֽסְפוּ֙ וְאַגִּ֣ידָה לָכֶ֔ם אֵ֛ת
that   to you   and I tell   the gather you   and he said

אֲשֶׁר־יִקְרָ֥א אֶתְכֶ֖ם בְּאַחֲרִ֥ית הַיָּמִֽים׃
the days   in last   that them   it will happen – which

49:1 And Jacob called unto his sons, and said, Gather yourselves together, that I may tell you that which shall befall you in the last days.

הִקָּבְצוּ וְשִׁמְעוּ בְּנֵי יַעֲקֹב
Jacob   sons   and you listen   gather you

וְשִׁמְעוּ אֶל־יִשְׂרָאֵל אֲבִיכֶם:
your father   Israel – unto   and you listen

2 Gather yourselves together, and hear, ye sons of Jacob; and hearken unto Israel your father.

רְאוּבֵן בְּכֹרִי אַתָּה כֹּחִי
my might   you   my first born   Reuben

וְרֵאשִׁית אוֹנִי יֶתֶר שְׂאֵת וְיֶתֶר עָז:
power   surplus   dignity   surplus   my virility   and first

3 Reuben, thou art my firstborn, my might, and the beginning of my strength, the excellency of dignity, and the excellency of power:

פַּחַז כַּמַּיִם אַל־תּוֹתַר
you will excel - not   like water   unstable

כִּי עָלִיתָ מִשְׁכְּבֵי אָבִיךָ אָז חִלַּלְתָּ יְצוּעִי עָלָה:
ascended   my couch   you profaned   then   your father   my bed   you went up   like

4 Unstable as water, thou shalt not excel; because thou wentest up to thy father's bed; then defiledst thou it: he went up to my couch.

שִׁמְעוֹן וְלֵוִי אַחִים כְּלֵי חָמָס מְכֵרֹתֵיהֶם:
their broadswords   violence   instruments   brothers   and Levi   Simeon

5 Simeon and Levi are brethren; instruments of cruelty are in their habitations.

בְּסֹדָם אַל־תָּבֹא נַפְשִׁי בִּקְהָלָם אַל־תֵּחַד כְּבֹדִי
my honor   you united – don't   in their assembly   my soul   it come – don't   in their secret

כִּי בְאַפָּם הָרְגוּ אִישׁ
man   they murder   in their anger   like

וּבִרְצֹנָם עִקְּרוּ־שׁוֹר:
bull - it essence   and in their will

6 O my soul, come not thou into their secret; unto their assembly, mine honour, be not thou united: for in their anger they slew a man, and in their selfwill they digged down a wall.

אָרוּר אַפָּם כִּי עָז
strong   like   their anger   cursed

וְעֶבְרָתָם כִּי קָשָׁתָה
towards hard   like   and their rage

אֲחַלְּקֵם בְּיַעֲקֹב וַאֲפִיצֵם בְּיִשְׂרָאֵל:
in Israel   and I will scatter them   in Jacob   I will apportion them

7 Cursed be their anger, for it was fierce; and their wrath, for it was cruel: I will divide them in Jacob, and scatter them in Israel.

פ

יְהוּדָה אַתָּה יוֹדוּךָ אַחֶיךָ
Judah _you_ _will praise you_ _your brother_

יָדְךָ בְּעֹרֶף אֹיְבֶיךָ יִשְׁתַּחֲווּ לְךָ בְּנֵי אָבִיךָ:
your hand _in neck_ _your enemies_ _they bow down_ _to you_ _sons_ _your father_

8 Judah, thou art he whom thy brethren shall praise: thy hand shall be in the neck of thine enemies; thy father's children shall bow down before thee.

גּוּר אַרְיֵה יְהוּדָה מִטֶּרֶף בְּנִי עָלִיתָ
grown cub _lion_ _Judah_ _from prey_ _my son_ _you ascend_

כָּרַע רָבַץ כְּאַרְיֵה וּכְלָבִיא מִי יְקִימֶנּוּ:
bows _reclines_ _like lion_ _and like parent lion_ _who_ _rouse him up_

9 Judah is a lion's whelp: from the prey, my son, thou art gone up: he stooped down, he couched as a lion, and as an old lion; who shall rouse him up?

לֹא־יָסוּר שֵׁבֶט מִיהוּדָה
depart – not _rod_ _from Judah_

וּמְחֹקֵק מִבֵּין רַגְלָיו עַד כִּי־יָבֹא שִׁילֹה
and law giver _from between_ _his feet_ _till_ _he comes – like_ _Shiloh_

וְלוֹ יִקְּהַת עַמִּים:
and to him _he will gather_ _peoples_

10 The sceptre shall not depart from Judah, nor a lawgiver from between his feet, until Shiloh come; and unto him shall the gathering of the people be.

אֹסְרִי לַגֶּפֶן עִירֹה [עִירוֹ]
binding _to vine_ _his foal_

וְלַשֹּׂרֵקָה בְּנִי אֲתֹנוֹ כִּבֵּס בַּיַּיִן לְבֻשׁוֹ
and to muskrat grape _son (colt)_ _his female donkey_ _washed_ _in wine_ _his clothes_

וּבְדַם־עֲנָבִים סוּתֹה [סוּתוֹ]:
grapes – and in blood _his covering_

11 Binding his foal unto the vine, and his ass's colt unto the choice vine; he washed his garments in wine, and his clothes in the blood of grapes:

חַכְלִילִי עֵינַיִם מִיַּיִן וּלְבֶן־שִׁנַּיִם מֵחָלָב:
blood shot _eyes_ _from wine_ _teeth – and white_ _from milk_

12 His eyes shall be red with wine, and his teeth white with milk.

פ

זְבוּלֻן לְחוֹף יַמִּים יִשְׁכֹּן
Zebulun _to port_ _seas_ _he dwells_

וְהוּא לְחוֹף אֳנִיֹּת וְיַרְכָתוֹ עַל־צִידֹן:
and he _to port_ _ships_ _and his flank_ _Zidon – upon_

13 Zebulun shall dwell at the haven of the sea; and he shall be for an haven of ships; and his border shall be unto Zidon.

פ

יִשָּׂשכָר חֲמֹר גָּרֶם רֹבֵץ בֵּין הַמִּשְׁפְּתָיִם:
the two burdens   between   reclining   rib   donkey   Issachar

14 Issachar is a strong ass couching down between two burdens:

וַיַּרְא מְנֻחָה כִּי טוֹב וְאֶת־הָאָרֶץ כִּי נָעֵמָה
pleasant   like   the land – and that   good   like   rest   and he saw

וַיֵּט שִׁכְמוֹ לִסְבֹּל וַיְהִי לְמַס־עֹבֵד:
servant – to tribute   and he be   to bear   his shoulder   and he turned

15 And he saw that rest was good, and the land that it was pleasant; and bowed his shoulder to bear, and became a servant unto tribute.

דָּן יָדִין עַמּוֹ כְּאַחַד שִׁבְטֵי יִשְׂרָאֵל:
Israel   tribes   like one   his people   he will judge   Dan

16 Dan shall judge his people, as one of the tribes of Israel.

יְהִי־דָן נָחָשׁ עֲלֵי־דֶרֶךְ שְׁפִיפֹן עֲלֵי־אֹרַח
road – ascends   adder   way – ascends   serpent   Dan – will be

הַנֹּשֵׁךְ עִקְּבֵי־סוּס
horse - heels   the bite

וַיִּפֹּל רֹכְבוֹ אָחוֹר:
backwards   his rider   and he falls

17 Dan shall be a serpent by the way, an adder in the path, that biteth the horse heels, so that his rider shall fall backward.

לִישׁוּעָתְךָ קִוִּיתִי יְהֹוָה:
ihvh   I waited   to your salvation

18 I have waited for thy salvation, O LORD.

ס

[חמישי]

גָּד גְּדוּד יְגוּדֶנּוּ וְהוּא יָגֻד עָקֵב:
to very end   he raids   and he   he will raid him   troop   Gad

ס

19 Gad, a troop shall overcome him: but he shall overcome at the last.

מֵאָשֵׁר שְׁמֵנָה לַחְמוֹ וְהוּא יִתֵּן מַעֲדַנֵּי־מֶלֶךְ:
king - dainties   he will give   and he   his bread   will be fat   from Asher

20 Out of Asher his bread shall be fat, and he shall yield royal dainties.

ס

נַפְתָּלִי אַיָּלָה שְׁלֻחָה הַנֹּתֵן אִמְרֵי־שָׁפֶר:

diplomatic – words   the giver   let loose   hind   Naphtali

21 Naphtali is a hind let loose: he giveth goodly words.

ס

בֵּן פֹּרָת יוֹסֵף בֵּן פֹּרָת עֲלֵי־עָיִן

[a] spring - ascends   fruitful   son   Joseph   fruitful   son

בָּנוֹת צָעֲדָה עֲלֵי־שׁוּר:

barricade – ascend   running onto   branches

22 Joseph is a fruitful bough, even a fruitful bough by a well; whose branches run over the wall:

וַיְמָרֲרֻהוּ וָרֹבּוּ וַיִּשְׂטְמֻהוּ בַּעֲלֵי חִצִּים:

arrows   masters of   they begrudging him   and they many   and they bitter him

23 The archers have sorely grieved him, and shot at him, and hated him:

וַתֵּשֶׁב בְּאֵיתָן קַשְׁתּוֹ

his bow   in area of power   and it returned

וַיָּפֹזּוּ זְרֹעֵי יָדָיו מִידֵי אֲבִיר יַעֲקֹב

Jacob   mighty   from hands   his hands   arms   and they supple

מִשָּׁם רֹעֶה אֶבֶן יִשְׂרָאֵל:

Israel   stone   shepherd   from there

24 But his bow abode in strength, and the arms of his hands were made strong by the hands of the mighty God of Jacob; (from thence is the shepherd, the stone of Israel:)

מֵאֵל אָבִיךָ וְיַעְזְרֶךָּ וְאֵת שַׁדַּי

Shadai   and that   and he will help you   your father   from El

וִיבָרֲכֶךָּ בִּרְכֹת שָׁמַיִם מֵעָל

from above   heaven   blessing   and he will bless you

בִּרְכֹת תְּהוֹם רֹבֶצֶת תָּחַת בִּרְכֹת שָׁדַיִם וָרָחַם:

and womb   breasts   blessings   under   lieth under   deep   blessings

25 Even by the God of thy father, who shall help thee; and by the Almighty, who shall bless thee with blessings of heaven above, blessings of the deep that lieth under, blessings of the breasts, and of the womb:

בִּרְכֹת אָבִיךָ גָּבְרוּ

prevailed   your father   blessings

עַל־בִּרְכֹת הוֹרַי עַד־תַּאֲוַת גִּבְעֹת עוֹלָם

everlasting   hills   yearning - till   progenitors   blessings - upon

תִּהְיֶיןָ לְרֹאשׁ יוֹסֵף וּלְקָדְקֹד נְזִיר אֶחָיו:

his brothers   separated   and to scalp (crown)   Joseph   to head   it be

26 The blessings of thy father have prevailed above the blessings of my progenitors

unto the utmost bound of the everlasting hills: they shall be on the head of Joseph, and
on the crown of the head of him that was separate from his brethren.

פ

[שְׁשִׁי]

בִּנְיָמִין זְאֵב יִטְרָף בַּבֹּקֶר יֹאכַל עַד
Benjamin   wolf   he tearing   in morning   he eats   prey

וְלָעֶרֶב יְחַלֵּק שָׁלָל:
and to evening   he will divide   booty

27 Benjamin shall ravin as a wolf: in the morning he shall devour the prey, and at night
he shall divide the spoil.

כָּל־אֵלֶּה שִׁבְטֵי יִשְׂרָאֵל שְׁנֵים עָשָׂר
all – these   tribes   Israel   ----twelve-----

וְזֹאת אֲשֶׁר־דִּבֶּר לָהֶם אֲבִיהֶם
and this   which – spoke   to them   their father

וַיְבָרֶךְ אוֹתָם אִישׁ אֲשֶׁר כְּבִרְכָתוֹ בֵּרַךְ אֹתָם:
and he blessed   to them   man   which   like his blessing   blessed   to them

28 All these are the twelve tribes of Israel: and this is it that their father spake unto
them, and blessed them; every one according to his blessing he blessed them.

וַיְצַו אוֹתָם
and he commanded   to them

וַיֹּאמֶר אֲלֵהֶם אֲנִי נֶאֱסָף אֶל־עַמִּי
and he said   unto them   I   gathered   unto – my people

קִבְרוּ אֹתִי אֶל־אֲבֹתָי אֶל־הַמְּעָרָה
you bury   to me   unto – my father   unto – the cave

אֲשֶׁר בִּשְׂדֵה עֶפְרוֹן הַחִתִּי:
which   in field   Ephron   the Hittite

29 And he charged them, and said unto them, I am to be gathered unto my people: bury
me with my fathers in the cave that is in the field of Ephron the Hittite,

בַּמְּעָרָה אֲשֶׁר בִּשְׂדֵה הַמַּכְפֵּלָה
in cave   which   in field   the Machpelah

אֲשֶׁר־עַל־פְּנֵי מַמְרֵא בְּאֶרֶץ כְּנָעַן
which – upon – face   Mamre   in land   Cannan

אֲשֶׁר קָנָה אַבְרָהָם אֶת־הַשָּׂדֶה מֵאֵת עֶפְרֹן הַחִתִּי
which   bought   Abraham   that – the field   from that   Ephron   the Hittie

לַאֲחֻזַּת־קָבֶר:
to possession – burying place

30 In the cave that is in the field of Machpelah, which is before Mamre, in the land of Canaan, which Abraham bought with the field of Ephron the Hittite for a possession of a burying place.

שָׁ֣מָּה קָֽבְר֞וּ אֶת־אַבְרָהָ֗ם וְאֵת֙ שָׂרָ֣ה אִשְׁתּ֔וֹ

his wife   Sarah   and that   Abraham – that   they buried   there

שָׁ֚מָּה קָֽבְר֣וּ אֶת־יִצְחָ֔ק וְאֵ֖ת רִבְקָ֣ה אִשְׁתּ֑וֹ

his wife   Rebekah   and that   Isaac – that   they buried   there

וְשָׁ֥מָּה קָבַ֖רְתִּי אֶת־לֵאָֽה׃

Leah – that   I buried   and there

31 There they buried Abraham and Sarah his wife; there they buried Isaac and Rebekah his wife; and there I buried Leah.

מִקְנֵ֧ה הַשָּׂדֶ֛ה וְהַמְּעָרָ֥ה אֲשֶׁר־בּ֖וֹ מֵאֵ֥ת בְּנֵי־חֵֽת׃

Heth – sons   from that   in it – which   and the cave   the field   from purchase

32 The purchase of the field and of the cave that istherein was from the children of Heth.

וַיְכַ֤ל יַעֲקֹב֙ לְצַוֺּ֣ת אֶת־בָּנָ֔יו

his sons – that   to commanding   Jacob   and he finished

וַיֶּאֱסֹ֥ף רַגְלָ֖יו אֶל־הַמִּטָּ֑ה וַיִּגְוַ֕ע

and he expired   the bed – unto   his feet   and he gathered

וַיֵּאָ֖סֶף אֶל־עַמָּֽיו׃

his people – unto   the gathered

33 And when Jacob had made an end of commanding his sons, he gathered up his feet into the bed, and yielded up the ghost, and was gathered unto his people.

CHAPTER 50

ספר בראשית פרק נ

וַיִּפֹּ֥ל יוֹסֵ֖ף עַל־פְּנֵ֣י אָבִ֑יו וַיֵּ֥בְךְּ עָלָ֖יו

upon him   and he wept   his father   face – upon   Joseph   and he fell

וַיִּשַּׁק־לֽוֹ׃

him – and he kissed

50:1 And Joseph fell upon his father's face, and wept upon him, and kissed him.

וַיְצַ֨ו יוֹסֵ֤ף אֶת־עֲבָדָיו֙ אֶת־הָרֹ֣פְאִ֔ים

the physicians – that   his servants – that   Joseph   and he commanded

לַחֲנֹ֖ט אֶת־אָבִ֑יו וַיַּחַנְט֧וּ הָרֹפְאִ֛ים אֶת־יִשְׂרָאֵֽל׃

Israel – that   the physicians   and they embalmed   his father – that   to embalm

2 And Joseph commanded his servants the physicians to embalm his father: and the physicians embalmed Israel.

וַיִּמְלְאוּ־לוֹ אַרְבָּעִים יוֹם כִּי כֵּן יִמְלְאוּ יְמֵי הַחֲנֻטִים
the embalming days they filled thus like day forty to him – he filled

וַיִּבְכּוּ אֹתוֹ מִצְרַיִם שִׁבְעִים יוֹם:
day seventy Egyptians to him and they mourned

3 And forty days were fulfilled for him; for so are fulfilled the days of those which are embalmed: and the Egyptians mourned for him threescore and ten days.

וַיַּעַבְרוּ יְמֵי בְכִיתוֹ
his mourning days and they passed

וַיְדַבֵּר יוֹסֵף אֶל־בֵּית פַּרְעֹה לֵאמֹר
to say Pharaoh house – unto Joseph and he spoke

אִם־נָא מָצָאתִי חֵן בְּעֵינֵיכֶם
in your eyes grace I found now – if

דַּבְּרוּ־נָא בְּאָזְנֵי פַרְעֹה לֵאמֹר:
to say Pharaoh in my ears now – you speak

4 And when the days of his mourning were past, Joseph spake unto the house of Pharaoh, saying, If now I have found grace in your eyes, speak, I pray you, in the ears of Pharaoh, saying,

אָבִי הִשְׁבִּיעַנִי לֵאמֹר הִנֵּה אָנֹכִי מֵת
die I am here to say caused me to swear my father

בְּקִבְרִי אֲשֶׁר כָּרִיתִי לִי בְּאֶרֶץ כְּנַעַן
Canaan in earth to me I dug which in my grave

שָׁמָּה תִּקְבְּרֵנִי
you bury me there

וְעַתָּה אֶעֱלֶה־נָּא וְאֶקְבְּרָה אֶת־אָבִי וְאָשׁוּבָה:
and I return my father – that and I bury please – I ascend and now

5 My father made me swear, saying, Lo, I die: in my grave which I have digged for me in the land of Canaan, there shalt thou bury me. Now therefore let me go up, I pray thee, and bury my father, and I will come again.

וַיֹּאמֶר פַּרְעֹה עֲלֵה וּקְבֹר אֶת־אָבִיךָ כַּאֲשֶׁר הִשְׁבִּיעֶךָ:
caused you to swear when your father – that and bury ascend Pharaoh and he said

6 And Pharaoh said, Go up, and bury thy father, according as he made thee swear.

וַיַּעַל יוֹסֵף לִקְבֹּר אֶת־אָבִיו
his father – that to bury Joseph and he went up

וַיַּעֲלוּ אִתּוֹ כָּל־עַבְדֵי פַרְעֹה זִקְנֵי בֵיתוֹ
his house elders Pharaoh servants – all with him and they ascended

וְכֹל זִקְנֵי אֶרֶץ־מִצְרָיִם:
Egypt – land elders and all

7 And Joseph went up to bury his father: and with him went up all the servants of
Pharaoh, the elders of his house, and all the elders of the land of Egypt,

וְכֹל בֵּית יוֹסֵף וְאֶחָיו וּבֵית אָבִיו
his father and house   and his brothers   Joseph   house   and all

רַק טַפָּם וְצֹאנָם וּבְקָרָם עָזְבוּ בְּאֶרֶץ גֹּשֶׁן:
Goshen   in land   they left   and cattle   and their flocks   little ones   only

8 And all the house of Joseph, and his brethren, and his father's house: only their little
ones, and their flocks, and their herds, they left in the land of Goshen.

וַיַּעַל עִמּוֹ גַּם־רֶכֶב גַּם־פָּרָשִׁים
horse men – also   chariot – also   with him   and they ascended

וַיְהִי הַמַּחֲנֶה כָּבֵד מְאֹד:
very   heavy   the camp   and it was

9 And there went up with him both chariots and horsemen: and it was a very great
company.

וַיָּבֹאוּ עַד־גֹּרֶן הָאָטָד אֲשֶׁר בְּעֵבֶר הַיַּרְדֵּן
the Jordan   in passing   which   the Atad   threshing floor – till   and they came

וַיִּסְפְּדוּ־שָׁם מִסְפֵּד גָּדוֹל וְכָבֵד מְאֹד
very   and heavy   great   lamentation   there – and they mourned

וַיַּעַשׂ לְאָבִיו אֵבֶל שִׁבְעַת יָמִים:
days   seven   mourning   to his father   and he did

10 And they came to the threshing floor of Atad, which is beyond Jordan, and there
they mourned with a great and very sore lamentation: and he made a mourning for his
father seven days.

וַיַּרְא יוֹשֵׁב הָאָרֶץ הַכְּנַעֲנִי אֶת־הָאֵבֶל בְּגֹרֶן הָאָטָד
the Atad   in foor   the mourning – that   the Canaanites   the land   dwellers   and he saw

וַיֹּאמְרוּ אֵבֶל־כָּבֵד זֶה לְמִצְרָיִם
to Egyptians   this   heavy – mourning   and they said

עַל־כֵּן קָרָא שְׁמָהּ אָבֵל מִצְרַיִם אֲשֶׁר בְּעֵבֶר הַיַּרְדֵּן:
the Jordan   in passing   which   mitzraim*   Abel   name   called   thus – upon

11 And when the inhabitants of the land, the Canaanites, saw the mourning in the floor
of Atad, they said, This is a grievous mourning to the Egyptians: wherefore the name
of it was called Abel-mizraim, which is beyond Jordan.

וַיַּעֲשׂוּ בָנָיו לוֹ כֵּן כַּאֲשֶׁר צִוָּם:
commanded them   when   thus   to him   his sons   and they did

12 And his sons did unto him according as he commanded them:

וַיִּשְׂאוּ אֹתוֹ בָנָיו אַרְצָה כְּנַעַן
Canaan   towards land   his son   to him   and they carried

וַיִּקְבְּרוּ אֹתוֹ בִּמְעָרַת שְׂדֵה הַמַּכְפֵּלָה

and they buried   to him   in cave   field   the Machpelah

אֲשֶׁר קָנָה אַבְרָהָם אֶת־הַשָּׂדֶה לַאֲחֻזַּת־קֶבֶר

which   bought   Abraham   the field – that   burying – to possession

מֵאֵת עֶפְרֹן הַחִתִּי עַל־פְּנֵי מַמְרֵא:

from that   Ephron   the Hittite   face – upon   Mamre

13 For his sons carried him into the land of Canaan, and buried him in the cave of the field of Machpelah, which Abraham bought with the field for a possession of a burying place of Ephron the Hittite, before Mamre.

וַיָּשָׁב יוֹסֵף מִצְרַיְמָה הוּא וְאֶחָיו

and he returned   Joseph   towards Egypt   he   and his brothers

וְכָל־הָעֹלִים אִתּוֹ לִקְבֹּר אֶת־אָבִיו

the ascenders – and all   with him   to bury   his father – that

אַחֲרֵי קָבְרוֹ אֶת־אָבִיו:

after   his burying   his father – that

14 And Joseph returned into Egypt, he, and his brethren, and all that went up with him to bury his father, after he had buried his father.

וַיִּרְאוּ אֲחֵי־יוֹסֵף כִּי־מֵת אֲבִיהֶם

and they saw   Joseph – brothers   dead – like   their father

וַיֹּאמְרוּ לוּ יִשְׂטְמֵנוּ יוֹסֵף

and they said   to him   he holding grudge us   Joseph

וְהָשֵׁב יָשִׁיב לָנוּ אֵת כָּל־הָרָעָה אֲשֶׁר גָּמַלְנוּ אֹתוֹ:

the return   he returns   to us   that   the bad – all   which   we requited   to him

15 And when Joseph's brethren saw that their father was dead, they said, Joseph will peradventure hate us, and will certainly requite us all the evil which we did unto him.

וַיְצַוּוּ אֶל־יוֹסֵף לֵאמֹר

and they commanded   Joseph – unto   to say

אָבִיךָ צִוָּה לִפְנֵי מוֹתוֹ לֵאמֹר:

your father   commanded   before   his death   to say

16 And they sent a messenger unto Joseph, saying, Thy father did command before he died, saying,

כֹּה־תֹאמְרוּ לְיוֹסֵף אָנָּא שָׂא נָא פֶּשַׁע אַחֶיךָ

you say it – thus   to Joseph   please   lift   please   sin   your brother

וְחַטָּאתָם כִּי־רָעָה גְמָלוּךָ

and their sin   bad – like   they forgive you

וְעַתָּה שָׂא נָא לְפֶשַׁע עַבְדֵי אֱלֹהֵי אָבִיךָ

and now   lift   now   to transgression   servants   Elohim   your father

וַיֵּבְךְּ יוֹסֵף בְּדַבְּרָם אֵלָיו:

unto him   in their speeches   Joseph   and he wept

17 So shall ye say unto Joseph, Forgive, I pray thee now, the trespass of thy brethren,
and their sin; for they did unto thee evil: and now, we pray thee, forgive the trespass of
the servants of the God of thy father. And Joseph wept when they spake unto him.

וַיֵּלְכוּ גַּם־אֶחָיו וַיִּפְּלוּ לְפָנָיו

before him   and they fell   his brothers - also   and they went

וַיֹּאמְרוּ הִנֶּנּוּ לְךָ לַעֲבָדִים:

to servants   to you   here we   and they said

18 And his brethren also went and fell down before his face; and they said, Behold, we
be thy servants.

וַיֹּאמֶר אֲלֵהֶם יוֹסֵף אַל־תִּירָאוּ

you fear it – don't   Joseph   unto them   and he said

כִּי הֲתַחַת אֱלֹהִים אָנִי:

I   Elohim   the in place of   like

19 And Joseph said unto them, Fear not: for am I in the place of God?

וְאַתֶּם חֲשַׁבְתֶּם עָלַי רָעָה

bad   upon me   you thought   and that you

אֱלֹהִים חֲשָׁבָהּ לְטֹבָה

to good   thought   Elohim

לְמַעַן עֲשֹׂה כַּיּוֹם הַזֶּה לְהַחֲיֹת עַם־רָב:

much – people   to the survive   the this   like day   do   to end

20 But as for you, ye thought evil against me; but God meant it unto good, to bring to
pass, as it is this day, to save much people alive.

[שביעי]

וְעַתָּה אַל־תִּירָאוּ אָנֹכִי אֲכַלְכֵּל אֶתְכֶם וְאֶת־טַפְּכֶם

your little ones – that   that you   I will sustain   I am   you fear it – don't   and now

וַיְנַחֵם אוֹתָם וַיְדַבֵּר עַל־לִבָּם:

to their hearts – upon   and he spoke   to them   and he confronted

21 Now therefore fear ye not: I will nourish you, and your little ones. And he comforted
them, and spake kindly unto them.

וַיֵּשֶׁב יוֹסֵף בְּמִצְרַיִם הוּא וּבֵית אָבִיו

his father   and house   he   in Egypt   Joseph   and he dwelt

וַיְחִי יוֹסֵף מֵאָה וָעֶשֶׂר שָׁנִים:

years   and ten   hundred   Joseph   and he lived

22 And Joseph dwelt in Egypt, he, and his father's house: and Joseph lived an hundred
and ten years.

[מפטיר]

וַיַּ֣רְא יוֹסֵ֤ף לְאֶפְרַ֙יִם֙ בְּנֵ֣י שִׁלֵּשִׁ֔ים
third generation   sons   to Ephraim   Joseph   and he saw

גַּ֗ם בְּנֵ֤י מָכִיר֙ בֶּן־מְנַשֶּׁ֔ה יֻלְּד֖וּ עַל־בִּרְכֵּ֥י יוֹסֵֽף׃
Joseph   knees – upon   they begotten   Manasseh – son   Machir   sons   also

23 And Joseph saw Ephraim's children of the third generation: the children also of
Machir the son of Manasseh were brought up upon Joseph's knees.

וַיֹּ֤אמֶר יוֹסֵף֙ אֶל־אֶחָ֔יו אָנֹכִ֖י מֵ֑ת
dead   I am   brothers – unto   Joseph   and he said

וֵֽאלֹהִ֞ים פָּקֹ֧ד יִפְקֹ֣ד אֶתְכֶ֗ם
to you   he visits   visitor   and Elohim

וְהֶעֱלָ֤ה אֶתְכֶם֙ מִן־הָאָ֣רֶץ הַזֹּ֔את
the this   the land – from   that you   and the ascend

אֶל־הָאָ֕רֶץ אֲשֶׁ֥ר נִשְׁבַּ֛ע לְאַבְרָהָ֥ם לְיִצְחָ֖ק וּֽלְיַעֲקֹֽב׃
and to Jacob   to Isaac   to Abraham   swore   which   the land – unto

24 And Joseph said unto his brethren, I die: and God will surely visit you, and bring you
out of this land unto the land which he sware to Abraham, to Isaac, and to Jacob.

וַיַּשְׁבַּ֣ע יוֹסֵ֔ף אֶת־בְּנֵ֥י יִשְׂרָאֵ֖ל לֵאמֹ֑ר
to say   Israel   sons – that   Joseph   and he swore

פָּקֹ֨ד יִפְקֹ֤ד אֱלֹהִים֙ אֶתְכֶ֔ם
that you   Elohim   he visit   will visit

וְהַעֲלִתֶ֥ם אֶת־עַצְמֹתַ֖י מִזֶּֽה׃
from this   my bones – that   and the you ascend

25 And Joseph took an oath of the children of Israel, saying, God will surely visit you,
and ye shall carry up my bones from hence.

וַיָּ֣מָת יוֹסֵ֔ף בֶּן־מֵאָ֥ה וָעֶ֖שֶׂר שָׁנִ֑ים
years   and ten   hundred – age   Joseph   and he died

וַיַּחַנְט֣וּ אֹת֔וֹ וַיִּ֥ישֶׂם בָּאָר֖וֹן בְּמִצְרָֽיִם׃
in Egypt   in coffin   and he put   to him   and they embalmed

26 So Joseph died, being an hundred and ten years old: and they embalmed him, and he
was put in a coffin in Egypt.

פ פ פ